BUDDHIST FUNERAL CULTURES OF SOUTHEAST ASIA AND CHINA

The centrality of death rituals has rarely been documented in anthropologically informed studies of Buddhism. Bringing together a range of perspectives including ethnographic, textual, historical and theoretically informed accounts, this edited volume presents the diversity of the Buddhist funeral cultures of mainland Southeast Asia and China. While the contributions show that the ideas and ritual practices related to death are continuously transformed in local contexts through political and social changes, they also highlight the continuities of funeral cultures. The studies are based on long-term fieldwork and cover material on Theravāda Buddhism in Burma, Laos, Thailand, Cambodia and various regions of Chinese Buddhism, both on the mainland and in the Southeast Asian diasporas. Topics such as bad death, the feeding of ghosts, pollution through death and the ritual regeneration of life show how Buddhist cultures deal with death as a universal phenomenon of human culture.

PAUL WILLIAMS is Emeritus Professor of Indian and Tibetan Philosophy and founding co-Director of the Centre for Buddhist Studies at the University of Bristol. He is author of *Mahāyāna Buddhism: The Doctrinal Foundations* (2nd edition 2009); *The Reflexive Nature of Awareness: A Tibetan Madhyamaka Defence* (1998); *Altruism and Reality: Studies in the Philosophy of Bodhicaryāvatāra* (1998); *The Unexpected Way: On Converting from Buddhism to Catholicism* (2001); and *Songs of Love, Poems of Sadness: The Erotic Verse of the Sixth Dalai Lama* (2004). He is co-author, with Anthony Tribe and Alexander Wynne, of *Buddhist Thought: A Complete Introduction to the Indian Tradition* (2nd edition 2012), and was sole editor of the eight-volume series Buddhism: Critical Concepts in Religious Studies (2005).

PATRICE LADWIG is Research Fellow at the Max Planck Institute for Social Anthropology (Halle, Germany) where he works in a research group focusing on historical anthropology. He has published articles in the fields of Anthropology, Asian Studies and Buddhist Studies. He is currently finalising a monograph entitled *Revolutionaries and Reformers in Lao Buddhism* and working on an edited volume on Buddhist socialism.

BUDDHIST FUNERAL CULTURES OF SOUTHEAST ASIA AND CHINA

EDITED BY

PAUL WILLIAMS

and

PATRICE LADWIG

CAMBRIDGE
UNIVERSITY PRESS

CAMBRIDGE
UNIVERSITY PRESS

University Printing House, Cambridge CB2 8BS, United Kingdom

Published in the United States of America by Cambridge University Press, New York

Cambridge University Press is part of the University of Cambridge.

It furthers the University's mission by disseminating knowledge in the pursuit of education, learning and research at the highest international levels of excellence.

www.cambridge.org
Information on this title: www.cambridge.org/9781107667877

First published 2012
First paperback edition 2013

A catalogue record for this publication is available from the British Library

Library of Congress Cataloguing in Publication data
Buddhist funeral cultures of Southeast Asia and China / edited by Paul Williams and Patrice Ladwig.
pages cm
ISBN 978-1-107-00388-0 (hardback)
1. Buddhist funeral rites and ceremonies – Southeast Asia. 2. Buddhist funeral rites and ceremonies – China. I. Williams, Paul, 1950– II. Ladwig, Patrice.
BQ5020.B83 2012
294.3′43880959–dc23
2012000080

ISBN 978-1-107-00388-0 Hardback
ISBN 978-1-107-66787-7 Paperback

Contents

List of figures — *page* vii
List of tables — viii
List of contributors — ix
Preface — xiii

1 Introduction: Buddhist funeral cultures
PATRICE LADWIG AND PAUL WILLIAMS — 1

2 Chanting as '*bricolage* technique': a comparison of South and Southeast Asian funeral recitation
RITA LANGER — 21

3 Weaving life out of death: the craft of the rag robe in Cambodian ritual technology
ERIK W. DAVIS — 59

4 Corpses and cloth: illustrations of the *paṃsukūla* ceremony in Thai manuscripts
M. L. PATTARATORN CHIRAPRAVATI — 79

5 Good death, bad death and ritual restructurings: the New Year ceremonies of the Phunoy in northern Laos
VANINA BOUTÉ — 99

6 Feeding the dead: ghosts, materiality and merit in a Lao Buddhist festival for the deceased
PATRICE LADWIG — 119

7 Funeral rituals, bad death and the protection of social space among the Arakanese (Burma)
ALEXANDRA DE MERSAN — 142

8 Theatre of death and rebirth: monks' funerals in Burma
FRANÇOIS ROBINNE 165

9 From bones to ashes: the Teochiu management of bad death in China and overseas
BERNARD FORMOSO 192

10 For Buddhas, families and ghosts: the transformation of the Ghost Festival into a Dharma Assembly in southeast China
INGMAR HEISE 217

11 *Xianghua foshi* 香花佛事 (incense and flower Buddhist rites): a local Buddhist funeral ritual tradition in southeastern China
YIK FAI TAM 238

12 Buddhist passports to the other world: a study of modern and early medieval Chinese Buddhist mortuary documents
FREDERICK SHIH-CHUNG CHEN 261

Index 287

Figures

4.1 Phra Malai takes the *paṃsukūla* cloth from a corpse. Phra Malai Manuscript, reproduced with permission of The Walters Art Museum, Baltimore. *page* 92

4.2 The practice of meditation on a corpse (Pali: *asubha-kammaṭṭhāna*). The corpse is devoured by birds (right side). Phra Malai Manuscript, reproduced with permission of The Walters Art Museum, Baltimore. 93

4.3 Two lay cremation assistants maintaining the fire over the coffin. Phra Malai Manuscript, reproduced with permission of The Walters Art Museum, Baltimore. 94

4.4 Monk pulling *paṃsukūla* cloth from a coffin. Detail from Phra Malai Manuscript, reproduced with permission of the Spencer Collection, The New York Public Library, Astor, Lenox and Tilden Foundations. 95

8.1 Process of separation and aggregation. 186

Tables

2.1 Chart of chanting sequences *page* 42
2.2 Index of verses and phrases 44
11.1 Ritual processes of the *Quanzhai* 246
11.2 Titles of Ten Enlightened Kings 253

Contributors

VANINA BOUTÉ is a lecturer at the University of Picardie Jules Verne (France) and a member of the Centre Asie du Sud-Est, Centre National de la Recherche Scientifique (CNRS, France). She completed her PhD in Anthropology at the École Pratique de Hautes Études (Paris, France) in 2005. Her dissertation, entitled 'Mirroring the power: the Phounoy of northern Laos – ethnogenesis and dynamics of integration', concentrates on the social changes among a highland border-guard group in northern Laos, from the colonial context to the post-colonial period. Her current research is focused on migration and the dynamic of change among ethnic groups in the borders of northern Laos. She is currently conducting anthropological research on ethnicity in contemporary Laos.

FREDERICK SHIH-CHUNG CHEN is currently a post-doctoral researcher at the Faculty of Oriental Studies, University of Oxford. His current post-doctoral project aims at the further development of his DPhil thesis at the University of Oxford which surveys the early formation of the Buddhist otherworld bureaucracy in early Medieval China. He has previously been awarded two MA degrees, in Study of Religions and in Cultural History of Medicine, from the School of Oriental and African Studies, University of London.

M.L. PATTARATORN CHIRAPRAVATI is Associate Professor of Art History and Director of the Asian Studies Program at California State University, Sacramento. She holds a PhD in Southeast Asian Art History from Cornell University. She is the author of *Votive Tablets in Thailand: Origin, Styles, and Uses* (1997), *Divination au royaume de Siam: Le corps, la guerre, le destin* (2011) and many scholarly articles on the arts of Thailand. She was co-curator of the Asian Art Museum's 2005 exhibition 'The Kingdom of Siam: the Art of Central Thailand 1350–1800' and the 2009 exhibition 'Emerald Cities: Arts of Siam and Burma 1775–1950'.

ERIK W. DAVIS is Assistant Professor of Asian Religions at Macalester College in Saint Paul, Minnesota. He holds a PhD from the University of Chicago. His dissertation, 'Treasures of the Buddha: Imagining Death and Life in Contemporary Cambodia', was based on three years of fieldwork on contemporary Cambodian funerary practices.

ALEXANDRA DE MERSAN has a PhD in Social Anthropology and Ethnology from the École des Hautes Études en Sciences Sociales (EHESS, Paris). She is the author of several articles on local social and religious practices of Buddhist societies. Her research in Burma has covered such subjects as religion, ritual, territory, migration and socio-religious dynamics, ethnicity and nation-building. She is an associate member of the Centre Asie du Sud-Est (CASE-CNRS, Paris), and is currently a researcher within a Franco-German team on a research programme entitled 'Local Traditions and World Religions: the Appropriation of "Religion" in Southeast Asia and Beyond'. She is also a lecturer in anthropology at the Institut National des Langues et Civilisations Orientales (INALCO, Paris).

BERNARD FORMOSO is Professor of Social Anthropology at the University of Paris Ouest – Nanterre – La Défense. He holds a PhD from the EHESS (1984) and an HDR from Paris Ouest University (1996). He has published several books on Thai society. His current research works focus on ethnicity and religious syncretism. His latest book on these topics is *De Jiao: a Religious Movement in Contemporary China and Overseas* (2010).

PATRICE LADWIG studied Social Anthropology and Sociology at the University of Muenster, the University of Edinburgh and the EHESS, Paris. He holds a PhD in Social Anthropology from the University of Cambridge (2007). In 2007–9 he was a research assistant at the University of Bristol and worked on the Arts and Humanities Research Council (AHRC) project on Buddhist death rituals. He is currently a member of the historical anthropology research group at the Max Planck Institute for Social Anthropology, Halle, Germany. His research interests include the anthropology of Buddhism (particularly in Laos and Thailand), the anthropology of the state, religious conversion, political theologies and the interaction of Marxism and Theravāda Buddhism in the post-colonial period.

RITA LANGER was educated at Hamburg University (MA, PhD in Indology) and Kelaniya University (Diploma in Buddhist Studies). She joined the Centre for Buddhist Studies at Bristol University as full time member of staff in January 2007 (research associate) and was appointed Lecturer in Buddhist Studies in August 2007. Her research focuses on two different but complementary areas of Buddhism: (1) theory of consciousness in the early Pāli sources and (2) Buddhist ritual and its origin (in South and Southeast Asia, particularly Sri Lanka). Her approach is interdisciplinary and combines textual studies with fieldwork. She is the author of *Buddhist Rituals of Death and Rebirth: A Study of Contemporary Sri Lankan Practice and its Origins* (2007).

INGMAR HEISE studied modern, classical Sinology and Asian history in Freiburg, Heidelberg and Leiden. He obtained an MA in Chinese Studies from Leiden University in 2005. Currently he is undertaking a PhD at the Centre for Buddhist Studies, University of Bristol on 'Buddhist Death Rituals in Fujian' as part of the Bristol AHRC-funded project 'Buddhist Death Rituals in Southeast Asia and China'.

FRANÇOIS ROBINNE holds a PhD in Social Anthropology from the École des hautes études en sciences sociales Paris (1985), and is a senior researcher at the Institute of Research on Southeast Asia (IRSEA-CNRS). He has published *Fils et Maîtres du Lac. Relations Interethniques dans l'Etat Shan de Birmanie* (2000) and *Prêtres et Chamanes. Métamorphoses* (2007).

YIK FAI TAM received his PhD from the Graduate Theological Union, Berkeley, California in 2005. His research interests focus on Chinese folk Buddhism and rituals. He is author of *The Xianghua Foshi Ritual Tradition and Xianghua Heshang of East Guangdong Province*, in *Minjian Fojia Yanjiu* (Studies on Folk Buddhism), edited by Wai Lun Tam (2007); 'The religious and cultural significances of *Xianghua foshi and Xianghua heshang*', *Guangxi Minzu Daxue Xuebao* (Journal of Guangxi University for Nationalities); special edition on *Kejia Minjian Xinyang Yanjiu* (Studies on Folk Beliefs in the Hakka societies); 'Religion in ethnic minority communities'; and a chapter in *Religion and Public Life in the Chinese World*, co-authored with Philip Wickeri.

PAUL WILLIAMS is Emeritus Professor of Indian and Tibetan Philosophy and founding co-director of the Centre for Buddhist Studies at the University of Bristol. A former president of the UK Association for Buddhist Studies, he was director (PI) of the University of Bristol's AHRC project on Buddhist Funeral Rites in Southeast Asia and China. He was sole editor of the eight-volume series for Routledge entitled *Buddhism: Critical Concepts in Religious Studies* (2005), and is the author of six books in Buddhist studies.

Preface

The centrality of death rituals has in anthropologically informed studies of Buddhism been little documented. The current volume brings together a range of perspectives on Buddhist death rituals including ethnographic, textual, historical and theoretically informed accounts, and presents the diversity of the Buddhist funeral cultures of mainland Southeast Asia and China. It arises out of the University of Bristol's Centre for Buddhist Studies research project *Buddhist Death Rituals in Southeast Asia and China*, funded by the UK's Arts and Humanities Research Council (AHRC). This project involved extensive new research in Thailand, Laos and China. Other items from that project included several public exhibitions, extensive stills photographs and several video films. The project team produced two 30-minute films on the Ghost Festival in Laos and China, one on urban funerals in Chiang Mai (Thailand) and several shorter clips dealing with funeral cultures in Laos, Thailand and China. Most of this material (and an extensive bibliography on the topic) is available free of charge from the project website located at the webpage of the Department of Theology and Religious Studies (Centre for Buddhist Studies) at the University of Bristol.

It gives us great pleasure to thank the AHRC for the funding that made this project possible. We also want to thank all those who contributed in different ways to its success, including those who took part in making and appearing in the films, all the contributors to this book and, in particular, the three research fellows/assistants who were involved during the lifetime of the project: Rita Langer, who originally conceived the project and saw its birth as well as undertaking some of the research involved; Patrice Ladwig, who was the research fellow throughout the body of the project and undertook a great deal of the research and organisation involved; and Ailsa Laxton, whose wonderfully efficient organisation and also expertise in putting on exhibitions came at just the right time. Thank you all so much not only for your impeccable efficiency but also for the sense of humour that made working on this project so much fun. We should thank, too, Ingmar Heise, who held the AHRC PhD research bursary for the project, and his supervisor, our colleague John Kieschnick. We would also like to thank John Kieschnick for preparing the Index. Thanks as well to our other colleague, Rupert Gethin, for all his encouragement, support and help, and to the University of Bristol for providing such an agreeable base for the project.

The project would have been impossible without all the people in Laos, Thailand and China who welcomed us into their homes and temples and allowed us to participate in their lives. In Laos we would like to express our gratitude to all the families and temples in Vientiane and Luang Prabang that aided us in our research, especially Duang Lattana Suphantong and Gregory Kourilsky, Khongma Pathoummy, and Michel Lorrillard and Achan Keo Sirivongsa of École Française d'Extrême-Orient (EFEO) Vientiane. Thanks also to the Section of Religion of the Lao National Front for Reconstruction in Vientiane and Huaphan province. In Chiang Mai we would like to thank Apinya Fuengfusakul, Nawin Sopapum and Suebsakun Kidnukorn for excellent hosting and research assistance. On the Chinese side we would like to express our gratitude to Zhang Han, Professor Xu Jinding of Quanzhou's Huaqiao University, Mao Wei and his friends and the monastics, monasteries and laypeople of Quanzhou.

Thank you Laura Morris and all those involved at Cambridge University Press for accepting this book and also for its production.

Funeral rites may not be a laugh a minute, but we hope the results – the 'outputs', as we are nowadays expected to call them – will still be informative, stimulating of further scholarly research, and perhaps even entertaining.

PATRICE LADWIG
AND
PAUL WILLIAMS

CHAPTER I

Introduction: Buddhist funeral cultures

Patrice Ladwig and Paul Williams

DEATH AT THE CENTRE OF BUDDHIST CULTURE

The statement that 'death is the origin and the center of culture' (Assmann 2005: 1) might at first sight seem like a simple generalisation that misses out on many other aspects of culture. However, when the study of death is not simply reduced to a rite of passage, we believe that approaching Buddhist cultures through their ideas, imaginaries and practices related to death can help us to understand crucial facts that reach beyond the domain of death and dying. First, death offers a unique departure for understanding the relations between people, monks, ritual experts and other entities that are commonly labelled as 'the dead', but can in fact comprise a multitude of entities of various ontological statuses. Second, death reaches out into such diverse domains as agricultural fertility, human reproduction, political cults and the economy and therefore constitutes a total social fact (Mauss 1990). Jan Assmann's statement also has a particular relevance for the history of Buddhism. Death indeed was and is at the centre of Buddhist culture and has on a ritual, ideological and even economic level played a crucial role in its development and spread. Death was from its beginning an event that was seen as particularly central to Buddhist interests. Throughout Asia it has always been recognised that Buddhists are specialists in death. One of the things that attracted Chinese (and Tibetans, for that matter) to Buddhism was its clarity about what happens at death, the processes needed to ensure a successful death – the welfare of the dead person and his or her mourners – and its clarity about what happens after death and its links with the whole way someone has lived their life. No other rival religion in Asia had at that time such clarity. It was a major factor in the successful transmission of Buddhism from its original Indian cultural context.

Why was Buddhism so successful in explaining death? Death was written into Buddhism from the beginning. It is universally accepted in the various hagiographies of Siddhārtha Gautama (died c. 400 BCE), the wealthy aristocrat who was to become the so-called 'historical Buddha', known as Śākyamuni, that one of the things which first gave him the existential crisis that led to his spiritual search was the sight of a dead man. This came as a shock, but much more was the shock when he applied the lesson to himself. *He too* would one day be as this man was – dead. The breakdown which resulted took from him all taste for the pleasures of life. Aware that there were others in north India who felt like he did, and who sought a state of being in which death would have ceased to be a problem for them, he renounced his life of luxury (and his wife and child) and joined them, a 'drop-out'. After many years in the forest, a homeless ascetic who lived on alms and practised physical austerities and deep meditation, he came to understand that if he could see in the deepest, most life-transforming way things the way they really are then *death would no longer be anything to him.* Seeing things that way, Buddhists hold, made Siddhārtha Gautama the Awakened One, the Buddha. This is a matter of the mind, understanding reality as it is, not physical asceticism but mental comprehension brought about through deep meditation. And that awakening was accompanied, so Buddhist tradition holds, by a triumph over Māra, the Buddhist 'tempter', whose very name suggests etymologically a personification of death.

So the Buddhist path from the beginning lay in a confrontation with death, at least for the spiritual virtuosi who could manage it. Doctrinally and philosophically speaking, there is also an intimate link between the notion of impermanence (Pali: *anicca*) and death. Things naturally arise and fall in accordance with impersonal causal processes. We suffer, we suffer all the time – including the unbearable but inevitable suffering of death – because we try to fix the processes of change, and we crave changeable things which in their cessation are bound to cause the one who craves them to be miserable. Applied to our lives, we are naturally bound to die, just as throughout life we were really inexorably dying all the time, from moment to moment, or even split moment to split moment. Our craving for our own permanence – something which is quite impossible – is one of the crucial factors that entail our deep existential suffering and misery. We are bound to die, and release comes when we let go in the deepest possible way and cease at even a subliminal level from resisting our inevitable impermanence. For, the Buddhist tradition argues, there is nothing about us unenlightened and hence inevitably suffering folk that could ever stand firm against the inexorable process of dissolution.

In this view, death is overcome through its deep acceptance, and its acceptance involves seeing that it is constantly occurring, from moment to moment to moment. Buddhist philosophy elaborated in great detail the different types of impermanence, and the complex causal connections between impermanent events. Impermanence and death are of the very essence of Buddhism. And it is this centrality of impermanence and death in Buddhism, reflected in the Buddhist doctrinal emphasis on change and absence of enduring identity – for death is a constant occurrence, we are really in many ways dead even while we are alive – when expressed in living cultures where close reciprocal relationships with the dead ancestors are essential to social identity and cohesion, that we shall see reflected in the studies contained in this book.

THE DEAD BETWEEN 'DOCTRINAL ABSENCE' AND 'ANTHROPOLOGICAL PRESENCE'

As many contributions in the present volume show, the dead continue to play a role in the life of the living; not only in the form of memory, but as 'active' members of a family or a community. They can live on in the form of other entities, as ancestors, spirits, ghosts. Therefore, what counts as dead, as being and agency has to be explored in very specific contexts. As Holt (2007) puts it for Sri Lankan Buddhism, the dead are 'gone, but not departed'. As classical and recent anthropological studies of death (Hertz 1960; Metcalf and Huntington 1991) have shown, in many societies death is usually conceived as a process of transformation, and less as the end of the agency of a deceased person, as is very often assumed in biological, 'Western'-inspired understandings. And yet the idea of 'the dead' as active members of the community, while undoubtedly very much present in the cultures covered by this book, provides an obvious paradox for anyone whose exposure to the study of Buddhism has been entirely or primarily its doctrine. For from the beginning, we have been taught, Buddhism holds that the dead have been reborn (or reincarnated – the attempt sometimes made to suggest some sort of difference between the two in 'Buddhist English' has little to recommend it). Whether the dead are reborn immediately after death, as is the doctrinal position of the Theravāda Buddhism of Southeast Asia, or there exists a short period of up to forty-nine days before rebirth, as is common in the Buddhism of e.g. Tibet or China, makes little difference. The fact is that soon after death the dead have gone beyond recall, reborn perhaps as happy beings known as 'gods' (*deva*), or as warlike 'anti-gods' forever jealous of the gods, or perhaps once more as humans, or non-human creatures such as animals, fish, cockroaches or wiggly worms, or hungry ghosts, or worst of all reborn in one of the many terrible hells of Buddhism in accordance with the moral quality of their past deeds while alive ('karma').

Of course, it is perfectly possible that one's dead family members have been reborn close to their living descendants, and hence are still capable one way or another of being in a dependence relationship with the living. But once more the majority doctrinal position of Buddhism has been to deny that these beings could be seen as actually still being our former family members who have passed on and to whom we hence preserve our familial duties of former times. This is because (we are told in so many introductory books on Buddhism) the Buddha did not hold that the reborn being is literally in all respects the *same* as the being who died. The reborn being is certainly not in any meaningful sense the same *person* as the one who died, and this point is recognised quite explicitly in several influential Buddhist philosophical traditions (Williams 1998: Chs. 3, 5). A cockroach cannot be the same person as one's grandfather.

The link between the 'reborn being' and the 'being that died' is explained in terms of causal dependence, where karmic causation is held to be a central factor in holding the whole process together. And it is essential to Buddhist doctrine that with causation there is absolutely no need for some sort of permanent, unchanging, enduring self-identical bearer of personal identity – a 'Self' – to link the one who dies and their rebirth (Collins 1982). All that happens is that at death the psychophysical bundle, made up out of a stream of physical events, sensations, conceptual activities, various other mental events including crucially one's intentions, and that awareness which is necessary to any conscious experience (i.e. the five classes of psychophysical events known as the 'aggregates') reconfigures. Doctrinally speaking, a living being is nothing more than a temporarily structured configuration of physical events, sensations, events of conceptualisation, various mental events such as intentions, and awareness, without any enduring Self (Pali: *attā*; Sanskrit: *ātman*) to glue him or her all together. Even when alive these aggregates (Pali: *khandha*; Sanskrit: *skandha*) form a flow, a stream, with no stability save that provided temporarily by the structuring causal force of previous actions. At death one configuration breaks down and another configuration takes place. Thus the person is reducible to a temporary bundle of events where all constituent events are radically impermanent, temporarily held together through causal relationships. Thus even if one's family members have been reborn in close relationship to their grieving family, this doctrinal position would entail that the rebirth cannot in any meaningful sense preserve enough identity to entail the normal social relationships and duties incumbent upon close or even fairly distant family members. The dead may be all around us, but they are no longer *our* dead.

And yet, as we shall see in the collection of papers published in this book, anthropological work in cultures where Buddhism plays a major part shows that the doctrinal scenario represented here must obviously be transformed and reinterpreted where reciprocal relationships with the dead ancestors is an essential part of living as a member of the group and its own social identity and cohesion. These dead ancestors are frequently felt to be present and still to be themselves for sometimes a considerable, if not indefinite, time after death, certainly more than forty-nine days. They continue to be present, albeit as transformed entities. Because Buddhism is in a society it necessarily performs a social role, and that role (a role of all religions) is one of caring and coping for the needs of society. As society also includes the dead, Buddhist funeral cultures comprise a multitude of ritual and other activities focusing on those who remain alive in some sense despite being considered dead. The deceased have to be cared for, they have to be fed, to be appeased or simply to be remembered as the duties to and relationships with the dead are essential to the flourishing of many, perhaps all, societies.

IMAGINING DEATH AND THE RITUAL PROCESS

With the expression 'Buddhist funeral cultures' we do not strictly limit ourselves to the domain of ritual or text, or an original idea of death in early Indian Buddhism. We understand the term in the sense of an imaginary, the latter term here denoting not something false or fantastic, but – similar to Steven Collins' notion of the 'Pali imaginaire' (1998: 72ff.) – as a concept referring to a capacity or faculty of the mind dealing with death and the dead. This imaginary is also created and expressed in ritual and everyday practices. Farrer (2006) has used the term 'deathscapes' in a very similar sense. On the one hand this can refer to concrete spaces of death like cemeteries, crematoria, monuments or, in general, material aspects of death (Sidaway and Maddrell 2010). On the other hand, this can deal with the complex conglomerate of abstract discursive and subjective spaces which death 'inhabits': texts, stories, emotions, but also rites and social practices are just a few examples. These stand in constant dialogue with the concrete spaces of death mentioned before. Due to these multiple links of death to various fields and domains, it cannot be understood as a timeless and universal idea or concept. Because 'society is not only made up of the living but also includes the dead' (De Coppet 1981: 198), death reflects the larger changes in society and history. Rituals, death imaginaries and deathscapes are open to transformations caused, for example, by political changes, sectarian divisions or religious purifications. In the chapters dealing with death and spirits in Laos (Bouté and Ladwig: Chapters 5 and 6) and

Heise on the Chinese ghost festival (Chapter 10) we see how socialist revolutions have led to certain rationalisations or even ritual restructurings that still have an influence in the present. Another example of the change of funerals is how the civil war in Sri Lanka has also left its traces in the preachings performed at funerals (Kent 2010). Robinne's chapter on theatre plays staged at a monk's funeral in Burma (Chapter 8) show that these performances are also commentaries on the present state of affairs. Besides dramatising the emotions of loss and mourning, imposed government propaganda (including the caricaturing of Westerners, for example) has been integrated into these plays. However, also a subversive and subtle critique of the Burmese junta can be aired in these performances.

What one encounters in the field, especially when dealing with local Buddhist funeral experts, is the claim that the rites – as prescribed and normative forms of behaviour – have changed little. Although Langer in her contribution (Chapter 2) proposes for the Sri Lankan case that 'death rituals appear to be quite resilient to change', closer inspection through a historical perspective often reveals a different picture. As in Chirapravati's contribution (Chapter 4), this might be expressed through a change in the role of objects in funerals, but might also be visible through deeper ritual restructurings. However, taking our informants seriously in that matter also means acknowledging that the *imaginary of continuity*, or the non-change of certain elements of these rites, is crucial for them. In the sense of Langer's quote above, death is considered a serious issue that demands regulation and the weight of a continuous tradition to be dealt with.

Death is a total social fact that cannot be cut out and analysed as a single-standing social event; it is rather a starting point of a long transformative process and an initiation into an afterlife (van Gennep 1960) of various deathscapes. Many studies of the volume therefore focus on the collective experience of death and how it is dealt with ritually. Death, as a disruption, the occurring of a sudden absence and non-presence, poses a threat to the social and cosmic order. Rites can be understood as instant and prophylactic measures to handle this exceptional situation and regain order. This process is most clearly expressed in Robert Hertz's classical study on the collective representations of death:

> The brute fact of physical death is not enough to consummate death in people's minds: the image of the recently deceased is still part of the system of things of this world, and looses itself from them only gradually by a series of internal partings. [. . .] Thus, if a certain period is necessary to banish the deceased from the land of the living, it is because society, disturbed by the shock, must gradually regain its balance. (Hertz 1960: 81–2).

This shock, or state of exception caused by death, is a confrontation that calls for ritual explication, but also a ritual smoothing of the transition. As Faure (1991: 184) has attested for Chan Buddhism, ritual is a form of mediation that 'simultaneously hides and reveals death: it marks its apotheosis, but also diffuses or defers its suddenness by turning the corpse or its substitutes into signifiers'. Ritual in that sense structures the space and time necessary for the movements and transformations of the corpse (Parkin 1992). This transformation of the corpse involves a number of stages such as the preparation and laying out of the corpse, recitation of texts, procession, and the final transformation of the corpse through incineration or burial. This process is accompanied by a 'care for the dead' by the living by providing food, merit, prayer and so forth. Obviously, there are large variations to this pattern. Even in one culturally relatively homogenous community differences caused through status distinctions can be huge: a monk has a very different funeral from a well-off layperson, and again this one is differentiated from the poor peasant. Langer's contribution starts with the (rhetorical) question 'Is there such a thing as Theravāda Buddhist funeral?', to which Tam in his contribution on Southeastern Chinese funeral rites (Chapter 11) gives us an indirect answer. For him, 'in the end defining a "standard" Chinese Buddhist death ritual is not a particularly useful project' (a similar point made for Tibet in Gouin 2010). It is not about the search for an original, historical blueprint of these rites, nor about defining a standard. So does the search for common patterns or a comparison between larger categories make sense at all?

COMPARISONS, CATEGORIES AND DIFFERENCES

Large-scale comparisons are, since the theoretical decline of grand narratives and the influence of deconstruction, a bit out of fashion. Recent research on the basic categories of Buddhist studies such as 'Theravāda' or 'Mahāyāna' have been critically scrutinised (Skilling and Carbine 2011). However, Williams argues that despite doctrinal diversity one can with appropriate caution speak of Buddhism and Mahāyāna as categories. Buddhism in that sense has 'doctrinal diversity and (relative) moral unity' (Williams 2009: 1). Although we cannot offer in this volume a systematic comparison between mainland Southeast Asian Theravāda Buddhist funeral cultures and Chinese cases, we believe the outcome of such an endeavour depends on the framework and scope of comparison. There is a whole spectrum between deconstructing categories such as Theravāda through, for example, the study of in-depth micro-histories, and the reflexive conceptualisation of categories that can serve as a basis for systematised and general comparisons. Neither the contributions in the volume nor this introduction deliver a systematic comparison, but we suggest that it is worth paying attention to several potential fields of comparison. First, there is a certain historical and regional affinity. Mainland Southeast Asia, especially the mountainous border regions of Yunnan, Laos and Burma, are a meeting place of both regions (Evans *et al.* 2000). Laos, for example, represents the eastern limit of Theravāda's expansion into Southeast Asia. In relation to funeral cultures, Gregory Kourilsky (2012) has, for example, suggested that certain elements found in the Lao Ghost Festival have clear parallels in the Chinese and Vietnamese festivals. Ladwig's and Heise's chapters deal with these festivals in their respective contexts and can serve as comparative examples. Here, the textual sources such as the story of Mulian in China and the Theravāda Moggallāna point to common origins that are ritually interpreted in different ways. Kapstein (2007) has also looked at the transformations of this narrative in the Tibetan-Chinese context.

A second example for the potential of comparison in the domain of funeral cultures can be advanced with regard to the importance of ancestor cults. Bouté's contribution on the Phunoy – a Tibeto-Burman minority living in the borderlands of Laos and China – suggests that their ancestor cult at least bears some resemblance to Chinese practices. The same can be said for the descriptions of bad or 'green' death, which also contains a comparative potential (see further below). We do not want to suggest that mainland Southeast Asian Buddhism is simply a mixture of Chinese and Indian influences, but that some partial connections exist and are worth following up in future research. Peter van der Veer's (2009) comparison between India and China as civilisations can here serve as a model.

Another level of comparison *inside* the Theravāda tradition is advanced by Langer. Looking at funerals and chants in Sri Lanka, Laos, Thailand and Burma, her comparative examination looks for 'core elements' of these rites and their variation. Langer gives us an overview of these elements: the presentation of a rag-robe (*paṃsukūla*), the giving of merit, the asking for forgiveness and religious wishes. She then discusses the 'optional elements' like Abhidhamma chanting and the use of protective *parittas*. With reference to Lévi-Strauss's idea of *bricolage*, Langer understands the performed rites and the chanted texts as a toolbox from which certain elements can be drawn. Although religious specialists might point to the coherence of chants and their genealogy from the Pali canon, variation and individual appropriation is rather the norm than the exception. Here, the canon (for the Theravāda case) and the chants used in funeral rites, are less a fixed compendium of texts, but rather an 'idea' that is efficacious through its imagined homogeneity and continuity (Collins 1995). Despite these variations, Langer – through a meticulous analysis of funeral chants – succeeds in uncovering common patterns across a vast temporal and spatial spectrum perhaps also based in the long tradition of regular exchanges between Southeast Asian and Sri Lankan Buddhism. Langer concludes her contribution with the statement, 'On the whole, Theravāda monks from Thailand would find little difficulty in joining into a chant of monks from Sri Lanka.'

Comparison, however, is also based on markers of difference. In contrast to the chapters dealing with Theravāda in mainland Southeast Asia, the two contributions by Tam and Chen (Chapters 11 and 12) both refer to the 'imperial metaphor' (Feuchtwang 1991) that becomes visible, for example, in the passport-like documents that the deceased need in order to cross the boundary to the afterlife. This is completely absent in the instance of Theravāda and the Chinese cases are marked by a different idea of orthopraxy. For Feuchtwang (2009: 103), China has 'a civilization of the government of conduct, its correction, exemplary performance and enforcement'. Although Ladwig has found similar ideas of the bureaucracy of hell in Laos that could be related to the imperial metaphor, the difference between them is still large. There is no bank of hell among Theravāda Buddhists and no burning of spirit money or houses can be observed. The sacrificial economy connecting the world of the living and the dead follows a different logic. The latter point is also visible in the different roles of monks. Whereas in China expert laypeople or half-official monks can also officiate at funerals (see the *xianghua heshang* in Tam's chapter), the Theravāda saṅgha seems to have a much more clearly defined position in death rituals. Without them, the contact to the dead is difficult whereas in China burning money or paper replicas of offerings can be done without the intermediary role of monks. On the whole, our volume has more contributions regarding mainland Southeast Asia, but the excellent volumes edited by Cuevas and Stone (2007), and Watson and Rawski (1988) present more information on East Asian funeral cultures. The material presented there can be contrasted and compared with the Theravāda cases presented here.

THE LOCALISATION OF BUDDHIST FUNERAL CULTURES

The majority of contributions look at Buddhism as being very much 'of a place', as all Buddhism really is and to which all study of Buddhism needs constantly to return. In cultures where Buddhism has been predominant, the relationship between Buddhist doctrine and social behaviour is a very complex one indeed (see, for example, Gombrich 1971). But it would be quite wrong to approach Buddhism as it occurs 'in a place' (and when does it not occur in a place?) with some sort of legislative model of what *should* happen or what Buddhists *must* do. Given the large variety of what has been called 'Buddhisms' (Ling 1993), we do not intend to reconstruct an original death ritual and then look at the local variations that have evolved. Instead, we want to examine the creative local appropriations that in a manner of a *bricolage* make use of certain elements already apparent, for example, in early Buddhism. The *Mahāparinibbāna Sutta*, recounting the last days, death and the funeral of the Buddha (cf. Strong 2007), could in this light be seen as a textual toolbox out of which certain elements are appropriated and are then translated into ritual practices constituted by partially prescribed, but also improvised actions accommodated to a local context.

Given the centrality of funeral rites in the development and spread of Buddhism, many of the contributions give us a detailed image of the localisation of Buddhism in the field of funeral culture. The interaction with pre-Buddhist ideas and cosmologies of the dead are, for example, exemplified in the multiplicity of concepts of what constitutes a person and how this entity, substance or conscience is transformed in the course of death. Conceptualising this interaction of Buddhist concepts and their transformation on the local level in a specific setting has a long history in anthropology and Buddhist studies. Discussions on the interaction of 'great and little tradition' (Obeyesekere 1963), the structural division of labour of Buddhism and spirit cults (Tambiah 1970), or more generally speaking notions of syncretism, have all examined the transformation of Buddhism on the local level. These discussions can also be applied to Buddhist funeral cultures.

However, like the concept of comparison discussed above, most of these discussions are currently somewhat out of fashion through the influence of a flexible hybridism model of culture. Shaw and Stewart (1995: 7), for example, propose that seeing a ritual or religion as syncretic 'gets us practically nowhere, since all religions have composite origins and are continually reconstructed through ongoing processes of synthesis and erasure'. Historical studies of Buddhism have proposed a less radical, but still similar, view. Buddhism was from its very beginning linked to a variety of local cults and entities that have been subsumed under the category of spirits or ancestors, as for example DeCaroli (2004) has shown. Through this flexible approach to funeral culture we can understand that there were also specific openings in Buddhist cosmology that allowed for an easy integration of indigenous cults. Reynolds (1976: 207) suggests that 'one of the reasons Buddhist cosmography fitted so well into mainland Southeast Asian societies is that it included a place for the creatures of animism'. Given the complex switches of ethnic and religious affiliation in mainland Southeast Asia (Leach 1954), this openness has probably contributed to Buddhism's successful spread.

Despite the widespread scepticism about concepts that try to understand the relationship of Buddhism and indigenous culture, the problem does not disappear. Just imagine a 'first contact situation' in the case of funerals. How did monks accommodate to a local situation? How did they enter into the local funeral traditions and what roles could be appropriated? In his contribution, Chen employs a historical perspective and through archaeological evidence reconstructs the meeting of Chinese Buddhist funeral culture with local burial customs. Like Schopen (1997), Chen argues that in order to avoid social censure, monks had a tendency to adjust their practice to local values. Chen also looks at current burial practices, in which monks, compared to the Theravāda cases we have discussed before, have a rather limited role. Moreover, he proposes that we have to look at a triangular relation that besides laity and saṅgha also includes funeral specialists, which in contemporary Taiwan still play a major role. An interesting case that moves outside the division of 'great and little tradition' is described in Formoso's contribution. He analyses the activities of Chinese funeral associations in Thailand and Malaysia that collect the bones of the victims of bad death. The activities and rites give rise to a very exceptional case of interethnic funeral cooperation. Although there are also differences and interethnic problems associated with the rite, Formoso thinks that 'Buddhism whatever the doctrinal differences between Theravāda and Mahāyāna traditions, is a key factor to bridge the differences between the groups in contact'. We see here again how Buddhism delivers a flexible template that can operate in various contexts and lives on its multiplicity of concepts.

Coming back to syncretism, we find in David Gellner's anthropology of Buddhism a line of argument that recovers some value in the concept of syncretism, namely as defining a certain hierarchy and interpretational sovereignty. Concerning the interaction of Buddhism and local traditions, he states that 'in order to find cohabitation acceptable, Buddhist specialists require that these other systems acknowledge Buddhism as the supreme overarching system, and as a path to salvation, and that their practices do not conflict too blatantly with Buddhism's own teachings' (Gellner 1997: 323). Applying Gellner's insight to funeral cultures results in what could be called an 'ordered multiplicity of concepts' instead of a random cultural hybridity. A good example for this ordered multiplicity can be found with reference to the immaterial components of a deceased person that features in many of the contributions. Although references to *viññāṇa* (Pali: 'consciousness') or its equivalent are to be found in most Buddhist funeral cultures, there are substantial overlaps with pre-Buddhist and indigenous concepts of soul, spirits and ancestor to be found. In contributions by de Mersan (Chapter 7) and Bouté (Chapter 5) we see multiple concepts of 'soul' (a term Buddhologists always try to avoid), or what survives death at work in funeral cultures. These concepts do not contradict each other, but open a space of interpretation. This complex amalgam of various concepts is well documented in Robinne's chapter. The theatrical performances that accompany the funerals of monks are a way of rewriting the Buddhist canon or filling the gaps, but only 'when the text's ambiguity leaves open this space'. In the sense of an ordered multiplicity this interpretative freedom is not random, and in his view 'these amalgams and confusions cannot be simply attributed to ignorance'. So it is not only that there is in many of the cases described in the volume a survival of certain aspects of a deceased person – a feature that was already present in early Indian Buddhism (Gellner 1997: 214; see also Gethin 1998: 159f.) – but, moreover, there is a multitude of ways to conceptualise this aspect of death. What is crucial when looking at these multilayered concepts is that their interaction is not necessarily random, but can be systemic. In many cases this syncretic multiplicity might affirm Buddhism's hegemony in the funeral business. However, there might also be cases when Buddhist concepts are pushed into the background, as in the case of the Tibeto-Burman Phunoy where there is neither a Buddhist concept of the 'soul' nor an idea of reincarnation predominant.

BAD DEATHS, GHOSTS AND POLLUTION

The fate of the immaterial components of a person is of crucial importance in Buddhist funeral practices. Besides the fact that someone died, it is also important to look at who died in which way. The pollution and dangerousness caused by a normal death is multiplied in the case of a bad death. Chanting and the 'magical power of words' (Tambiah 1968) are often considered an indispensable part of a funeral rite and battle the potential pollution caused by death. Schopen (1997: 219) points out that death and pollution have always been central to Hinduism and that certain elements were appropriated by early Buddhism in order to fit into the cultural landscape of Hinduism and avoid criticism and opposition. Although the overarching importance of notions of purity and pollution, for example as proposed in the heavily criticised account of Hinduism by Dumont (1980), is not observable in Southeast Asia and China, the domain of funerals is to a certain extent always marked by pollution. As Davis states in his contribution on Khmer funeral culture (Chapter 3), monks are considered to be socially dead and are therefore equipped to deal with death as an exceptional situation, but the laity is still exposed to the dangers of death. Pollution, according to Mary Douglas' (2002) study *Purity and Danger*, is a result of the contact or presence of an anomaly, a break in the flow of things that resists classification and endangers the community. Although death is in some sense completely natural, it at the beginning 'resists' integration and is shocking, especially in the case of bad death; a notion widely spread in Asia and understood as an untimely, premature or violent death (Baptandier 2001; Feuchtwang 2010: 135f.). Douglas states that pollution has to be understood as the 'interplay between form and formlessness' (2002: 150). Ritual can be seen as the struggle to give bad death a form, work it through and combat pollution.

Several contributions in this volume deal with the case of bad death, but the two cases of 'ethnic minority Buddhism' – by De Mersan on the Arakhanese in Burma and Bouté on the Phunoy in Laos – are perhaps most exemplary. De Mersan's chapter contains an impressive description of a rite called 'to introduce the word action' intended to drive out evil forces and spirits in case of bad death. Among the Arakhanese, bad deaths 'give rise to an immaterial component of a person in search of a base, which therefore endangers the living'. Here the ritual actions redefine the social space and boundaries of the village and the chants purify it and expel evil spirits. Another example of how death threatens the social cohesion and purity of the village is given in Bouté's contribution. Here, the yearly rites for the ancestors have the main goal of securing the purity of the village and regenerating its potential for fertility of humans and the land. The idea of reincarnation – in popular imaginary perhaps the *sine qua non* of Buddhist funeral cultures – according to Bouté remains quite foreign to the Phunoy. Ancestor cults are far more important for them due to their protective qualities.

Heise's and Ladwig's contributions on China and Laos respectively connect the themes of bad death and ghosts. Ghosts are from a doctrinal perspective often the outcome of bad karma or negative deeds towards one of the members of the saṅgha, but in practice they are often associated with bad death. Ghosts can point to unresolved conflicts, trauma and bad death; to a life that through violence and untimeliness has not had a proper ending and has yet to be finalised. Persons who have died a bad death are denied the passage and are caught inbetween the worlds. Nevertheless, ghosts are social beings that are addressed and play a role in the lives of the living, or indeed can be seen, heard or spoken to in specific contexts and have specific desires. Therefore, one should not approach ghosts as remnants of a 'primitive belief', but as important figures of the social fabric. Morris (2008: 31) suggests that 'ghostliness in Southeast Asia offers itself as an idiom with which to address issues about the difficult delineation of a boundary between the living and the dead'. This is especially exemplified in cases where political violence, war or rapid and forced social change has happened (Kwon 2008; Mueggler 2001). Here, the line between the living and the dead is blurred through hauntings, and ghosts in that sense stand in defiance of binary oppositions such as presence and absence, body and spirit, past and present, life and death (Derrida 1994). The ambiguity exemplified by ghosts calls for ritual action either as part of the ritual cycle (as described by Heise and Ladwig), or demanding even greater ritual action in order to appease, for example, the abandoned souls of soldiers who have never found peace due to their bad death on the battlefield (Kwon 2008).

THE MATERIALITY OF FUNERAL CULTURES

But not only ritual actions, words and beliefs are topics of research when dealing with Buddhist funeral cultures. Gregory Schopen (1991) can be considered one of the first who seriously took into account the study of certain material evidence in early Indian Buddhism and in recent studies, the materiality of religion has been highlighted as a long-neglected field of inquiry. Things and objects also have a social life (Appadurai 1986) that can be important for funeral cultures. Objects dealing with the dead are crucial for performing rituals, but also for recalling the presence of the dead. Hallam and Hockey (2001: 7) propose that 'in the absence suggested by death we find potent cultural materials and strategies including objects, visual images and texts that constitute systems of recall'. The objects dealt with in funeral rites – may they be quotidian things or ritual objects – have a lot to say about how death is imagined and dealt with. It is important what people and texts tell us, but we must not forget that ritual actions are carried out with the objects that often play a crucial role in these performances. Davis, Langer and Chirapravati deal with a specific material aspect of Buddhist funeral culture, namely with the *paṃsukūla* robe. By looking at depictions of funerals in Thai murals in a historical perspective, Chirapravati is able to detect important changes in Thai funeral culture. Here, the shift from *paṃsukūla* as rag-robe taken from the dead to an offering of a new robe at Thai funerals attests the transformation of monks from scavengers to recipients of gifts (Schopen 2006: 337). Davis explores the meanings of the *paṃsukūla* in the Khmer context and proposes that 'the ritual actions of the *paṃsukūla* are mirrored in ritual and technical actions performed in other contexts, in which non-Buddhist spirits are controlled and made useful by Buddhist monks'. Langer examines the, at first sight, contradictory modern image of the *paṃsukūla* with its sources in Buddhist history by looking at the chants associated with it.

The topic of the materiality of funeral cultures is also a topic dealt with by Patrice Ladwig. He focuses on the post-mortem fate of victims of bad death, who among the ethnic Lao become *phiphed*, a liminal ghost being sharing many characteristics with the *peta* of the *Petavatthu*, but also exposing specificities of the local cosmology. Although the ritual discussed by Ladwig has its textual references in Pali Buddhism, he proposes that certain Buddhist key concepts linked to the funeral culture such as the widely discussed transfer of merit are relevant, but can only be understood in relation to Lao notions of food and corporality. The materiality of the offerings given to ghosts has nourishing qualities that largely derive from a local cosmology, but is ritually integrated into the transfer of merit.

DEATH AND THE REGENERATION OF LIFE

The role of beings labelled 'dead' also becomes important in relation to fertility and the regenerative potential that death contains. Death is, almost on a universal level, a ritual separation from the living, but also a celebration and reproduction of fertility not only in the human domain. In that sense, the 'rebirth which occurs at death is not only a denial of individual extinction but also a reassertion of society and a renewal of life and creative power' (Bloch and Parry 1982: 5). Death is always a signifier of the potential breakdown of fertility through finitude and decay and demands ritual action aiming at reestablishing order and reproduction. Hertz already noted in his comparative study on death that, 'In establishing a society of the dead, the society of the living regularly recreates itself' (Hertz 1960: 72). Many of the funeral cultures discussed in the book are still predominately situated in societies that make their living out of or from agriculture. Here, the fertility of the land is intimately linked to the dead as protective spirits or ancestors. Paul Mus (1975) already proposed this link of Buddhism with Southeast Asian 'cadastral cults'. Indian religions took root in Southeast Asia by establishing a link to chthonic forces and fertility. In his contribution on Khmer funeral culture, Davis conceptualises the monk as a master and farmer of the dead who is capable of controlling and containing the worlds of spirits. With reference to the *paṃsukūla* robe and its role in ritual practice and the imaginary of death,

Davis proposes that the rites involving the *paṃsukūla* and other objects aim at binding indeterminate vitality unleashed by death into a useful form. These 'ritual technologies' link death practices to agricultural fertility. Human fertility and sexual symbolism is also a theme often encountered in funeral rites. Robinne's contribution also refers to sexual symbolism in Burmese funerals. Death and the regeneration of human life are crucial themes of the Burmese theatre plays performed. Erect phalli are paraded around during the funeral thereby performatively acting out the relationship between conception, death and rebirth.

But what is exactly reproduced in the case of death might differ significantly in Buddhist funeral cultures. Bloch and Parry (1982: 7) argue that, 'In most cases what would seem to be revitalised in funerary practices is that resource which is culturally conceived to be the most essential to the reproduction of the social order.' Whereas in many Theravāda Buddhist societies and also in the Chinese case described by Yik Fai Tam we can identify merit (Pali: *puñña*; Sanskrit: *puṇya*) as a crucial resource to reproduce social order, the link between fertility and death looks different among the Tibeto-Burman Phunoy. For the Phunoy, the dead are not receivers of merit, as commonly found among most groups in the region like the ethnic Lao described by Ladwig. For the Phunoy, the reactivation of fertility and protection through transforming the dead into protective ancestors is more crucial than transferring merit.

FUTURE RESEARCH PROSPECTS

Although the single contributions also refer at times to the modernisation of Buddhist funeral cultures (the influence of political changes, for example), the scope of most of these essays is rather 'traditional' and remains focused on the collective representations of Buddhist funeral cultures. This might be explained by several factors: First, the data collected by our contributors often derive from field-sites and timeframes that have only to a certain extent been exposed to 'modernity'. Second, for the sake of the coherence of the volume we have limited ourselves to such cases and decided not to include studies that deal, for example, with urban funeral associations, new ways of dying or new cosmologies of the afterlife. We believe that before embarking on such studies, more groundwork has to be covered. Therefore, our own volume and that of Cuevas and Stone (2007) also leave many questions open that will hopefully be addressed in future research. A lot remains to be said about the transformations that have and will occur in Buddhist funeral cultures through increasing urbanisation, the use of new medical technologies or the economy of funeral businesses. The field is wide open and here we only want to mention some examples that could be seen as widening the scope of this volume.

A good example for expanding the research in Buddhist funeral cultures is Suzuki's study (2001) of the changes of Japanese funeral culture. Here, the professionalisation of the funeral business through modernisation and new divisions of labour has led to profound changes. His project clearly reflects how death becomes modernised and is connected to wider social and economic changes in Japanese society. Another fine example for widening the study of death in a Buddhist context is the project of Felicity Aulino, who is currently completing a PhD at Harvard focusing on the contemporary palliative care movement and hospices in contemporary northern Thailand. We would also like to mention Gregory Delaplace's (2008) excellent work *L'Invention des Morts. Sépultures, Fantômes et Photographies en Mongolie Contemporaine.* His study deals with the transformations of Mongolian Buddhist funeral culture. Here, the everyday relations with the spirits of the dead and the use of photographs for remembering and visualising the dead are dealt with in innovative ways. Finally, we would like to mention that Buddhist funeral cultures have already reached cyberspace. One can now practise Buddhist death and afterlife in a computer game. The 'Religion in Virtual Worlds Study Group' at Front Range Community College in Colorado tested out the 'Second Life Bardo Game' created by the company EduPunx. The game '[. . .] virtually creates the in-between state of the dead person as described in the Tibetan Book of the Dead, challenging the player to find her way to enlightenment' (Davies-Stofka 2009: n.p.). Reading this book might not lead to enlightenment, but we ask our readers and other researchers to continue the 'game'. Please press *Enter.*

BIBLIOGRAPHY

Appadurai, A. (1986), 'Introduction: commodities and the politics of value', in ed. A. Appadurai, *The Social Life of Things. Commodities in Cultural Perspective*, New York: Cambridge University Press.

Assmann, J. (2005), *Death and Salvation in Ancient Egypt*, Ithaca, NY: Cornell University Press.

Baptandier, B. (ed.) (2001), *De la Malemort en Quelques pays d'Asie*, Paris, Karthala.

Bloch, M. and Parry, J. (1982), 'Introduction', in eds. M. Bloch and J. Parry, *Death and the Regeneration of Life*, Cambridge University Press.

Collins, S. (1982), *Selfless Persons: Imagery and Thought in Theravāda Buddhism*, Cambridge University Press.

(1995), 'On the very idea of the Pāli Canon', *Journal of the Pāli Text Society* XV, 89–126.

(1998), *Nirvana and other Buddhist Felicities: Utopias of the Pali Imaginaire*, Cambridge University Press.
Cuevas, B. and Stone, J. (2007), *The Buddhist Dead: Practices, Discourses, Representations*, Honolulu: University of Hawai'i Press.
Davies-Stofka, B. (2009), 'Inside the genesis of a serious game: creating the Second Life Bardo Game', unpublished draft paper, Front Range Community College.
DeCaroli, R. (2004), *Haunting the Buddha: Indian Popular Religions and the Formation of Buddhism*, Oxford University Press.
De Coppet, D. (1981), 'The life-giving death', in eds. S. C. Humphreys and H. King, *Mortality and Immortality: the Anthropology and Archaeology of Death*, London: Academic Press, 175–204.
Delaplace, G. (2008), *L'Invention des Morts. Sépultures, Fantômes et Photographies en Mongolie Contemporaine*, Paris: Collection Nord-Asie.
Derrida, J. (1994), *Specters of Marx, the State of the Debt, the Work of Mourning, and the New International*, London: Routledge.
Douglas, M. (2002), *Purity and Danger: an Analysis of the Concepts of Pollution and Taboo*, London: Routledge.
Dumont, L. (1980), *Homo Hierarchicus: the Caste System and its Implications*, The University of Chicago Press.
Evans, G., Hutton, C. and Khun, K. (eds.) (2000), *Where China Meets Southeast Asia: Social and Cultural Change in the Border Region*, Bangkok, White Lotus.
Farrer, D. (2006), 'Death scapes of the Malay martial artist', *Social Analysis* 50 (1), 25–50.
Faure, B. (1991), *The Rhetoric of Immediacy: a Cultural Critique of the Chan/Zen Tradition*, Princeton University Press.
Feuchtwang, S. (1991), *Popular Religion in China: the Imperial Metaphor*, London: Routledge.
(2009), 'India and China as spiritual nations: a comparative anthropology of histories', *Social Anthropology* 17, 100–8.
(2010), *The Anthropology of Religion, Charisma and Ghosts: Chinese Lessons for Adequate Theory*, Berlin, New York: de Gruyter.
Gellner, D. N. (1997), 'For syncretism: the position of Buddhism in Nepal and Japan compared', *Social Anthropology* 5 (3), 275–89.
Gethin, R. (1998), *Foundations of Buddhism*, Oxford and New York: Oxford University Press.
Gombrich, R. (1971), *Precept and Practice: Traditional Buddhism in the Rural Highlands of Ceylon*, Oxford: Clarendon Press.
Gouin, M. (2010), *Tibetan Rituals of Death*, Abingdon and New York: Routledge.
Hallam, E. and Hockey, J. (2001), *Death, Memory and Material Culture*, Oxford: Berg.
Hertz, R. (1960), 'A contribution to the study of the collective representation of death', in eds. R. Needham and C. Needham, *Death and the Right Hand*, New York: Free Press.
Holt, J. (2007), 'Gone but not departed: the dead among the living in contemporary Sri Lanka', in eds. B. Cuevas and J. Stone, *The Buddhist Dead: Practices, Discources, Representations*, Honolulu: University of Hawai'i press, 326–44.

Kapstein, M. T. (2007), 'Mulian in the land of snows and King Gesar in hell: a Chinese tale of parental death in its Tibetan transformations', in eds. B. Cuevas and J. Stone, *The Buddhist Dead: Practices, Discourses, Representations*, Honolulu: University of Hawai'i press, 345–77.

Kent, D. W. (2010), 'Onward Buddhist soldiers: preaching to the Sri Lankan army', in eds. M. Jerryson and M. Juergensmeyer, *Buddhist Warfare*, New York: Oxford University Press, 157–78.

Kourilsky, G. (2012), *Parents et Ancêtres en Milieu Bouddhiste Lao: Étude de Textes Choisis et de Leurs Applications Rituelles*, PhD thesis, Paris: École Pratique des Hautes Études.

Kwon, H. (2008), *Ghosts of War in Vietnam*, Cambridge University Press.

Leach, E. (1954), *Political Systems of Highland Burma: a Study of Kachin Social Structure*, Cambridge, MA: Harvard University Press.

Ling, T. (1993), 'Introduction', in T. Ling, *Buddhist Trends in Southeast Asia*, Singapore: Institute of Southeast Asian Studies, 1–5.

Mauss, M. (1990). *The Gift: Form and Reason for Exchange in Archaic Societies*, London: Routledge.

Metcalf, P. and Huntington, R. (1991), *Celebrations of Death*, 2nd edn, Cambridge University Press.

Morris, R. (2008), 'Giving up ghosts: notes on trauma and the possibility of the political from Southeast Asia', *Positions* **16** (1), 229–58.

Mueggler. E. (2001), *The Age of Wild Ghosts: Memory, Violence, and Place in Southwest China*, Berkeley: University of California Press.

Mus, P. (1975), *India Seen from the East: Indian and Indigenous Cults in Champa*, trans. I. W. Mabbet and D. P. Chandler, Clayton, Victoria, Australia: Monash University Centre of Southeast Asian Studies.

Obeyesekere, G. (1963), 'The Great Tradition and the Little in the perspective of Sinhalese Buddhism', *Journal of Asian Studies* **22**, 139–53.

Parkin, D. (1992), 'Ritual as spatial direction and bodily division', in ed. D. de Coppet, *Understanding Rituals*, London: Routledge.

Reynolds, C. (1976), 'Buddhist cosmography in Thai history, with special reference to nineteenth-century culture change', *Journal of Asian Studies* **35** (2), 202–20.

Schopen, G. (1991), 'Archaeology and protestant presuppositions in the study of Indian Buddhism', *History of Religions* **31** (1), 1–23.

(1997), 'On avoiding ghosts and social censure: monastic funerals in the Mulasarvastivada-vinaya', in G. Schopen, *Bones, Stones, and Buddhist Monks – Collected Papers on the Archaeology, Epigraphy, and Texts of Monastic Buddhism in India*, Honolulu: University of Hawai'i Press, 204–37.

(2006), 'A well-sanitized shroud: Asceticism and institutional values in the middle period of Buddhist monasticism', in ed. P. Olivelle, *Between the Empires: Society in India 300 BCE to 400 CE*, New York: Oxford University Press.

Shaw, R. and Stewart, C. (eds.) (1995), *Syncretism/Anti-Syncretism: the Politics of Religious Synthesis*, London: Routledge.

Sidaway, J. and Maddrell, A., (eds.) (2010), *Deathscapes: Spaces for Death, Dying and Bereavement*, Aldershot: Ashgate.

Skilling, P. and Carbine, J. (eds.) (2011), *How Theravāda is Theravāda? Exploring Buddhist Identities*, Bangkok/Taipeh: Dharma Drum.

Strong, J. S. (2007), 'The Buddha's funeral', in eds. B. Cuevas and J. Stone, *The Buddhist Dead: Practices, Discourses, Representations*, Honolulu: University of Hawai'i Press, 32–59.

Suzuki, H. (2001), *The Price of Death: the Funeral Industry in Contemporary Japan*, Stanford University Press.

Tambiah, S. J. (1968), 'The magical power of words', in *Man* (NS) 3/2, 175–208.

(1970), *Buddhism and the Spirit Cults in North-east Thailand*, Cambridge University Press.

van der Veer, P. (2009), 'The comparative sociology of India and China', *Social Anthropology* 17 (1), 90–108.

van Gennep, A. (1960), *The Rites of Passage*, University of Chicago Press [1st edn. 1909 in French].

Watson, J. and Rawski, E. (eds.) (1988), *Death Ritual in Late Imperial and Modern China*, Berkeley, London: University of California Press.

Williams, P. (1998), *Altruism and Reality: Studies in the Philosophy of the Bodhicaryāvatāra*, Richmond: Curzon.

(2009), *Mahāyāna Buddhism: the Doctrinal Foundations*, 2nd edn, London: Routledge.

CHAPTER 2

Chanting as 'bricolage *technique*': *a comparison of South and Southeast Asian funeral recitation*

Rita Langer

INTRODUCTION

There is no ancient prescriptive text outlining in detail how a Theravāda funeral is to be conducted. Nevertheless, contemporary Theravāda funerals seem to follow a recognisable pattern. Some information on funerals in the countries of South and Southeast Asia is available in regional studies and anthropological surveys, but these contain very little on the Pāli chants, which form an integral part of the ceremonies. Considering that Pāli is the sacred language shared by the Theravāda countries, these texts might provide a clue to a better understanding of how a Theravāda funeral is constructed. In the first part of this chapter funeral chanting is approached in terms of a '*bricolage*' – a patchwork of heterogeneous elements with the monk as 'bricoleur', the skilled craftsman. The main part of the chapter is based on a number of ritual 'snapshots' – recordings of ceremonies in Sri Lanka, Laos, Thailand and Myanmar. The chanting sequences of these ceremonies are analysed one by one and their composition is investigated. A chart of chanting sequences (Table 2.1) and a verse index (Table 2.2) are added to facilitate comparison and to provide a complete record and reference. The final part of the chapter offers some tentative suggestions as to why, against all odds, the pattern of Theravāda funeral chants is not more varied than it is, along with open questions and possible avenues of further inquiries concluding the study.

CHANTING AS A *BRICOLAGE* TECHNIQUE

Anyone interested in ancient Indian funeral rites has a host of prescriptive literature from which to choose as a starting point for research. The Vedic *sūtras* contain a wealth of details on how the cremation is to be performed, depending on the status of the deceased and the chief mourner.[1] The

[1] Caland (1896) records the variations in the prescribed ritual of the various Vedic schools.

situation is very different when we look at Theravāda Buddhism.[2] The countries of South and Southeast Asia, which understand themselves to belong to the Theravāda tradition of Buddhism (Sri Lanka, Myanmar, Thailand, Cambodia and Laos) share a reliance on the Buddhist canon (and its commentaries) composed in Pāli, the sacred and ritual language of the Theravādins. However, there are no ancient, prescriptive Pāli texts (canonical or post-canonical) outlining how to conduct a Theravāda Buddhist funeral. Considering this lack of prescriptive literature one might expect to find differences between the various Theravāda countries as well as regional and sectarian differences.[3] The question is just how substantial are these differences? Is it possible that the common sacred language brings with it a shared ritual heritage?[4] Or, to phrase it differently, is there such a thing as a Theravāda Buddhist funeral?

In order to explore these questions I compared a number of funeral ceremonies from Sri Lanka, Laos, Thailand and Myanmar with regard to the Pāli chants utilised.[5] As this is not an ethnographic study, research for the present paper did not require doing interviews, reading pamphlets in the vernacular languages and, strictly speaking, not even my presence in the field.[6] My intention was to create a record and reference (by way of a chart and verse and phrase index) of a number of real chanting events and analyse them. I concentrate on the Pāli chanting rather than the chanting in the vernacular, because it is a common denominator (there are others, to be sure) of Theravāda ritual and it might even be said that it defines a ritual as Theravāda. It should be understood, however, that any observations I make are merely on the basis of these ritual snapshots and not meant as general conclusions about Buddhism in Sri Lanka, Laos, Thailand and Myanmar.

[2] The complex question of what constitutes Theravāda was the topic of a panel at the International Association of Buddhist Studies (IABS) in Atlanta 2008 and a volume on the topic (edited by Peter Skilling) is forthcoming.

[3] Among the people who increased my understanding of Theravāda and its regional forms are: Rupert Gethin, Hiroko Kawanami, Gregory Kourilsky, Patrice Ladwig, Mudagamuwe Maitrimurthi and Justin McDaniel. It goes without saying that any mistakes and misconstructions in this paper are entirely my own responsibility.

[4] See also Collins (1998: 40–89) on the concept of 'Pāli imaginaire'.

[5] I would like to take this opportunity to express my gratitude to the families who let me share the funerals of their loved ones and the many members of the saṅgha who assisted me in my research. They shall remain unnamed for reasons of privacy.

[6] While I observed most of the ceremonies myself, it is also entirely possible to extract the chanting sequences from good film footage, such as the one provided by my colleague, Patrice Ladwig, for Laos 2 and Thai 2.

Bricolage

The picture that emerged from my research is a patchwork of different elements, drawn, however, from a somewhat confined pool: in other words, a *bricolage*.[7] The French term *bricolage* was in the early sixties applied to the field of religion (more specifically myths and rites) by Lévi-Strauss (1966: 17ff.) who defined the *bricoleur* as:

> adept at performing a large number of diverse tasks; but, unlike the engineer, he does not subordinate each of them to the availability of raw materials and tools conceived and procured for the purpose of the project. His universe of instruments is closed and the rules of his game are always to make do with 'whatever is at hand', that is to say with a set of tools and materials which is always finite and is also heterogeneous because what it contains bears no relation to the current project, or indeed to any particular project, but is the contingent result of all the occasions there have been to renew or enrich the stock or to maintain it with the remains of previous constructions or destructions.

Lévi-Strauss discusses this in relation to myths, but the concept – or rather process – of *bricolage* seems to be quite suited to explain the dynamics of Theravāda Buddhist funeral chanting as well. To begin with we shall examine the materials and sets of tools, which are used in the funeral chanting, and then the *bricolage* itself and the Buddhist monk as '*bricoleur*'.

The toolbox of the performer: canonical and non-canonical chants

There might not be one authoritative text prescribing how to conduct a Theravāda funeral, but there are numerous handbooks for novices, containing the basic chants for all kinds of occasions. The handbooks are probably the first contact a young novice has with Pāli chants and most monks have their own copy of some edition of a chanting handbook.[8] They might draw on a variety of other resources or people for their knowledge and inspiration, but as far as funeral chants are concerned, the handbook is for all intents and purposes the 'closed tool box'.[9] But while the handbooks contain all the chants – the building blocks – from which Theravāda ceremonies are constructed, there is still need for an experienced

[7] I am grateful to Patrice Ladwig who drew my attention to the concept of *bricolage*. Other ways to describe the dynamic of a ritual are 'ritual syntax' (see Staal 1996) or jazz composition (Ladwig, personal communication).

[8] Some examples of handbooks for novices: (1975) *Book of Chants* (for Thailand); Liambounrueang (2003), Wannaphoupa (2001) for Laos and (1995) *Sāmaṇera Baṇa Daham Pota* (for Sri Lanka).

[9] See also Samuel (2004) who discusses the novices' way of learning in Sri Lanka.

instructor to explain to novices on what occasion, in which order, etc. the chants are used.

The handbooks themselves have a long recorded history as one such, the Khuddakapāṭha, made it into the Tipitaka as the first of the fifteen books that constitute the Khuddaka Nikāya.[10] Geiger and Ghosh (1943: 19) states that it is 'clearly a prayer book for daily use' and Norman (1983: 58) speculates that 'the whole work was probably compiled as an extract from the canon to serve as a handbook for novices'. Schalk (1972: 97), comparing it to one such contemporary Sri Lankan *paritta* chanting book, observes that seven of the nine texts of the Khuddakapāṭha are found in the contemporary handbook and, with one exception, even the order of texts is kept.

Blackburn (1999a: 355) distinguishes between 'formal' and 'practical' canon:

> By formal canon I mean the Pāli canon as the ultimate locus of interpretive authority in the Theravāda. Practical canon refers to the collection of texts used in a particular time and place. The practical canon may include portions of the *tipiṭaka* with their commentaries as well as texts understood by their authors and audience consistent with, but perhaps not explicitly related to, the *tipiṭaka* and its commentaries.[11]

The practical canon, and in particular the handbook, is for an ordinary monk or novice what the Pāli canon is for the tradition as a whole – a comprehensive collection.[12]

Handbooks over the centuries have grown considerably in size: new chants, transcriptions, explanations and translations have been added. And just as historically there were attempts to standardise the formal canon by way of councils, there was also an attempt to standardise the practical canon. McDaniel (2006: 129) relates King Mongkut's attempts in the mid-nineteenth century to create a universal sense of Theravāda identity. He invited foreign Theravāda monks to Thailand, designed a universal script for Pāli (Ariyaka) to be used by all Theravādins and also tried to create 'a standard Pāli liturgy for the Theravāda Buddhist world' containing only the basic chants shared by all countries, but no vernacular instructions. Later these attempts were given up and the bewildering number of different handbooks in contemporary Thailand alone seems to show that far from

[10] The texts that make up the extremely short Khuddakapāṭha are (in order): Saraṇattaya; Dasasikkhāpada; Dvattiṃsākāra; Kumārapañha; Maṅgalasutta; Ratanasutta; Tirokuḍḍasutta; Nidhikaṇḍasutta; Karaṇīyamettasutta.

[11] See Collins (1995) and McDaniel (2008: 191).

[12] While the latter is an 'exclusive, closed list' (Collins 1995: 91), the former is 'fluid and open' (McDaniel 2006: 122).

unifying Theravāda on an international level, it failed even to establish conformity on a national level.[13]

The toolbox of the researcher: the field data

The rituals connected with death are very complex, can extend over several days and include very diverse practices such as chanting, preaching, confusing the spirit of the deceased, gambling, inviting gods, giving merit to the dead and feeding the spirit of the deceased. Of course, not all of these involve monks' participation, or the use of Pāli texts, but even when concentrating on the monks' involvement there are a number of different events. A monk or monks are invited after the death to chant Abhidhamma (in Thailand and Laos) or to preach for an hour (in Sri Lanka). Then there is usually an alms giving on behalf of the dead, which is done on the day of the cremation (in Thailand and Laos) or on the seventh day after the death (in Sri Lanka) and at regular intervals after that. There are also ceremonies (e.g. chanting and ritual near the coffin) that take place on the day of the cremation or burial at home, at the temple or even at the cremation ground. And finally there is a ceremony performed over a figurine made of the bones in Thailand and Laos. The focus of this chapter is on the chanting and ritual that is performed on the funeral day itself, which for convenience I will refer to as 'funeral'. Apart from the great complexity of the death rites, there is also the issue of geography and history to take into account. The area covered or touched by Theravāda is vast, incorporating diverse ethnic and sectarian groups, and spans over 2000 years of history.[14] Obviously a comprehensive study of all the relevant material is not possible, but a pilot study, concentrating on selected locations in order to create a number of 'snapshots', remains practical.

In this chapter I will closely examine the chanting sequences of eight funeral ceremonies: a simple laywoman's burial (SL1) and an elaborate monk's cremation (SL2) from Sri Lanka;[15] a simple burial in Sagaing (Myanmar 1);[16] a simple

[13] These handbooks are not exclusively for novices and monks. There are a great number of these widely available in print or online now, some of them produced by temples for their supporters. To name but a few examples: Nārada (2008); (2008) *Samatha Chanting Book*; (2000–10) *A Chanting Guide*; (2007) *Morning Chanting Guide*.

[14] The modern state boundaries do not reflect the distribution of different ethnic and sectarian groups.

[15] Detailed descriptions of the two funerals can be found in Langer (2007). The fieldwork in Sri Lanka was funded by the Deutscher Akademischer Austauschdienst.

[16] I am very grateful to Hiroko Kawanami, U San, Ven. Ashin Dhammapiya and the Sagaing Funeral Society for their support. The field trip to Myanmar (2009) as well as the field trips to Laos (2007) and Thailand (2008) were in part funded by the University of Bristol Research Fund.

cremation in Luang Prabang (Laos 1); an elaborate cremation of a government official in Vientiane in three parts and locations: at his home, at the cremation ground, near the incinerator (Laos 2.A-C);[17] a simple cremation conducted by Thai monks in a crematorium in the UK (Thai 1); an elaborate cremation in Chiang Mai in three parts and locations: at his home, at the cremation ground, near the incinerator (Thai 2.A-C); and a medium-sized cremation (Thai 3).[18] In addition I included five other ceremonies for comparison: an alms giving from Sri Lanka (SL 3); an alms giving from Myanmar (Myanmar 2); a 'bone collection ceremony' from Laos performed over a figurine (Laos 3); and from Thailand an 'Abhidhamma evening chant' (Thai 4) and a 'coffin ritual' (Thai 5), which is essentially a healing ritual involving the client lying in a coffin while monks conduct 'funeral rites'.

I have entered the chanting sequences of the ceremonies into a chart (see Table 2.1), where every row (comprising four lines) represents one ceremony or distinct part of a ceremony. Each line contains the first word of a Pāli verse or phrase or the name of a *sutta*, which can be looked up in the verse/phrase index (Table 2.2).[19] My intention was to create a record and reference of a body of funeral and funeral-related ceremonies in South and Southeast Asia. Of course, condensing complex ceremonies into a single chart leaves out the performance aspects, some of which will be discussed below, but it allows one to identify the different elements as well as highlight 'gaps'. I will first introduce the elements one by one before looking at the bigger picture.

THE ELEMENTS OF THE *BRICOLAGE*

The data will be analysed in two parts: first, the basic framework which is found in all the funeral ceremonies (and represented in the short, Sri Lankan, sequence), and second, some further elements as found in Southeast Asia.

The core of a funeral ceremony

Preliminaries and honouring of the Triple Gem

Under this category I subsume first the verses of honouring the Buddha and the Triple Gem (*namo tassa* . . . and *iti pi so bhagavā*) as well as the invitation to the gods to come and listen to the Dhamma (*sagge kāme ca*

[17] My brief field trips to Laos and Thailand were timed to coincide with Patrice Ladwig's longer research stays and I am grateful to him and Nicole Reichert for their support. For an overview of Lao funerary rites see Ladwig (2003) and Zago (1972: 237–55).

[18] For an overview of Thai funerary rites see Wells (1960: 211–28) and Terwiel (1979).

[19] Any Pāli words or phrases in brackets refer to verses and passages, which can be found in the index.

rūpe ...).[20] In Sri Lanka, however, the verse is shortened to the simple statement 'It is time to listen to the Dhamma' (*dhammassavana-kālo*) until the seventh day after the death, when the home of the dead person ceases to be regarded as the 'house of the deceased'.[21] Next comes the formal request for the precepts or preaching (*mayaṃ bhante* . . .), which is in essence a re-enactment of the Dhammacakkappavattanasutta (S V 420), when Brahma asks the Buddha to teach, and is very common in Thailand, Laos and Myanmar, but less so in Sri Lanka. All the above verses and phrases are usually chanted by a layman, an *upāsaka*, who is familiar with the Pāli verses. The monks then lead the chanting of the three refuges (*buddhaṃ saraṇaṃ* . . .) and the Five Precepts (*pāṇātipātā* . . .), which are canonical (Khp I).[22] As these preliminaries are not specific to funerals I have omitted them from the chart.

The offering of the 'refuse rag' (Pansukul)

Next comes the chanting of a verse (*aniccā vata saṃkhārā* . . .) and the offering of a white piece of cloth or robes. The verse was famously uttered by the god Sakka in the Mahāparinibbāna sutta (D II 157) after the Buddha's passing away:

> Impermanent are conditioned things! It is their nature to arise and fall.
> Having arisen, they cease. Their stilling is happy.[23]

This verse is, at least in Sri Lanka, very well known by laypeople and so closely associated with funerals and death that one might suspect it would be virtually impossible to use it in any other context. The chanting of this verse is nearly always accompanied by the offering of a new piece of cloth/ robes to the monks. This cloth is commonly referred to either as a 'refuse rag' (*paṃsukūla*) or in Sri Lanka sometimes also as a 'cloth of the dead/ remembrance' (*matakavastra*).[24] This former term links back to an ancient ascetic practice of only wearing robes made from refuse rags (*paṃsukūla*)

[20] On *iti pi so* . . . see also Harrison (1992) and on inviting the gods see Skilling (2002).

[21] I was told in Sri Lanka that gods do not like funeral houses, and passages such as Khp-a 117 seem to confirm the gods' dislike of smelly humans: 'For when deities come for any purpose to the human world, they do so like a man of clean habits coming to a privy. In fact, the human world is naturally repulsive to them even at a hundred leagues' distance owing to its stench, and they find no delight in it.' Ñāṇamoli (1960b: 127).

[22] Ñāṇamoli (1960b: 5; of *The Illustrator of Ultimate Meaning*). Khp-a 14. See also Ñāṇamoli (1960a).

[23] Gethin (2008: 90).

[24] The etymology of the Pāli word *paṃsukūla* (also used in Sinhala), is not very clear, but the term and concept is widely known in South and Southeast Asia as *pansukul* and seems to be used not just for a cloth, but also for the ritual sequence of chanting and offering of the cloth (and it is in this sense that I use the word in the chart) or even just for the chant that accompanies the offering (see also Chapter 3 by Davis).

found in unclean places, one of thirteen ascetic practices described in the Visuddhimagga, a post-canonical work (fifth century CE).

Most Buddhists in South and Southeast Asia are not only familiar with the term and concept of the *paṃsukūla*, but seem to be rather fond of it despite, or may be precisely due to, the fact that more often than not the reality of monastic life is far from that of a 'refuse-rag wearer'.[25] The link between the verse (*aniccā vata* ...) and the offering of cloth/robes to the monks is so commonly known that in Thai chanting books the verse itself is referred to as '*pansukul*', even though the actual wording does not hint at the practice at all. The verse sometimes 'attracts' other, similar verses such as 'Soon this body will lie on the ground ...' (*aciraṃ vat* ...) or 'In the present every being dies ...' (*sabbe sattā maranti* ...), which are fairly well known and go well with the theme of impermanence and death.[26] In the ceremonies I observed in Laos and Thailand, it is also closely connected with the next element (see below), the giving of merit symbolized by pouring water and sometimes even combined with a brief paritta chant. In Sri Lanka the verse is usually chanted by itself and constitutes something of a climax in the proceedings while the giving of merit is performed at the very end. Interestingly at Myanmar I the canonical verse was chanted at the very end of the ceremony and turned into a triplet (*aniccā vata saṃkhārā ... dukkhā vata saṃkhārā ... anattā vata saṃkhārā*).

It is impossible to tell when the chanting of the verse and offering of the cloth became linked, but they are not only a feature of nearly every Theravāda Buddhist funeral in South and Southeast Asia, but constitute, in fact, the core and only funeral-specific aspect.

The giving of merit

The giving of merit to the deceased is marked by the chanting of Pāli verses, which are found in two canonical works: the Petavatthu (Tirokuḍḍapetavatthu, Pv 5) and the Khuddakapāṭha (Tirokuḍḍasutta, Khp 7).[27] The latter has already been mentioned above, but the former needs a word of introduction. The Petavatthu is a collection of 'ghost stories', which deal with the themes of karma and retribution and follow a fixed pattern: a miserable creature approaches a human being, reveals him/

[25] I have argued elsewhere (Langer 2007: 84) that the offering of a new cloth at funerals might have originated in the Vedic ritual and been given a new, Buddhist interpretation. For other interpretations see also Schopen (2007) and contributions by Davis (Chapter 3) and Chirapravati (Chapter 4) in this volume.

[26] The latter (*sabbe sattā* ...) is most commonly chanted by the Thammayut monks (Ven. Bhatsakorn Piyobhaso, personal communication).

[27] In the Myanmar ceremonies the giving of merit was accompanied by pouring water and chanting in Burmese.

herself as a hungry ghost (*peta/petī)* and asks for help. The intent of benefiting the dead is usually understood as giving of merit, even though the canonical verses of the Tirokuḍḍapetavatthu do not mention merit. The giving of merit is, doctrinally, not unproblematic as it seems to run counter to the accountability of the individual. The Abhidhamma solves the dilemma by proposing a two-way process: the giver can only 'offer' merit (*pattidāna*) and the receiver can only 'rejoice' in the merit offered (*pattānumodanā*).[28] Both these acts are themselves meritorious acts and both the giver and the receiver are better off karmically.[29]

The Tirokuḍḍapetavatthu (Pv 4f) is very topical (filial duty) and its popularity as a funeral chant is not surprising. Individual verses, couplets or quadruplets are chanted at various points in the proceedings, but two of its verses became associated with the giving of merit:

As water rained on the uplands flows down to the low land,
even so does what is given here benefit the petas. (*unname udakaṃ* . . .)

Just as swollen streams swell the ocean,
even so does what is given here benefit the petas. (*yathā vārivahā* . . .)[30]

The chanting is always accompanied by the ritual pouring of water from a cup or jug into a bowl as a solemn act, possibly indicating a promise or vow. Here there is a clear link between the wording of the chant and the ritual act of pouring water. Interestingly the order of the two verses is often reversed (*yathā vārivahā* . . . and *unname udakaṃ* . . .) when compared to the two canonical versions. This raises the question of whether there was possibly another version of the *Sutta* in circulation or whether the ritual tradition simply chose this order for rhythmic or musical reasons. Whatever the case, the fact that the Tirokuḍḍasutta also occurs in the canonical handbook, the *Khuddakapāṭha*, might be an indication that its ritual use might be as old as that of the *parittasuttas* in the same collection.

Asking for forgiveness and religious wishes

I group these two together (under the heading of 'wishes' in the chart) as, in my view, they represent two sides of the same coin: the asking for forgiveness by the laypeople in order to remove obstacles and the subsequent

[28] See Abhidhammatthasaṅgaha 25.
[29] For a more detailed discussion of merit see Langer (2007: 156–85).
[30] Dhammapāla (1980: 26, Pv 5).

'granting' of a wish by the monks to further improve one's lot.[31] In Southeast Asia a short chant of three verses asking the Triple Gem for forgiveness for wrong deeds of body, speech and mind (*kāyena vācāya vā cetasā vā . . .*) was recited at some of the ceremonies in Laos and Thailand immediately before the giving of merit.[32]

The verses are not canonical, but the motif of asking for forgiveness from a Buddha is. In the Sāmaññaphalasutta King Ajātasattu addresses the Buddha:

> Sir, foolish, deluded, and weak man that I am, I have done something wrong. In pursuit of power, I have taken the life of my father, the righteous and lawful king. Let the Blessed One accept this confession of my wrongdoing and in the future there will be restraint.[33]

Interestingly, Ajātasattu does not ask for his karmic slate to be wiped clean, but that he may be more restrained and better equipped to avoid such deeds in the future.[34] Asking for forgiveness – like giving of merit – is at first glance at odds with the responsibility of karma and doctrinally confession merely serves to aid a more wholesome state of mind in the future. It is, however, likely that on an affective level people perceive the act of confession as freeing them from past bad deeds.

The religious wishes (*icchitaṃ patthitaṃ . . .*) are, again, part of nearly every ceremony and immediately follow the giving of merit. Here the collectively generated merit is the basis of a wish that is 'granted' by the monks to everyone present. The content of the wish is personal, but in Sri Lanka it is quite common for the monk to preformulate the wish to be reborn under the future Buddha and attain Nibbāna. The oldest source for the verses that I have found is Vedeha's Rasavāhinī, which is usually dated to the thirteenth century, but goes back to older Sinhala works. Its stories illustrate the workings of karma and the virtue of generosity and it is similar in style to the Jātaka and Apadāna literature. Bretfeld (2001: xli) points out that the great number of existing manuscripts indicate its extremes popularity in Sri Lanka and Southeast Asia. The story in which the verses occur (Rv I 38) is rather long and rambling, but the immediate context is that a honey merchant gives a pot of honey to a solitary buddha (*paccekabuddha).*

31 Indeed these two aspects seem to be combined in the Burmese formula of asking permission (*Okāsa*), which is uttered at the beginning of ceremonies.

32 The asking for forgiveness is also common in Sri Lanka in connection with offerings to the Buddha statue or relic (Maithrimurthi, personal communication).

33 Gethin (2008: 35; D I 85). The similarity in phrasing between the verse and the passage in D I 85 is interesting.

34 Killing a parent is, of course, classed as 'weighty kamma' (*garuka kamma*), which bears fruit in the immediate next existence. Vism XIX, 15 (Warren), Buddhagosa (1991: 620).

While doing so, he remembers a story from the Mahāvaṃsa (chapter V, verse 57) which also involves a honey merchant pouring honey for a *paccekabuddha* until the vessel overflows and making a wish to become ruler of Jambudīpa. The first honey merchant tells this story to the *paccekabuddha* who then utters the verses (*icchitaṃ patthitaṃ* ...; see Norman 1910). Interesting here are two things: the image of the overflowing bowl in connection with an earnest wish (overflowing bowls are a feature of the giving of merit ceremony in Sri Lanka) and second, the wish is for better rebirth in a powerful position, not for Nibbāna.

The verses leave the content of the wish open which makes it akin to a boon that is granted by the monks. Again, doctrinally speaking there can only be a shift in mental make-up (caused by merit-making activity), but it is anyone's guess how people perceive their wishes to be fulfilled. It is also quite common towards the end of a ceremony for merit to be shared with all beings. In Sri Lanka this is done by way of a monk formulating the wish that all beings may benefit from the merit generated on this occasion. In Myanmar, too, merit is shared with all beings at the end of the ceremony and the same goes for Laos (*yaṃ kiṃci kusalaṃ* ...).[35] After the sharing of merit follow the sermons in the Sri Lankan sequence, but as this paper is about chanting the important topic of preaching will not be discussed here.

Further elements

The previous section, 'The core of a funeral ceremony', focused on elements commonly found in most Theravāda funerals. The present section, on the other hand, deals with elements that are not found in all countries (specifically not in Sri Lanka) but shared nevertheless widely.

Abhidhamma chanting

The chanting of Abhidhamma is very popular and well known in Thailand and Laos where it is mostly associated with funerals. It was not easy to establish what parts of the Abhidhamma are actually chanted and in what order.[36] McDaniel (2008: 307 n16) lists the works that can be chanted at funerals:

[35] Another Pāli formula for giving of merit to all beings seems to be popular in Lao, Thai and Khmer Buddhist communities (Gregory Kourilsky, email communication). The initial part of this chant (*iminā puññena* ...) is found in 'Yogāvacara's Manual' see Rhys Davids (1896: 3).

[36] For a similar observation in Cambodia see Davis in this volume (Chapter 3). As far as I am aware the chanting of Abhidhamma is in Myanmar not associated with funerals and in Sri Lanka it is not part of the chanting repertoire at all.

The *Abhidhamma chet kamphi*, excerpts from *Abhidhammasaṅgaha* and the *mātikā* are not the only texts chanted at funerals. Funerals, like most Thai and Lao rituals, also include the recitation of texts like the *Nāmo tassa, Itipiso, Tisaraṇa*, *Bahum* and other standard liturgical texts. Additional texts can be chanted upon request of the family of the deceased. When I performed funerals, my abbot instructed the other monks and me (a quorum of four is standard) to chant Abhidhamma texts, standard liturgical texts and often a text of his choosing. These extra texts, which we had to commit to memory, were based on my abbot's preference rather than on a standard liturgical prescription or tradition.[37]

What is chanted or utilised in the funeral context will, no doubt, also depend on the occasion. It is customary to place a piece of paper inside the dead person's mouth on which are written the syllables *ci ce ru ni*, signifying the four major topics of the Abhidhammatthasaṅgaha: consciousness (*citta*), associated mentality (*cetasika*), physical phenomena (*rūpa*) and nirvāṇa (*nibbāna*; see also McDaniel 2008: 238). It is also common in the days leading up to the funeral to invite monks to chant Abhidhamma in the evening (see Thai 4). However, for the present paper the focus shall be on the funeral day. The main two Abhidhamma chants utilised are the initial passages from the first and last of the seven books of the Abhidhamma: the *mātikā* of the Dhammasaṅgaṇī (Dhs 1f) and the initial passage of the Paṭṭhāna, the *paccāyuddesa* (also referred to as the Paṭṭhāna mātikā). The chanting of a passage from the beginning and a passage from the end might well be intended to represent the whole of the Abhidhamma.

The Dhammasaṅgaṇī *mātikā* is a summary, an outline expanded on in the rest of the Dhammasaṅgaṇī. By itself, its twenty-two triplets are unintelligible to the 'untrained' ear (be it monk or scholar) and even more so to the ordinary person attending a funeral. When looking more closely, it becomes apparent that these texts deal with the deconstruction of the body in much the same way as the *aniccā vata* ... verse does. There is, however, another line of argument that attempts to explain the connection between Abhidhamma and funerals, namely that Abhidhamma is needed for the construction of the new person. Gethin (1992: 161) argues that rather than merely being a summary, the *mātikā* is the 'mother', a creative force 'pregnant with Dhamma', but confines his observation to the function of the *mātikā* within texts. McDaniel (2008: 232) takes this further and argues that it is this creative force that made the Dhammasaṅgaṇī *mātikā* such an

[37] According to McDaniel (2008: 233), Abhidhamma chet kamphi is a well-known work containing excerpts from the seven books of the Abhidhamma. See also Swearer (1995).

intrinsic part of the funerals: it was needed for the creation of the new person (see also Davis' chapter).

The other Abhidhamma passage comes from the Paṭṭhāna and the relationship between those two great works of Abhidhamma could be illustrated best in terms of a comparison: if the Dhammasaṅgaṇī was a dictionary, the Paṭṭhāna would be the grammar (Rupert Gethin; personal communication). The passage chanted is, again, the *mātikā*, the beginning of the book, and lists the twenty-four conditions to which the realities are subjected and the various possible combinations, which would, according to the commentaries and subcommentaries that Nārada (1969: xv) quotes, add up to almost half a billion questions. Even though not all relations and questions are discussed, the Paṭṭhāna is by far the biggest volume of the Abhidhamma and is highly regarded (particularly in Myanmar) for its content and position within the Abhidhamma. In terms of the Abhidhamma as a whole, the two texts, the Dhammasaṅgaṇī and the Paṭṭhāna, are the beginning and end of the Abhidhamma.

In an interesting variation (Laos 2.A) a list of *devas* was sandwiched between the two Abidhamma parts and then followed by the last three verses of the Karaṇīyamettasutta. The different elements (*kusalā dhammā, cātummahārājikā devā, hetupaccayā* and *mettañ ca*, . . .) are chanted without pause as if they were of one piece. When examining the list of *devas* more closely, it turned out to be an elaborated version of a passage from the Dhammacakkappavattanasutta (Vin I 10–12 and S V 420–4), where the gods spread the news that the wheel of *dhamma* has been set in motion again through the various levels of the cosmos.[38] This could be seen as a re-enactment of that moment when the wheel of Dhamma was set in motion in the same way as Brahmā's request is still re-enacted at ceremonies every time laypeople request the teaching from the monks. Gethin (1998: 203–4) describes the 'general attitude' to Abhidhamma as follows:

> Hearing it being recited – even without understanding it – can have a far reaching effect. The Abhidhamma catches the very essence of the Dhamma, which means that its sound can operate almost as a charm or spell.

This function as 'charm or spell' brings it closer to *paritta* chanting (see below) and might explain why the Paṭṭhāna recitation is followed immediately by verses from the Karaṇīyamettasutta.

[38] The chanting names all the gods individually while the canonical passages group the Brahmā gods together as *brahmakāyikā devā*.

Chants of protection – the Paritta sequences

Paritta or *pirit* is a ceremony in its own right, which may last from an hour to seven days and which has a long history.[39] It serves a multitude of purposes from protection from danger to the acquisition of something desired. Schalk (1972: 44) gives countless examples to show how some *parittas* are associated with a particular function (e.g. Aṅgulimālasutta with easing childbirth), while others (e.g. Ratanasutta) are multifunctional. Apart from the canonical *parittas*, which are found scattered about in the Pāli Canon, there are a number of post-canonical *parittas*. Norman (1983: 173) gives different lists of *parittas*: six (as mentioned in Milindapañha); nine (as commonly found in Sri Lanka), as well as lists of twenty-two and twenty-eight. Schalk (1972: 112) observes that it is by no means clear why some *suttas* make it into the lists of *parittas*, while others (such as the Satipaṭṭhānasutta) do not. He also introduces an interesting category of Meta-*parittas*, which are essentially *parittas* praising other *parittas* (for example the Ratanasutta) and thereby drawing on their authority.

Paritta chanting enjoys enormous popularity in South and Southeast Asia and beyond. Blackburn (1999b: 354) observes:

> Broadcast daily on radio, chanted for hours by monks at the installation of cabinet ministers and in short or all-night ceremonies to mark major transitions in human lives and to bring good fortune in a variety of circumstances, the recitation of these texts is one of the most common forms of ritual practice in the Theravāda tradition.

Most Theravāda Buddhist ceremonies contain a '*paritta* sequence' and this is also true for the funeral ceremonies in Thailand and Laos. In Sri Lanka and Myanmar, however, any hint of *paritta* is noticeably absent in the funeral ceremonies, even though it constitutes part of the seventh day alms giving (included in the chart for reasons of comparison). The reason for this might be that in Sri Lanka *pirit* ceremonies are strongly associated with chasing away troublesome ghosts and spirits. The first seven days after a death has occurred are popularly (though not doctrinally) believed to be an in-between stage when the spirit of the deceased (Sinhala: *malagiyaprānakārayā*) is still about and his/her afterlife destiny can still be influenced. Besides, there are a great many types of 'ghosts' in Sri Lanka (*preta, yak⊠a, bhūta*, etc.) that the deceased might have been reborn as and the categories are not always very fixed. Whatever the case may be, the deceased should not be chased away by

[39] Even the paraphernalia of the *pirit* ceremony, such as *pirit* thread (J I 399) and *pirit* water (Sn-a 204f) go back a long way, and in the Mahāvaṃsa VII 8 and 9 the Buddha entrusts god Sakka with water and thread and sends him off to look after the island of Lankā. See also Langer (2007: 19–23).

pirit and thereby be excluded from the beneficial effect of his own funeral ceremony.[40] In Thailand and Laos there do not seem to be the same reservations, and in fact these *paritta* elements are included throughout the funeral ceremonies and it also seems to be quite common to invite monks for *paritta* chanting in the evening after the cremation.

Let us take a brief look at what *parittas* are chanted. At two funerals recorded in Chiang Mai (Thai 2.B and Thai 3) the nine verses of the Jayamaṅgalasutta were chanted.[41] In most ceremonies the religious wishes (see above) are immediately followed by two verses, which seem often to be chanted together: the first verse (*sabbītiyo vivajjantu* . . .) is from the non-canonical Mahājayamaṅgalagāthā and the second verse (*abhivādanasīlissa* . . .) is from the Dhammapada (verse 109). Both verses go together very well and wish the beings present a long life.[42] Finally most funerals, as well as the alms givings in Sri Lanka and Myanmar (SL 3 and Myanmar 2), end either with a triplet from the Mahājayamaṅgalagāthā (*bhavatu sabbamaṅgalam* . . .), or with the last three verses of the Karaṇīyamettasutta.[43] Schalk (1972: 41) has already pointed out that the Karaṇīyamettasutta, which culminates in the highest achievement, adds another, meditative, dimension to the *paritta* ceremony. And Blackburn (1999b: 357) takes this one step further and critically and convincingly argues that *paritta* is an integral part of monastic education and identity rather than a concession, a part of 'Buddhism's "accommodation" to society', as a great number of scholars seem to suggest.[44]

GENERAL OBSERVATIONS AND CONCLUSIONS

Chanting as bricolage

A patchwork of individual verses, couplets, triplets (canonical and non-canonical) are often combined into one chanting sequence whereas the

[40] Maithrimurthi (personal communication). Interestingly I encountered the same reasoning in Sagaing with regard to the observation that Abhidhamma was not chanted at funerals.

[41] Not to be confused with the canonical Maṅgalasutta or the non-canonical Mahājayamaṅgalasutta. According to Schalk (1972: 190) the Jayamaṅgalasutta and the Mahājayamaṅgalasutta are particularly associated with weddings (*maṅgala* in Sinhala means 'blessing, wedding') in Sri Lanka.

[42] The commentary on the Dhammapada verse (Dhp-a II 235ff) is particularly interesting, because it legitimises and asserts the efficacy of *pirit* chanting. According to the story, a boy who was promised to a *yakkha* was saved from certain death by the Buddha and the community of monks who chanted without interruption for seven days until the danger had passed.

[43] The Karaṇīyamettasutta (Khp 8), which is said to help with contemplation by way of expelling fear, is often confused with two other Suttas by the name of Mettasutta (A V 342 and A IV 150).

[44] The scholars whose position Blackburn discusses include de Silva, Spiro, Tambiah and Gombrich.

recitation of a whole sutta is rare. Some combinations of individual verses (*sabbītiyo* . . . and *abhivādana* . . .) are common in Sri Lanka, Laos and Thailand. Sometimes a verse on the Buddha seems to prompt the chanting of parallel verses on the Dhamma and Saṅgha (*kāyena* . . .), or a verse starting with *aniccā* is followed by verses starting with *dukkhā* and *anattā* (Myanmar 1) to make up triplets. Some verses occur in more than one *paritta* sequence or even form a new *paritta* in their own right (e.g. see Abhayaparitta in the verse index). There are also at times slight variations in order (the *unname* and *yathā vārivahā* verses), or in the verses themselves (*icchitaṃ patthitaṃ* . . .).

But why is such a patchwork of verses chanted at funerals? The most plausible explanation would seem to be that each individual verse is regarded as representing a whole *sutta* and by chanting a patchwork of verses more ground can be covered. Similarly the recitation of the two Abhidhamma sequences (*mātikā* and *paccayuddesa*) could be seen as representing the whole of the Abhidhamma.

It is, according to Lévi-Strauss (1966: 18), a principle of *bricolage* that some elements are more versatile than others and while the *bricoleur* uses 'whatever is at hand' there are certain parameters given:

> A particular cube of oak could be a wedge to make up for the inadequate length of a plank of pine or it could be a pedestal – which would allow the grain and polish of the old wood to show to advantage. In one case it will serve as extension, in the other as material. But the possibilities always remain limited by the particular history of each piece and by those of its features, which are already determined by the use for which it was originally intended or the modifications it has undergone for the purpose. The elements which the 'bricoleur' collects and uses are 'pre-constrained' like the constitutive units of myths, the possible combinations of which are restricted by the fact that they are drawn from language where they already possess a sense which sets a limit on their freedom of manoeuvre.

To give a concrete example: most blessing verses such as 'May all distresses be averted . . .' (*sabbītiyo vivajjantu* . . .) are relatively multifunctional and can be used in a variety of contexts, whereas other elements, such as the verse 'Impermanent are conditioned things . . . ' (*aniccā vata saṃkhārā* . . .), have become so closely linked with the funeral context (at least in Sri Lanka) that their use seems to be more restricted.

The selection of verses is important, but does not of itself make a ceremony; their order and sequence has to be determined, too. To give a simple example: it is not accidental that the passage concerning the various gods proclaiming that the wheel of Dhamma has once more been set in motion (Laos 2A and Laos 3) is chanted right after the Dhammasaṅgaṇī *mātikā* as a re-enactment of the Dhammacakkappavattana Sutta.

The funeral *bricolage* is, of course, a live performance, and a chart and verse index cannot do justice to it: some parts, like the initial requesting of the precepts, are performed as a dialogue between the monks and a lay specialist, while other parts, such as the refuges and precepts, involve the whole audience. In Sri Lanka it is common at certain moments throughout the ceremony for laypeople to join in with exclamations of '*sādhu, sādhu, sā*'. Some verses (*icchitam* . . . for example) are chanted by only one monk (the chief monk) who is then joined again by the other monks on the next verse (*sabbītiyo* . . .). This is particularly interesting as this was a common feature in all the ceremonies recorded in Sri Lanka, Thailand and Laos.

Aspects of ritual performance

The sound is not the only aspect that is missing from this study; there is also the lack of a visual dimension. I have already mentioned the two main ritual acts performed in the funeral context. The first one is the offering of a white piece of cloth to the monks, which is always closely associated with the chanting of a canonical verse (*aniccā vata* . . .). In Thailand and Laos the monks touch the parcels which have been placed in front of them, while at the same time reciting the funeral verse (*aniccā vata* . . .), which has nothing in its wording that might suggest the practice. The second ritual act is the pouring of water from a cup or jug into a bowl to symbolise the giving of merit. The friends and family of the deceased sit on the floor in a circle holding a jug (Sri Lanka) or in a line in front of the monks (Thailand and Laos) while pouring the water as a solemn act. Here the situation is reversed in that the act of pouring water is accompanied by two canonical verses which actually do speak of water. Throughout the ceremony other verses from the Tirokuḍḍasutta are chanted, and considering that this *sutta* was already included in the Khuddakapāṭha, one might speculate that its ritual use could belong to the older stratum of the funeral rites.

There is often a hiatus in the ceremonies (somewhere between the *aniccā vata* verse and the giving of merit), which is so subtle that it is easily missed. In some ceremonies there is a break for lunch at this point, or parcels are offered or sermons delivered (under the heading of 'transition' in the chart). A comparison with two other ceremonies – the 'bone ceremony' and the 'coffin ritual' – might provide a clue: this is the moment when the 'bone figure' or the 'client' is turned around from the original position (head to the west signifying death) to the new position (head to the east signifying life).

From then on they are quite literally 'heading for life'. Applied to the funeral chant it now becomes apparent that the first half of the ceremony is mainly concerned with death and the deconstruction of the person, whereas the second half is about life and providing merit for the dead (and everyone else).[45] There are many more ritual acts, which are performed during the ceremonies, but the focus of this article is on chanting.

Some comparisons

In Sri Lanka the ceremonies during the first seven days after the death were shorter and more clearly separated: the funeral takes place on the third or fourth day, a special one-hour sermon on the sixth day and the alms giving on the seventh day. The funeral ceremonies I recorded in Sri Lanka were all short and all took place in the afternoon in one location (at the home of the deceased or, in the case of the monk's cremation, at the temple and nearby school ground). Of the short funerals I recorded in Myanmar, one took place at home, one at the roadside and one at the cemetery, where a sheltered place had been built for the purpose. In Thailand and Laos, on the other hand, there was a tendency to hold various ceremonies such as alms giving and ordination (as merit-generating activities) on the funeral day and to include *paritta* elements for protection. As a result the funeral is sometimes divided into several distinct parts (morning and afternoon) or locations (home and cemetery).

In these longer ceremonies there seems to be a certain amount of repetition built in. To give an example, the core elements of the chanting of the funeral verse (while touching the parcel), giving merit (while pouring the water), wishes and blessings occur several times at home and at the cemetery in Laos 2 and Thai 2. The most poignant of these sequences is performed near the coffin in front of the incinerator. In Sri Lanka and Myanmar, on the other hand, there are no repeat sequences, but where the occasion required a 'bigger' event (for example the monk's cremation in SL 2), it was simply a case of more monks chanting together or more people offering parcels at the same time.

Other features that seem to be missing in the Sri Lankan (and Burmese) funeral ceremony have already been mentioned: inviting the gods (they do not like funeral houses); chanting of any *paritta* (which might keep away the spirits for whose benefit the ceremony is conducted) and, of course, the

[45] However, in Myanmar 1 the verse is chanted at the very end after the sharing of merit with all beings, and forms an almost self-contained, optional sequence.

Abhidhamma. All this accounts for the fact that the chanting time at funerals in Sri Lanka and Myanmar is much shorter (see gaps in the chart in Table 2.1) than in Thailand and Laos. Even taking into account the preaching sequences, which are interspersed with the chanting but not noted in the chart, it can be said that the funeral ceremonies I recorded in Myanmar and Sri Lanka were on the whole rather short. In Sri Lanka it appeared that what is lacking in 'ceremonial time' is made up for in 'speaking time', which seems to be in direct proportion to the perceived 'importance' of the departed. In short the repeat sequences in Thailand and Laos and the speeches in Sri Lanka are basically techniques designed to 'pad out' an otherwise brief core ceremony.

CONCLUSIONS

In comparing the ceremonies, it seems noticeable how many similarities were present and how the differences seemed generally rather slight and concerning matters of details. There were, however, two exceptions to this. First, the ceremonies recorded in Myanmar seem to conform less to the general pattern that emerged on the basis of observing funerals in Sri Lanka, Thailand and Laos. This needs further investigation, but also confirms by contrast just how similar the liturgical practice of the ceremonies recorded in the three other countries is. Second, the use of Abhidhamma in the funeral context in Thailand and Laos, but not in Myanmar and Sri Lanka, is significant and shall be discussed further below. Nevertheless, on the whole a Theravāda monk, say, from Thailand would find little difficulty joining in the chanting in Sri Lanka. This seems to me rather remarkable, considering (a) the lack of authoritative, prescriptive ritual literature; (b) the great number and variety of liturgical handbooks; and (c) the failure to standardise the liturgical literature nationally and internationally. I would like to examine these points one by one.

(a) There might not be prescriptive ritual literature, but there is a body of Theravāda chants and Suttas for ritual use that has been preserved by the tradition over the centuries. Most of the texts in the canonical Khuddakapātha are still found in the contemporary handbooks of the various Theravāda countries. And even when it comes to the additional, non-canonical *parittas* and verses, there seems to be a considerable overlap.

(b) It appears that the undoubtedly great number and variety of contemporary chanting books has not resulted in a great variety of chanting in the funeral context. The reason seems to be that the recorded ceremonies were all constructed from a relatively small number of fairly common chants found in all the contemporary handbooks.[46] It is possible that differences are more apparent in other ceremonies, but, as I have argued elsewhere, death rituals appear to be quite resilient to change (Langer 2007). Interpretations might change, but generally people seem reluctant to deviate from the well-known ritual. Also, there is nothing 'offensive' in the funeral ceremony, either doctrinally (once giving of merit was accepted), or ethically (no Vinaya rules are infringed) and it is unlikely that it might have caught the attention of any reformer (see McDaniel 2006: 120).

(c) King Mongkut might not have succeeded in establishing a universally accepted standard Theravāda liturgical handbook, but maybe his effort of inviting foreign Theravāda monks contributed in some way to a standardisation of the liturgical practice. Throughout the history of Theravāda Buddhism (and long before King Mongkut's attempt to bring together Theravāda monks) there has been a considerable amount of cross-fertilisation between Sri Lanka, Myanmar, Thailand and Laos. This is most tangible in the revival of ordination lineages as discussed by Bizot (1988) and Blackburn (2003), but even outside these crisis situations, there would have been a certain amount of travelling done by Theravāda monks, which might have contributed to a 'levelling out' of diversity in funeral rites.

This goes some way to explain the similarities in the ceremonies. What it does not explain, however, are the variations, since no two funerals are identical. Here the concept of *bricolage* provides a useful model. Given the same task and utilising a similar set of tools, materials and skills, two *bricoleurs* might make similar choices, but it is unlikely they would come up with an identical result. In the same way two monks faced with the task of conducting a ceremony will have the experience and skill to choose appropriate chants and combine them into a recognisable, but not necessarily identical, pattern. Again, one might compare the monk to a native speaker who is intuitively familiar with the syntax, or a musician who is able to improvise without losing sight of the main theme.

The character of this study is preliminary and I would like to conclude by posing some questions and raising some issues. First, the most obvious next

[46] McDaniel (2006) speaks of many different books: 'chanting books', 'recitation anthologies', 'liturgical chanting books', 'funeral books' etc. It would be interesting to examine whether and to what extent the different books were intended to be prescriptive for liturgical practice and how successful they were in doing so.

step would be to examine the Burmese rituals more closely and extend the study to include the Cambodian rituals. Second, the chanting of Abhidhamma in the funeral context requires more attention. McDaniel (2008: 136) states that Abhidhamma sections have been 'commonly chanted (especially at funerals) in this form in Laos and northern and central Thailand for over 230 years'. One might take this as an indication that the Abhidhamma chanting was a later addition to funerals. It is not immediately obvious why the Abhidhamma became associated with funerals, but the *aniccā vata* verse might have attracted the Abhidhamma passages as a thematic elaboration of the verse itself. The question then becomes not why was the Abhidhamma added (it seems to be a perfectly fitting piece in the *bricolage*), but rather why is it not part of the funeral ceremony in Sri Lanka or Myanmar? Finally, to really do this topic justice, a more detailed investigation on a greater scale would be necessary, involving members of the saṅgha as well as Buddhist specialists of the various Theravāda countries working together to unravel the *bricolage* that is the Buddhist funeral rite. Alas, research does not always work out ideally (in fact it rarely does), funding and time are limited, and the researcher is more often than not left to make do with the data, time and skills he has at his disposal: in short, he, too, is not dissimilar to a *bricolage* artist.

Table 2.1 *Chart of*

event	start	Abhidhamma	paritta	pansukul±Pv	repeat	repeat	transition
SL 1 + 2				*imaṃ mataka* ANICCĀ×3			sermon instructions
SL 3 alms giving	*nivedayāmi* sermon			*saparikkhāraṃ* *imaṃ* *tāmbula*→			*icchitaṃB*×2 *icchitaṃA* || *ayu-r-ārogya* lunch + sermon
Myan 1							sermon
Myan 2 alms giving							sermon
Laos 1		*namo* kusalā hetu-→		ANICCĀ×3 *namo* adāsi2||			sermon parcels
Laos 2.A		*namo* kusalā cātummahā→ hetu-→	Mettasutta3 →	*namo*+10 sec ***ACIRAM×3*** ANICCĀ×3 ***SABBE***×3||		10 secs; ANICCĀ ***SABBE*** *sādhu*||	
Laos 2.B			Mettasutta3 →	7 secs ANICCĀ×3		*namo* ANICCĀ ***SABBE*** *sādhu*||	sermon
Laos 2.C				4 monks: ANICCĀ ***SABBE***→ adāsi4→ Mettasutta3||		new set: ANICCĀ ***SABBE*** adāsi 4	people to pyre speeches
Laos 3 bone ceremony		kusalā cātummahā →	Mettasutta3 →	ANICCĀ×3 ***AṬṬHI***-ANICCĀ			parcels 2 mins no turning
Thai 1	sermon	*namo* kusalā hetu-||		ANICCĀ×3			chief monk: on merit
Thai 2.A							layperson: 2.5 mins
Thai 2.B	*namo* iti pi so *Jayamaṅgala* *Jayaparitta*→	kusalā (3) hetu-|	|				layman: 1.5 mins
Thai 2.C				senior monk: ANICCĀ→ so ñāti- water	set of monks: ANICCĀ Mettasutta3||	4 new monks: ANICCĀ×2 so ñāti- 1 monk: repeat	
Thai 3	*namo* iti pi so *Jayamaṅgala* *Jayaparitta*→	kusalā hetu-||		layperson: 3 mins ANICCĀ		ANICCĀ×2 so ñāti- repeat (at cemetery)	
Thai 4 evening chant		Abhidh-sam|		senior monk: ANICCĀ→			
Thai 5 coffin ritual		*namo* kusalā hetu-→	*Nando (×3)*→ 15 secs	ANICCĀ *aciraṃ*||			turning around offering

key: italics-non-canonical Pāli; secs/mins-unidentified chant; || = end of chanting sequence; → = chanting continued without break;

chanting sequences

wishes	Pv-merit	wishes	paritta/wishes	Pv	paritta	finish	event
	idaṃ me yathā vāri-2→ water	*icchitaṃB*×2 *icchitaṃA* ||				sermon + wishes	SL 1 + 2
	idaṃ me yathā vāri-2→ water	*icchitaṃB*×2 *icchitaṃA*||	all monks: *sabbītiyo* *bhavatu* abhivādana||			monks leave	SL 3 alms giving
	giving merit water	giving merit to all beings				ANICCĀ *dukkhā* *anattā*	Myan 1
	giving of merit water	giving merit to all beings	*samantā* *yassānubhāvato* Mettasutta		iti pi so + evaṃ *yan dun-* *bhavatu*		Myan 2 alms giving
a monk: *kāyena*→	chief monk: yathā vāri→ water	*icchitaṃA* *icchitaṃB*→	all monks: *sabbītiyo* abhivādana-→		*bhavatu*→	yam kiñci *okāsa* *vandāmi*	Laos 1
a monk: *kāyena*→	chief monk: yathā vāri→ water	*icchitaṃA* *icchitaṃB*→	all monks: *sabbītiyo* abhivādana-→	adāsi 4→	Mettasutta3||	monks leave contd at pavilion	Laos 2.A
a monk: *kāyena*→	chief monk: yathā vāri→ water	*icchitaṃA* *icchitaṃB*→	all monks: *sabbītiyo(×3)* abhivādana-→	adāsi 4||		contd at pyre	Laos 2.B
							Laos 2.C
	chief monk: yathā vāri→ water	*icchitaṃA* *icchitaṃB*→	all monks: *sabbītiyo* abhivādana-→	adāsi 4→	Mettasutta3||	monks leave; people take bones	Laos 3 bone ceremony
	chief monk: yathā vāri→	*icchitaṃA* *icchitaṃB*→	all monks: *sabbītiyo* abhivādana-→	ayañ ca so ñātidh→	*bhavatu*	sermon monks leave	Thai 1
	chief monk: yathā vāri→ water	*icchitaṃA* *icchitaṃB*→	all monks: *sabbītiyo* abhivādana-→	adāsi 4→	*bhavatu*	contd without break next line	Thai 2.A
layman: *kāyena*→	parcels cleared lunch		all monks: *sabbītiyo* abhivādana-→	ayañ ca so ñātidh||		contd at pyre	Thai 2.B
							Thai 2.C
	chief monk: yathā vāri→ water	*icchitaṃA* *icchitaṃB*→	all monks: *sabbītiyo* abhivādana-→	adāsi 4→	*bhavatu* layperson: 2 mins		Thai 3
	yathā vāri→	*icchitaṃA* *icchitaṃB*→	all monks: *sabbītiyo* abhivādana→	so ñātidh→	*bhavatu*	layperson: 2.5 mins	Thai 4 evening chant
			jayanto 3→ *yan dun-* *sabbītiyo* abhivādana-||			monks leave woman leaves	Thai 5 coffin ritual

boxing (single line) = pansukul sequence.

Table 2.2 *Index of verses and phrases*

Abbreviations for titles are in accordance with the Critical Pāli Dictionary (CPD) unless stated otherwise. Verses and passages were quoted from websites listed in the bibliography or from the editions and translations of the Pāli Text Society with the exception of Visuddhimagga (Vism), which is quoted from the edition by H. C. Warren and D. Kosambi (1950), Cambridge, MA: Harvard University Press. Where no reference is given, the translation is mine.

First word(s)	Pāli	English
Abhayagāthā	*yan dunnimittaṃ avamaṅgalañ ca yo cāmanāpo sakuṇassa saddo,* *pāpaggaho dussupinaṃ akantaṃ buddhānubhāvena vināsamentu!* *. . . dhammānubhāvena . . .* *. . . saṅghānubhāvena . . .* Abhayaparitta or Abhayagāthā.	Whatever unlucky portents and ill omens, And whatever distressing bird calls, Evil planets, upsetting nightmares: By the Buddha's power may they be destroyed. . . . by the Dhamma's power . . . . . . by the Saṅgha's power . . . (2000–10), *A Chanting Guide*.
Abhidhamma-saṃkhepa	*kusalā dhammā akusalā dhammā abyākatā dhammā. [further 21 triplets and 54 dhammas left out] avikkhepo hoti ye vā pana tasmiṃ samaye aññe pi atthi paṭicca-samuppannā arūpino dhammā: ime dhammā kusalā.* Dhammasaṅgaṇī 1 (square brackets are mine).	States that are good, bad, indeterminate. [further 21 triplets and 54 states left out]. Now these – or whatever other incorporal, causally induced states there are on that occasion – these are states that are good. Rhys Davids (1900: 1–5; (square brackets are mine).
	pañca-kkhandhā: rūpa-kkhandho . . . ayaṃ vuccati rūpa-kkhandho. Vibhaṅga 1.	The five aggregates are: the aggregate of material quality . . . this is called the aggregate of material quality. Thiṭṭila (1969: 1).
	saṅgaho asaṅgaho . . . vippayuttena sampayuttaṃ. Dhātukathā 1.	Classification and unclassification . . . dissociated and associated. Nārada and Thein (1962, xlvii).
	cha paññattiyo: khandha-paññatti . . . arahā arahattāya paṭipanno. Puggalapaññatti 1–3.	The six designations: (1) The notion of the groups . . . (50) An Arahant walking in Arahantship. Law (1924: 1–5).
	puggalo upalabbhati saccik'aṭṭha-paramatthenā ti? . . . ti micchā.	Is there a person known in the sense of a real and ultimate fact? – . . . That which you say here is wrong.

	Kathāvatthu I.	Aung (1915: 8).
	ye keci kusalā dhammā sabbe te kusala-mūlā ye; vā pana kusala-mūlā sabbe te dhammā kusalā. ye keci kusalā dhammā sabbe te kusala-mūlena eka-mūlā; ye vā pana kusala-mūlena eka-mūlā sabbe te dhammā kusalā. Yamaka I.	Are all states that are wholesome wholesome roots? Or are all wholesome roots states that are wholesome? Do all states that are wholesome share the same wholesome roots? Are all states that share the same wholesome roots wholesome?
	hetu-paccayo, ārammaṇa-paccayo, adhipati-paccayo . . . avigata-paccayo. Mahāpaṭṭhāna I.	Root condition, object condition, predominance condition . . . non-appearance. Nārada (1969: 1).
abhivādana- . . .	*abhivādanasīlissa niccaṃ vaddhāpacāyino cattāro dhammā vaḍḍhanti āyu vaṇṇo sukhaṃ balaṃ.* Dhp 109 (cf. Skilling 1994: 748).	To him who practises respectful salutation, constantly respecting his elders, four things increase: age, beauty, happiness and strength. Norman (1997: 17).
aciraṃ . . .	*aciraṃ vat' ayaṃ kāyo paṭhaviṃ adhisessati chuddho apetaviññāṇo niratthaṃ va kaliṅgaraṃ.* Dhp-a I 321.	Soon this body will lie on the ground, thrown away, deprived of consciousness, like a useless piece of wood. Adapted from Burlingame (1921: II 21).
adāsi (+4) . . .	See last four verses of the *Tirokuḍḍapetavatthu.*	
ahaṃ bhante. . .	See *mayaṃ bhante* . . .	
anattā . . .	See *aniccā* . . .	
aniccā . . .	*aniccā vata saṃkhārā, uppādavayadhammino uppajjitvā nirujjhanti tesaṃ vūpasamo sukho.* D II 157, D II 199, *et al.* Appears as triplet: *dukkhā vata . . . ; anattā vata . . .* (Myanmar 1) Prefixed with *aṭṭhi* (bone) at bone ceremonies (Laos 3).	Impermanent are conditioned things! It is their nature to arise and fall. Having risen, they cease. Their stilling is happy. Gethin (2008: 90).
aparājita- . . .	See *Jaya Gāthā* . . .	
arahan . . .	See *iti pi so* . . .	
aṭṭhi-aniccā . . .	See *aniccā* . . .	
āyu-r-ārogya-	*āyu-r-ārogyasampatti sagga-sampatti-m-eva ca atho nibbāṇasampatti iminā te samijjhatu*	May there be the attainment of long life and good health, and of heaven and by this may you be successful in the attainment of Nirvāṇa! Langer (2007: p. 131).

Table 2.2 (*cont.*)

First word(s)	Pāli	English
bhavatu . . . (all three)	*bhavatu sabbamaṅgalaṃ – rakkhantu sabbadevatā* *sabbabuddhānubhāvena – sadā sotthi bhavantu te* [or *me*]. *sabbadhammānubhāvena* . . . *sabbasaṃghānubhāvena* . . . Mahājayamaṅgala Sutta 13–15.	May there be for me all blessings, may all the devas guard me well, by the power of all the Buddhas ever in safety may I be. by the power of all the Dhammas . . . by the power of all the Sanghas Nārada (2008).
Brahmā . . .	*Brahmā ca lokādhipatī Sahampatī katañjalī anadhivaraṃ ayācatha:* *santīdha sattā 'ppa-rajakkha-jātikā* *desetu dhammaṃ anukamp' imaṃ pajaṃ.* Bv 1 (reminiscent of M I 168).	Then Brahmā Lord of the World with joined palms made his request to the Unsurpassed One: 'There are beings here with little dust (in their eyes), so out of compassion teach this world.'
buddhaṃ . . .	*Buddhaṃ saraṇaṃ gacchāmi* *dhammaṃ saraṇaṃ gacchāmi* *saṃghaṃ saraṇaṃ gacchāmi* *dutiyam pi* . . . *tatiyam pi* . . . Khp 1; M I 24; Vin I 22.	I go for refuge to the Awakened One. I go for refuge to the Dharma. I go for refuge to the Community. For the second time, . . . For the third time, . . .
Cātummahā . . .	*Cātummahārājikā devā saddam anussāvesuṃ.* *Cātummahārājikānaṃ devānaṃ saddaṃ sutvā Tāvatiṃsā devā saddam anussāvesuṃ* . . . *Akaṇiṭṭhakā devā saddam anussāvesuṃ.* S V 420–4, Vin I, 10–12 *et al.*	[Having heard the cry of the earth-dwelling *devas*] the *devas* of the realm of the Four Great Kings raised a cry ['At Bārāṇasī in the Deer Park at Isipatana, this unsurpassed Wheel of the Dhamma has been set in motion by the Blessed One . . . ']. Having heard the cry of the *devas* of the realm of the Four Great Kings, the Tāvatiṃsa *devas* . . . the Yāma *devas* . . . the Tusita *devas* . . . the Nimmānaratī *devas* . . . the Paranimmitavasavattī *devas* . . . [the *devas* of Brahmā's company . . . here S V 423 and Vin I 12 have *Brahmakāyikā devā* while the chanting continues with the formula naming all the Brahma gods individually]. Bodhi (2000: 1,846; square brackets are mine).

dukkhā . . .	See *aniccā* . . .	
evaṃ Buddhaṃ . . .	*evaṃ Buddhaṃ sarantānaṃ,* *dhammaṃ saṅghañ ca bhikkhavo;* *bhayaṃ vā chambhitattaṃ vā,* *lomahaṃso na hessati.* S I 220, (last paragraph of the Dhajaggasutta S I 219–20).	For those who thus recall the Buddha, the Dhamma, and the Saṅgha, bhikkhus, No fear or trepidation will arise, nor any grisly terror. Bodhi (2000: I 320f.).
hetu- . . .	See *Abhidhamma-saṃkhepa*	
icchitaṃ A . . .	*icchitaṃ patthitaṃ tuyhaṃ khippam eva samijjhatu,* *[sabbe] pūrentu cittasaṃkappā cando paṇṇaraso yathā.*	May whatever is desired and wanted quickly come to be. May [all] your wishes be fulfilled like the moon on the full moon day.
icchitaṃ B . . .	*icchitaṃ patthitaṃ tuyhaṃ khippam eva samijjhatu,* *[sabbe] pūrentu cittasaṃkappā maṇijotiraso yathā.* Rasavāhinī (B^{e}) 151 (Mahāsenavagga, story 38).	May whatever is desired and wanted quickly come to be. May [all] your wishes be fulfilled like a radiant wish-fulfilling gem. See also Norman (1910: 61).
idaṃ me . . .	See *Tirokuḍḍapetavatthu*	
imaṃ mataka- . . .	*imaṃ matakavatthaṃ bhikkhusaṃghassa dema!*	We offer this 'cloth of the dead' [or 'cloth of remembrance'] to the community of monks!
imaṃ tāmbū- . . .	*imaṃ tāmbūlagilānapaccayadānaṃ bhikkhusaṃghassa dema!*	We offer this gift of betel and refreshments to the community of monks!
imāni mataka-	*imṃ matakavatthaṃ* . . .	
imāni pañca . . .	*Imāni pañca sikkhāpadāni sīlena sugatiṃ yanti, sīlena bhogasampadā sīlena nibbutiṃ yanti. Tasmā sīlaṃ visodhaye.*	These are the five training rules. Through virtue they go to a good bourn. Through virtue is wealth attained. Through virtue they go to liberation. Therefore we should purify our virtue. (2000–10) *A Chanting Guide*.
iti pi so . . .	*iti pi so bhagavā: arahaṃ, sammāsambuddho* . . . *svākkhāto bhaghavatā dhammo* . . . *supaṭipanno bhagavato sāvakasaṃgho* . . . S I 219–20 (Dhajaggasutta), M I 37f, A III 285f, *et al.*	The Blessed One is an arahant, perfectly enlightened . . . The Dhamma is well expounded by the Blessed One . . . The Saṅgha of the Blessed One's disciples is practising the good way . . . Bodhi (2000: I 320f.); see also Ńāṇamoli and Bodhi (1995: 118).
Jaya Gāthā . . .	*mahā-kāruṇiko nātho hitāya sabba-pāṇinaṃ* *pūretvā pāramī sabbā patto sambodhim-uttamaṃ*	(The Buddha), our protector, with great compassion, For the welfare of all beings,

Table 2.2 (*cont.*)

First word(s)	Pāli	English
	etena sacca-vajjena hotu te jayamaṅgalaṃ.	Having fulfilled all the perfections, Attained the highest self-awakening. Through the speaking of this truth, may you have a victory blessing.
	jayanto bodhiyā mūle sakyānaṃ nandi-vaḍḍhano *evaṃ tvaṃ vijayo hohi* [or: *tuyhaṃ jayo hotu*] *jayassu jaya-maṅgale* [or: *jayamaṅgalaṃ*]. Also: Mahājayamaṅgala Gāthā verses 1+2. *aparājita-pallaṅke sīse paṭhavi-pokkhare* *abhiseke sabba-buddhānaṃ aggappatto pamodati.*	Victorious at the foot of the Bodhi tree, Was he who increased the Sakyans' delight. May you have the same sort of victory, May you win victory blessings. At the head of the lotus leaf of the world On the undefeated seat Consecrated by all the Buddhas, He rejoiced in the utmost attainment.
	sunakkhattaṃ sumaṅgalaṃ supabhātaṃ suhuṭṭhitaṃ *sukhaṇo sumuhutto ca suyiṭṭhaṃ brahma-cārisu.* *padakkhiṇaṃ kāya-kammaṃ vācā-kammaṃ padakkhiṇaṃ* *padakkhiṇaṃ mano-kammaṃ paṇidhī te padakkhiṇā.* *padakkhiṇāni katvāna labhantatthe padakkhiṇe.*	A lucky star it is, a lucky blessing, a lucky dawn, a lucky sacrifice, a lucky instant, a lucky moment, a lucky offering: i.e. a rightful bodily act a rightful verbal act, a rightful mental act, your rightful intentions with regard to those who lead the chaste life. Doing these rightful things, your rightful aims are achieved. (2000–10) *A Chanting Guide.*
Jayamaṅgala Gāthā.	*1. bāhuṃ sahassam ahabhinimmitasāvudhan taṃ* *Girimekhalaṃ uditaghorasasenaMāraṃ* *dānādidhammavidhinā jitavā munindo* *taṃ tejasā bhavatu te* [or *no*] *jayamaṅgalāni* . . . [plus five more verses]	The Lord of Maras conjured up a thousand-armed form while riding on his elephant Girimekhala brandishing in every hand a weapon fit to kill surrounded by his soldier-hosts shrieking frightfully: The Lord of Munis conquered him by Generosity and the rest. By the power of that victory may I win all success! . . .

	7. Nandopanandabhujagaṃ vibudhaṃ mahiddhiṃ *puttena therabhujagena damāpayanto* *iddhūpadesavidhinā jitavā munindo* *taṃ tejasā bhavatu te jayamaṅgalāni.*	The Naga-king of potency, Nandopananda named, of power and perverted views, the Lord permission gave his son the elder Moggallana to tame in Naga-form, and he so tamed perceived his faults, by magic taught the way: The Lord of Munis conquered him through Moggallana's might. By the power of that victory may I win all success!
	9. etā 'pi buddhajayamaṅgalaaṭṭhagāthā *yo vācako dinadine sarate matandi* *hitvānanekavividhāni c'upaddavāni* *mokhaṃ sukhaṃ adhigameyya naro sapañño.* Jayamaṅgala gāthā (verses 1, 7 and 9).	The man sincere of wisdom sure will recollect each day these stanzas eight of victories won by the Buddha's might and chanting them he will avoid all dangers, accidents, to come at last to happiness when liberation's found. Nārada (2008).
jayanto . . .	See *Jaya Gāthā . . .*	
Jayaparitta	See *Jaya Gāthā . . .*	
Karaṇīyamettasutta	*8. mettañ ca sabbalokasmiṃ mānasam bhāvaye aparimāṇaṃ* *uddhaṃ adho ca tiriyañ ca asambādhaṃ averaṃ asapattaṃ*	And loving-kindness towards all the world. One should cultivate an unbounded mind, above and below and across, without obstruction, without enmity, without rivalry.
	9. tiṭṭhaṃ caraṃ nisinno vā sayāno vā yāvatassa vigatamiddho *etaṃ satiṃ adhiṭṭheyya brahmam etaṃ vihāraṃ idha-m-āhu.*	Standing, or going, or seated, or lying down, as long as one is free from drowsiness, one should practise this mindfulness. This, they say, is the holy state here.
	10. diṭṭhiñ ca anupagamma sīlavā dassanena sampanno *kāmesu vineyya gedhaṃ na hi jātu gabbhaseyyaṃ punaretī ti* Sn 24f; Khp 8 (last three verses).	Not subscribing to wrong views, virtuous, endowed with insight, having overcome greed for sensual pleasures, a creature assuredly does not come to lie again in a womb. Norman (2001: 19).
kāyena . . .	*kāyena vācāya vā cetasā vā* *buddhe kukammaṃ pakataṃ mayā yaṃ* *buddho patigganhātu accayantaṃ* *kālantare samavarituṃ va Buddhe!* *. . . dhamme!* *. . . saṅghe!*	Whatever bad kamma I have done to the Buddha by body, by speech, or by mind, may the Buddha accept my admission of it, so that in the future I may show restraint toward the Buddha. . . . toward the *dhamma!* . . . . . . toward the *saṅgha!* (2000–10) *A Chanting Guide*.

Table 2.2 (*cont.*)

First word(s)	Pāli	English
kusalā . . .	See *Abhidhamma-saṃkhepa*	
mayaṃ bhante. . .	*mayaṃ bhante visuṃ visuṃ rakkhanatthāya ti-saraṇena saha pañca sīlāni yācāma.*	Venerable Sir, for [our] protection we individually request the Five Precepts along with the Three Refuges.
	dutiyaṃ pi . . .	For the second time, . . .
	tatiyaṃ pi . . .	For the third time, . . .
	anuggahaṃ katvā sīlaṃ detha no bhante	Out of kindness grant us the precepts.
Mettasutta 3	See last three verses of the *Karaṇīyametta Sutta*.	
na hi ruṇṇaṃ . . .	See *Tirokuḍḍapetavatthu*.	
namo . . .	*namo tassa bhagavato arahato sammāsambuddhassa.*	Homage to Him, the Blessed One, the Worthy One, the Fully Awakened One!
Nandopanand . . .	See *Jayamaṅgala Gāthā*.	
nivedayāmi . . .	*nivedayāmi sambuddhaṃ vītarāgaṃ mahāmuniṃ, nimantayāmi sugataṃ lokaseṭṭhaṃ narāsabhaṃ*	I address the Buddha, who is free of passion, the great sage. I invite the well-gone, the most excellent in the world, the lord of men.
	sugandhaṃ sītalaṃ kappaṃ pasanna-madhuraṃ subhaṃ, pāṇīyam etaṃ bhagavā patigaṇhātu-m-uttamaṃ.	May the Blessed One accept the best, this water, fragrant, cool, proper, clear, sweet and pleasant.
	adhivāsetu no bhante bhojanaṃ parikappitaṃ, anukampaṃ upādāya patigaṇhātu-m-uttamaṃ.	May he accept from us, the venerable one, this prepared food, may he receive the best with compassion.
	. . . *vyañjanaṃ parikappitaṃ*. . .	. . . prepared curry . . .
	. . . *khajjakaṃ parikappitaṃ* . . .	. . . prepared sweet meats . . .
	. . . *rasavantaṃ phalāphalaṃ* . . .	. . . tasty fruits . . .
	. . . *parikkhāraṃ parikappitaṃ* . . .	. . . prepared utensils . . .
	. . . *sabbaṃ saddhāya pūjitaṃ* . . .	. . . all things offered in faith . . . see Langer (2007: 129).
okāsa . . .	*okāsa vandāmi bhante*	Asking your leave, I revere you, Venerable Sir
	sabbaṃ aparādhaṃ khamatha me bhante	May you forgive me all my guild, Venerable Sir
	mayā kataṃ puññaṃ sāminā anumoditabbaṃ	May the master rejoice in the merit I have done
	sāminā kataṃ puññaṃ mayhaṃ dātabbam	May the master transmit te merit to me, he has done
	sādhu sādhu anumodāmi	Well (said), well (said); I rejoice in it. (2007) *Morning Chanting Guide*; see also Bernon (2000: 488).

padakkhiṇaṃ . . .	See *Jaya Gāthā* . . .	
pāṇātipātā . . .	*pāṇātipātā veramaṇī-sikkhāpadaṃ samādiyāmi* *adinnādānā* . . . *kāmesu micchācārā* . . . *musāvādā* . . . *surāmerayamajjapamādaṭṭhānā* . . . KhP 1; Vin I 83–84; Vbh 285ff.	I undertake the training precept of abstention from killing breathing things . . . from taking what is not given . . . from unchastity . . . from speaking falsehood . . . from any opportunity for negligence due to liquor, wine and besotting drink. Ñāṇamoli (1960b: 1).
sabbe . . .	*sabbe sattā maranti ca mariṃsu ca marissare,* *tath'ev' ahaṃ marissāmi, n'atthi me ettha saṃsayo.*	In the present every being dies, they will die in future, always died. In the same way then I shall surely die. There is no doubt in me regarding this. Nārada (2008).
sabbītiyo . . .	*sabbītiyo vivajjantu sabbarogo vinassatu* *mā te bhavatv antarāyo sukhī dīghāyuko bhava* *Mahājayamaṅgala Gāthā* verse 12.	May all distresses be averted, may all diseases be destroyed, may no dangers be for me, may I be happy living long. Nārada (2008).
sagge . . .	See *samantā* . . .	
samantā . . .	*samantā cakkavāḷesu,* *atrāgacchantu devatā.* *saddhammaṃ muni-rājassa* *suṇantu sagga-mokkhadaṃ.* *sagge kāme ca rūpe giri-sikharataṭe c' antalikkhe vimāne,* *dīpe raṭṭhe ca gāme taruvana-gahane geha-vatthumhi khette;* *bhummā cāyantu devā jala-thala-visame* *yakkha-gandhabba-nāgā.* *tiṭṭhantā santike yaṃ muni-vara-vacanaṃ* *sādhavo me suṇantu.*	From around the galaxies may the devas come here. May they listen to the True Dhamma of the King of Sages, Leading to heaven and emancipation. Those in the heavens of sensuality and form, On peaks and mountain precipices, in palaces floating in the sky, In islands, countries and towns, In groves of trees and thickets, around homesites and fields. And the earth-devas, spirits, heavenly minstrels and nagas In water, on land, in badlands and nearby: May they come and listen with approval As I recite the word of the excellent sage.

Table 2.2 (*cont.*)

First word(s)	Pāli	English
	dhammassavanakālo ayam bhadanta (X3).	This is the time to listen to the Dhamma, Venerable Sirs. (2000–10) *A Chanting Guide.*
saparikkhāraṃ	*saparikkhāraṃ sāṭṭhaparikkhāraṃ imaṃ bhikkhaṃ bhikkhusaṃghassa dema! (2x)*	We offer this alms food to the community of monks together with the eight requisites and other utensils! See Langer (2007: 131).
so ñāti- . . .	See *Tirokuḍḍapetavatthu.*	
sunakkhattaṃ . . .	See *Jaya Gāthā*	
supaṭipanno . . .	See *iti pi so . . .*	
svākkhāto . . .	See *iti pi so . . .*	
Tirokuḍḍapetavatthu	*3. . . . Idaṃ vo ñātīnaṃ hotu sukhitā hontu ñātayo!*	'Let this be for our relatives! May our relatives be happy!'
	7. unname udakaṃ vaṭṭhaṃ yathā ninnaṃ pavattati, evam eva ito dinnaṃ petānaṃ upakappati.	As water rained on the uplands flows down to the low land, even so does what is given here benefit the petas.
	8. yathā vārivahā pūrā paripūrenti sāgaraṃ, evam eva ito dinnaṃ petānaṃ upakappati.	Just as swollen streams swell the ocean, even so does what is given here benefit the petas.
	9. adāsi me akāsi me ñātimittā sakhā ca me, petānaṃ dakkhiṇaṃ dajjā pubbe katam anussaraṃ.	'He gave to me, he worked for me, he was a relative, friend and companion to me' – (thus) recalling what they used to do one should give donations for the petas.
	10. na hi ruṇṇaṃ va soko vā yā c'aññā paridevanā, na taṃ petānamatthāya evaṃ tiṭṭhanti ñātayo.	No amount of weeping, sorrow or any lamentation benefits the peta though their relatives persist in them.
	11. ayañ ca kho dakkhiṇā dinnā saṅghamhi suppatiṭṭhitā, dīgharattaṃ hitāyassa ṭhānaso upakappati.	But this donation that has been made and firmly planted in the Saṅgha will serve, with immediate effect, their long term benefit.
	12. so ñātidhammo ca ayaṃ nidassito petāna pūjā ca katā uḷārā, balañ ca bhikkhūnamanuppadinnaṃ tumhehi puññaṃ pasutaṃ anappakan ti. Pv 5f; see also Khp.	Now this, the duty to one's relatives, has been pointed out and the highest honour has been pain to the petas; strength has been furnished to the monks and not trifling the meritorious deed pursued by you. Dhammapāla (1980: 26); see also Ñāṇamoli (1960b: 7).

tissaraṇa-gam	*tissaraṇa-gamanaṃ niṭṭhitaṃ/paripuṇṇaṃ.*	This end the going for refuge. (2000–10) *A Chanting Guide.*
ukkhitta . . .	See *Jayamaṅgala Gāthā.*	
unname . . .	See *Tirokuḍḍapetavatthu.*	
yam kinci . . .	*yaṃ kiñci kusalaṃ kammaṃ kattabbaṃ kiriyaṃ mama,* *kāyena vācāmanasā tidase sugataṃ kataṃ,* *ye sattā saññino atthi ye ca sattā asaññino,* *kataṃ puññaphalaṃ mayhaṃ sabbe bhāgī bhavantu te.* *ye taṃ kataṃ suviditaṃ dinnaṃ puññaphalaṃ mayā,* *ye ca tattha na jānanti devā gantvā nivedayuṃ,* *sabbe lokamhi ye sattā jīvantāhārāhetukā,* *manuññaṃ bhojanaṃ sabbe labhantu mamaṃ cetasā ti.* Ap I 4 *(Tilokavijayarājapattidānagāthā)*	Whatever wholesome deeds that were my duty to perform, I have properly performed them in body, speech and mind with rebirth among the thirty [gods] in mind. Whatever sentient and insentient beings there are, may they all share in the fruits of my good actions. To those who are well aware of my actions, I give the fruit of that merit; and those who don't know about them, the gods will come and inform. By the power of my mind may all beings in the world who live in dependence on food gain all delightful foods.
yan dun- . . .	See *Abhayagāthā.*	
yassānubhāvato . . .	*yassānubhāvato yakkhā n'eva dassenti bhiṃsanaṃ* *yaṃhi c'evānuyuñjanto rattin-divam atandito* *sukhaṃ supati sutto ca pāpaṃ kiñci na passati,* *evam-ādi-guṇopetaṃ parittan taṃ bhaṇāmahe* (reminiscent of A V 324).	By its power supernatural beings do not appear in frightful forms; The person who untiringly devotes himself to it day and night, sleeps soundly and has no bad dreams – let us recite this protective sutta possessing these and other qualities. Introductory chant to the *Karaṇīyametta Sutta.*
yathā vāri-. . .	See *Tirokuḍḍapetavatthu.*	

BIBLIOGRAPHY

(1975), *The Book of Chants: a Compilation being the Romanized Edition of the Royal Thai Chanting Book*. Bangkok, Mahāmakut Rājavidyālaya Press.

(1995), *Sāmaṇera Baṇa Daham Pota*, Sri Sarananda Maha Pirivena.

(2000–10), *A Chanting Guide*. The Dhammayut Order in the United States of America, www.accesstoinsight.org/lib/authors/dhammayut/chanting.

(2007), *Morning Chanting Guide*. Wat Lao Buddhamamakaram, Columbus. www.theravadapgco.org/Liturgy.htm.

(2008), *Samatha Chanting Book*. Llangunllo, The Samatha Centre, Greenstreet.

Adikaram, E. W. (1946), *Early History of Buddhism in Ceylon: or, State of Buddhism in Ceylon as Revealed by the Pāli Commentaries of the 5th Century A.D.*, Migoda, Ceylon: D. S. Puswella.

Aung, Shwe Zan and Mrs. Rhys Davids (trans.) (1915), *Points of Controversy or Subjects of Discourse: Being a Translation of the Kathā-Vatthu from the Abhidhamma-Piṭaka*, Oxford: Pāli Text Society.

Bareau, A. (1964), *Der Indische Buddhismus*, Stuttgart: W. Kohlhammer.

Bernon, O. de (2000), 'Le rituel de la "grande probation annuelle"', *Bulletin de l'École Française d'Extrême-Orient* **87** (2), 473–510.

Bizot, F. (1988), *Les Traditions de la Pabbajjā en Asie du Sud-Est: Recherches sur le Bouddhisme Khmer IV*, Paris: Publications de l'École Française d'Extrême-Orient.

Blackburn, A. M. (1999a), 'Looking for the *Vinaya*: monastic discipline in the practical canons of the Theravāda', *Journal of the International Association for Buddhist Studies* **22** (2), 281–309.

(1999b), 'Magic in the monastery: textual practice and monastic identity in Sri Lanka', *History of Religions* **38** (4), 354–72.

(2003), 'Localizing lineage: importing higher ordination in Theravādin South and Southeast Asia', in eds. J. Holt, J. N. Kinnard and J. S. Walters, *Constituting Communities: Theravāda Buddhism and the Religious Cultures of South and Southeast Asia*, Albany, NY: State University of New York Press, 131–49.

Bodhi, Bhikkhu (2000), *The Connected Discourses of the Buddha: A New Translation of the Saṃyutta Nikāya; Translated from the Pāli*, Somerville, MA: Wisdom Publications.

Bretfeld, S. (2001), *Das Singhalesische Nationalepos von König Duṭṭhagāmaṇī Abhaya: Textkritische Bearbeitung und Übersetzung der Kapitel VII.3-VIII.3 der Rasavāhinī des Vedeha Thera und Vergleich mit den Paralleltexten Sahassavatthuppakaraṇa und Saddharmālaṅkāraya*, Berlin: Dietrich Reimer Verlag.

Buddhaghosa (1950), *Visuddhimagga of Buddhaghosācariya*, ed. H. C. Warren, Cambridge, MA: Harvard University Press.

(1991), *The Path of Purification: Visuddhimagga*, trans. B. Ñāṇamoli, Kandy: Buddhist Publication Society.

Burlingame, E. W. (1921), *Buddhist Legends*, Cambridge, MA: Harvard University Press.

Caland, W. (1896), *Die Altindischen Todten und Bestattungsbräuche*, Wiesbaden: Dr. Martin Sändig oHG.

Carter, J. R. (1993), *On Understanding Buddhists: Essays on the Theravāda Tradition in Sri Lanka*, Albany, NY: State University of New York Press.

Collins, S. (1995), 'On the very idea of the Pāli Canon', *Journal of the Pāli Text Society* **XV**, 89–126.

(1998), *Nirvana and Other Buddhist Felicities: Utopias of the Pāli Imaginaire*, Cambridge University Press.

Cuevas, B. J. and Stone, J. I. (eds.) (2007), *The Buddhist Dead: Practices, Discourses, Representations*, Honolulu: University of Hawai'i Press.

De Silva, L. (1981), Paritta: a historical and religious study of the Buddhist ceremony for peace and prosperity in Sri Lanka, *Spolia Zeylanica (Bulletin of the National Museums of Sri Lanka)* **36** (1).

Dhammapāla (1980), *Elucidation of the Intrinsic Meaning: So Named the Commentary on the Peta-stories (Paramatthadīpanī nāma Petavatthu-aṭṭ hakathā)*, P. Masefield trans., London: Pāli Text Society: distributed by Routledge and Kegan Paul.

Dhammatilaka, P. (ed.) (1997), *Theravāda Sāmaṇera Baṇadaham Pota*, Colombo: M. D. Gunasena.

Freiberger, O. (2004), 'The Buddhist Canon and the Canon of Buddhist Studies', *Journal of the International Association of Buddhist Studies* **27** (2), 261–83.

Geiger, W. and Ghosh, B. (1943), *Pāli Literature and Language*, Calcutta: University of Calcutta.

Gethin, R. (1992), 'The Mātikās: Memorization, Mindfulness and the List' in ed. J. Gyatso, *In the Mirror of Memory: Reflections on Mindfulness and Remembrance in Indian and Tibetan Buddhism*, Albany, NY: State University of New York Press, 149–72.

(1998), *Foundations of Buddhism*, Oxford and New York: Oxford University Press.

(2008), *Sayings of the Buddha: a Selection of Suttas from the Pāli Nikāyas*, Oxford and New York: Oxford University Press.

Gombrich, R. F. (1981), 'A new Theravādin liturgy', *Journal of the Pāli Text Society* **9**, 47–73.

(1988), *Theravāda Buddhism: a Social History from Ancient Benares to Modern Colombo*, London and New York: Routledge and Kegan Paul.

(1991), *Buddhist Precept and Practice: Traditional Buddhism in the Rural Highlands of Ceylon*, Delhi: Motilal Banarsidass Publishers (reprint).

Gonda, J. (1977), *The Ritual Sūtras*, Wiesbaden: Harrassowitz.

Gyatso, J. (ed.) (1992), *In the Mirror of Memory: Reflections on Mindfulness and Remembrance in Indian and Tibetan Buddhism*, Albany, NY: State University of New York Press.

Harrison, P. (1992), 'Commemoration and identification in buddhānusmṛti', in ed. J. Gyatso, *In the Mirror of Memory: Reflections on Mindfulness and Remembrance in Indian and Tibetan Buddhism*, Albany, NY: State University of New York Press, 215–38.

Holt, J., Kinnard, J. N., Walters, J. S. (eds.) (2003), *Constituting Communities: Theravāda Buddhism and the Religious Cultures of South and Southeast Asia.* Albany, NY: State University of New York Press.

Keyes C. and Anusaranasasanakiart, Phrakhru (1980), 'Funerary rites and the Buddhist meaning of death: an interpretative text from northern Thailand', *Journal of the Siam Society* **68** (1), 1–28.

Klima, A. (2002), *The Funeral Casino: Meditation, Massacre, and Exchange with the Dead in Thailand*, Princeton, NJ: Princeton University Press.

Ladwig, P. (2003), *Death Rituals among the Lao: an Ethnological Analysis*, Berlin. Seacom Edition, Tai Culture Interdisciplinary, Tai Studies Series 15.

Langer, R. (2007), *Buddhist Rituals of Death and Rebirth: Contemporary Sri Lankan Practice and its Origins*, Abingdon and New York: Routledge.

Law, B. C. (1924), *Designation of Human Types*, London, New York: Oxford University Press.

Lévi-Strauss, C. (1966), *The Savage Mind*, University of Chicago Press.

Liambounrueang, M. (2003), *Handbook of Rituals and Chants*, Vientiane: Committee for the Education of Monks.

Lopez, D. S. (1995), *Buddhism in Practice*, Princeton, NJ: Princeton University Press.

McDaniel, J. (2002), 'The curricular Canon in northern Thailand and Laos', *Manusya: Journal of Thai Language and Literature Special Issue*, 20–59.

(2006), 'Liturgies and cacophonies in Thai Buddhism', *Aséanie* **18**, 119–50.

(2008), *Gathering Leaves and Lifting Words: Histories of Buddhist Monastic Education in Laos and Thailand*, Seattle: University of Washington Press.

Ñāṇamoli, Bhikkhu (1956), *The Path of Purification (Visuddhimagga) by Bhadantācariya Buddhaghosa*, Colombo: R. Semage.

(1960a), *The Three Refuges*, Kandy: Buddhist Publication Society.

(1960b), *The Minor Readings (Khuddakapātha) the first book of the minor collection (Khuddakanikāya) and The Illustrator of Ultimate Meaning (Paramatthajotikā); Commentary on the Minor Readings*, Oxford: Pāli Text Society.

Ñāṇamoli, Bhikkhu and Bodhi, Bhikkhu (1995), *The Middle Length Discourses of the Buddha: a New Translation of the Majjhima Nikāya*, Boston, MA: Wisdom Publications.

Nārada (1969), *Conditional Relations (Paṭṭhāna.): Being vol. 1 of the Chatthasangāyana Text of the Seventh Book of the Abhidhamma Piṭaka*, London: published for the Pāli Text Society by Luzac.

(2008), *The Mirror of the Dhamma: a Manual of Buddhist Chanting and Devotional Texts*, revised by Bhikkhu Khantipalo (ed.), The Wheel Publication No 54 A/B, Colombo: Buddhist Publication Society. www.bps.lk/new_wheels_library/wh054-p.html.

Nārada, U. and Thein, N. (1962), *Discourse on Elements (Dhātu-kathā) the Third Book of the Abhidhamma Piṭaka*, London: published for the Pāli Text Society by Luzac.

Norman, H. C. (1910), 'Buddhist legends of Asoka and his times. Translated from the Pāli of the Rasavāhinī by Lakṣmaṇa Śāstrī', *Journal of the Asiatic Society of Bengal*, New Series **6**, 57–72.

Norman, K. R. (1983), *Pāli Literature: Including the Canonical Literature in Prakrit and Sanskrit of all Hinayana Schools of Buddhism*, Wiesbaden: Otto Harrassowitz.

(1997), *The Word of the Doctrine (Dhammapada)*, Oxford: The Pāli Text Society.

(2001), *The Group of Discourses (Sutta-Nipāta)*, Oxford: The Pāli Text Society.

Pandey, R. B. (1969), *Hindu Saṃskāras: Socio-religious Study of the Hindu Sacraments*, Delhi: Motilal Banarsidass.

Rhys Davids, C. A. F. (1900), *A Buddhist Manual of Psychological Ethics of the Fourth Century BC: Being a Translation, now made for the First Time, from the original Pāli, of the First Book in the Abhidhamma Piṭaka, entitled Dhamma-sangaṇi (Compendium of States or Phenomena)*, New Delhi: Oriental Books Reprint Corp; Distributed by Munshiram Manoharlal Publishers.

Rhys Davids, T. W. (ed.) (1896), *The Yogavacara's Manuel of Indian Mysticism as Practised by Buddhists*, London: publication for the Pāli Text Society by H. Frowde.

Samuel, J. (2004), 'Toward an action-oriented pedagogy: Buddhist texts and monastic education in contemporary Sri Lanka', *Journal of the American Academy of Religion* 72 (4), 955–71.

Schalk, P. (1972), 'Der Paritta-Dienst in Ceylon', PhD dissertation. Lund: Lunds Universitet.

Schopen, G. (2007), 'Cross-dressing with the dead: asceticism, ambivalence, and institutional values in an Indian monastic code', in eds. B. J. Cuevas and J. I. Stone, *The Buddhist Dead: Practices, Discourses, Representations*, Honolulu: University of Hawai'i Press, 60–104.

Skilling, P. (1992), 'The Rakṣā Literature of the Śrāvakayāna', *Journal of the Pāli Text Society* **15**, 110–80.

(1994), *The Mahāsūtras: Great Discourses of the Buddha*. Oxford: Pāli Text Society.

(1998), 'Sources for the study of the Maṅgala and Mora Suttas', *Journal of the Pāli Text Society* **24**, 185–93.

(2002), 'Arādhanā Tham: Invitation to teach the Dhamma', Manusya: *Journal of Humanities* Special Edition (4), 84–92.

Skilling, P. and Pakdeekham, S. (2002), *Pāli Literature Transmitted in Central Siam: A Catalogue Based on the Sap Songkhro*, Bangkok: Fragile Palm Leaves Foundation/Lumbini International Research Institute.

Skilling, P. and Prapod, A. (2002), 'Tripiṭaka in practice in the fourth and fifth reigns', *Manusya: Journal of Humanities* Special Edition (4): 60–72.

Spiro, M. E. (1982), *Buddhism and Society: a Great Tradition and its Burmese Vicissitudes*. Berkeley, CA: University of California Press.

Staal, F. (1996), *Ritual and Mantras: Rules without Meaning*, New York: P. Lang and Delhi: Motilal Banarsidass.

Swearer, D. K. (1995), 'A summary of the seven books of the Abhidhamma', in ed. D. S. Lopez, *Buddhism in Practice*, Princeton, NJ: Princeton University Press, 336–42.

Tambiah, S. J. (1970), *Buddhism and the Spirit Cults in North-east Thailand*, Cambridge University Press.

Terwiel, B. J. (1979), 'Tai funeral customs: towards a reconstruction of Archaic-Tai ceremonies', *Anthropos Freiburg* 74 (3–4), 393–432.

Thera, V. (1898), *Rasavāhinī*, Hunupitiya: Jinalankara Yantralaya.

Thiṭṭila (Seṭṭhila), U (1969), *The Book of Analysis (Vibhaṅga): the Second Book of the Abhidhamma Piṭaka*, London: published for the Pāli Text Society by Luzac.

Walshe, M. O' C. (1987), *Thus Have I Heard: the Long Discourses of the Buddha* (*Dīgha Nikāya*), London: Wisdom Publications.

Wannaphoupa, D. (2001), *Buddhist Prayers and Chants, Assembled by Douangchan Wannaphoupa*, Vientiane: State Printing House.

Wells, K. E. (1960), *Thai Buddhism, its Rites and Activities*, New York: AMS Press.

Wijeratne, R. P. and Gethin, R. (2002), *Summary of the Topics of Abhidhamma (Abhidhammatthasaṅgaha) by Anuruddha and Exposition of the Topics of Abhidhamma (Abhidhammatthavibhāvinī) by Sumaṅgala being a Commentary to Anuruddha's Summary of the Topics of Abhidhamma*, Oxford: Pāli Text Society.

Zago, M. (1972), *Rites et Cérémonies en Milieu Bouddhiste Lao*, Rome: Università Gregoriana.

CHAPTER 3

Weaving life out of death: the craft of the rag robe in Cambodian ritual technology

Erik W. Davis

INTRODUCTION

A monk's robe made of a shroud rests at the heart of the Theravādan Buddhist funeral of Southeast Asia. This robe, called the *paṃsukūla*, (Khmer: *bangsukol*) refers to two objects.[1] The first is the physical object of the *paṃsukūla*, a cloth offering given as part of the central action during a Khmer funeral ritual, invested with a surfeit of meaning. The second is the ritual practice termed *paṃsukūla* in everyday Khmer speech. This *paṃsukūla*, while related to the physical cloth termed *paṃsukūla*, is not identical. Instead, it refers to a subritual within the funeral process in which Buddhist monks intone a chant that refers to the Abhidhamma, one of the divisions of the Pāli canon, and perform important associated actions. The material robe connects to the funerary imagination in a way that highlights the importance of grounding our observations in the materiality of funerary cultures. I will connect these two *paṃsukūla*s, and proceed to concentrate on the centrality of the *paṃsukūla* in Southeast Asian Buddhism, and the basis of this centrality in the Cambodian ritual imagination.

My argument has three parts. First, the ritual actions of the *paṃsukūla* are mirrored in ritual and technical actions performed in other contexts, in

[1] Debate exists as to the best way to represent Khmer words in roman text. Transliteration properly renders Khmer spelling, and makes clear the connection to Indic languages. However, it poorly represents the way the words are pronounced compared to the various available transcription systems. I have opted for the transliterative approach, drawing largely on the American Library Association's chart. In the first instance of each word, I have italicised it and given a parenthetical Khmer-language transcription. For purposes of consistency, quoted words transcribed differently have been altered in quotation. This article is largely based on dissertation fieldwork conducted in Cambodia from 2003–6. There are many similarities and comparisons that may be fruitfully made between the Cambodian practice and Thai or Lao practice. See Chapter 4 by Chirapravati in this volume. However, except where made clear in the text, this chapter concerns itself solely with the Khmer *paṃsukūla*. Special thanks are due to my co-conspirators Pattaratorn Chirapravati and Patrice Ladwig for their stimulating conversations on the subject of *paṃsukūla*, and to David Chandler for his helpful comments on an earlier draft.

which non-Buddhist spirits are controlled and made useful by Buddhist monks. Second, these actions are based on, and receive their social force from, the agricultural work, inclusive of agricultural rituals, involved in the farming of rice in Khmer Southeast Asia. Finally, the previous two points position the Buddhist monk as a master and 'farmer' of the dead, capable of containing and controlling the world of spirits, on the basis of the monks' ability to resist death's contagion. I will take up the last point first.

When death takes one of the living, most of us feel concern and anxiety. We continue to care for the deceased, but most also feel a certain fear of the dead – their physical or remnant spiritual energies. The fear of death strongly resembles the fear of contagion.[2] Khmer are not exceptional in this regard, and have a well-developed anxiety about the spirits who inhabit a surprising amount of the world of the living, especially in the forests and waters. To live a civilised life – in villages, growing rice and participating in Buddhist ritual – requires a means of mediating and controlling these spirits, who may take offence at the insults civilisation commits against the natural world. Spirits have more power than the living over the energies of the world, and their disapproval and wrath must either be appeased or contained. New fields, homes and buildings must therefore be built with permission from the spirits of the land and water. Such buildings also commonly have a dangerous spirit bound within them for protection (Ang Choulean 1988: 38).

The ritual *paṃsukūla* appears to address both of these attitudes towards the spirits of the dead, where they are seen as powerful, dangerous and, if properly managed, useful. For when the family of the deceased offers the cloth representing the funerary shroud, the monk accepts it, presumably to turn it into another monastic robe. We are faced with a situation in which Buddhist monks engage in precisely those morbid activities that engender fear and avoidance for most.

Anthropologically speaking, the honoured reception of an impure robe by a presumably pure Buddhist monk strongly resembles Douglas' description of dirt as 'matter out of place' (Douglas 1966: 44). It appears as a confusion of antithetical categories. This seeming problem is in fact the key to Buddhist monastic authority. Just as the waxy lotus flower repels the muck in which it grows, the Buddhist monk's authority is grounded in his vocationally unique and special impunity to the impurity of death, which is the monk's

[2] Thus, in one of the foundational works on funerary custom in anthropology, Robert Hertz's primary metaphor for mourning taboos is to describe the mourners as living under the contagion of death (Hertz 1960).

primary concern and obstacle. This paradox grounds the authority of the Buddhist monk. As Bond (1980: 237) writes of Buddhism and death:

> Death has a paradoxical status in Theravāda Buddhism for it stands both at the heart of the human predicament and at the heart of the solution to that predicament.

Buddhist monks represent a social – and socially approved – power immune to the dangers of death. They prove their fearlessness and real power by publicly accepting funeral shrouds to wear as robes, which those afraid of death's contagion would be loath to do. This conquest and management of death is at the core of Buddhist monastic authority. Where the *paṃsukūla* cloth serves as evidence of the monk's vocational conquest of death, the *paṃsukūla* ritual appears as the practical means by which the monks deploy their powers over the world's spirits. The *paṃsukūla* ritual is one of a wide range of rituals – Buddhist and non-Buddhist – which order the Khmer world through the containment of spirits; this practice is based on the everyday experiences of rice farmers, who have composed the vast majority of the Khmer population since the adoption of agriculture.[3]

PAṂSUKŪLA: THE RAG ROBE

In Pāli texts, the *paṃsukūla* means a 'rag-robe' or 'dust-heap robe'.[4] According to these texts, the *paṃsukūla* robe may be obtained from various sources, ranging from trash heaps to charnel grounds. However, as Gregory Schopen notes, the notion of *paṃsukūla* as 'rubbish heap cloth' is a 'perfectly legitimate, if almost entirely rhetorical, Buddhist monastic ideal' (Schopen 2006: 336). Instead, the *paṃsukūla* was in almost every case a robe made from cloth associated with a corpse – a shroud, or a pall (*ibid.*: 337). The *paṃsukūlika* – the Buddhist monk wearing a *paṃsukūla* – wears a shroud he has sewn into a monk's robe.

In the Pāli texts which serve as the major source of information about supposedly early *paṃsukūla* practices, it is abundantly clear that early *paṃsukūla* cloths were collected from the charnel grounds where families

[3] It would be more proper to say that agriculture 'created' the Khmer, rather than that they 'adopted' it. Even today, somewhere between 80 and 90 per cent of Cambodians give their primary occupation as 'farmer'. Despite a rapidly growing urban population, 85 per cent of Cambodia's citizens live in the countryside (World Bank 2006).

[4] Translators for the Pāli Text Society routinely use one of these two translation options. The Pāli Vinaya (*Mahāvagga* VIII, 34–5) presents all of the Buddha's early disciples as *paṃsukūlikas*, or rag-robe wearers, until the presentation of new-cloth robes to the saṅgha by a lay-disciple, a full twenty years into the Buddha's teaching.

abandoned corpses wrapped in cloth. Taking cloth from an abandoned corpse renders such monks vulnerable to accusations of grave robbing. Given the fear of death-contagion in non-monastic society, the *paṃsukūlika* 'would seem, in short, not to be decreasing but increasing in its social offensiveness' (*ibid.*: 319).

> The message here may be not that radical ascetic, socially dangerous practices must be covered up, but rather than even beneath the appearance of a conventionally 'proper' monk there is a body wrapped in a shroud, and that in fact the latter is the foundation of the former, that in spite of appearances, radical ascetic and socially dangerous practices still underlie Buddhist monasticism (*ibid.*: 321–2).

The source of the monk's power to negotiate and control death and the spirits is founded in his triumphant conquest of death, and his fearlessness in its face. This conquest, in turn, comes as the result of Buddhist monastic training, and is potently represented by the *paṃsukūla.*

The syncretic gift

The most in-depth study of the *paṃsukūla* of which I am aware is François Bizot's (1981) work *Le Don de Soi-même*, where he examined a range of rituals in which the *paṃsukūla* is employed. His argument draws on the symbolism of the *paṃsukūla* cloth as a pregnant womb, and understands the rite of *paṃsukūla* as that which makes the cloth both a shroud and a matrix for a better rebirth or recovery in this life. This is accomplished, Bizot suggests, through the symbolic identification of the cloth with the individual's body, which is then given to the saṅgha as a substitute for the self. The *paṃsukūla* is therefore, for Bizot, not an abandonment or renunciation of the self, but a 'gift of the self' to the saṅgha, with enormous rewards.

Rita Langer (2007: 178; 183–4) argues that the practice of the *paṃsukūla* combines the Vedic funeral rite with a gift offering.[5] Schopen makes the point that the ceremony transforms Buddhist monks from cemetery scavengers to honoured recipients of gifts (Schopen 2006: 337–9). Thus, while the scriptural representation of the *paṃsukūla* portrays wearing it as a form of isolated ascetic autonomy, the transfer of the gift at funerals transforms it into a symbol of relationship between the saṅgha and the laity at the moment

[5] Langer quotes Richard Gombrich, who notes a similar fusion (Gombrich 1991: 283). There is a notable similarity between the stated function of the white cloth offering made during Vedic funerals and the Khmer *dâṅ praliṅ*, or 'spirit flag', which also plays a role in the funeral ritual, but is separate from the *paṃsukūla*. Both the *dâṅ praliṅ* and the Vedic cloth offering are said to serve as a component of entry to the realm of Yama, lord of the dead. In the case of the Vedic offering, it is supposed to act as a garment in that realm, whereas in the case of the *dâṅ praliṅ* it is said to act as a 'sort of passport'.

of death. Insofar as the transfer of the *paṃsukūla* during the funeral is a gift, it is a gift that only Buddhist monks are capable of receiving. There is no general denial of death's contagion or impurity, but merely a denial that the Buddhist monk is subject to its laws and its influence. The *paṃsukūla* could hardly be given to anyone else. Only a monk could be so brazen as to wear a shroud without fear.[6]

The *paṃsukūla* as object makes a very clear, symbolic, point about the ability of monks to remain untouched by death. The ritual performance termed '*paṃsukūla*' makes no semantic point but accomplishes a task: to influence the death and rebirth of others. A magico-technical power exists for the monks on the basis of their relationship with death. This relationship, based on the presumption of the Buddhasaṅgha that Buddhist monks ought to be able to subdue spirits, is in turn the basis for Buddhism's self-representation in its relationship to other domains, such as that termed 'Brahmanism'.[7]

As we turn now from a consideration of the *paṃsukūla* as object to the ritual in which it plays a central but by no means the only role, I will stress that the *paṃsukūla* is consistently associated with monastic actions that transform an item of no value – a funeral pall, dust-heap rags – into an item of great value. I will further argue that this is accomplished through practices that evoke other cultural representations that are central to the ordering of the moral and practical world. The most fundamental of these are the rituals and techniques underlying agricultural practices, which in many ways resemble those of the funeral *paṃsukūla* ritual.

Paṃsukūla *as ritual*

If the primary textual referent of the word *paṃsukūla* is to a cloth object offered or appropriated by Buddhist monks in the context of funeral rituals, *paṃsukūla* in colloquial usage refers to a ritual chant, called alternately merely *paṃsukūla*,

6 Similar concerns attend the offering of funerary gifts to Hindu funeral professions, in which the receipt of such gifts 'amounts to man-eating or partaking of a corpse' (Heesterman 1962: 25, quoted in Parry 1994: 132–3).

7 It is part of a larger argument, not rehearsed here, that mainland Southeast Asia, especially in the modern reform period, has drawn upon pre-existing elements within the Buddhist imagination, especially those having to do with death, to formulate a new religious superiority, and that in so doing, they actually created the imaginary domains to which they now refer. Thus, contemporary 'Brahmanism' in Cambodia appears as an amalgam of various practices, all placed on an equivalent plane in relation to Buddhism, and termed 'Brahmanism'. The relationship between Brahmanism and Buddhism in Southeast Asia has been the subject of enormous amounts of ink, but see especially (Tambiah 1970; Spiro 1996; Mus 1975, 1978).

paṃsukūla-mātikā or *sattappakaraṇa-mātikā*.[8] *Mātikā* is a word, cognate with matrix and mother, which denotes the mnemonic verses of sūtra contents. The *sattappakaraṇa-mātikā* is the collection of these mnemonic verses from the seven books (*sattappakaraṇa*) of the Abhidhamma. The chant is performed by an even number of Buddhist monks (four is the most common), who are collectively referred to as the *mātikā-buon*, 'the four-part *mātikā*'.[9] These references to *mātikā* over-represent the extent to which the actual content of the chant has anything to do with the Abhidhamma.[10] The *paṃsukūla-mātikā* is not chanted in a pedagogical or analytical manner; instead, it is chanted and stands metonymically for the Abhidhamma in moments when the ritual efficacy of the Abhidhammic perspective is required.

How is this ritual efficacy of the Abhidhamma imagined, and why should it, merely by allusion, have the sort of power in funerals ascribed to it? Part of the answer has to do with a conception of the Abhidhamma 'throughout the region as a life-giving mother' (McDaniel 2008: 241), and as a 'mother that bears new children' (*ibid.*: 244). The Abhidhamma's power is embryological, naturally of the mother, but is here in the possession of celibate male monks, who employ this power of new life to positively affect the rebirth station of the deceased.[11] The Abhidhamma enumerates and investigates the basic 'elements' of life and explains how they combine into the conditioned entities we experience as the phenomenal world; the *paṃsukūla-mātikā* seems to have some concrete effect on the disintegration and recombination of these elements into new bodies of life. The allusions to the Abhidhammic perspective in this context invoke the presumed conquest of death performed by the Buddhist monk.[12] It is his presumed conquest and resulting technical

[8] When Cambodians speak of the *paṃsukūla* they almost always mean the ritual act of chanting the *paṃsukūla-mātikā* and its allied ritual actions. I conducted extensive surveys of Buddhist lay-members, both those with and without specialist knowledge of funerary ritual. Asked what part of any funeral is the most important, two-thirds responded that the performance of the *paṃsukūla* was the most important. Although the other third did not mention the *paṃsukūla*, neither did any other response receive more than one suggestion.

[9] In all cases except the funeral, monks take care to avoid visiting lay-people as a group of four, or in multiples of four, since this is understood to represent death.

[10] The content of the chant varies, especially along lines of national and linguistic tradition. It does indeed contain some of the Abhidhamma *mātikā* content, but this is actually a rather minor portion of the actual chant, which is taken largely from a collection of standard chants, and a single verse from the *Mahāparinibbānasutta*. A Khmer manuscript of the *paṃsukūla-mātikā* has been reproduced with an excellent scholarly apparatus as a major part of Bizot's work (Bizot 1981).

[11] Readers curious about the logic of the gendered inversion evident in such an appropriation may find Nancy Jay's book on similar aspects in other rituals stimulating (Jay 1992).

[12] McDaniel writes that 'Often there is a disjuncture between the contents and the purposes of texts in monastic education. However, it is only a disjuncture if one values texts only for their semantic meaning and not for their usefulness in ritual transformation' (McDaniel 2008: 228).

control over death that allows the *paṃsukūla* ritual to be elaborated into initiatory and healing rituals (see Ladwig, Chapter 6 of this volume).

More specifically, the *paṃsukūla* ritual is most required during moments of change, transfer and transformation of the human being. The chant is typically intoned during moments in the funeral process when the corpse or post-cremation remains are moved.[13] The Khmer express considerable concern over these moments, for the disruption of the corpse – especially during the first seven days after death, when the deceased is supposed to be unaware that he or she has died – can result in the freeing of the spirit, which may then return to molest the living. The chanting of *paṃsukūla* takes place primarily at such moments when the danger of the freeing of malevolent spirits is greatest, and we may thus interpret it as partially addressing this concern.

The notion that the *paṃsukūla* ritual addresses fears of the dead, and specifically fears of freeing malevolent spirits, is strengthened by the associated ritual actions that take place during the chanting of the *paṃsukūla-mātikā*. When Cambodians discuss the *paṃsukūla* ritual, most of the time a necessary part of that discussion explicitly involves creating a boundary, or *sīmā*, around the corpse or its remains. This vocabulary of binding pervades the engagement of Buddhist monks with death. At all moments where the *paṃsukūla-mātikā* is chanted, there is an accompanying ritual gesture of binding. Most commonly, this involves the use of raw cotton thread called *aṃboḥ* to literally bind the corpse and to create a border around the body or its remains. This act prevents malevolent spirits from forming, or from returning home from the place of cremation or burial. When this thread is not in evidence, an equivalent binding is accomplished by at least four monks who stand around the corpse, such that they themselves function as the boundary when they chant *paṃsukūla-mātikā*.

VITAL, NON-BUDDHIST SPIRITS

The spirits composing a human being in the Khmer imagination are not limited to the Buddhist *viññāṇa*. Buddhism identifies death as the disintegration of a living being into its constituent components, commonly referred to as aggregates (Pāli: *khandha*). A human is composed of five of these, including

[13] At a minimum, during the following moments: (1) immediately before and during the moment of death; (2) immediately prior to moving the corpse out of the house; (3) during the entire parade or movement of the corpse to the place of its interment or cremation; (4) prior to and during the very beginning of the cremation itself; and (5) during the interment of the remains in a grave or urn.

the part identified with consciousness as such, the *viññāṇa*, thought of as that which takes rebirth.[14]

For Cambodians, however, the identification of *viññāṇa* with the spiritual stuff that remains after death is insufficient. While it remains the dominant model for Khmer thought about consciousness and identity, it appears to require the supplementation of a notion of vital power, called *praliṅ*. *Praliṅ* appears to predate *viññāṇa* as a model for spirit and self in Cambodia, and Ang Choulean has convincingly tied it to Śaivite cults of the *liṅga*, such that the word itself derives from two words meaning 'sacred liṅga' (*vraḥ liṅga* = *praliṅ*; Ang Choulean 2004: 173). The *liṅga* is 'not simply limited narrowly to a meaning associated with the male sexual organ, but also cover[s] connotations of strength and vigor which open onto the idea of dynamism and fecundity' (*ibid.*).

Praliṅ is the vitalism of fecund power, a role commandeered by the king who both encourages rice agriculture and eats the fruits of the kingdom that he metaphorically consumes in his role as sovereign.[15] The king's domain over fertility and lifepower connect to the vitality and mode of power of the *praliṅ*. In contrast, the king has no claim to *viññāṇa*, which exists solely in reference to the Buddhist philosophical system. He cannot eat it, or hold it. When a person dies, the *viññāṇa* immediately flies to a new birth via a process inaccessible to the king's sovereign power. Where the king's role is to promote and ensure fecundity, the monks' dominant association is with death and the refusal of constant rebirth.

Funerals, as the paradigmatic rite of Buddhist passage, must take into account not only the Buddhist conception of the self, but also address the spirits of the *praliṅ*. Buddhist funerals seem partly to be about separating these different powers from each other and treating them differently. These acts of separation and incorporation through binding are elaborated into acts of healing as well.[16] When a Khmer person falls ill, all sorts of causes are considered. Nevertheless, and especially when the illness is accompanied by a sudden fall, fright, or illness, the presumption is often that some of the patient's vital spirits, called *praliṅ*, have fled his or her body to the wild forests and deep waters where they originate. These *praliṅ*, of which most

[14] The best discussion of the self in rebirth thought can be found in Collins 1982.

[15] Porée-Maspero's works on Cambodian agrarian rites and private ceremonies confirm these observations: '[F]rom many rites and many symbolisms rise the idea that Cambodians call the vital spirits, or *praliṅ*'. The king's relationship to the kingdom is culinary: he is said to 'eat the kingdom': *saoy reach*. The king encourages rice agriculture most potently (in the symbolic realm – violence is more effective in the short term) through the yearly ritual of the Royal Ploughing.

[16] Rites of separation and incorporation find their classic exposition in Van Gennep (1960).

humans possess nineteen, are the vital spirits that enliven the body and the senses. Vitality, which does not transmigrate with the *viññāṇa* for all that it moves constantly, is instead accounted for by the presence or absence of these *praliṅ*.[17] Some may prefer to see a contradiction between the treatment of such spirits and the primary Buddhist concern with the *viññāṇa*, the Buddhist element that is reborn after death. Certainly, Buddhist texts do not discuss *praliṅ*.

More illuminating distinctions emerge from comparison with the *viññāṇa* managed during a funeral ritual. Where *praliṅ* are omnipresent, multiple and Brahmanist; the *viññāṇa* is located only in beings, is singular and Buddhist. Where the *viññāṇa*, as that which is reborn, is associated with karmic morality and moral choices, *praliṅ* are associated with vitality. A fat baby is greeted with cries of 'She's got *praliṅ*!', and saying that I have 'lost *praliṅ*' means that I feel weak or sick. The *viññāṇa*'s location is as part of the body until death, at which point it immediately becomes part of a new rebirth; the *praliṅ*'s location is uncertain and difficult to ascertain even in life. At death the *praliṅ* do not accompany the *viññāṇa* to the new identity.[18]

In Cambodia, *praliṅ* are vital spirits endowing every growing thing, sentient or not, and many things that are not even growing but special in other ways: rice, trees, termite mounds and often the soil itself have *praliṅ*. None of these have *viññāṇa*. For this reason the belief in *praliṅ* has been properly considered an animist one by Bizot (1981: 99) and others, although Porée-Maspero (1958: 22) suggests a more complicated history. The most common healing ritual, the calling of the *praliṅ*, summons the *praliṅ* back into the body of the patient and resembles the *sukhwan* rituals of Thailand and Laos.[19] After the *praliṅ* have returned to the body, they are bound into the patient's body symbolically by tying string around the wrist, the same *aṃboḥ* string used in funerals to bind and create boundaries around the corpse.[20] Regarding the use of this thread, Porée-Maspero (1958: 23) writes that:

> After collecting the vital spirits, one must proceed to the rite of caṅ dae (tying the wrist), which consists in binding the wrist of the patient with unbleached cotton string soaked in holy water . . . By tying the cotton string, it is also possible to form

[17] The best treatment of *praliṅ* I have encountered exists in the paired texts by Ang Choulean and Ashley Thompson (Thompson 1996, 2005; Ang Choulean 2004).

[18] The textual and specialist doctrines of rebirth, especially within the Abhidhammic perspective, are considerably more complicated than this description, based on interviews with contemporary Cambodian monks and lay-funerary specialists, *ācārya yogī*.

[19] These are essentially identical rites. The local names for these rites are semantic doubles: *su khwan* means to call the vital spirits in Thai and Lao, as does *hov praliṅ* in Khmer.

[20] In contrast, Sino-Khmer who participate in the calling of the *praliṅ* rite typically tie a length of red yarn around their wrist.

a kind of mystical bond: thus in the inauguration of a house, cotton bracelets are tied to the owners, and strings are attached to the column inhabited by the house's guardian deity.

Porée-Maspero makes one crucial allusion beyond her main point that tying this string creates a mystical bond: she notes that spirits are bound into non-beings, such as the column of a house. This is indeed true, and points us towards a resolution of the role of the *aṃboḥ* in the *paṃsukūla* rite. A minor deity called the *nāṅ pdaḥ*, or the young lady of the house, is bound into the central post of a building during rituals inaugurating it as a home. Similarly, specially empowered Buddhist temples, especially those referred to as having *pāramī* ('perfection') or being from the pre-modern period (*purāṇa*), are thought to have used similar rites to forcibly endow temples with a protective spirit, which was bound into the pedestal of the temple's central Buddha image.

This spirit is typically imagined as a *brāy*, a powerful malign female spirit created when a woman dies pregnant or in childbirth. *Brāy* are the most dangerous spirits of all, which is perhaps why pregnant women are widely imagined to have been sacrificed in the foundation of important and empowered royal buildings and temples (Ang Choulean 1988: 37). When such spirits are 'liberated' from a body and bound into a building's columns, the 'brāy changes from an eminently malevolent spirit into a guardian of correct Buddhist cult [. . .]. One of her names means the "brāy residing in the pedestal"' (*ibid.*: 38).

I have so far offered three examples of rituals that appear to partake of a singular shared logic, in which cloth, and especially unbleached raw cotton string called *aṃboḥ*, is used to bind potentially malevolent non-Buddhist spirits into a safe location. The funeral, the calling of the spirits, and the inauguration of a house, as well as the installation of a *brāy* into an important building or Buddhist temple, all draw on the imagery of Buddhist monks binding and controlling non-Buddhist spirits.

Let us now consider two further examples that will clarify not only the logic that underlies the examples we have already seen, but which may have a role in their origin. The first is the inauguration of a temple, regardless of whether that temple contains a *brāy*. This ceremony is called *pañcuḥ sīmā*, the 'burying of the boundary', and follows in both the general logic thus outlined of binding, but also the more specifically sacrificial imagery of the building sacrifice previously mentioned. Further, this ritual is the event where the *aṃboḥ* string is gathered for use in other rituals, including funerals. In many ways, this ritual is the birthplace of the *aṃboḥ* string that plays such a significant role in the *paṃsukūla* binding.

THE *SĪMĀ*: ORDERING THE COSMOS

Khmer routinely describe the *pañcuḥ sīmā* ceremony as the 'biggest' ceremony in Buddhism, by which they typically mean that it is the most popular and well attended of the occasional ceremonies (as opposed to calendrical or life-cycle ceremonies). After a new central sanctuary – *vihāra* – is completed, *aṃboḥ* is tied around it in a boundary. This boundary is further connected to eight buildings around the perimeter of the temple, and to nine large round stones, called *sīmā* stones, which will be buried in eight pits dug either around or inside the sanctuary, along with a central stone – the most important of them, which will be buried into a central pit. Until the conclusion of the ceremony, however, the strings continue to bind the stones, which are suspended over the pits from large wooden planks or branches.

Before the ceremony begins, novices are excluded from entering the *aṃboḥ*-demarcated border, and the laity make small offerings into the pits. These offerings partake of a clear sacrificial logic of return: the laity offer symbolic tokens of what it is they desire more of in their next life. A young woman who wishes she was more beautiful, or smarter, or wealthier, might drop makeup, notebooks, or small currency into the hole. Men, especially younger men, occasionally cut their fingers and offer a few drops of blood into the pits, along with currency or other types of objects.[21]

After asking for permission from the non-Buddhist spirit of the land (*kruṅ vālī*), the ceremony begins. At the conclusion of the ceremony, a representative of the king – nowadays most commonly a minor political official or businessman – takes a large machete and a cudgel to the central *sīmā* stone, suspended over the central pit. Placing the blade on the *aṃboḥ* thread holding the stone, he then takes the cudgel and hammers it against the blade, severing the *aṃboḥ* and freeing the stone. At the same time, lower-status officials sever the threads on the other eight stones. Immediately after the stones drop, the temple's inauguration is complete, and a mêlée often breaks out as throngs compete for as much of the *aṃboḥ* as they can lay their hands on. Monks engage in the grabbing as well, though they tend to comport themselves somewhat more respectfully than do their lay counterparts.

[21] When asked what return they hope for, from the sacrifice of their blood, such men are rarely specific beyond hoping for generalised 'health and happiness'. I suspect, however, that this generalised well-being is more an appropriate response to such a question posed by a stranger, than it is a proper representation of their hopes.

Some power has impregnated the *aṃboḥ* with the severing of the stones.[22] Some ancient temples are believed to have a specific spirit – the spirit of a sacrificed woman, usually – captured within the temple grounds (often in the pedestal of the central Buddha image). The sacrificial imagery of the *pañcuḥ sīmā* ceremony shows that this is imagined as a ritual murder sacrifice, where the released spirit is bound and put to work in the service of Buddhism. This transfer of spiritual energy is a common part of the Cambodian religious imagination. Mao Sengyan and Ang Choulean, for instance, have argued that ritual cloths are frequently imagined as enlivened. They write (2007–8: 31) that:

> [S]ome flags are alive. That is, an ācārya must 'open the eye' of the flag first.[23] Except when these flags are being sewn, they must be ordained prior to being used in any important religious ceremony, and have their ordination removed after the ceremony is completed.

Understood in this way, we can see that the *paṃsukūla* cloth offered to the saṅgha during the funeral ceremony does not merely *represent* the gift of the self to the saṅgha, but *is*, in fact, the gift of the self to the saṅgha, where the vital spirits of the person impregnate the cloth.

Michael Wright believes that the *sīmā* ceremony of Southeast Asia, so unlike that of Sri Lanka in its practice, makes symbolism of human sacrifice central to its performance. He argues that the cutting of the *aṃboḥ* to release the *sīmā* stones mimics and replaces the decapitation of a human head, a performance of a type of royal fertility rite, to ensure abundant harvests (Wright 1990: 45). We may also note the relationship between the sacrifice implied in the *sīmā* and the building sacrifices referred to earlier, which bind the *brāy* into the Buddha's pedestal.

AGRICULTURAL FIELDS AND BASES

A connection between the 'binding' of a *sīmā* and agriculture appears very early in the expansion of Buddhism, even where the sacrificial component was absent, as in the Sinhalese Buddhist rites. In all these texts, the action monks

[22] The above description is based on my own fieldwork, during which time I attended many *pañcuḥ sīmā* ceremonies. However, it is confirmed and may be compared to the following articles, which deal with the ritual in a more central manner (Kent 2007; Harris n.d.; Giteau 1969). A thoroughly reform interpretation of *sīmā* rules and practices can be found in Huot That (1953) and Lās' Lāy (2003).

[23] Just as one must to enliven or empower a central Buddha image in a temple.

take in order to create a boundary is to *bind* it.[24] The connection with agriculture exists at both the level of the purely symbolic and at the practical organisation of life. The *Mahāvaṃsa*, the great chronicle of Sinhalese kings, records that 'in the second century B.C. King Devanampiya Tissa ploughed a furrow around the Maha Vihara and that furrow became its sīmā' (*ibid.*).

But although the monarch is the sacrificial agent whose action renders the *sīmā* rite effective, it is the saṅgha whose sovereignty symbolically rules that area henceforth.[25] From this perspective we can see that the binding of a *sīmā* around the central sanctuary, or vihāra, of a Buddhist temple 'effectively exorcises the immediate influence of the king's power but paradoxically retains the presence of the monarchy as a symbol of protection' (Harris n.d.: 5). This opinion, although it has been the subject of learned dispute among historians of Burma, is nevertheless clear and consistent, at least at the level of symbol, regionally: the binding of a *sīmā* alienates land from the king's control and power.[26]

Further, monks are not permitted by vinaya to engage in plough agriculture, since it may cause the death of soil-dwelling animals. Responsible for agricultural fertility, the king cedes control and power over monastic land symbolically in the rite of burying the *sīmā*. The *sīmā* ritual thus assists in demarcating and ordering the world along lines of symbolic supernatural powers – the world of the king (the *āṇācakra*) and the world of the dhamma (the *dhammacakra*), the world of the kingdom and the world of the monastery, of the king and of the monk. While these realms are theoretically separated, there is also, from the Buddhist point of view, a critical and unquestionable superiority of the Buddhist monk to the spirits of the non-Buddhist world.[27]

Where the king releases vital and potentially dangerous spirits through his acts of violence, the Buddhist monk should have the ability to face them

[24] Thus, in these texts, temple *sīmā* are referred to as 'bound' or unbound. The word used, *baddha*, is in Pāli a past passive participle meaning 'bound', but in Khmer usage, is adopted as an active verb as well. Thus, to *baddha sīmā* in Khmer means 'to bind a *sīmā*'. The Pāli past passive participle is used as an active verb in Khmer, or translated directly by its Khmer equivalent, *caṅ*.

[25] In fact, this corresponds well with the distinction between sacrifier and sacrificer made by Hubert and Mauss in their famous monograph on sacrifice. In this example, the king or his agents act as the sacrificer and the saṅgha as the sacrifier, a reversal of the norm. Thus, the king commits the sacrificial violence for the benefit of the saṅgha (Hubert and Mauss 1981).

[26] This description is accurate regardless of its correspondence to any historical reality; I attend here to the symbolic import of the ritual and its simplifying representations, rather than to the historical landholding regimes debated by Aung-Thwin and Lieberman for Burma (e.g. Aung-Thwin 1979; Lieberman 1980).

[27] Far from being merely a traditional stance overcome by contemporary Buddhist modernism, it is precisely this ability to vanquish spirits that is attributed to many of those who can be considered 'patron saints' of Buddhist modernism, such as Somdet To in Siam.

without fear and to control them. It is this power that is most clearly proffered in all of the rituals surveyed above. This power of controlling spirits and vital essences in turn relies on an apparent imagination of a technique in which spirits are gathered into a body or some other object and bound there. Such a technique appears as the common thread in all the examples. This power may in social fact not exist in particular members of the saṅgha, and certainly some monks are recognised and famed as more skilled than others in the application of powers over the spirit world. Nonetheless, their power does not reside in their person, but in their robes. These robes are of course approximated to the *paṃsukūla* gift of the shroud to the saṅgha.

The connection between the monastic robe and agriculture is quite direct in the Pāli texts as well. In one Vinaya story, the Buddha and his cousin and personal attendant Ānanda are walking in Magadha's rice fields, when the Buddha, inspired by the sight, asks Ānanda to make robes in the same way (Horner 1951: 407–8):

Then the Lord, having stayed in Rājagaha for as long as he found suitable, set out on tour for Dakkhiṇagiri. The Lord saw the fields of Magadha, laid out in strips, laid out in lines, laid out in embankments, laid out in squares, and seeing this, he addressed the venerable Ānanda, saying:

'Now, do you, Ānanda, see the field of Magadha laid out in strips . . . laid out in squares?'
'Yes, Lord.'
'Are you able, Ānanda, to provide robes like this for the monks?'
'I am able, Lord.'

The modern form of the monastic robe comes to us based on this auspicious inspiration. The descriptors used for these fields identify the technique used to order the fields: bunding, just as in the rainfed contemporary Cambodian rice agriculture. In the above quotation, in each place where the translator used the phrase 'laid out in', the word translated was some form of the Pāli word for 'bound': *baddha*. The seams of thread used to sew the robes together form the bunds of the robe, just as dredged dirt pressed into place forms the bunds of the rice field. The monk truly is a field of merit, in Buddhism's consistent metaphor.[28]

The appearance of agricultural resonance in the *sīmā* ceremony presents a solution to the initially confusing practices of binding that pervade these rituals. Why should monks contain these spirits with binding actions? Indeed, since these spirits are not amenable to the moral discipline and

[28] Horner herself notes this in her footnote on the passage (Horner 1951: 408 n1).

practices of Buddhism and its karmic perspective, why are monks engaging with these spirits at all? I argue that the practice of gathering indeterminate vitality and binding it into a useful form is based on the agricultural fertility rites which may be the earliest version of this practice, found in the *paṃsukūla* rite, and even identified by many laypeople *as* the *paṃsukūla* rite itself, that of calling of the spirits of the rice.

The strong cultural correlate between the production of rice and the practices of death should not surprise anthropologists. Maurice Bloch and Jonathan Parry write in the introduction to their volume *Death and the Regeneration of Life,* 'In most cases what would seem to be revitalised in funerary practices is that resource which is culturally conceived to be the most essential to the reproduction of the social order' (Bloch and Parry 1982: 7).

Khmer civilisation would have been impossible without the intensive production of rice. Rice has been the staple food and dominant commodity for most of Cambodian history, and most Khmer were and remain engaged in the production of rice in their daily lives.[29] As I have argued elsewhere, it is the intimate relationship with the techniques of gathering and binding water into rice, along with the rituals that mark key points in the cycle, that appear to provide the paradigm for the other appropriations of that practice (Davis 2008a, 2008b, 2009). Without the constant production and appropriation of surplus rice stocks, Cambodian civilisation would collapse.

In the actual production of rice, there are many moments, such as transplanting, when dispersed and non-useful vitality is gathered and bound. Unlike relatively non-intensive forms of rice production (flood retreat or shifting cultivation), intensive rice production in Cambodia means primarily using various methods to control water. Water flexibly represents the world's flows of power and energy. Necessary for life, too much of it – in the form of floods – can bring disaster. Cambodian peasants have typically relied on bunding rice fields in order to collect water for rice production. This practice is widespread enough that, in connection with other forms of water preservation, Richard O'Connor (1995a) has characterised the Khmer as people who hoard water, as opposed to others (like the Thai, Lao and Vietnamese) who manage flows.

There is also a ritual correlate, still practised by some, the calling of the *praliṅ* of *vraḥ me*, or 'Holy Mother Rice', referring to living, unhusked rice (Ang Choulean 2004: 166). As Ang Choulean writes of the ceremony:

[29] This close connection between rice, rice-agriculture and cultural identity has been noted repeatedly over the years. Note especially (Fox and Ledgerwood 1999; Piper 1994; Samaddar 2006; Terwiel 1994; Hanks 1972; Hanks 1964).

> [A] representative of each household brings this bunch of stalks to the house of the anak ta [*neak ta*] . . . where all the villagers organise the ceremony of calling the *praliṅ* of the rice . . . When the ceremony ends, they go to the shed in which the rice will be stored and fasten the bunch of stalks to a chram, or tube-like container used for putting offerings, which is then tied to the central column of the shed (*ibid.*: 166–8).

Before the stalks are fastened to the shed as a premonition of a successful harvest, they must first be offered to the regional spirits called *anak tā* (Khmer: *neak ta*), in a first-fruits ceremony where the potential surpluses are offered to the lord of the land. The growth and ripening of the rice in the fields is imagined in a life-cycle that mirrors the life-cycle of a young woman. The rice is gendered as a woman, and goes through various phases, including self-ornamentation and pregnancy (*ibid.*).

The Khmer farmers I interviewed about the *praliṅ* of rice described it not as an amorphous quality that pervades the entire seed, but something that can be physically located. An unhusked kernel of rice is 'alive, because it has *praliṅ*', whereas husked rice was 'dead, and without *praliṅ*'. Husking the rice 'kills' it, an act that deprives it of its *praliṅ* and simultaneously renders it useful for human consumption.

The binding of a temple and the installation of its boundary stones is necessary for its constitution as a place for the creation of merit, an act which at the same time alienates its creative and productive capacity from the appropriation of the king. The *praliṅ* of the body must be recalled and bound into the body for a person to recover from ills and accidents. The *praliṅ* of the rice is called into a sheaf, bound and installed in the home, at the same time that the major portion of the rice crop is cut from the fields which nourish it, tied into sheaves, and threshed to make it edible. Remembering that rice is called Vraḥ Me and compared to a pregnant young woman, we will see that the process of making rice edible also entails her symbolic murder.

In the example of the *sīmā* ceremony, I indicated the ways in which the imagination of a sacrificed pregnant woman empowers and vitalises a new temple and removes the land from consumption by the king. Similarly, the murder of a living rice kernel makes the *praliṅ* of the rice available to those who would consume it. I have termed 'binding' all these activities that make clear the boundaries of energy that are otherwise conceived to be in flux and movement, following local usage. Having bound energy into place – a temple, milled rice, or a person – care must be taken to ensure that the energy does not succumb to its natural proclivities towards excursion and adventure: bound vitality obeys the law of entropy, constantly slipping its bounds and disappearing beyond human use. Unbound vitality does not similarly degrade simply because it is not manifested anywhere in particular. Only that which is bound into place decays. This observation again accords very well with established notions in the field of anthropology on the links between fertility, food and death: 'Whether gifts, knowledge or food, that which is retained rots, festers and corrupts the body; and here it is clearly the digestion of food which provides the root metaphor' (Bloch and Parry 1982: 213–14).

This agricultural style produces more than rice, undoubtedly Southeast Asia's most valuable and important commodity; it also produces aspects of culture.

CONCLUSION: RITUAL TECHNOLOGIES AND THE AUTHORITY OF CONQUERING DEATH

In Cambodia, the root metaphor of binding power into valuable end-products seems to have emerged in agricultural practices, and to underwrite much of non-agricultural practice, including the ritualisation of death by Buddhist monks. Georges Condominas wrote compellingly of the shifting cultivation culture of highland Vietnam, and developed the notion of 'ritual technology'. He argues that the division between agricultural and religious activity with which outsiders are concerned is largely irrelevant to the Mnong Gar he studied. For them, instead, both are experienced as 'work'.

> For the Mnong Gar mind . . . work whose end is both to reproduce the individual and his society comprises the two technologies not just as two complementary elements but two continuous procedures whose accomplishments are both essential to the achievements of man's ultimate ends, however these ends are defined (Condominas 1986: 40).

Inspired by the approach of Condominas and the work of fellow Southeast Asian anthropologists, Richard O'Connor (1995b: 969) wrote of the vital importance of agriculture and imitative technique to the reproduction of both crops and society:

> Agriculture is a locus of meaning, not just a means to subsist. As these societies arise performatively … farming's technical practices easily become ritual acts … that constitute a moral stance … and define ethnic identity.

Following these two, I suggest that the *paṃsukūla* ritual actions of binding have social force because they treat the world of non-Buddhist spirits in the same way that farmers treat water. Buddhist monks are endowed with the potency to accomplish such technical management by their own conquest of death, symbolised by the association of their robes with the shrouds of the dead. Both are work, and both contain elements of ritual. Ritual technology in Cambodia, as often elsewhere, roots itself in broader cultural imaginaries.

I have offered here the general outlines of a core imagination of power and its control in Cambodian society, and established a basis for its transfer from the everyday agricultural practices in which most Cambodians are still engaged, and the ritual specialist actions of Buddhist monks performing '*paṃsukūla*', which appears at first to have little to do with the robe with which it shares its name. As an example of what Condominas (1986) and O'Connor (1995b) term 'ritual technology', the rite of *paṃsukūla* connects with the *paṃsukūla* robe in the same way that Buddhism, and the Buddhist monk, connect to Brahmanism, and the lay-person.

The connection among agricultural ordering, geographical ordering, religious ordering and spirit ordering, all of which take the form of 'binding' activities, on the one hand, and the *paṃsukūla* robe, on the other, is made possible by the saṅgha's relationship to the rest of the world. As Schopen (2006) noted of another Buddhist school's Vinaya, the primary audience for which Buddhist monastic rules of comportment and conduct were constructed was not Buddhist, but Brahmanist.[30] Similarly today, Buddhist monks are the exceptional actors whose authority and power may be useful in controlling and appeasing the non-Buddhist spirits of the dead. This control of the dead, which takes place in the agricultural metaphor of binding, is possible for Buddhist monks because of the robes they wear. These robes – whether they are genuinely former shrouds or not – identify them as socially dead men, renunciants of the household life, those who, like the spirits of the dead, must survive on gifts from the living.

BIBLIOGRAPHY

Aung-Thwin, M. (1979), 'The role of Sasana reform in Burmese history', *Journal of Asian Studies* **38**: 671–88.

Bizot, F. (1981), *Le Don de Soi-même: Recherches sur le Bouddhisme Khmer III*, Paris: École Française d'Extrême-Orient.

Bloch, M. and Parry, J. (1982), 'Introduction', in eds. M. Bloch and J. Parry, *Death and the Regeneration of Life*, Cambridge University Press.

Bond, G. (1980), 'Theravada Buddhism's meditations on death and the symbolism of initiatory death', *History of Religions* **19** (3): 237–58.

Choulean, A. (1988), 'The place of animism within popular Buddhism in Cambodia: the example of the monastery', *Asian Folklore Studies* **47**: 35–41.

[30] The point appears confirmed in Cambodia today. Most Khmer engage, even if relatively rarely, in 'Brahmanist' practices and ritual, though they identify as 'Buddhists'.

(2004), *Braḥ Liṅg*, Phnom Penh: Reyum Publishing.
Collins, S. (1982), *Selfless Persons: Imagery and Thought in Theravāda Buddhism*, Cambridge University Press.
Condominas, G. (1986), 'Ritual technology in Mnong Gar swidden agriculture', *Rice Societies: Asian Problems and Prospect*, ed. I. Nørlund, S. Cederroth and I. Gerdin, Riverdale, MD: The Riverdale Company.
Davis, E. W. (2008a), 'Between forests and families: a remembered past life in pre-DK Cambodia', in A. Kent (ed.), *Reconfiguring Religion, Power, and Moral Order in Cambodia*, Copenhagen: Nordic Institute of Asian Studies (NIAS).
(2008b), 'Imaginary conversations with mothers about death', in A. R. Hansen and J. Ledgerwood (eds.), *At the Edge of the Forest: Essays on Cambodia, History, and Narrative in Honor of David Chandler*, Ithaca, NY: Southeast Asian Program Publications (Cornell University).
(2009), *Treasures of the Buddha: Imagining Death and Life in Contemporary Cambodian Religion*, Divinity School, University of Chicago.
Douglas, M. (1966), *Purity and Danger: an Analysis of Concepts of Pollution and Taboo*, New York: Praeger.
Fox, Jeff and Ledgerwood, Judy (1999), 'Dry-season flood-recession rice in the Mekong Delta: two thousand years of sustainable agriculture?' *Asian Perspectives* **38** (1): 37–50.
Giteau, M. (1969), *Le Bornage Rituel des Temples Bouddhiques au Cambodge*, Paris: École Française d'Extrême-Orient.
Gombrich, R. (1991 reprint), *Buddhist Precept and Practice: Traditional Buddhism in the Rural Highlands of Ceylon*, Delhi: Motilal Banarsidass.
Hanks, J. Richardson (1964), 'Reflections on the ontology of rice', in S. Diamond (ed.), *Primitive Views of the World*, New York: Columbia University Press.
Hanks, L. M. (1972), *Rice and Man: Agricultural Ecology in Southeast Asia*, Chicago: Aldine-Atherton.
Harris, I. (n.d.), 'Monastic and state boundaries in Cambodia'. No further details of publication.
Heesterman, J. C. (1962), 'Vratya and sacrifice', *Indo-Iranian Journal* **6**: 1–37.
Hertz, R. (1960), 'A contribution to the study of the collective representation of death', in R. Hertz (ed.), *Death and the Right Hand*, Aberdeen University Press.
Horner, I. B. (1951), *The Book of the Discipline*, vol. 4, London: Pāli Text Society.
Hubert, H. and Mauss, M. (1981), *Sacrifice: its Nature and Functions*, University of Chicago Press. Original edition 1898.
Huot That (1953), *Sīmā Vinicchaya Saṅkhepa (an abbreviated analysis of the Sīma)*, Phnom Penh: Editions de l'Institut Bouddhique.
Jay, N. (1992), *Throughout Your Generations Forever*, University of Chicago Press.
Kent, A. (2007), 'Purchasing power and pagodas: the Sīma monastic boundary and consumer politics in Cambodia', *Journal of Southeast Asian Studies* **38** (2): 335–54.
Langer, R. (2007), *Buddhist Rituals of Death and Rebirth: Contemporary Sri Lankan Practice and its Origins*, London and New York: Routledge.
Lās' Lāy (2003), *Sīmā Vaṇṇanā*, Phnom Penh: L'Institut Bouddhique.
Leach, E. (1965), *Political Systems of Highland Burma*, Boston: Beacon Press.

Lieberman, V. (1980), 'The political significance of religious wealth in Burmese history', *Journal of Asian Studies* **39**: 753–69.

Mao Sengyan and Choulean, A. (2007–8), 'Dâṅ', *Khmer Renaissance* **3**: 31–5.

McDaniel, J. T. (2008), *Gathering Leaves and Lifting Words: Histories of Buddhist Monastic Education in Laos and Thailand*, Seattle and London: University of Washington Press.

Mus, P. (1975), *India Seen from the East: Indian and Indigenous Cults in Champa*, trans. I. W. Mabbet and D. P. Chandler, Clayton, Victoria, Australia: Monash University Centre of Southeast Asian Studies.

(1978), *Barabudur*, New York: Arno Press.

O'Connor, R. A. (1995a), 'Indigenous urbanism: class, city and society', *Journal of Southeast Asian Studies* **26** (1): 30–45.

(1995b), 'Agricultural change and ethnic succession in Southeast Asia states: a case for regional anthropology', *The Journal of Asian Studies* **54** (4): 968–96.

Parry, J. (1994), *Death in Benares*, Cambridge University Press.

Piper, J. M. (1994), *Rice in South-East Asia: Cultures and Landscapes*, Oxford University Press.

Porée-Maspero, E. (1958), *Cérémonies Privées des Cambodgiens*, Phnom Penh: Institut Bouddhique.

Sahlins, M. (1985), *Islands of History*, University of Chicago Press.

Samaddar, A. (2006), 'Traditional and posttraditional: a study of agricultural rituals in relation to technological complexity among rice producers in two zones of West Bengal, India', *Culture and Agriculture* **28** (2): 108–21.

Schopen, G. (2006), 'A well-sanitized shroud: asceticism and institutional values in the middle period of Buddhist monasticism', in P. Olivelle (ed.), *Between the Empires: Society in India 300 BCE to 400 CE*, New York: Oxford University Press.

Spiro, M. (1996), *Burmese Supernaturalism*, expanded edition, Piscataway, NJ: Transaction Publishers.

Tambiah, S. J. (1970), *Buddhism and the Spirit-cults of North-East Thailand*, Cambridge Studies in Social Anthropology, Cambridge University Press.

Terwiel, B. J. (1994), 'Rice legends in mainland Southeast Asia: History and ethnography in the study of myths of origin', in A. R. Walker (ed.), *Rice in Southeast Asian Myth and Ritual*, National University of Singapore.

Thompson, A. (1996), *The Calling of the Souls: a Study of the Khmer Ritual Hau Bralin*, Clayton, Australia: Centre of Southeast Asian Studies, Monash University.

(2005), *Calling the Souls: a Cambodian Ritual Text*, Phnom Penh: Reyum Publishing.

van Gennep, A. (1960), *The Rites of Passage*, University of Chicago Press.

World Bank (2006), *Cambodia: Halving Poverty by 2015? Poverty Assessment 2006*, World Bank.

Wright, M. (1990), 'Sacrifice and the underworld: death and fertility in Siamese myth and ritual', *The Journal of the Siam Society* **78** (1): 43–54.

CHAPTER 4

Corpses and cloth: illustrations of the paṃsukūla *ceremony in Thai manuscripts*

M. L. Pattaratorn Chirapravati

INTRODUCTION

Before the Bangkok period (1782–present), funeral scenes were not commonly portrayed in Thai art. However, around the end of the eighteenth century, pre- and post-scenes of the Buddha's cremation, which were drawn from the Pāli version of the *Mahāparinibbānasutta* text and Buddhaghosa's Commentary, respectively, became important parts of scenes from the life of the Buddha as depicted in Thai mural paintings and manuscripts.[1] By around the first quarter of the nineteenth century, although there are only a small number of examples, other funeral subjects, such as cremations, funeral processions and monks performing funeral rituals, appeared in mural painting and manuscripts. The subjects were drawn from different textual sources and appear to reflect important contemporary ritual practices of that time. While some practices continue to be conducted at present, others are no longer extant. Thus the illustrations in mural paintings and manuscripts help us to understand Thai funeral rituals of the past.

This chapter discusses a specific aspect of these depictions of Thai funeral culture, the *paṃsukūla* and the rituals linked to it. I shall here focus on the *paṃsukūla* as an aspect of the materiality of Thai funeral culture, but also its embeddedness into ritual practices and the ideas attached to it. The *paṃsukūla* ceremony is considered one of the most important parts of a Thai Buddhist funeral. It is believed that when a monk removes the *paṃsukūla* cloth (made of white cotton) from the corpse (or in

This chapter would not have been possible without the valuable advice and kind help of my colleagues: Venerable Anil Sakya, Erik Davis, Patrice Ladwig, Justin McDaniel, Arthid Sheravanichkul, Peter Skilling and Hiram W. Woodward. I would also like to thank Richard Breedon for editing this article.

[1] I presented two papers on 'Funeral of the Buddha in Thai Art: Texts and Interpretation of the Roles of Mahakasappa and Dona Brahmana', at the American Committee for Southern Asian Art conference at the Asian Art Museum of San Francisco (2007) and at the International Association of Buddhist Studies conference at Emory University (2008). This chapter will be published in my forthcoming book, *Thai Funeral Culture: Studies of Images and Texts in Thai Art*.

contemporary practice from the coffin or a table placed close to the coffin) and chants a verse from the *Mahāparinibbānasutta*, great merit is transferred to the deceased. At the same time, it also helps bring awareness to the living of their own impermanence. This chapter examines illustrations of the *paṃsukūla* ceremony, an exceptionally rare subject, depicted in two Buddhist manuscripts in the collection of the Walters Art Museum (in Baltimore) (Figures 4.1–4.3) and the Spencer Collection of the New York Public Library (in New York) (Figure 4.4), both dating to around the 1830s.[2,3] So far these are the only two manuscripts I have found depicting this subject.[4] In addition, a similar rite portrayed in murals and manuscripts concerns the practice of meditation on a corpse (Pāli: *asubha-kammaṭṭhāna*) that was popular with forest monks (Figure 4.2).[5] Illustrations showing the offering of a white cloth in the *paṃsukūla* ceremony, which is no longer practised, clearly reflect how the ritual was performed before the second half of the twentieth century. Presently a monk's robe is used for this purpose. To understand the nineteenth-century *paṃsukūla* practice portrayed in the manuscripts, and for analysing the change this important object of Thai funeral culture underwent, the ceremony in present-day central Thailand will be used for comparison.

MANUSCRIPTS, MURALS AND FUNERAL CULTURE

Thai manuscripts were usually commissioned and donated to temples for the purpose of merit making. The manuscripts are made of handmade paper from the inner bark of the *khoi* bush (scientific name: *streblus asper*). The text of the manuscripts and the illustrations seldom have any direct correspondence: the text was chanted during Buddhist ceremonies such as funerals and weddings, while the illustrations depicted themes such as the life of the Buddha, his previous lives (*jātakas*) and the story of Phra Malai, a monk who travelled to heaven and hell by the power he achieved through

[2] I am grateful for the kind help and advice of Dr. Hiram Woodward regarding the Walters manuscript. The accession number of this manuscript is W.716. I am indebted to the late Henry Ginsburg, who did pioneering work on Thai painting, for bringing this manuscript to my attention. The Library of Congress system is used in this article for the transcription of Thai to English.

[3] The latter manuscript is published in Henry Ginsburg (2000: 102–3).

[4] I have not yet had sufficient opportunity to study Thai paintings in European or private collections.

[5] Two examples of the *paṃsukūla* in meditations on a corpse (*asubha-kammaṭṭhāna)* illustrations can be found on the mural of Wat Somanat in Bangkok and two manuscripts in the collections of Wat Lai in Phetchaburi Province and Wat Suwannaphum in Suphanburi. The two manuscripts were published by Khrongkan Supsan Moradok Wattanatham Thai (1999).

meditation and great merits. The illustrations served as reminders of the Buddha's teachings and exemplary models for practitioners. The donors and artists were thus free to choose the themes they preferred. A specific category of manuscripts used in funeral culture often explains the anatomy and function of organs of the human body and are called the *Seven Books of the Abhidhamma (Abhidhamma Chet Khanphi Ruam).*[6] Other common texts include the *Abhidhamma Dhammasaṅgaṇi* (Enumeration of Phenomena), *Abhidhammavaṇṇanā* (a Pāli text that uses terms from the *Abhidhamma Dhammasaṅgaṇi*) and *Phra Malai*.

Because of the fragility of paper to humidity, tropical heat and insects, no example of a manuscript older than the seventeenth century has survived in Thailand. Thus it is not clear when illustrations of funeral rituals and depictions of corpses became subjects of Thai mural paintings and manuscripts. During the reign of Rama III (r. 1824–51) the main school (or ordination lineage) of Buddhism was an old order continued from the Ayutthaya period called *Mahanikai* ('lineage of long-standing habit' *Mahānikāya*). Prince Mongkut was ordained as a monk in 1824 in this lineage and remained in monkhood until 1851. In the 1830s, Mongkut (King Rama IV, r. 1851–68) established the new lineage of *Thammayutika* ('lineage adhering to the *Dhamma*'), which was based on a stricter idea of monastic discipline. King Rama III appointed him the Abbot of Wat Boworniwet and the head of the *Thammayutika* (Wyatt 1982: 175–6). The changes in lineages, and increased contact with Chinese, Persian, British and other peoples, as well as the rise in the Siamese economy, led in part to new Buddhist art. This art reflects popular Buddhist practices and the interest of royal patrons and lay society in Bangkok at the time, and new subject matter was portrayed in mural painting and manuscripts. Popular novels such as the *Rammakian* (the Thai version of a Hindu epic, *Rāmāyaṇa*), *Samkok* (the Thai version of a Chinese novel, *Romance of the Three Kingdoms*) and *Inao* (a Javanese novel) were chosen by royal patrons for their temples. It is interesting to note that the majority of the funeral episodes from Thai novels that are depicted on the murals of temples in Bangkok such as the *Rammakian* (at the Emerald Buddha temple, Bangkok) and *Inao* (at the Sommanat Temple, Bangkok), and the manuscripts with funeral scenes (e.g. *asubha-kammaṭṭhāna* and Phra Malai), are associated with the reign of

[6] The *Abhidhamma Chet Kamphi* ('Seven Books of the Abhidhamma') is a genre of texts composed before the eighteenth century, used as a funerary text in Thailand. This text does not contain the entire seven volumes of the *Abhidhamma*. See Swearer (1995: 336–42). See also McDaniel (2008: 229–45) for the use and composition of this text in funerals and its link to the construction of a new 'embryo' (i.e. new life) during funeral rites.

King Rama III and the early years of King Rama IV.[7] The scenes can be dated to around the first half of the nineteenth century.

ILLUSTRATIONS OF *PAṂSUKŪLA*

Why did funeral ceremonies become the subject of mural paintings and manuscripts in the beginning of the nineteenth century? Do the illustrations of *paṃsukūla* reflect the actual ceremony as performed in the nineteenth century and earlier? And do paintings of *paṃsukūla* and cremations contain any special symbols in the manuscripts?

Paṃsukūla (Thai: *bansakul)* are commonly referred to as 'dusty rags' (Phra Khru Anusaranasasanakiarti and Keyes 1980: 12). The word means 'stained' or 'covered with dirt' (*paṃsu* means dirt, dust, and *kūla* means stain). The practice of wearing *paṃsukūla* cloths can be traced to the time of the Buddha. Later in the Buddha's life, however, the Buddha allowed monks to accept new robes donated by lay-practitioners. The *paṃsukūla* rags were commonly found at charnel grounds, where bodies wrapped in a cloth were left for wild animals to eat.[8] Forest monks therefore took real *paṃsukūla* shrouds from corpses. Gregory Schopen differentiates the *paṃsukūla* cloth from the *śmaśanika* cloth (cemetery cloth). He points out that in early Indian Buddhism *paṃsukūla* cloth is 'cloth from a highway or thrown out in the forest or on a river bank, etc., cloth that is torn or rotten, eaten by rats, etc.' (Schopen 2006: 337). Thus monks wore the *paṃsukūla* cloth to practise detachment from the body as well as the world.[9]

Let us now turn to the depictions of the *paṃsukūla* in manuscripts and their analysis. The first manuscript is from the Walters Art Museum and has been in the collection of Henry Walters since before 1938 (Figure 4.1). The illustrations are executed in watercolour on paper. It measures 66 × 137.8 cm (26 × 54$\frac{1}{4}$ in). Based on the style of the realistic portrayal of the monk, the deep coloured background and the decorative motifs on the textile, the Walters Art Museum manuscript can be dated to 1800–40.[10]

[7] For further information on funeral scenes of the *Rammakian* mural see Chirapravati (forthcoming-a and -b).

[8] Rita Langer (2007: 180–2). See Bizot (1981: 5) for this. He also discusses the (in his opinion) partially problematic etymology of the term (*ibid.*: 106).

[9] For further study on *paṃsukūla*, its history and the associated ideas such as healing through 'symbolic death' see François Bizot (1981), and Chapter 2 by Davis in this volume.

[10] Henry Ginsburg did extensive studies on the manuscripts in the Walters Art Museum collection. For further information see Ginsburg (2006–7: 135).

This accordion-folded manuscript has sixteen illustrations: on each leaflet the text is written in the centre, accompanied by an illustration on each end. The text is written in Cambodian Mul script in the Pāli language, with some commentary in Thai. Its content is the *Abhidhamma-vaṇṇanā-piṭaka*, a commentary on the *Abhidhamma* scriptures.[11] The *paṃsukūla* ritual and the cremation, the focus of this chapter, are illustrated on the left end of leaflets nine and ten. Illustrations number one, fifteen and sixteen are decorated with pairs of monks, female practitioners and male practitioners, respectively, with their hands performing the adoration hand gesture. While illustrations two to eight depict the meditations on a rotting corpse *(asubha-kammaṭṭhāna)*, illustrations eleven to fourteen portray the story of Phra Malai, the monk who travelled to heaven and hell by the power he achieved through meditation and great merit.[12,13]

The painting of the *paṃsukūla* scene depicts a monk who may also represent Phra Malai. The traditional highlighted scenes of Phra Malai's story are depicted after the cremation scene in the following leaflet. Here two lay cremation assistants are busy maintaining the fire over the coffin (Figure 4.3). The monk is dressed in a traditional monk's robe that is worn in two layers: the under lower garment and the outer robe. He is standing in three-quarter view facing an ornate coffin. The monk is looking at the corpse while pulling (Thai: *chak)* the end of a white cloth *(pha paṃsukūla)* out of the coffin, and chanting the blessing (Figure 4.4). Here even though the corpse is not depicted, it is clear that the monk is performing the *paṃsukūla* rite. The monk's right hand is placed on his stomach and is supported with his left arm. A male figure, probably a relative of the deceased, is seated with his hands held in the adoration gesture near to the monk and the coffin. An offering of a set of monk's robes for merit-making for the deceased is placed in a container *(phan wenfa)* beside the

[11] I would like to thank Justin McDaniel for reading and checking the content of this manuscript. The text was identified in 1938 in Horace Poleman's *Census of Indic Manuscripts in the United States and Canada* with the title *Abhidhammavaranapitaka*.

[12] For an anthropological account of *asubha-kammaṭṭhāna* practices and spaces of death see Klima (2002: 169 ff.).

[13] Illustrations eleven to fourteen portray the story of Phra Malai. They cover the standard scenes of the Phra Malai story (essentially a Thai version of Maleyyadevathera; see Chapter 6 by Ladwig in the present volume): illustration eleven shows Phra Malai visiting hell, illustration twelve represents the woodcutter picking lotus blossoms and offering them to Phra Malai, illustration thirteen shows Phra Malai's visit to Indra's heaven and the Chulamani chedi and illustration fourteen depicts the discourse of Indra and Phra Malai and the arrival of Maitreya, the future Buddha. For examples of Phra Malai manuscripts and further information see Ginsburg (1989: 72–88, 2000: 92–111). Also see McGill (2009: 173–9).

coffin. Hence it is clear that by this time, monks' robes had not replaced white *paṃsukūla* cloth and the robes were being offered to the monk.

As rare as the *paṃsukūla* scene, the cremation scene is depicted on the left end of leaflet ten. On the opposite end, a traditional musical group is performing at the funeral, a practice that continued to around the middle of the twentieth century.

The second example of the *paṃsukūla* illustration is in the Phra Malai Manuscript of the Spencer Collection, New York Public Library (Thai MS12). It is also an accordion-folded manuscript made of *khoi* paper (Figure 4.4). The manuscript is 67.5 cm wide. It illustrates ten episodes of the story of Phra Malai. The text is written in Cambodian script in black ink. The colophon lists the family members and dates the book to 1839.[14] Henry Ginsburg comments that in this manuscript 'the artist presents the usual Phra Malai scenes in a conventional way, but also includes the subject of a funeral'. Even though he did not identify the *paṃsukūla* scene, he was probably struck by its unusual subject matter and further explains that the funeral scene is appropriate because Phra Malai texts were commonly recited at funerals (Ginsburg 2000: 102).

The Phra Malai text was typically recited at funerals from the end of the Ayutthaya period (1350–1767) to the middle of the nineteenth century. It was used for chanting as entertainment at funeral wakes in Thailand. Because monks often dramatised and embellished the story of Phra Malai while chanting, it was later considered inappropriate behaviour. Thus during the reign of King Mongkut, monks were forbidden from chanting the Phra Malai story. However, recitations of the Phra Malai text continued at funerals by former monks who dressed up like monks for the occasion. As Bonnie Brereton states (1995: 2):

> While this tale is known throughout Theravāda Buddhist Southeast Asia, it has been especially popular in Thailand, where its teachings have for centuries influenced the content of sermons and the practice of a number of different rituals . . . It is through the growth and dissemination of the story that grisly hell scenes, fantastic wish-fulfilling trees, and visions of the glorious city of *nibbāna* became affixed on the walls of the temples and in the minds of the faithful.

Unlike the Walters Art Museum manuscript, the illustrations of the *paṃsukūla* scene and the cremation scenes are depicted on the same leaflet. The *paṃsukūla* is placed on the left side and the cremation on the opposite ends. In comparison to the *paṃsukūla* illustration in the Walters Art

[14] Unfortunately I have not been able to examine this manuscript. Thus I have depended on the information in Ginsburg's book. For further information, see Ginsburg (2000).

Museum manuscript – where the cloth is not visible to the viewer because of the casket – the Spencer Collection manuscript clearly portrays Phra Malai pulling the white cloth from a corpse. Here the monk takes the *paṃsukūla* cloth with his right hand and holds a monastic fan *(talaphat)*, one of his attributes, in his left hand.[15] His eyes are engaged with the deceased families who are mourning besides the coffin. The face of the corpse is depicted with his right eye opened wide, perhaps reflecting the facial features of the dead. It was a custom that the coffin was left open so the family could see the deceased for the last time before the cremation. Here the deceased body is covered from its neck down with a beautiful textile decorated with traditional floral motifs. It is important to note that from around the 1940s it became more common for the coffin to be covered with a wooden lid, as seen in the Spencer manuscript. Thus the corpse is not visible.

Even though it is not shown in either *paṃsukūla* illustration, traditionally the white cloth was tied to the corpse. According to Charoen Indraket, the corpse was tied with raw thread, called *trasang* or *doinai*, in three places: around the face and neck, the arms and hands and the feet (Charoen Indraket 1973: 7,435–7). An example of *trasang* can be seen on leaflet seven in the Walters Manuscript (Figure 4.2).[16] The hands are generally formed in the adoration hand gesture and sometimes hold a flower, incense or candle. The whole body would be covered with two long white cloths, one cloth covered from the head down to the feet with the ends of the cloth tied around the back of the head, another tied around the body from the feet up to the head. The long ends were then connected to the 'connecting cloth'(*phusayong*), which was then lightly tied to the *paṃsukūla* cloth. In some cases, the *paṃsukūla* cloth was the same as the one that was wrapped around the corpse.

Venerable Anil Sakya mentions that certain ethnic groups in Nepal have a similar practice.[17] The corpse's hands are tied with raw thread in the gesture of adoration on his chest and the end of this thread is left outside the coffin before the lid is closed. Thus when the monk performs the *paṃsukūla* ritual, the deceased receives the blessing directly through his hands. Similar is a description by Karl Dohring in his article, 'Cremation in Siam',

[15] Phra Malai's attributes are a monastic fan, an umbrella and an alms bowl.

[16] Two illustrations are depicted on leaflet seven. The illustration on the left depicts a monk meditating on a male corpse whose body is tied with *trasang* in three places: the toes, the hands and the neck. An inscription above the corpse reads *pul.lavakam*, meaning 'meditation on a worm-infested corpse'. The illustration on the opposite end depicts a male corpse being tied by *trasang*. The inscription above the corpse reads *vikkhaayitakam*, which means 'meditation on a gnawed corpse'.

[17] Personal communication with Venerable Anil Sakya, secretary of the Thailand Supreme Patriarch, Wat Bovornnitwet, Bangkok.

published in 1923: for a royal funeral, the body is placed in an urn (*kot*) in a kneeling position, with the hands in a praying gesture holding a lotus flower, and a broad long prayer ribbon is left emerging from between the cover and the rim of the urn.[18] He explains that the monks recite funeral prayers while holding the prayer ribbon, which hangs out from the urn between their hands. This rite allows the deceased to take part in their prayers and meditation. This description helps explain parts of the ritual that monks performed during the *paṃsukūla* rite that were not depicted in the illustrations of either manuscript.

CHANTING FOR THE DEAD: *PAṂSUKŪLA*, CREMATION AND CORPSES

For contextualising the ritual use of the *paṃsukūla* cloth, it is worth mentioning that in the moment when the monk is taking the *paṃsukūla* cloth, *Mahanikai* monks chant the following verse from the *Mahāparinibbāna sutta*:

Impermanent, alas, are all conditions,
Arising and passing away
Having been born they all must cease
The calming of conditions is true happiness.[19]

Thammayutika nikāya monks chant the same verse with an additional section. This last section emphasises and reminds us that even monks will not escape this cycle of life. It sums up the blessing as follows:

All beings surely die, have always died and will always die.
In the same way I shall surely die; doubt about this does not exist in me.[20]

[18] Dohring (1923: 243–4).

[19] I am grateful for the valuable advice and translation of Pāli texts by Venerable Anil Sakya. This text is chanted by *Mahanikai* (*Mahānikāya*) monks up to the present:

Aniccā vata saṅkhārā,
Uppādavaya dhammino
Uppajjitvā nirujjhanti,
Tesaṃ vūpasamo sukho.

[20] According to Venerable Anil Sakya, the Pāli version of this additional line is:

Sabbe sattā maranti
Ca mariṃsu ca marissare
Tath'evāhaṃ marissāmi
natthi me ettha saṃsayo.

Venerable Anil Sakya also mentions that 'However, there are parts when monks chant different chants, for example, during the cremation after the *paṃsukūla*, while everyone [relatives] go to lay sandal-wood flowers as a symbol of cremation, there are four monks who provide background chanting until the last person lays the flower' (personal communication). The common chanting for this part of *paṃsukūla* is the *Seven Books of the Abhidhamma* (*Abhidhamma Chet Khanphi Ruam*). The *Seven Books of the Abhidhamma* is generally utilised during the merit-making funeral ceremony in the evening at the temples and the number of monks varies depending on the rank of the deceased and the family. In popular conceptions the chanting is often associated with merit transfer, however, there is also a link between ideas of the *Abhidhamma* being crucial for the creation of mental processes and to construct 'new life' through the formation of a new embryo through the sounds of the chanting, as McDaniel has shown (2008: 229–45). This can also be set in relation to the interpretation of Bizot (1981: 66), who thinks that the use of the *paṃsukūla* in certain healing ceremonies can be compared to that of a 'ritual womb', creating a new and healthy body for the initiated person.

Coming back to the visual representations of the subject, it is interesting to note that the *paṃsukūla* and the cremation scenes seem to have been depicted as a transition between two subjects: Phra Malai and meditations on a corpse. The former commonly portrayed corpses in the underworld during Phra Malai's trip to hell, which again reflected the subject of death. As mentioned earlier, the *asubha-kammaṭṭhāna* meditation was popularly practised by monks in Thailand, Burma, Cambodia and Laos from around the eighteenth to the middle of the twentieth century. It is not clear, however, if this practice had anything to do with the interest in portraying funeral subjects in mural paintings of temples and in manuscripts.

The meditations on the corpse *(asubha-kammaṭṭhāna)* were depicted on leaflets two to eight of the Walters Art Museum manuscript. It helps to aid practitioners to realise the truth of the Buddhist doctrine of impermanence (*anicca*; Phra Khru Anusaranasasanakiarti and Keyes 1980: 12). Even though this meditation technique was still relatively popular by the time the Walters Art Museum manuscript was produced (Figure 4.2), it is a subject rarely portrayed on mural paintings and manuscripts. It is remarkable that murals in Wat Sommanat and Wat Bovorniwet, two very important temples that were fully patronised by King Mongkut, depict the *asubha-kammaṭṭhāna* scenes and the thirteen ascetic austerities *(dhutaṅgas)*, respectively. Wat Sommanat was built in memory of Queen Sommanat, a consort of King Rama IV, who died in 1852. The *asubha-kammaṭṭhāna* is depicted on a mural in the ordination hall.[21] The congregational walls highlight funerary scenes in their mural, which are drawn from the queen's favourite literature, *Inao*.[22] These scenes clearly reflect funeral practices during the reign of King Rama IV.

Note also the thirteen ascetic austerities depicted in a small congregational hall *(wihan)* of Wat Bovorniwet, where Mongkut was an abbot.[23] Mongkut was known for being an avid practitioner of the meditation style of the *dhutaṅga* (forest monks). It is widely known that he wore robes made out of rags from cremation grounds. It is likely that when he was a monk, Mongkut also practised *asubha-kammaṭṭhāna*.[24]

REPLACEMENT OF THE WHITE CLOTH WITH MONK'S ROBES

From the *paṃsukūla* paintings portrayed on the Walters Art Museum and the Spencer Collection manuscripts, it is clear that around the 1840s the white cloth was still used for *paṃsukūla* and monk's robes were presented to monk(s) for merit-making. It is not clear exactly when the *paṃsukūla* ritual changed, why it changed and why the white cloth was replaced with monk's robes. However, by taking a closer look at accounts of funeral rites and *paṃsukūla* practices one may be able to delineate a rough time-frame and in a speculative manner link the wider cultural changes taking place in the late nineteenth and early twentieth century with the transformation of funeral practices.

From Western accounts, it seems that the white cloth, as seen in the illustrations (Figures 4.1 and 4.4), continued to be used in the *paṃsukūla* rite during the reign of King Chulalongkorn (Rama V; r. 1868–1910). Karl Dohring, who served in Siam at the Royal Siamese Railway Department and the Ministry of Interior between 1906 and 1913, wrote about Siamese cremation as follows: 'If a Siamese has died and the loud laments of the next of kin have stopped, the deceased is washed and wrapped in ribbon of white cloth. They put the body in a coffin, which has four sidewalls and a cover,

[21] The temple was built in 1856. For further information on the mural paintings of Wat Sommanat see Listopad (1995).

[22] *Inao* was translated from a Javanese novel during the reign of King Rama I (r. 1782–1809). It became a popular source of Thai literature and theatre.

[23] At Wat Bovorniwet, the mural of the thirteen ascetic austerities appears on the wall of Wihan Phra Sasada.

[24] King Rama IV's adviser, Somdet Phra Archan Tho Prommarangsi, was a famous practitioner of *asubha-kammaṭṭhāna*. In addition several of the high-ranking monks who were appointed by King Mongkut also practised *asubha-kammaṭṭhāna*. I would like to thank Justin McDaniel for his advice on this subject. For further information on Somdet Phra Archan Tho Prommarangsi see McDaniel (2011).

but instead of a bottom there is an iron grill on which the body is placed' (Dohring 1999: 36). Dohring further explains that for prominent people the body was first embalmed because the preparations for the cremation took a long time. The body was wrapped very tightly with narrow ribbons of white cloth while spices, incense, myrrh and honey were added to it. He said also that the corpse looked like a mummy except that the head was left uncovered (*ibid.*: 37). The 'ribbon of white cloth' probably referred to *trasang*, which is connected to *phusayong* and the *paṃsukūla* cloth as mentioned earlier. Although Dohring did not mention the *paṃsukūla* rite, his descriptions provide evidence of the use of long white cloth on the corpse. Dohring's references on funeral subjects came from his observations of cremation and funeral ceremonies and from Captain Werner who stayed in Bangkok in 1861.

In his book, *The Mons of Burma and Thailand*, Robert Halliday, a missionary who resided in Burma and Thailand before 1917, mentions the use of white cloth in Mon funerals: 'The coffin is then placed in front of the priest who is to perform the ceremony [. . .] Before the service begins, a white cloth is drawn out of the coffin and the end of it is placed in the hands of the priest. A coconut is broken and the water is poured out at the head of the coffin' (Halliday 2000: 74). This description clearly matches the illustrations in the Walters Art Museum and the Spencer Collection manuscripts.

Dohring and Halliday's accounts describe the procedure of the *paṃsukūla* rites practised at the beginning of the twentieth century towards the end of the reign of King Rama V until the end of King Rama VI's (r. 1910–25). Significant transformations occurred in Thailand after King Rama VII (r. 1925–35) abdicated the throne in 1935.[25] Not only was a Western type of government established, but also significant cultural conversions affected every aspect of Siamese lives.[26] Perhaps the basis for these changes were already created earlier and influenced by an intense look towards the West filtered through the Thai elite in Bangkok. For example, ideas about hygiene and discourses about what constitutes 'real' Buddhism were already apparent earlier. The religious centre in Bangkok was pushing for a purification and centralisation of Buddhist practices, exemplified, for example, in the 1902 saṅgha act.[27] With funerals being a central monastic

[25] The name of the country was changed from Siam to Thailand in 1939.

[26] For further information on this subject, see Wyatt (1984: 234–60).

[27] See for example Tiyavanich's account (1997: 254) of wandering forest monks and the reshaping of their practices such as *asubha-kammaṭṭhāna* through the authorities in Bangkok.

practice, and *asubha-kammaṭṭhāna* being a rather 'unhygienic' form of meditation, the change of funeral practices and meditation on corpses can perhaps also be explained by the long-term influence of these reforms.

Regarding the *paṃsukūla* ceremony in central Thailand, in around 1974–5 Kenneth E. Wells wrote that 'at present the *paṃsukūla* cloth is presented to monks who chant funeral services, and consists of fresh new robes laid across the coffins – not the dusty rags once left at cremation grounds' (Wells 1975: 112). Wells was obviously aware of the traditional ceremony but did not mention when the white cloth was replaced by monk robes. A decade earlier, when my grandfather passed away in 1963, the *paṃsukūla* rite was already performed the same way as Wells described in his article. In the northern region, Phra Khru Anusaranasasanakiarti and Charles Keyes attended a funeral ceremony in 1978, observing (1980: 12) that 'the clergy who have gone to send off the corpse pull the *paṃsukūla* cloth'. The 'clergy' Phra Khru Anusaranasasanakiarti and Charles Keyes refer to are laypersons who perform cremations at a temple (Thai: *sappaler*). It is these lay cremation assistants and not the monks who performed the rite. They also remark (*ibid.*) that 'when the *paṃsukūla* cloth is pulled, no one else is nearby [for it is an occasion solely] for the clergy to reflect [*phitcarana*] on the corpse as a meditation on impurity [Pāli: *asubha-kammaṭṭhāna*]'. This is interesting because again it was the cremation assistants – not monks – who performed both the *asubha-kammaṭṭhāna* and the *paṃsukūla* rite. Was the corpse considered by the monks to be unclean and polluted by this time?

Another interesting account of the *paṃsukūla* can be found in Rita Langer's book, *Buddhist Rituals of Death and Rebirth*. Langer states that the *paṃsukūla* derived from the Vedic tradition. Regarding the *paṃsukūla* in Sri Lanka, Langer (2007: 184) explains that:

> The offering of a piece of cloth does require a recipient, a priest or a monk to act as mediator between the living and the dead. And, at least in modern practice, it constitutes the only formal involvement of the monks that is specific to the funeral rites (other than chanting and giving of merit, which are both rather unspecific and occur in post-funerary and other contexts).

Phra Khru Anusaranasasanakiarti, Keyes and Langer point out similar funeral practices in northern Thailand and Sri Lanka. It seems that while the lay cremation assistants dealt with the corpse, the monk's roles were mainly focused on blessing and chanting. Schopen also supports this idea in his analysis of the shroud cloth as an indication of the transformation of the role of monks from scavengers to the recipients of gifts (2006: 337). In addition, he explains that it separated the monks from the cemetery and thus from impurity (*ibid.*: 338).

CONCLUSION

A transformation of funeral rites in central Thailand seems to have occurred after the 1940s. At present the coffin is commonly covered with a wooden lid so the corpse is not visible. In this case the monk does not take the white cloth that is tied to the deceased's hands as depicted in the Walters Art Museum and the Spencer Collection manuscripts. In some temples in Bangkok, the temple assistants will ask the family members if they desire to see the face of the deceased for the last time. If they do, the lid will be left open for a short time before it is taken inside the crematorium. The family members will then place sandalwood flowers inside the coffin as their last offerings to the deceased. Because the ritual has changed, the white robe no longer has any function in the ceremony. Thus monk's robes, commonly offered to the monk who performs the *paṃsukūla*, as can be seen depicted in the Walters Art Museum manuscript, eventually replaced the white cloth. If the corpse is considered impure and polluted, and the role of monks now concerns blessing and the transferring of merits to the deceased and their families, it is no longer necessary for monks to receive an offering from the corpse.

The illustrations of the offering of the white cloth in the *paṃsukūla* ceremony, which is no longer practised in the central region of Thailand, clearly reflect how the ritual was performed before the second half of the twentieth century. The *paṃsukūla*, the *asubha-kammaṭṭhāna*, and Phra Malai all seem to be related and symbolise different stages of transformation after death. While the forest monk takes a real *paṃsukūla* shroud from a corpse as depicted in the *asubha-kammaṭṭhāna* illustration, the other monks portrayed in the Walters Art Museum and the Spencer Collection manuscripts (Figures 4.1 and 4.4), take conventional *paṃsukūla* in a ritual context of a funeral. Hence the cloths have the same function.[28] Thus the *asubha-kammaṭṭhāna* scenes represent the transformation of the body after death. Phra Malai represents what one achieves when one mentally conquers death through meditation and from the Buddha's teaching. The promise of heaven and the chance of being reborn in the time of the Future Buddha,

[28] I appreciate Peter Skilling's advice on this concept.

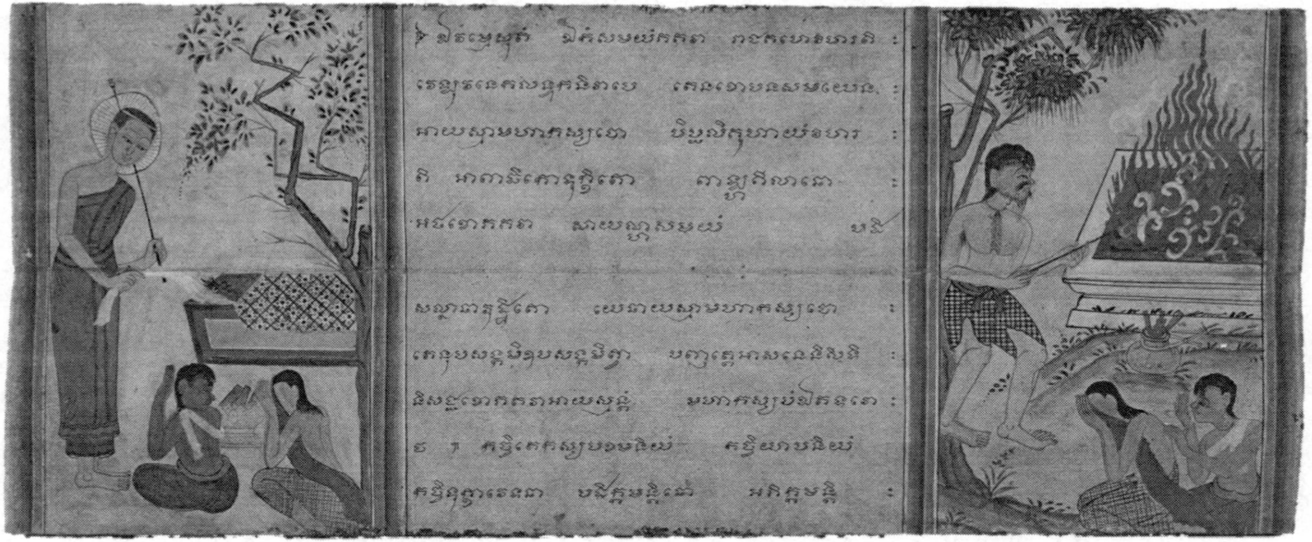

Figure 4.1 Phra Malai takes the *paṃsukūla* cloth from a corpse. Phra Malai Manuscript, reproduced with permission of The Walters Art Museum, Baltimore.

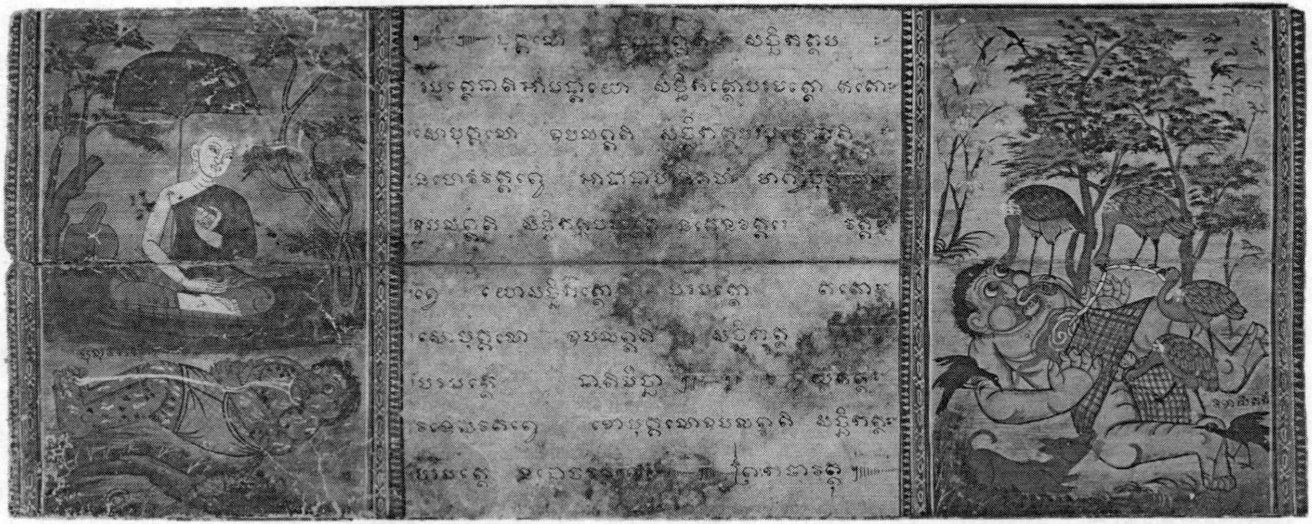

Figure 4.2 The practice of meditation on a corpse (Pali: *asubha-kammaṭṭhāna*). The corpse is devoured by birds (right side). Phra Malai Manuscript, reproduced with permission of The Walters Art Museum, Baltimore.

Figure 4.3 Two lay cremation assistants maintaining the fire over the coffin. Phra Malai Manuscript, reproduced with permission of The Walters Art Museum, Baltimore.

Maitreya (Thai: Phra Si An), was thought to follow from listening to the Phra Malai text and Vessantara *jātaka*.

The *paṃsukūla* ceremony, performed by a monk as depicted in the Walters Art Museum and the Spencer collection manuscripts, symbolically

Figure 4.4 Monk pulling *paṃsukūla* cloth from a coffin. Detail from Phra Malai Manuscript, reproduced with permission of the Spencer Collection, The New York Public Library, Astor, Lenox and Tilden Foundations.

represents the conquest of the fear of death as is supported by the meaning of the chants and, in addition, reflects the actual blessing before the cremation. The *paṃsukūla* cloth is, at the cremation of a person's present physical body, the last offering of merit-making.

Transferring this specific transformation of Thai Buddhist funeral culture to the wider anthropological study of rituals, Catherine Bell very well sums up the dilemma the study of ritual poses. Rituals, and the use of certain 'objects' in those, like, for example the *paṃsukūla*, are often understood as unchanging due to their imagined inherent conservative nature (1997: 210):

> Part of the dilemma of ritual change lies in the simple fact that rituals tend to present themselves as the unchanging, time-honoured customs of an enduring community. Even when no such claims are explicitly made within or outside the rite, a variety of cultural dynamics tend to make us take it for granted that rituals are old in some way.

By applying a Buddhist concept to the study of culture, Venerable Anil Sakya points out that an important aspect of Thai Buddhism is that 'everything is *aniccam* or impermanent. Rituals are not always static, especially in Theravāda Buddhism. Many rituals are recently invented and we keep inventing rituals all the time to go with the changing situation' (personal communication). As I have shown for the case of the *paṃsukūla* and the associated rites, an analysis of the changing roles of ritual objects has to be embedded in larger historical changes. Despite the fact that the *paṃsukūla* continues to be an important part of Thai funeral rites and is still imagined as having the same function as in the past, its various depictions have revealed remarkable shifts in Thai Buddhist funeral culture.

BIBLIOGRAPHY

Bell, C. (1997), *Ritual: Perspectives and Dimensions*, New York: Oxford University Press.

Bizot, F. (1981), *Le Don de Soi-même: Recherches sur le Bouddhisme Khmer III*, Paris: Publications de' École Française d'Extrême-Orient.

Brereton, B. P. (1995), *Thai Telling of Phra Malai: Texts and Rituals Concerning a Popular Buddhist Saint*, Tempe: Arizona State University Program for Southeast Asian Studies.

Chirapravati, P. (forthcoming-a), *Thai Funeral Culture: Studies of Images and Texts in Thai Art*.

Chirapravati, P. (forthcoming-b), 'Funeral scenes in the Ramayana mural painting at the Emerald Buddha Temple', in ed. Marijke Klokke, *Recent Studies in Southeast Asian Archaeology*, International Institute for Asian Studies (IIAS) Publication Series, Amsterdam University Press.

Dohring, K. (1923), 'Lijkverbranding in Siam [Cremation in Siam]', *Nederlandsch-Indie Oud&Nieuw*, 243–4. (For English translation see J. P. M. Bloemhard (1985), 'Cremation in Siam', in ed. Somphop Phirom, *Phramerutmat Phra Meru Lae Meru: Samai Krung Ratanakosin* [Phra Merutmat Phra Meru and Meru in Ratanakosin Period], Bangkok: Samnakphim Amarin, 468–9.

Dohring, K. (1999), *The Country and People of Siam*, trans. Walter E. J. Tips, Bangkok: White Lotus.

Ginsburg, H. (1989), *Thai Manuscript Painting*, London: British Library.

(2000), *Thai Art and Culture: Historic Manuscripts from Western Collections*, London: British Library, 92–111.

(2006–7), 'Thai Painting in the Walters Art Museum', *The Journal of the Walters Art Museum*, A Curator's choice: Essay in Honor of Hiram W. Woodward, Jr., **64**/65, 99–148.

Halliday, R. (2000), *The Mons of Burma and Thailand*, vol. 1, reprint from the 1917, ed. Christian Bauer, Bangkok: White Lotus.

Indraket, C. (1973), *Salanukhromthai Chabap Ratchabunditsathan* [Thai Encyclopedia, the Royal Thai version], Prachineburi: Rongpim sune kanthahanrap, vol. 12.

Khrongkan Supsan Moradok Wattanatham Thai (1999), *Samut Khoi: Moradok Thai* [Buddhist manuscripts: Thai Heritage], Bangkok: Khurusapha.

Klima, A. (2002), *The Funeral Casino: Meditation, Massacre, and Exchange with the Dead in Thailand*, Princeton, NJ: Princeton University Press.

Langer, R. (2007), *Buddhist Rituals of Death and Rebirth: Contemporary Sri Lankan Practice and its Origins*, Abingdon and New York: Routledge.

Listopad, J. (1995), *The Process of Change in Thai Painting: Khrua In Khong and the Mural Paintings of Wat Somanat Vihan*, unpublished Masters thesis, University of Michigan.

McDaniel, J. (2008), *Gathering Leaves and Lifting Words: Histories of Buddhist Monastic Education in Laos and Thailand*, Seattle: University of Washington Press.

(2011), *The Lovelorn Ghost and the Magical Monk: Practicing Buddhism in Modern Thailand*, New York: Cambridge University Press.

McGill, F. (2009), *Emerald Cities: Arts of Siam and Burma, 1775–1950*, San Francisco: The Asian Art Museum of San Francisco.

Phra Khru Anusaranasasanakiarti and Keyes, C. F. (1980), 'Funerary rites and the Buddhist meaning of death: an interpretative text from northern Thailand', *Journal of the Siam Society* **68** (1), 1–28.

Schopen, G. (2006), 'A well-sanitized shroud: asceticism and institutional values in the middle period of Buddhist monasticism', in ed. Patrick Olivelle, *Between the Empires: Society in India 300 BCE to 400 CE*, New York: Oxford University Press.

Swearer, D. K. (1995), 'A summary of the seven books of the Abhidhamma', in ed. D. S. Lopez, *Buddhism in Practice*, Princeton, NJ: Princeton University Press.

Tiyavanich, K. (1997), *Forest Recollections: Wandering Monks in Twentieth-century Thailand*, Honolulu: University of Hawai'i Press.

Wells, K. E. (1975), *Thai Buddhism: its Rites and Activities*, 3rd rev. edn, Bangkok: Suriyabun Publishers.

Wyatt, D. K (1984), *Thailand: a Short History*, New Haven and London: Yale University Press.

CHAPTER 5

Good death, bad death and ritual restructurings: the New Year ceremonies of the Phunoy in northern Laos

Vanina Bouté

Research on Buddhism in Laos has principally focused on the Buddhism practised by the Lao, the main population of the country. There are, however, other Buddhist populations (the Sö, the Kasak, the Phunoy, etc.) usually designated as 'minority groups' whose religious practices are still little known. The aim of this chapter is to discuss how Buddhism is intertwined with spirit cults among the Phunoy, a Tibeto-Burmese society of highlanders living in northern Laos, with a special focus on local funeral rituals. The Phunoy draw a distinction between two types of dead: the 'good dead' – i.e. those with an 'ordinary' death that allows them to join the community of the ancestors – and the 'bad dead' – i.e. those with an abnormal death – accident or suicide – who will form the group of the malevolent spirits.[1] Traditionally, the funeral rituals for the former are performed exclusively by Buddhist monks, while spirit priests usually perform those for the latter. However today, a specific ceremony – a sort of 'second funeral' led by monks – associates them all. It is part of the New Year festival, *Bun Pimay*, which is one of the most important events in the Lao Buddhist calendar. During this ceremony, the good and the bad dead receive similar offerings to secure their life in the hereafter. They are also prayed to together to protect the living and to provide them with prosperity and fertility for their fields, also reflecting the embeddedness into agricultural practices. Nevertheless, there remain obvious differences in the ritual devices according to the kind of dead involved. It appears that this specific ceremony unifying all the dead is an outcome of a changing conception of Buddhism, partly imposed by the Communist Party in the 1960s. However, this sort of official Buddhist ritualism and ritual restructuring does not prevent the Phunoy from continuing with spirit cults.

[1] See Hertz (1928) for classical work on good and bad death and Baptandier (2001) for a discussion of various Asian cases.

In the Phunoy villages one can observe a new and original linkage between various religious elements borrowed from Buddhism as well as from spirit cults. Indirectly, we will in this way reopen the age-old debate about the supposed general opposition between the 'great and little tradition' (Redfield 1956), and more specifically between the 'religion of Buddha' (*sasana phut*, L) and 'the religion of spirits' (*sasana phi*, L).[2] I will in my case start to analyse this opposition from the apparent borderline example of Buddhism in a minority population.

THE PHUNOY: FORMER BUDDHISTS AND RECENT CONVERTS

The Phunoy, a group of approximately 35,000 people, live in the north of Laos in the mountainous area of the province of Phongsaly, crossed from north to south by a major river, the Ou. They make a living from shifting cultivation (swidden) and animal breeding, even though, over recent years, government policies have questioned this way of life. The Phunoy were long ago converted to Theravāda Buddhism, and have borrowed from their lowland neighbours, the Tay Lue, the monastic code of discipline, the order of Buddhist ceremonies and the manuscripts in Tay Lue, which differ slightly from those of the Lao.[3]

In the 1920s, Roux noted that four ceremonies (*bun*, L) were celebrated regularly by the Phunoy: the Lao New Year (Pimay, celebrated in the fifth Lao month, i.e. in April), the beginning and end of the Buddhist lent (Khao Phansa and Ok Phansa, in July and October respectively) and in September, Khao Salak (literally 'rice drawn by lot'), a festival for the dead and considered by the Phunoy to be 'the most important festival of the year' (Roux 1924: 482). As with the Tay Lue and the Lao, where ceremonies led by monks in the pagoda were associated with rites in honour of the spirits that protected the village (*phi ban*, L) and the territory (*phi mùang*, L), the Phunoy Buddhist rituals cohabited with the totality of the rites addressed to spiritual entities protecting the land and were led by two major officiating priests: the *tjaotjam* and the *maphè*. The former was the intermediary between the guardian spirit of the village and its

[2] Note on the transcription: the words between brackets not followed with indications are Phunoy words; the words in Lao are indicated with an 'L'. There is no Lao official system of transcription so I chose my own. The *ù* is pronounced as in the word *fluent*, the *u* as in *shoot*, *ng* as in *camping*, *tj* as in *tiara*, *gn* as in *Kenya*, *y* as in *yoyo*. To simplify reading, the tones (five in Lao, six in Phunoy) and the differences between long and short vowels have not been retranscribed.

[3] For Roux, it would seem that 'the religion of Buddha was introduced to the P'ou-Noi by Lu bonzes [Tay Lue], in an era that it is impossible to ascertain' (1924: 486). Many Phunoy stories date their adoption of Buddhism from when they arrived in the Phongsaly region, at the end of the eighteenth century.

inhabitants. Every year, the *tjaotjam* carried out a rite at sowing time, asking the guardian spirit of the village to protect the growth of the rice. At the same time, all the villagers prayed to their own ancestors, who were revered on the altars existing in each house. He also carried out rituals when a change occurred in the composition of the village or when a problem threatened its integrity. The *maphè* was responsible for two collective rites associated with the agricultural cycle (one carried out when the land was cleared for cultivation and the other before the harvest) and was addressed to the spirits of metals and of the sky and the earth. The rites carried out by the two priests, addressed to the ancestors (who included the guardian spirit of the village) and to other spirits, were therefore mainly linked to the agricultural cycle, whereas the ceremonies carried out in the pagoda were to honour Buddha and give offerings to the dignitaries in the village at the time of New Year, to oneself at the time of Khao Salak (offerings that the giver would like to find after his death in the hereafter) or to the monks during the Buddhist lent.

Today, the number of Buddhist festivals celebrated by the Phunoy, their finalities and their importance has changed. So the New Year celebrations which, at the beginning of the twentieth century, consisted mainly of readings of Buddhist texts in the pagoda (*ibid.*) now include new ritual sequences and have progressively replaced, by their importance, the Khao Salak festival. The ancient collective cults to the spirits which opened and concluded the agricultural cycle have disappeared, as has the *maphè* priest. With the disappearance of the ritual carried out at the time of sowing, the role of the *tjaotjam* is now limited to carrying out the special rituals addressed to the guardian spirit of the village, who is no longer seen as an ancestor, but as a combination of forces of the locality.

These transformations partly result from religious purges carried out by the new government throughout the country from 1975. The Party decided to restructure the Buddhist religious community so that it would be in a position to promote the new national socialist identity, and rejected everything that could prove an obstacle to the constitution of a 'modern' socialist nation (i.e. in the religious field, all that had to do with spirits, the *phi*). For the Phunoy, the religious purges began in the 1960s as the Communists came into power in the Phongsaly province in 1954. The new administration considered that the practices of the Buddhist populations in the region, qualified as 'superstitions' were a hindrance to the economic development of the region. Groups of monks who had joined the revolutionary movement, coming from Sam Neua and Vientiane and accompanied by soldiers, went into the Phunoy villages to urge the inhabitants to 'reject the spirits in the forest' (*thim phi yu pa*, L). The altars to the ancestors and the *maphè*, who were the priests responsible for the cults addressed to a certain number of spirits, became the main targets. The Lao monks obliged the villagers, from then on, to go and nourish their ancestors in the pagoda during the Buddhist festivals such as *Khao Padapdin* which is a Lao festival for the dead.

However, this was not the festival principally chosen by the Phunoy to honour their dead. They gave preference to the New Year, which also celebrates the 'second funerals'. I will therefore describe this Buddhist ceremony, which has become today, on the Lao mode, the most important in the Phunoy Buddhist calendar, first by describing the ordinary funerals of which it is supposed to be the prolongation. We shall see how this festival has been transformed in the villages where the collective cults to the spirits have been banished.

RITUALS FOR GOOD AND BAD DEATH

I have previously mentioned the existence of a distinction between the rites carried out in the pagoda and the spirit cults – even if a certain number of the latter have disappeared further to the religious purges carried out by the Pathet Lao. There are consecutively two categories of priests: the Buddhist priests – the monks and the secular head of the pagoda (the *atjan*, a former monk) – and the priests in charge of the spirit cults, the *tjaocam*, and the soothsayer.[4] This distinction between different cults, carried out by distinct priests, can be observed in the funeral rites for the deceased.

When a person dies, the body is taken out through the main door, but beforehand it is washed, perfumed and dressed in its finest clothes. All its favourite things are placed in the coffin: pipes, certain objects, food and a duck (which has previously been knocked out) to carry it to the beyond. In the house, the monk reads the kusala sutta (*sut Kossala*, L) so that the deceased can find the path to heaven. This text will be read again in the cemetery. At the same time, outside the house, several of the elders and a soothsayer sacrifice some animals at the foot of the ancestor's pole, located at the back of the house. The deceased will feed on their meat and the animal's right back leg will be given to the elder brother of the mistress of the house. Once these preparations have been carried out, the members of the lineage of the deceased and his allies, preceded by the monk, carry the coffin to the cemetery in the southwest of the village. As we shall see in the passages devoted to the

[4] On the function and the transformation of Phunoy religious officiants, see Bouté (2008).

Buddhist ceremonies, other ceremonies linked to the funeral will later be celebrated in the pagoda.

In the cemetery considered to be for the 'good dead' (*la pum*, 'the place for souls', in opposition to the cemetery for the 'bad dead', cf. infra) the tombs of children under ten years of age are separate from those of adults. The place of each tomb is determined by a divination using grains of rice and carried out by the elders the day before the burial. When the place has been settled upon, the master of the deceased's house (or the son, if it is the master who has died) throws an egg and if it breaks, the place is declared to be propitious. Bamboo constructions are built over the tombs and covered with straw hut grasses, which rot and disappear quickly. When they have completely disappeared, the tomb's place will no longer have any importance. In this way, when a village changes its location, the former cemetery becomes an ordinary piece of land and can be cultivated.

The treatment of those considered to be 'bad dead' is very different. This time, the Buddhist priests take no part in the ceremony. The bad dead are children under ten, women who die in childbirth and those who die a violent death (by suicide or accident). If they die in the village, they are buried in a location next to the cemetery, considered to be the cemetery of the bad dead. If they die outside the village, they are buried at their place of death. These types of dead are said to be particularly dangerous. As death took them by surprise, their soul cannot return to the land of their ancestors and they stay and haunt the place in which they died. As they are angry, they try to lure the living into joining them. Their funeral consists of a simplified form of ordinary ceremonies, except for those who drowned, who are considered to be the most dangerous of the bad dead (the head of a drowned person is laid face down to prevent its rebirth). The deceased's belongings are buried with him, but nothing is built over the tomb. The Phunoy say that with this category of dead, all family links must be severed and, during the funeral ceremony, the bad deceased is asked not to draw the family members down with him. The elders, who must be as many as possible in order to protect themselves from the spirit of the deceased, carry out a ritual led by a soothsayer at the place of the tomb, then at the gate of the village, to be sure that the souls of the deceased have not followed the living and do not try to go into the village with them. The elders repeat to the deceased: 'Now, you are no longer one of us; you are a spirit (*dat*), we are people (*sang*). We can no longer stay together. You must go away.' A divination using rice is then carried out to verify that the spirit has left. As long as the grains of rice thrown form an uneven number, the spirit is again asked to leave. In the future, these dead will not be fed with the ancestors on the altar found in each house.

The Phunoy say that they have become the spirits of the forest (*tchitchong seu*, lit. 'the dead of the old forest'), and the villagers will avoid cultivating the land where they died. The offerings which, in the course of ceremonies related to the agricultural cycle, are made to this type of dead are laid outside the village, but we will return to this later.

Afterwards, the souls of the dead (for the Phunoy, there are nine) develop in different ways. Those of the bad dead are said to prowl around and try to drag other accidental deaths down with them. The souls of the 'good dead' are meant to find their way to paradise (*mùang savane*, L). However, this is only made possible if a second funeral ceremony is carried out for the dead after the first funeral.[5] This second ceremony is organised by the members of the deceased's family when they have the financial means, as it is fairly costly. It can therefore be carried out in the year of the deceased's death, or several years later. But it takes place systematically during one of the major yearly Buddhist ceremonies. Although previously carried out during the Bun Khao Salak festival in September, it now takes place during the New Year ceremonies. It is therefore this celebration that we will now study.

DESCRIPTION OF THE NEW YEAR CELEBRATIONS: CHRONOLOGY OF A RITE

For the Lao, the New Year, *Pimay* – which according to the descriptions of Condominas (1998 [1968]) in the 1960s was not the most important ceremony in the Buddhist ritual cycle – consisted mainly of the sprinkling of lustral water by the villagers onto statues of the Buddha so that their New Year would be favourable (Nginn, 1967: 12), purification of houses and recitations by monks to bring righteousness to the dead.[6] Similar ritual sequences can be found in the Phunoy population with, however, a particular emphasis on the offerings made to the ancestors.

Contrary to the Lao, who invariably celebrate the New Year on 13 April, for the Phunoy the time of its celebration varies, according to the village and the year, between the beginning of April and mid-May. None of the Phunoy I questioned could explain the reasons for this variation, but it should be

[5] On the phenomenon of the second burial and its integrative meaning see Hertz's comparative examination (1928).

[6] Tambiah (1970: 154). In the capitals of ancient Lao realms, New Year celebrations would involve other ritual sequences, such as the territory's refoundation and the regeneration of time, linked to a purification ritual (Archaimbault 1973: 20–62 for Luang Prabang, 1971 for Bassak). In Luang Prabang, sprinklings of the Buddha statue named Phra Bang and founder ancestors' mask dances would take place. (Archaimbault 1973: 48–9 n 36 and 46, 49–53); Méridat (1943: 112–17).

noted that within what used to make up the domains, the village considered to be the oldest is the first to celebrate New Year, followed by the other villages in an order based on the supposed date of their foundation.[7] The celebration is always preceded or followed by sowing, clearly demonstrating the relationship of agriculture practices and the ritual cycle. If the ground is considered to be 'warm' (*ang lang*), i.e. the first rains have not yet fallen after the land has been burnt for fire-fallow cultivation, the ceremony will take place after sowing. If the land is considered to be 'cold' (*ang tcho*), it will take place beforehand.

In the village of Thongpi, where I observed the New Year celebrations in 2000 and 2002, the ceremonies invariably began on 13 April. The long and complex festival lasts for three days. As with the Lao, the first day is considered to be the last day of the year (*mù sangkhan pay*, L); the second (*mù nao*, L) is an intermediary day (depending on the year, there can be two intermediary days). The third is the first day of the New Year (*mù sangkhan khùn*, L). A fourth day, which is not considered to be part of the actual celebrations, is devoted to various rituals.

First day: the building of the phasat *and the 'bringing down' of the Buddhas*

On the last day of the year, the villagers who have decided to make an offering to the dead prepare the *phasat*, a sort of small maisonette built for them, which they carry to the temple (i.e. the building that constitutes the location of the cult).[8,9] Made from bamboo, they are built on tiny stilts, surrounded by a little platform with a garden and enclosed by a barrier. They are large enough for a man to sit in. Inside, the families put everything the deceased might require: a mat, mattress, pillow, material and reels of coloured cotton (so that the deceased can make his clothes). In front of the door, they place a basket of rice, a cooking pot, kettle, tripod for the fire and perhaps some fans, identical to those offered to the monks. On the outside, in what represents the garden, there are two small replicas of rice granaries – one containing

[7] Up until the 1960s, most Phunoy villages were organised in what I call 'domains'. A domain would comprise a group of villages originating from the dissemination of a first village. This organisation disappeared after the Pathet Lao came into power. On ancient domains, see Bouté (2007).

[8] The word *phasat*, which I translate as *maisonette*, comes from Pāli, *prasāda*, which means 'offering, favour made to a divinity' and, by extension, refers to a stūpa (*that*), a building reproducing the cosmos and likened to mount Meru (Mus 1978: 355). In the Lao population, the *Prasat* is a building forming a little temple which is used to present the offerings to the monks (Zago 1972: 98, 295).

[9] The Phunoy refer to this building by using the same word they use to refer to all the pagoda's buildings, 'vat'. I will now use the word 'temple' to name this building and 'pagoda', the group of religious buildings (temple, monks' house, etc.).

paddy and the other rice. On the barriers around the garden they tie fruit, vegetables and bags filled with materials and sweets. There are also small trunks of banana trees decorated with wax flowers (*khan tham*, L). The number of trunks placed there corresponds to the number of prayers that will be paid for by the person who offers the house to the deceased. Lastly, the flags (*sao thung*, L) are attached, into which are pinned many bank-notes and some sticks (*um tjêk*) bearing three different layers of material. These will be 'loaded' with the prayers recited and are brought to the deceased through the undulations of the material.

While the villagers build their maisonette and install it in the temple, several of the elders deal with the preparations relating to the statues of the Buddha which will be 'brought down' (*ao phatjao lum*, L) from their altar. To do this, in the courtyard of the pagoda, they install a wooden house on stilts, normally kept in the corner of the temple, and place on it a large Nāga in painted wood.[10] Then, as the villagers start to file into the courtyard, the elders go to fetch the statues of the Buddha. They place them in the courtyard and shower them with water. The secular head of the pagoda (*atjan vat*) then turns around the statues three times while sprinkling them with water, followed by the men and then the women. The latter also sprinkle water over the pagoda drums then, when inside the temple, the four corners of the room. The men throw water in the direction of the village (the pagoda is always built above the village, on a ridge) then on the monk's house. The statues are then placed in the wooden house and are once more showered by pouring water on the Nāga that is above them. All the participants then go in procession to pour water over different places: the entrance to the clump of trees where the village's guardian spirit lives, the altars of the *thevada* (the divinities that protect the four corners of the pagoda), the monk's house and the drums and finally the banyan tree located outside the pagoda and in front of which each villager also lays a wooden stick. The elders go to the gates of the village and put sticks of wood on the ground across them, a sign to any strangers passing by that the village is closed to them.[11] In the evening

[10] The Nāga, a well-known figure in Theravāda Buddhism, is a snake, master of the chthonian world, but it is also said to live in the sky from where it would help to obtain rain. In tales on the life of Buddha, the Nāga protects the Buddha by sheltering him from the flood caused by the demon Māra in order to injure him (Tambiah 1970: 169–75); on the rites to obtain rain and the role of the Nāga among the Lao, see Archaimbault (1968).

[11] A little way beyond the fence which often encloses Phunoy villages are four 'doors' (*keu tan*), which are just simple wooden posts. One leads to the pagoda located above the village, one to the cemetery below the village and the two others to the path crossing the village. All have protecting trellises or sculptures representing arrows or knives, protecting the villagers from wild animals, malevolent spirits and other types of evil powers.

(and the following day) each of the families who have placed a maisonette in the temple organises in turn a meal, to which all of the villagers are invited.

Second day: the prayers to the dead in the pagoda

The next day is the day of prayers for the dead. In the morning, various purification operations are carried out by individuals or by all the members of a household in order to get rid of any bad luck (*kho*, L) they may have had in the previous year. These rituals are carried out on the second day of the celebration as this is a sort of intermediary phase, a liminal day that does not really exist because it is neither part of the old year nor of the new one. In the afternoon, all the villagers go to the pagoda to lay down candles and flowers in front of the Buddha altar, the statues in the courtyard, the altars of the *thevada*, the monks' house and the banyan tree. Then they all try to fit into the crowded temple. The monk, the novices and the *atjan* arrange the books to be read. On a sign from the holy men, the families throw water onto the maisonettes that they dedicate to their deceased. This is the beginning of the ceremony. The monk recites the *vandana*, then the *tisarana*, which are repeated by the villagers.[12] Then the religious participants (monks, novices, *atjan*) each go into one of the maisonettes to start the prayers, which will soon be rapidly transformed into a confused and indistinct brouhaha. On a metal support, the families honouring their dead tie and burn cotton threads. This operation will be carried out before each prayer, to inform the *thevada* of the pagoda that the recitation is about to begin. After each prayer, the assembly throws rice onto the maisonette and the person reciting the prayers receives a small sum of money from the owner of the maisonette. The former change regularly, so that one maisonette does not exclusively receive the prayers of a novice while another receives the prayers of a monk. This ceremony will last until nightfall.

Third day: the 'raising up' of the Buddhas, 'dead and born again'

The third day is the first day of the New Year. It is the time for washing and repainting the statues of the Buddha, which have been brought into the courtyard, then reinstalling them on their altars in the temple

[12] These are two prayers in Pāli. The *vandana* is the prayer of salutation to Buddha, by which all Buddhist ceremonies begin. The *tisarana* is a recitation concerning the veneration of the 'Three Jewels' (the Buddha, the Dhamma and the Saṅgha).

(*ao phatjao khùn*, L, literally 'raising up the Buddha' but this operation has also been described to me as when 'the Buddha dies and is born again'). The *atjan* recites a prayer asking the Buddha to bless the New Year, inviting him to admire the renewal of nature (in this case, branches representing trees which have been planted all around the statues), while the men repeat his words. The villagers then erect many small nine-storey clay stūpas covered with bamboo shoots. On some of them, the owners of the maisonettes plant flags (*sao thung*, L) which, linked by a cotton thread to the temple, are for the dead to whom the maisonettes are dedicated. On their pole many other small flags are stuck, and a bamboo platform on which food (rice, alcohol, sweetmeats) are laid. The material hanging down from the top will enable the dead, as did the Buddha, to 'rise' to heaven, using the flag as a ladder and taking the bird for a mount or the wooden dragon that sits in state on the top. The villagers not only put flags out for the dead, they also feed them. To this end, each mistress of the house brings a plate of offerings with different foods as well as receptacles full of water (kettles, bottles) and protective trellises in bamboo (*kra bia*), that she first presents to the statues of the Buddha, then to the banyan tree and finally to the altars of the *thevada*. She then lays these platters close to the altar of the Buddha in the temple. On each platter there is a piece of paper on which is written in Lao: 'the spirits of the house of so and so are . . .' followed by the names of the different dead people in each house (for three generations). The *atjan* then reads the names written and will say a prayer for the dead. This ceremony lasts for several hours.

The statues of the Buddha are then brought down from the wooden house and laid in the courtyard, while the branches representing trees are cut down. The novices and certain men from the village bang the cymbals and drums in the pagoda and, in front of them, the elders perform the 'dance of the big drum' (*tum ba djien gê*) using two sticks. From time to time, rifles are fired. All this is intended to frighten the malevolent spirits who would like to take advantage of the Buddhas descending from their pedestal to attack them. The monks, the men and then the women shower the statues with water. The men repaint the statues, dress them in small orange clothes identical to the robes of monks, and slip bank-notes inside.[13] The statues are then carried into the temple. The women take off their scarves

[13] By contrast with the Lao, where women are not allowed to touch the statues of Buddha, among the Phunoy, old women take part in those operations. It should also be noted that the individuals who personally offered a statue to the pagoda have to take it down themselves and wash it before the others.

and make them into a sort of carpet going from the monks' house to the courtyard in which the statues were placed.[14] The monks and the novices come down from their cells, walk across the improvised carpet and disappear beneath floods of water thrown at them by the villagers. They are then dried off and carried ('like statues', I am told) into the courtyard where the statues of the Buddha have been placed. Here, they are sprinkled with perfumed water.

The maisonettes are then dismantled. The pieces making up their structure are thrown away below the village and the objects which decorated them are sold cheaply to the villagers the following day. The money will be divided into four parts: one for the Buddha (administered by the *atjan* and one of the elders, this money goes towards the upkeep of the pagoda), one for the monks, one for the novices and one for the *atjan*. A ritual supervised by the monk concludes the ceremonies of the day. This enables all the misfortunes of the past year to be expelled. The elders, led by the monk and the *atjan*, make a sort of tray (*kro tang kao*, L) with a bamboo frame and a base made of banana leaves. This tray has nine compartments, each of which contains black rice, white rice, dried meat, small bones, flowers, some gold and silver (represented by bits of shiny paper) and a different animal in clay (buffalo, chicken, pig, dog, horse, snake, cow, elephant).[15] A human figurine is placed in the central compartment, named the Lord of the Days (*Phanya van*, L). It is then said that the former Lord, burdened with all the bad things that have happened in the community, must be thrown away to make place for the new one. This tray, which has a door on each side, is in fact a spirit trap. They run to get the food and the doors are then destroyed. The monk, then the *atjan*, begin a prayer to imprison the spirits in the trap, which is then thrown away outside the village, towards sunset.

In the evening, the families that offered a maisonette to a deceased person invite the villagers to other festivities. They notably jointly organise firework displays, which are set off from the village square. These 'fire flowers' (*dok fay*, L) are addressed to the dead and the *atjan* sends up a prayer with each firework.

[14] Lafont and Bitard (1957: 201, 209) noticed a similar practice during the ordination of Tay Lue monks. Women's headdresses and men's turbans were, in this context, seen as substitutes of the bodies of the devotees, alluding to the legend according to which the hermit Sumedha offered his back as a bridge to a Buddha. Such a practice would enable the devotees to obtain merit.

[15] The model of this square is very prevalent in the Buddhist communities of the peninsula, but the ritual procedures related to its use differ according to types of population. On the use of this square among the Intha (Shan State, Burma), see Robinne (2000: 119–25).

Fourth day: the tributes of the day following the celebrations

The next day, the second day of the New Year, relatives who had come to visit go home. But for the villagers, this is the day for sending off rockets (*bang fay*, L) and paying tribute to the elders.[16] In Thongpi, rockets are let off in the afternoon a short way away from the village, on a large flat area. This is one of the rare occasions during the New Year celebrations when all the villagers without exception (and not just one representative from each household) are present, dressed in their finest clothes. The women and the children crowd together in the school buildings and comment on each firing while eating sweetmeats. The young men take care of the preparation and the firing of the rockets, which is accompanied by the banging of drums and cymbals. The elders, installed on benches in front of the rockets, recite prayers for the rockets to take off well and fly high, and invite the dead to come and get them. Each time a rocket flies really high, the assembly shouts for joy and the happy owner is carried in triumph.

The rockets are made for the dead, those that have been given maisonettes on the previous days and those who died recently, and who have not yet received offerings in the pagoda. If the rockets fly high and far, it is said that the deceased has already reached paradise and that he is drawing the rocket to him. If, on the contrary, the rocket falls quickly or burns up before taking off, it is a bad sign: the deceased is still wandering sadly on earth. His family will send up a rocket the following year to see if, in the meantime, he has managed to reach paradise. The firing of rockets is therefore an important event which is the object of a lot of discussions over the following days.

After the rockets have been sent up, there are then tributes (*soma*, L) to the elders, the monks and the dignitaries, in exchange for their blessing. These tributes can be carried out on the evening following the firing of the rockets, or the next day, which is the day on which sowing commences. These little ceremonies take place in several stages. The sons and their wives first pay tribute to their parents. The son lays in front of his father a plate and a piece of material containing a little money and some flowers, while his wife (or sometimes the unmarried girls) washes the feet of her father-in-law. The elder touches the plate and recites prayers aimed to protect the members of the household and to obtain wealth and fertile fields.

In the afternoon, the gong is struck to warn villagers that the *soma* ceremony will be carried out in the pagoda. Few people go to this. Some old women bring

[16] In a Lao context, the firing of rockets (*Bun Bang Fay*) is a distinct celebration, generally celebrated around June (Condominas 1998 [1968]: 87).

four platters (*pha khao,* L) on which each newcomer places some yellow and red flowers, some paddy, small candles and a little money.[17] The elders dance around the drum. Two or three women wash the monk's feet and then the elders come to bring him some candles, flowers and some material containing a small sum of money. The monk then recites prayers aimed to protect the community. In the evening, a small procession of elders and young people carrying cymbals go to the houses of the *atjan* and the head of the village to pay tribute to them. They receive the same offerings as the monk, pronounce in return wishes for prosperity and invite the participants to a meal. Once this final stage of the New Year celebrations has been completed, the men, having the protection of the dead and the Buddha, can begin to plant the rice.

THE UNION OF THE INSIDE AND THE OUTSIDE: THE RENEWAL OF A PACT

The main beneficiaries of the festival are the Buddha and all the dead of the community and in the forefront, those to whom maisonettes are offered. The most important objective of the rites is to make the deceased happy (unhappy, they would make the living sick), by feeding them, dressing them, etc. It is here significant to point out that this is achieved in a very specific way: contrary to Lao Buddhist ceremonies, no one speaks of transferring the merits of the dead. The term *bun*, 'merit', is not used. The dead are honoured in the hope of a counterpart: they are expected to bring protection and fertility. There is therefore a fundamental difference to the observations of Hayashi and Tambiah in Lao Issan Buddhism (see below). According to Tambiah, there is no cult of ancestors. If the Lao Issan transfer merit to their dead during the Buddhist festival this is not, according to Tambiah, a cult to the ancestors in the sense of a systematic propitiation of the deceased and a formalised relation by which the deceased interacts with the living. He notes that there are also no sanctions on the part of the dead. The accent is solely put on the help the living give to their dead through Buddhist festivals (Tambiah 1970: 191; Hayashi 2003: 139–49). On the contrary, not to punish and to bring fertility are the actions that the Phunoy ask of their dead but also, to a certain extent, of the Buddha, in exchange for the offerings given to them.[18] Let us now examine the way in

[17] Four is a number pertaining to the dead and also to the village and its inhabitants, which is divided into four sections.

[18] For the Phunoy, the effigies of the Buddha are also ambivalent elements. If they are no longer worshipped, they are capable of becoming very angry with the villagers and bringing destruction in the form of epidemics.

which these two requests are precisely expressed during the New Year celebrations.

Even though the New Year is a festival dedicated to the dead, it is also a festival of renewal: of the coming year, symbolised by the new 'Lord of the Days', of the surrounding nature that is presented to the statues of the Buddha, the Buddha himself 'dead and born again', explain the villagers, referring to the fact that after they have been bathed, the statues are painted and dressed in little clothes into which money is slipped.[19] This renewal is also for the rice fields to come, the village and its inhabitants, a renewal which, as we have seen, is achieved through sending away misfortunes and by prayers for protection to have a prosperous year. In the more precise case of the village, we will see how the ritual expression of these requests seems to take place around a rite of re-creation, implying a shutting and opening of the village, two moments when the recipients of the celebrations, other than the Buddha and ancestors, are revealed indirectly.

The renewal of the village supposes expelling any bad elements which might be found there, and appears to be carried out through a sort of refounding of the village. This is shown in various ways. The villagers say explicitly that the itinerary they follow is similar to one carried out when the villages are founded. The rite shows a reenactment of this process performed in social space: the villagers go successively to the most important places in the village, which are the pagoda, the banyan tree located close by and the clump of trees where the guardian spirit lives. According to the Phunoy, the precincts of the pagoda and the four corners represent the village and its four gates. The banyan tree, which is a vital stage in the circuit, is compared by the villagers to the 'heart of the village' (*lak ban*, L, 'village pillar', the first spot from where the men start to clear and build a new site). In certain villages, this refoundation is more obvious. In the village of Xay, for example, on the second day of the New Year celebrations, the monk recites the text of the founding of villages, *ton ban*, which is only pronounced at times when the integrity of the village comes under threat (by a fire, an epidemic, a bad death) and when it is therefore necessary to redefine its limits.

By using various symbols that demarcate the transformation of social space, the refounding ritual also implies closing and then opening the village. It is surrounded by cotton threads and the gates are closed. The villagers then place crossed bamboo sticks through the threads to forbid passage. The water sources, which are located at the entrance of the village

[19] Slipping money into the statues seems to be a reference to the enthroning rites for new statues, during which their power is activated by giving them a heart made of gold.

(they must not run inside the village for fear of letting in the spirits of the spring), are also shut down. On the first day, the little canal formed by the waste water is cleaned and dug out, and the bamboo that drains the spring is changed. On the second day, little wooden bridges are built over this canal, but their access is forbidden by two crossed bamboo sticks at their entrance (on the outside of the village). They are also surrounded with cotton threads and bamboo trellises. The village is thus shut on the first day of the New Year celebrations (which is the last day of the year) and on the second day, which is the intermediary day, outside the year, and particularly propitious for changing the order of things and opening up to the outside world. For if this opening enables the bad things to be expelled from the village, it also makes it possible for other spirits to enter.

On the third day of celebrations, the village opens the gates again. The old gates, considered to be no longer efficient, are thrown away and replaced by new ones that have been made effective by their former stay in the temple. The little bridges placed over the springs are also opened. For the first time, the ceremonies do not take place exclusively within the village, but also outside. The rockets are sent up from a large flat area and the villagers go briefly into the fields to start the first stages of sowing.[20] The opening up of the village therefore not only results in the villagers going out, but also brings the outside world back in. This is signified in the direction in which the bridges are crossed, not from the village to the outside but from the outside into the village. The bridge is not only used by women who want to have a child, but also by the rest of the villagers. 'It is to obtain good fortune, strength' (*ga tchanibeu*) one of the villagers told me, who was impatient to be first over the bridge. This also seems to be the significance of the branches planted in the courtyard and presented to the Buddha, which come from the clump of trees in the sacred area where the guardian spirit of the village (*dat tu*) is said to live, outside the village precincts.

These operations seem therefore to imply a temporary opening up of the village to the outside, as if fertility were obtained through the intrusion of external forces, associated with the rites pertaining to the benevolent figures of the Buddha and the ancestors, and among which the guardian spirit of the village seems to occupy an important role. For it is indeed the figure of this spirit that emerges in certain of the ritual stages of the ceremony.

[20] Each head of a household marks off a small square about 2 × 2 metres in the area of land that he has cleared, next to the hut in the field. He surrounds it with cotton threads and bamboo trellises. On it he sows a few handfuls of rice and then builds a small altar on which he puts some of the meat that was offered to the dead in the temple. It is said that in this way, the spirit of rice, Apitchaba, is laid in the field as up until then, she was in the rice granary.

In another village named Kiu, where I observed the New Year celebrations, the link between the guardian spirit, the 'outside' brought into the village and the Buddha was even more evident. The elders and the *tjaotjam* first lay offerings of meat on the altar of the guardian spirit in the clump of trees just outside the village. Carrying so many branches that they almost disappear beneath them, they then lead a procession around the altar. Then they make a sort of stretcher on which seems to be a real reconstituted tree, but that the villagers present as being a stūpa. The stretcher is carried around the spirits' altar three times, then taken through the village where the inhabitants sprinkle it copiously with water, and finally laid at the foot of the Buddha statue in the courtyard of the pagoda. As with the bridges in Thongpi, which were crossed from the outside to the inside of the village, so the procession in the village of Kiu goes from the forest (or more precisely from the altar of the guardian spirit of the village) to the pagoda located here in the very centre of the village. The important role played by the guardian spirit in these ceremonies is not surprising if one remembers that it was formerly this spirit that was honoured before the sowing and to whom villagers prayed for fertility. It should also be remembered that if the offerings are now addressed to the dead, the guardian spirit was previously considered to be the spirit of the first head and founder of the village.

If the village is temporarily open in order to expel misfortunes (via the ceremony of the tray) and to underline the link with the village's guardian spirit, other more ambivalent figures could also make their way in. The third day is the moment when the elders perform the dance of the drum in order to prevent malevolent spirits penetrating the village. There are usually considered to be many of these evil spirits roaming around outside the village but on this particular day only certain of them are considered likely to appear: the spirits of metals (*sam pum dat)* and the chthonian snakes (*piahong dat*), are indeed ambivalent spirits as in some villages they were and still are considered to be the distributors of gifts or blessings. These chthonian spirits were formally closely linked with the 'spirits within the village' (*khong thon dat*) and to which the *maphè* paid worship before the land was cleared and after the harvest. During these two rites, the *maphè* built two altars for the spirits of the sky and the earth, but on which he also gave offerings to the spirits of metals and the bad dead. The propitiation of these forces was thought to be necessary to enable work in the fields to progress well and harvests to be plentiful.

Today, the spirits of metals are only brought offerings before the clearing of the land but they remain, on several points, closely linked to the village that they threaten to enter during the Buddhist holy days (*van sin*, L, i.e. the eighth and the fifteenth days of the waxing and waning moons) which occur between the New Year celebrations and the harvests. A parallel could be drawn here between the telluric spirits and the village guardian spirits in the Lao Buddhist populations, who roam freely in the village on holy days: the women cannot hull the rice, the villagers cannot cut or bring in wood and they must also not take any vehicles into or out of the village.[21] In the Phunoy populations, similar restrictions are observed by the villagers on holy days. However, it is not the guardian spirit that wanders around freely, but the spirits of metals and chthonian snakes, due to the pact made in olden days with the first inhabitants of the village. The history of this pact tells that a chthonian spirit came in olden times to get his food by killing men. They made a pact by offering him, instead of human flesh, animals that they sacrificed and made him promise only to come near the village again on holy days. This pact made with an animal spirit brings to mind figures of the ogres, demons etc. which, once pacified, become the guardian spirits of the Tay people's territory (see for example Kraisi 1967). It is true that the Phunoy do not consider these chthonian spirits to be the guardian spirits of the village, but the time when they come back to the village corresponds to the villagers' prayers to protect the growing rice. The ritual opening of the Phunoy villages on the holy days following the New Year also addresses the spirits that are feared but are necessary to obtain a primordial fertility indispensable to the regeneration of the villages, the men and the fields.

CONCLUSION

The New Year is therefore presented as a festival of rebirth, namely of the Buddha but also of the village and its occupants, who carry out certain rites of purification and reestablishment of the village. It is shut then opened again to the outside world, and its unity is reconfirmed (each villager places a stick representing themselves in 'the heart' of the village: the four sections of the village celebrate together the last day of the festival). This ceremony is today mainly directed towards the dead who were previously given offerings of food outside the house, then in the fields, before the sowing period began. Today, say the Phunoy, they are solely given nourishment in the pagoda.

This process of 'Buddhisation' of the ancestors is accompanied by another, more recent, phenomenon: the inclusion of certain bad dead in Buddhist ceremonies. In theory, the bad dead are buried in a separate

[21] Tambiah (1970: 267). Zago adds to these prohibitions, hunting, fishing (killing animals does not please Buddha) but says that any works of public interest are allowed (1972: 116).

cemetery and a special rite is carried out to sever the links between the bad dead and the living, especially their close relatives. However, in recent years, once these rites have been carried out, those who suffered a violent death are also entitled, during the New Year celebrations, to a ceremony almost identical to the one previously reserved for the ordinary dead.

On the first day of the New Year celebrations in 2002, two maisonettes (*phasat*, L) were built: one for a woman who had committed suicide a few days earlier, the other for a little girl who had been mortally wounded by gunshot from a rifle with which she had been playing. In and around the maisonettes were all the offerings usually made to the 'normal' dead: there was food and the wooden bird on top of the mast to carry her to the beyond. The ceremony did not take place in the temple or even in the pagoda, but nearby, a cotton thread linked the two masts addressed to the dead to the roof of the temple. 'This means that the Buddha authorises the ceremony and that he is watching over it', the monk told me. In short, the entirety of this ceremony seemed to be aimed at honouring the bad dead as if they had been good dead, and the people I talked to confirmed this. 'In the olden days, we would not have been able to do this. A bad dead was a bad dead. But today, it does not matter so much. The bad dead who died in the village are not very dangerous and we can carry out the same rituals for them as for the others. The families are very unhappy to think that their relatives are condemned to wander eternally and never find rest. So by carrying out this ceremony, we turn them into good dead.'

These ceremonies can be interpreted in several ways. For the anthropologist R. Hamayon, the 'recovery' of the bad dead often seems to happen in minority groups with a small population.[22] The 'advantage' of reintegrating the bad dead and turning them into good dead is that they are reborn into the group. This proposition corroborates the fact that the integration of bad dead goes hand in hand with a distinct decrease in population in the area. The Phunoy would carry out these new rites to 'recover' the souls of the bad dead, as ancestors were diminishing in number. Finally, reintegrating the bad dead is also a sign that the ancestors are necessary for the reproduction of the group. This is not only through their reincarnation within the community – as the whole idea of reincarnation, very present in Theravāda Buddhism, remains quite foreign to the Phunoy – but more importantly by obtaining the fertility that is bestowed upon them by the ancestors. The New Year

[22] Oral communication, third workshop in the programme *Dynamiques de l'identité et de l'ethnicité en Asie du Sud-Est et en Chine du Sud*, IRSEA-CNRS, University of Provence, 18–19 December 2004, 'Présence et usage de l'autre dans l'imaginaire religieux'.

ceremony can therefore be seen not only as a festival where the ancestors are prayed to for fertility, but also an occasion to 'make' dead, be they good or bad, who will become ancestors.

Finally, it is also as if the prayers for fertility of the people and the fields addressed to the ancestors under the auspices of the Buddha were indissociable from a prayer addressed to the 'other' forces linked to the wild. Formerly the founding ancestor of the village, the figure of the guardian spirit has become the representative of the forces of nature surrounding the village but also of the chthonian forces prayed to in olden times when the land was cleared, and at harvesting time. The 'opening' of the village during the New Year celebrations therefore seems to signify that the contribution of the outside world is necessary for the regeneration of the inside world. We find again here elements related in Phunoy tales concerning the establishment of the first villages, when two clans were necessary, one notably being associated with the outside world and the fertilising rain. The description of the multiple facets of the New Year ceremonies therefore shows that the transformation and addition of new ritual sequences to this cult results, on the one hand, from the integration of ancestral figures and, on the other, from taking into account the finalities of ancient collective cults, which are to ensure the fertility of the fields and the fecundity of the people.

BIBLIOGRAPHY

Archaimbault, C. (1968), 'Les rites pour l'obtention de la pluie à Luong P'rabang', *Bulletin de la Société des Etudes Indochinoises* **43** (3), 1–17.

(1971), *The New Year Ceremony at Bassak (South Laos)*, Afterword by Prince Boun Oum, trans. Siman B. Boas, Ithaca, NY: Cornell University, Southeast Asia Program, Data Paper 78.

(1973), *Structures religieuses lao (rites et mythes)*, Vientiane: Vithagna.

Baptandier, B. (ed.) (2001), *De la Malemort en Quelques Pays d'Asie*, Paris: Karthala.

Bouté, V. (2007), 'The political hierarchical processes among some highlanders of Laos', in eds. M. Sadan and F. Robinne, *Changing or Exchanging? Dynamics of Transformation among the Highlanders of Southeast Asia*, Brill: Leiden, 187–208.

(2008), 'Cultes aux esprits et bouddhisme chez les Phunoy du nord Laos', in eds. Y. Goudineau and M. Lorillard, *Nouvelles Recherches sur le Laos*, Paris: Publications de l'École Française d'Extrême Orient, 579–93.

Condominas, G. (1998), *Le Bouddhisme au Village: Notes Ethnographiques sur les Pratiques Religieuses dans la Société Rurale Lao (Plaine de Ventiane)*, Vientiane: Editions des Cahiers de France [(1968), 'Notes sur le bouddhisme populaire en milieu rural lao', *Archives de Sociologie des Religions* **25**, 81–110 and **26**, 111–50].

Hayashi, Y. (2003), *Practical Buddhism among the Thai-Lao: Religion in the Making of a Region*, Kyoto: Kyoto University Press.

Hertz, R. [1907] (1928), 'Contribution à une étude sur la représentation collective de la mort', in ed. R. Hertz, *Mélanges de Sociologie Religieuse et de Folklore*, Paris: Félix Alcan, 1–98 (1st edn. *Année Sociologique*, 1st series, vol. 10).

Kraisi, Nimmanhaeminda (1967), 'The Lawa Guardians Spirits of Chiangmai', *Journal of the Siam Society* **55** (2), 185–202.

Lafont, P.-B., and Bitard, P. (1957), 'Ordination de deux dignitaires bouddhiques Tay Lu', *Bulletin de la Société des Études Indochinoises* **32** (3), 199–223.

Meridat, L. (1943), 'La nouvelle année laotienne', *Bulletin de la Société des Études Indochinoises* **18** (1/2), 107–17.

Mus, P. (1978), *Barabudur*, New York: Arno Press.

Nginn, P. S. (1967), *Les Fêtes Profanes et Religieuses au Laos*, Vientiane: Editions du Comité Littéraire.

Redfield, R. (1956), *Peasant Society and Culture*, University of Chicago Press.

Robinne, F. (2000), *Fils et Maîtres du Lac: Relations Interethniques dans l'État Shan de Birmanie*, Paris: Centre National de la Recherche Scientifique/Maison des Sciences de l'Homme.

Roux, H. (1924), 'Deux tribus de la région de Phongsaly', *Bulletin de l'Ecole Française d'Extrême-Orient* **24**, 373–500.

Tambiah, S. J. (1970), *Buddhism and the Spirit Cults in North-east Thailand*, Cambridge University Press.

Zago, M. (1972), *Rites et Cérémonies en Milieu Bouddhiste Lao*, Rome: Università Gregoriana.

CHAPTER 6

Feeding the dead: ghosts, materiality and merit in a Lao Buddhist festival for the deceased

Patrice Ladwig

INTRODUCTION: CARING FOR THE DEAD

In his classical study on the anthropology of death rituals, Robert Hertz (1960) pointed out that a movement of ritual integration follows the separation process that society has to accomplish in relation to the dead. It is also crucial to acknowledge that in many societies these post-mortem relationships are not only established once, but have to be continuously reproduced. The dead – as ancestors, divinities or ghosts, for example – are not located in a realm that is purely 'beyond' and inaccessible through a sort of metaphysical wall, but are social entities intrinsic to the workings of society. A comparative study on the anthropology of death (De Coppet *et al.* 1994: 112) states that these 'boundaries are not insuperable barriers, but rather loci of relations of exchange, that is, of the transformations essential to the perpetuation of being'. The regeneration or perpetuation of life is an important part of many funeral cultures (Bloch and Parry 1982) and often implies the revitalisation of domains such as agriculture or human fertility.

Among the ethnic Lao, Buddhism plays a major role in the upkeep of these relationships through ritual exchanges with the dead.[1] The deceased are a focus of ritual attention ranging from everyday acts of food donation to monks to

The ethnographic data were collected in the urban setting of Vientiane and surrounding villages. I first observed the rituals between 2003 and 2005 during my first PhD fieldwork sponsored by the German Academic Exchange Service (DAAD). A more detailed study was carried out in September 2007 in the context of the project 'Death rituals of Southeast Asia and China' at the University of Bristol, funded by the Arts and Humanities Research Council (AHRC). I would especially like to thank all Lao monks and laypeople that helped us in our project. Thanks also to Gregory Kourilsky (L'École Practique des Hautes Études [EPHE] Paris) and Rita Langer (University of Bristol) for sharing the joys and troubles of ghostly haunting with me during fieldwork.

[1] I here focus on the Buddhism of the ethnic lowland Lao occupying the lowlands of the present-day nation state of Laos. Most ethnic Lao today live in the northeast of Thailand and sources relating to them will also be used. Comparative data on very similar rituals, especially on northern Thailand and Cambodia, will supplement my account. For an analysis of related rites among a Lao Buddhist 'ethnic minority' see Bouté's contribution in this book (Chapter 5).

larger festivals dedicated to the dead that are part of the ritual cycle. The first kind of care for the dead came to my attention while going on alms rounds with fellow monks from the local monastery in Vientiane. Later interviews with the donors feeding me every morning dealt with the motivation of giving and elaborated on topics such as the cultivation of good thoughts, generosity and transfer of merit (*boun*) to the dead while giving to monks.[2] However, a quite significant proportion directly mentioned their deceased relatives and described the act of giving to the monks as a 'feeding of the dead' (*liang phu day*). Members of the saṅgha are therefore transmitters; a 'conveyor belt' for exchanges with the aim of transferring merit and feeding the dead.

More ritually elaborated forms of caring for the dead by transferring merit and feeding can be observed in the context of larger rituals, which are the subject of this chapter. Among the Lao, two festivals of the yearly ritual cycle (*hit sip song*) explicitly address the dead and demonstrate their continuing entanglement in society. The first ritual, 'the festival of rice (packets) decorating the earth' (*boun khau padab din* – hereafter BKPD) takes place at new moon of the ninth month (usually in September) and marks the beginning of a special two-week period, the end of which is marked by the second festival, called *boun khau salak* ('the festival of rice baskets drawn by lot' – hereafter BKS). Both festivals aim at the reconstruction and perpetuation of a multitude of relations with different kinds of deceased such as recently deceased relatives, ancestors and ghosts. At BKPD, for example, ghosts are popularly believed to be freed from hell and enter the world of the living. These ghosts have to be distinguished from the various protective and agricultural spirits that are also addressed during the ritual. Although both festivals are to be understood as one ritual complex, I shall focus only on BKPD as the main topics of this chapter – the care for the dead and ghosts, merit and feeding – are most clearly exemplified in this festival.

In most of the anthropological and buddhological literature dealing with Southeast Asian societies marked by Theravāda Buddhism, the relationships with the dead are often explained via the notion of the 'transfer of merit'. In some accounts of doctrinal Buddhism, but also for some more orthodox Lao monks, this process of transferring merit is far from unproblematic.[3] Although the existence of this transfer is clearly visible in Lao

[2] There is no standardised transcription system for Lao and I use my own transcriptions. Most words, however, should be easily identifiable.

[3] White (1986: 206), for example, speaks of 'the thorny problem of merit transfer' and Agasse (1978: 312) proposes that 'the existence of the practice of merit transfer [. . .] constitutes a problem'. A few orthodox Lao monks I have met also have an individualistic stance on merit and karma and do not support the idea of a transfer. Karma, which depends on the amount of merit accumulated, is by them understood as a strictly individual quality that cannot be influenced by a transfer.

Buddhist practice, I want to expound some problems of Theravāda doctrine in relation to merit transfer and focus on alternative perspectives with which the linkages between the living and the dead might be explored. An emphasis on the kind of exchanges taking place, their 'materiality' as food, and their concrete context shall supplement the often too general analysis of the transfer of merit and lead to a broader understanding of the construction of post-mortem relationships. I will start with an investigation of the ritual entanglements with the various dead and discuss their ontological status. I will then focus on the feeding of ghosts and the textual backgrounds of the festivals in local Lao and doctrinal sources.[4] I want to conceptualise their apparition in the festival as a form of haunting in which care for the dead is expressed through establishing a kinship bond and their feeding. I will demonstrate that seeing food in its mediating materiality is crucial for a wider understanding of the festival, which a sole focus on merit could not accomplish. Finally, I argue that the ritual feeding of different kinds of deceased is constitutive for nurturing and protecting the well-being of a community, which comprises the living and various forms of the dead.

ONTOLOGICAL AND RITUAL FUZZINESS: FEEDING ANCESTORS, PROTECTIVE SPIRITS AND GHOSTS

Rituals provide a framework in which the living and the dead can interact in a more elaborate and effective manner than usual. The spheres of separation and the channels of communication take on a different quality in these periods, but this intensification also produces a certain kind of fuzziness regarding the ontological status and ritual addressing of the various deceased. Before describing the ritual practices and defining the category of ghosts and spirits addressed more thoroughly, it must be mentioned that the ritual addresses a multitude of deities and different categories of deceased hard to distinguish, as their ontological status is marked by a high degree of fuzziness. Lambek (1996: 242) mentions that we should 'not expect spirits to follow a Linnean model of distinct "species", notable for the discreteness of their identities' and reminds us that 'multiple and sometimes competing constructions of spirits can coexist in the same society' (*ibid.*: 246).

[4] I will try to distinguish the Lao and doctrinal conceptions of ghosts by referring to their differences. At the same time, however, there is also a substantial overlap between these concerning the textual references used, for example. This opens up the still ongoing discussion between practice and text, between great and little tradition, which cannot be dealt with here. See Rozenberg (2005) for an overview of these discussions.

Although BKPD and BKS are distinguished by their ritual practices, they overlap to a certain degree and are marked by rather blurred distinctions: elements found in one ritual may appear in the other, and they both address a multitude of beings which are not neatly distinguishable due to an ontological and ritual fuzziness. Older sources dealing with the festivals in Laos slot the rituals together and state their similarity (Nginn 1961: 32). Examining the rituals in the culturally very close context of northern Thailand, Premchit and Doré (1992: 283) report of two rituals for the dead. During the first ritual 'people dedicate a part of the merit to the dead', whereas they describe the second ritual (BKS) as a 'pure' Buddhist ceremony. The Cambodian Ghost Festival bears strong resemblances to the Lao one; it lasts for two weeks and is marked by an opening and closing ritual that could be said to correspond to the Lao BKPD and BKS.[5] Concerning the recipients of the offerings and beings addressed in the ritual, most ethnographic accounts simply refer to the dead as a rather homogeneous category. The gifts of food 'are destined for the late sister and brother, for the great uncles and the grandfathers who have passed away' (Abhay and Kene 1958: 14–15). Tambiah (1970: 156–7) states that 'the dead are allowed to visit the earth' during the festivals, but is less specific about the different kinds of deceased. Zago (1972: 315–18) subsumes both rituals as being 'for the favour of the dead', but additionally links them with the worship of agricultural divinities; a point also found in Archaimbault's (1973: 222–3) short account of the rites. Tambiah (1970: 156) also builds up a link to agricultural fertility and remarks that among the ethnic Lao of north-east Thailand the rituals take place 'at the critical time when the rice grains are forming in the fields'.[6]

In Vientiane, where the two festivals were observed, they are distinguished by the ritual practice that gives them their names. BKPD is the opening ritual for the special period and BKS closes it.[7] I want to focus my

[5] In Cambodian Buddhism *kan pen* is understood as a 14- or 15-day period (Porée-Maspero 1950: 47–58). Gregory Kourilsky (personal communication) has suggested that there are strong parallels to the Lao festival, but due to a calendar shift the timing is different. Ang Choulean (2006: 238), however, argues that in neighbouring Buddhist countries there is no comparable ritual to the Khmer one. Despite the fact that some important details are actually different, the resemblances concerning textual background and ritual practice make this a disputable position.

[6] Both rituals have an explicit agricultural character and are saturated with symbols deriving from rice culture. This would deserve an examination on its own and cannot be accomplished here. I will only refer to this form of the 'regeneration of life' with reference to the spirit of the rice field and the meaning of food offerings. For comparison, see Erik Davis' contribution in this volume (Chapter 3).

[7] BKS involves a ritual with labelled baskets with the names of the donor (sender) and deceased relatives (receiver). Through a lottery system that involves drawing sticks (*salak*) they are distributed among the monks who then transfer them to the dead. For the use of the *salākā* in various contexts, see Strong (1992: 141f.).

ethnography on the first ritual. The day before the ritual, special food packets are prepared by the families and almost the entire day is dedicated to the production of special offerings and decorations. Packets made from banana leaves, called *ho khau* ('rolled rice packet') contain sticky rice, several fruits and sometimes cigarettes. Other packets, labelled *khau dom*, contain sweet rice and pieces of fruit wrapped in banana leaves. Today, in the urban setting of Vientiane, it is also common to buy these offerings on the market. The following day, during the early morning of new moon in the ninth lunar month (usually September), at around 4am, the temple bell is struck. Continuing for over an hour, this signifies the opening of the doors of hell and the coming of the *peta*, or *phiphed*, hungry ghosts.[8] Laypeople flock to the temple and deposit the small packets on the temple grounds to be consumed by hungry ghosts. These parcels 'decorate the earth' – hence the name of the ritual – and are eagerly looked for by the hungry ghosts. Many informants have mentioned the movement of searching (*ha sawaeng*) when I asked about the *phiphed* and the food offerings. They thereby emphasised the needs of the *phiphed* and their hunger. Offerings are also placed in front of the *stūpas* (*that khaduk*) containing the bones of deceased relatives. People light candles, kneel down and speak to the deceased relatives with invitations such as these excerpts I recorded during the ritual:

> 'All ancestors and deceased! Every one of you! Please come to take these offerings of food so that we can receive well-being. Sathu!'
>
> 'My family and relatives. Come to take the gifts and eat. May you be reborn in better circumstances and in prosperous conditions because of these gifts.'
>
> 'These rice packets are for the four of you [his deceased relatives]. Please come and get them.'

If the temple has a shrine for the first abbot of the monastery (*phi cau khun vat*) rice packets will also be presented there. Later that day the spirit of the rice field (*phi dta haek*) will receive rice packets from the head of the family at the small shrine located at the edge of the field.[9] The Lao words used in this context also entail references to the movement of the offerings: *hai* (give to), *hab* (to receive) and *song* (to send). Whereas in this part the monks have no direct ritual role, the second part of the ritual – the temple service at 7am – involves the monks

[8] Some monks told me that this is also a kind of 'warning' that the *phiphed* are coming. For more details on the ontological status of *peta* and *phiphed* see the following section.

[9] The shrines of the spirit of the first abbot of the monastery have often disappeared in urban temples due to their ambivalent status after the purification efforts under socialism following the revolution in 1975. I could not witness this ritual in the temple. The *phi dta haek* has often been a victim of modernisation – only a few families still have rice fields where his shrine is usually located. I was able to see this very short ritual in the countryside, however.

receiving offerings from the laypeople. Here a standardised almsgiving to the monks is performed. The merit gained through the offerings is then 'transferred', or better 'dedicated' to the 'souls' (*vinyan*, Pāli: *viññāṇa*) of the deceased.

Focusing on BKPD, it becomes obvious that among the Lao the deceased are not a homogenous category as the aforementioned accounts present them. The result is a rather complex ontology of the dead comprising a multitude of beings with different characteristics.[10] However, dissecting these entities into neatly arranged categories also poses problems as this ontology is based on a certain fuzziness. During the first part of the BKPD ritual I was able to distinguish at least three kinds of beings that were addressed. The first category is constituted by ancestors, which are generally labelled either as *phu day* (dead people), or as *puutaa*, which can be translated as 'ancestor'. This category also includes the dead whose names have been forgotten, and also recently deceased relatives that are specifically addressed at their bone *stūpas*.[11] The second category of deceased consists of ghosts that have fallen into hell due to their lack of merit and are waiting for a better rebirth, but are according to Lao local cosmology on the day of BKPD released from hell and can receive food from the living. Interestingly, the Lao use the word *phed* (from Pāli *peta*) to describe them, but one more often encounters the word *phiphed*. This is a compound word merging the Pāli term with Tai-Kadai concepts of ghosts and spirits (*phi*) also found among non-Buddhist groups in this ethnolinguistic family.[12] Pottier (2007: 508) translates *phiphed* as 'phantom' and 'revenant', which describes well their coming from hell. Finally, the third category contains protective spirits that are sometimes identifiable persons that have passed away (like the *phi cau khun vat)* or the *phi dta haek*, whose shrine in the rice field is usually not associated with a person.

Ritual handbooks and books on Lao culture in Lao (which can be bought on every market in Vientiane and give short information on each rite of the yearly cycle) designate various recipients of the offerings prepared the day before the ritual. Duangmala (2003: 74) simply says that the dead, one's living relatives and the monks receive the *ho khau*. Simphon (2007: 72) is

10 Here ontology is understood as dealing with questions concerning what entities exist, and how these can be classified according to similarities, differences and positions in a hierarchy of beings.

11 These *stūpas* contain the bones of the cremated dead and are in Laos often to be found in the temple, and therefore at the centre of Lao social space (Ladwig 2002).

12 The word *phi* encompasses a multitude of spirits, also among non-Buddhist Tai-Kadai groups. This can include protective spirits of a certain place, but also malicious spirits such as the *phi phob* that feeds on people's organs and leads to illness or even death. For an overview of the Lao concepts of *phi* see Condominas (1975) and for a detailed classification of various *phi* see Pottier (2007: 15–42).

more specific and states that BKPD has two goals, the first being to honour the protective spirit of the rice field and the earth goddess, Nang Tholanee, 'who both care for the rice fields and are the lords of the land'.[13] The second goal is to give the *ho khau* to 'the souls of the ancestors, mothers, fathers and the deceased, and to those who are caught in the rebirth cycle – those who are already dead but have not yet been reborn. They come to receive the food and drink which their offspring has prepared and transfer to them' (*ibid.*). With the latter Simphon probably means the *phiphed*, which Philavong (1967: 67) and Viravong (1996: 33–4) mention more explicitly because they relate the festival to the textual background to the story of Bimbisāra.[14] Philavong (1967: 68) explains: 'the relatives of King Bimbisāra died and were born as *phed* [. . .] they fell into hell for ninety-one aeons. The *phed* who are relatives can also receive merit deriving from the offerings.' He explains the popularity of the festivals by the fact 'the Lao people really like this ritual because they take it as a day of commemoration' (*ibid.*). Lao socialist modernity has also left its mark on the interpretation of the ritual. In a book written by one of the leading monks of the Lao Buddhist Fellowship Organization – the official association of all Lao Buddhist monks founded after the Communist revolution – we find a secularised and rationalised explanation of the festival. References to ghosts, which in conversations and ritual practice are perceived as crucial elements of BKPD, are not found in this rather ideological account. The solidarity of peasant culture is pointed out, and the 'feeding of oneself, family, friends and society' (Buakham 2001: 44) is described, but the dead are completely absent in this account. The shallow remark 'that in the old [political] system there were many things that were not practiced according to the truth' (*ibid.*) might explain this conscious eradication of the traces of the dead even in rituals dedicated to them.[15]

Taking into account that the presentation of offerings to the *phed*, or *phiphed*, in the morning of the ritual has given the latter its name and is the central act of BKPD, I now want to focus on ghosts as a form of the

[13] Nang Tholanee has a substantial functional overlap with the *phi dta haek* (spirit of the ricefield) and the cult of the mother of rice (*mae phosop*). For the latter and the link to agriculture see Rajadhon (1955).

[14] More information on the textual background of the festivals follows.

[15] Adorno's and Horkheimer's (1997: 215) interesting thoughts in a text concerning this kind of modernity, 'On the theory of ghosts', fits very well here: '[. . .] the disturbed relationship with the dead – forgotten and embalmed – is one of the symptoms of the sickness of experience today'. They think that in these systems of thought the deceased's 'trace is hated as irrational, superfluous, and "overtaken" in the literal sense of the word'. The seemingly rational socialist ideology in regard to the kind of Buddhism promoted by the Lao government by and among some leading monks just seems to confirm this sceptical stance towards modernity. See also Bouté's contribution on ritual change on the influence of Lao socialist politics in this volume (Chapter 5).

deceased. First, it is crucial to elaborate on the concept of *phiphed* in Lao culture and its link to various concepts of *peta* in Pāli Buddhism. The word *peta* in Pāli usually signifies 'hungry ghost', but its uses in early Theravāda Buddhism are far from clear. The term can denote ancestor (from Sanskrit *pitṛ*), but also hungry ghost. Further discussions of this will exemplify that this double meaning is also on some level alive in the Lao expression. Historically speaking the offering to *peta* is linked to the Brahmanic ritual practice of *śrāddha*, in which the ghost as a liminal being is transformed into an ancestor. In Sri Lankan Buddhism this transformation process is ritually still fairly tangible (Langer 2007: 188).[16]

However, one must take into account that Buddhism also redefined this ancestral role and *peta* are referred to as a specific rebirth category (Holt 1981). In many sources of Theravāda Buddhism the *peta* realm is understood as one of the five (or six) realms (*gati*) in which one can be reborn. Moreover, the difference between the *peta* and the *phiphed* in popular Lao and other Southeast Asian accounts is based mainly on their location in the Buddhist cosmology. In Laos the *phiphed* are understood as hell beings that can wander the earth as revenants. The *peta* of the canonical sources and the *phiphed* also have many things in common. *Peta* and *phiphed* are ghosts that are anomalous creatures, strange and shocking in appearance, even threatening. Congruently, Lao and Thai depictions show them as tormented beings that suffer constant hunger and thirst. In the narratives and commentaries of the *Petavatthu* they are exposed to tortures often related to the misdeeds in their lives: birds pick out flesh from their bodies, they vomit constantly, are forced to eat faeces etc.[17] Because it is impossible to consume any food or drinks in their realm, the *phed* are completely dependent on humans and their provisions. Their thirst and hunger is sometimes expressed in visual depictions in which they are shown to have huge bellies and needle-like necks. The living are supposed to pity them and show charity towards them, either by directly feeding them through food offerings or by presenting gifts to the monks who then send the merit produced to them.[18]

[16] For *śrāddha* and death rituals in Hinduism see Parry's (1994: 195–6) seminal study. The genealogy of Hindu and Buddhist rituals for the dead and ghosts is a complex one and cannot be discussed here in detail.

[17] The *Petavatthu* is a collection of stories in the Khuddaka Nikaya that describe the effects of negative deeds as a rebirth of the peta realm. See Kyaw and Masefield (1980) for a translation. The story of King Bimbisāra (to be discussed later) is also part of this collection. Whereas in early Buddhist studies these stories were dismissed as a lower type of Buddhism, recently Jeff Shirkey (2008) has developed a more thorough reading of the stories beyond the simplicity of moral tales showing the workings of karma. My text is very much indebted to his reading of the material.

[18] The question of whether the monks are actually necessary intermediaries is an important one discussed later in the chapter.

THE *PHIPHED* AS VISITORS FROM HELL: TEXTUAL BACKGROUNDS OF THE FESTIVAL

From where does this image of *phiphed* as beings from hell derive? And why are they allowed to enter the realm of the humans on the day of BKPD? Let us turn to the textual backgrounds of the festival. Two narratives are mentioned frequently by Lao informants and the Lao texts dealing with the ritual. The first relates to the story of the monk Mahā Moggallāna. This story is often equated, or even mixed with, the figure of Māleyyadevatthera, which in Laos and Thailand is widely known by the local adaptation in the form of Phra Malai. The second, the story of King Bimbisāra and his encounters with the *peta*, is also crucial and will be discussed later. Let us first turn to Mahā Moggallāna and Māleyyadevatthera and consider their inclusion in the local Lao cosmology and their roles as explanatory narrative frameworks for the ritual.

Touring hell: Moggallāna and Māleyyadevatthera

Mahā Moggallāna is described as one of the chief disciples of the Buddha with extraordinary abilities acquired through meditation.[19] He uses his supernatural powers to travel through the cosmos. He surveys each location, travels to the different hells and also enters the *peta* realms. He questions the *peta* about their fate and their deeds and reports this in the world of the living. According to Louis Finot (1917: 54f.) these travels appear in Laos in localised forms in stories and manuscripts such as 'Moggallāna visits hell' or 'Moggallāna interrogates the *peta*'. In a short Lao version printed in a popular book (Simphon 2007: 73), a slightly modified story establishes a link with BKPD: Moggallāna travels to hell in order to see the creatures there, but when he arrives there are none. He asks the Chief of Hell (Yamarāja) where all the hell creatures are. Yamarāja tells Moggallāna that on the day of new moon in the ninth month he, the Lord of Hell, opens the gates so the creatures can go out and search for food and drink.[20] Moggallāna is told that some of the creatures did not receive any offerings and had to return to hell, while others received offerings and were liberated. When Moggallāna hears this, he returns to the world of humans and

[19] I cannot give a full account of Moggallāna here. His travels and life are described in various canonical sources and their local adaptations. See the paragraph on comparative potential below.

[20] Viravong (1996: 34) mentions Yama's act could be seen as analogous to 'the liberation of convicts'. Hell is here equated with a jail and Yama with a king who gives the order of a general pardon.

converses with the Buddha about this. The Buddha then reminds the believers that they have to worship the three gems, care for older people and the deceased by thinking of them and giving food to them on the day of BKPD.

According to Julie Gifford (2003: 72), Moggallāna's travels are 'intended to guide others by providing a cosmological and karmic map of saṃsāra' and he derives his popularity from his extraordinary abilities and his sainthood. What Gifford misses out on, however, is the fact that the liberation from hell associated with the Lao and Thai versions of these stories gives people the chance to feed *petas* as potential relatives, soothe their suffering and even liberate them from their existence in hell.[21] The abbot of the monastery where I observed the festival stated in an interview:

> Today the spirits are released from hell. They wander around and search for food. They come here to receive food and merit from their relatives. If there is an opportunity some of them may be reborn as humans. If there is no opportunity like this, they might be reincarnated as deities. If the relatives do not feed them, they might have to return to hell again.

I think it is important to mention that the various narratives of Moggallāna contain a comparative potential that has yet to be researched. Although the Lao and Thai versions of *Phra Malai* – a text also recited at funerals – are based on the figure of Māleyyadevatthera, they seem to have merged to a certain degree with the figure of Moggallāna due to their similar themes. The accounts of Phra Malai are more widely known than those of Moggallāna, but I think they should be discussed together and seen as a unit.[22] Both are quite popular in Southeast Asia. Moreover, the parallels with the Chinese version of Moggallāna, Mulien and the practice of filial piety, are one example. The Chinese and Vietnamese Ghost Festivals bear strong resemblances to the Lao one. Despite difference concerning ritual practice and kind of offerings – the Lao have no ghost money and don't burn offerings for them, for example – the textual references partially overlap. A Lao story (Genau and Thammamone 2000) about children who are able to liberate their parents from hell through

[21] See the next part for an explication of the status of *peta* as potential relatives that are integrated through a remembrance of kinship.

[22] Denis (1964: 66) concludes that 'It seems most likely that the descents of Phra Malai into the hells are born out of a local adaptation of the descents of Moggallāna into the hells, as encountered in Laos and Siam' and Bonnie Brereton (1995: 123f.) in her excellent study of Phra Malai comes to a similar conclusion. However, Denis (1964: 40) also acknowledges that the development of the different versions is rather complex and the transitions from South Asia to Southeast Asia are hard to trace. For further discussions see also Steven Collins' (1993) discussion of Eugene Denis' work and Anatole Peltier's (1982) study on the visual representations of Phra Malai.

donating to the monks, indeed shows Chinese characteristics and therefore could be used to work out a more comparative framework.[23]

Coming back to the Lao case, the image of *phiphed* is that of 'strange' creatures. Their physical appearance marked by mutilated bodies and their inability to consume food due to their thin mouths make them objects of pity. If we examine the status of ghosts in relation to notions of belonging, it becomes clear that *phiphed* actually do not belong to the world of the living; they are just granted the right to enter this world by Lord Yama. Moreover, this sojourn takes place in a limited time-frame. In some sense they are strangers that invade a space that is actually not their home, but then get socialised. Heonik Kwon (2008: 16) coined a term for the ghosts of war in Vietnam, 'ontological refugees', which I think can also be applied to the Lao *phiphed*: fleeing from hell, they search for food, recognition and a chance to escape into the world of the living. They are 'asylum seekers' and strangers, hoping to receive food through hospitality in the world of humans so that they can escape from hell and be reborn in another realm.[24]

But are there other strategies to socialise the *phiphed*? How is a bond with them established? The other textual basis of the BKPD might help us to understand how *peta* and *phiphed* are ritually incorporated.

Kinship with strangers: Bimbisāra

Many Lao informants relate BKPD to the narrative of King Bimbisāra (Lao: *phimbisan*), also told in the *Petavatthu*.[25] Several monks also assured me that in the past – when people had more time to attend temple services – the story was told during the festival. However this might have changed, we encounter with Bimbisāra a narrative that socialises the *phiphed* as strangers in another way. In this story a group of *peta* is told by the monk Kassapa that in one Buddha-aeon, during the time of the Buddha Śākyamuni, a king

[23] I am very much indebted to Gregory Kourilsky for the lengthy discussions we had on this topic in Laos. See his analysis of filial piety and the role of Moggallāna in Lao Buddhism and beyond (Kourilsky 2012). Moggallāna also plays an important role in Mahāyāna Buddhism: the Japanese Ghost Festival is inspired by the Ullambana Sutra describing the actions of Moggallāna. For the Chinese Ghost Festival see the seminal study by Stephen Teiser (1988) and his description of Mulien as a 'shaman' (*ibid.*: 140) saving his mother from hell. For a Tibetan version see the highly interesting account of Kapstein (2007). See also Ingmar Heise's piece in this volume (Chapter 10).

[24] The notion of hospitality, I think, is also very useful to understand the interaction of the *phiphed* and the living. See Ladwig (forthcoming) for an analysis of BKPD with a central focus on hospitality and ghosts as strangers.

[25] There are various adaptations of the Petavatthu in Lao which I have not read. The section used here, however, was told to me orally many times and does not deviate much from the ones in the canonical sources and the translation by Kyaw and Masefield (1980: 23ff.).

named Bimbisāra will dedicate offerings to them. When the moment finally arrives, Bimbisāra knows nothing of his responsibilities and gives to the Buddha without dedicating the gift to the *petas*. At night, the *petas* 'wailed in utter and dreadful distress', and the king was 'filled with fear and trembling' (Kyaw and Masefield 1980: 25). In the morning the Buddha clarifies the situation and tells Bimbisāra about his former relatives who have arisen in the *peta* realm and have been waiting for the gift for so long. Bimbisāra simply did not know about them. The Buddha makes the *petas* visible for the king and they are described as 'extremely ugly, deformed and terrible to behold' (*ibid.*). Another alms-giving is organised and through the dedication the *petas* receive abundant food, drink and clothes.

Important here is that the *peta* are relatives of Bimbisāra who have been forgotten, but are brought back to memory, identified as kin and socialised through food. The miraculous intervention of the Buddha lays bare a kinship bond that extends beyond families and village units: from the Buddha's superior perspective we actually all have kinship bonds stretching back to a very distant past. Buddhism thereby constructs an almost *infinite universe of kinship relations* of which the *peta* are one vital segment. The moral cosmos and also that of ritual obligations could be described as what Jonathan Walters (2003: 14) has called 'communal karma' or 'socio-karma'. This strategy of making kin out of others through a karmic community can be said to represent a transposition from family-centred ritual hospitality to ghosts in Hinduism (caring only for one's own *peta* relatives after death) to a universal, Buddhist one, in which every one of us has *peta* relatives.[26] This is by no means limited to the textual accounts used here, but is also visible in ritual practice. Hayashi (2003: 148), for example, points out that for the Lao living in northeast Thailand rituals in which the dead are addressed are based on rather fuzzy ideas about their afterlife as the living cannot know the post-mortem fate of their relatives, but nevertheless offer food at various rituals for them.

Coming back to the ritual practices of BKPD, we might say that the *phiphed* take on the appearance and position of strangers and liminal beings that do not belong to the world of humans. However, both stories of

[26] This construction of a kinship bond between the living and the *peta* is also elaborated in the Buddha's discourse given to Bimbisāra (Kyaw and Masefield 1980: 28–9), in which the duty of relatives is mentioned in various forms. Here it again has to be pointed out that Bimbisāra does not know about these relatives, but the Buddha states that they must not be forgotten. Also in the *Petavatthu* (Kyaw and Masefield 1980: 30) we find a further hint to this that relates to unknown kinship bonds. Here the Buddha is asked if the *śrāddha* rites of Brahmins are efficacious even when one does not have a *peta*-relative. The Buddha replies that it is impossible. Among the mass of kin, everyone *must* have relatives among the *peta*, even if they do not realise it.

Moggallāna and Bimbisāra point out that they have relatives. In the case of Moggallāna and Phra Malai the living are informed about their relatives' fate in hell and, in Lao understandings, receive a chance to help them on the day of BKPD. The *peta* are here then not real strangers, but already have a vague connection to the world of the living through Moggallāna's tours in hell. In the case of Bimbisāra this connection is made through a kinship bond that extends over a whole Buddhist aeon. The intrusion of the stranger into the world of the living and their welcome through offering food can therefore also be understood as a reminder of relationships that have been forgotten. Ghosts in that sense want to be recognised and be reminded that they were once humans as well, an expression of their longing for escaping their miserable state. This integration into the social fabric could in anthropological terms be labelled 'artificial kinship'. This kinship bond is in ritual practice primarily expressed through the offering of food.

MERIT, MATERIALITY AND FOOD

Most Buddhist rituals that expose features of care for the dead need members of the saṅgha to act as ritual intermediaries. As we have seen, however, the ritual performed at BKPD in the morning happens without the mediation of monks; the *phiphed* are fed directly. The second part of the ritual – involving a transfer of merit – requires the monks' participation. How can we then imagine this feeding of the *phiphed* and the *petas*? And given the importance of food offerings and nourishment, how is the interplay of food and merit to be understood according to textual sources and ritual practice? The literature on the transfer of merit is vast and I do not want to tackle the problem as a whole here, but I think it worth pointing out that as the prime way of communicating with the dead it might be worth reconsidering at least some aspects of the complex development of the doctrine and relating them to the ritual practice as observed in BKPD.[27]

First looking at the canonical sources, one recognises that the *Petavatthu* and its commentary contain stories in which direct giving to the *peta* without a monk fails. As we have seen, Bimbisāra forgets to dedicate the gift to his *peta* kin and the transaction only becomes successful with the help of the Buddha. In the Nanda *peta* story a husband wants to give something to the *peti* of his deceased wife directly, but this and many other stories, such as that of Culasetthi (Kyaw and Masefield 1980: 113), follow the

[27] In a very useful analysis Schmitthausen (1986: 212) traces some of these complex developments up to the *Petavatthu*. See also Bechert (1992) and Hayashi (1999) for further discussions of merit.

same line: direct gifts to *petas* are doomed to fail.[28] Given to the *peta* directly, the food offered turns to filth and the cloth into stinking rags (cf. White 1986: 201–2). However, not all sources and ritual practices are so clear on that point. Many *Petavatthu* stories seem to suggest the possibility of a direct giving of food, while the post-canonical commentaries (*Petavatthu-aṭṭhakathā*) lean more towards a transfer of merit. Langer points out that early sources expose a lack of 'unambiguous passages' in relation to the materiality of the gifts transferred, or their abstraction into a concept of merit (Langer 2007: 168). She argues that there are three possibilities when discussing the transfer of food and/or merit to the *peta* of the deceased: (1) direct giving; (2) giving to monks who act as intermediaries in a process similar to the *śrāddha* rite; and (3) merit is generated by way of offering food to monks, the fruits (*phala*) of this act to benefit the *peta* (Langer 2007: 170). Some sources of the Theravāda tradition also suggest there is a direct transfer of food, and not of merit, towards the *petas* (Gombrich 1971: 203).

In the first part of BKPD, there are only direct offerings of food by laypeople. The offering cannot therefore be understood as a kind of *dakkhiṇā*, a donation given to a holy person with reference to unhappy beings in the *peta* realm (Agasse 1978: 313), as the monks play no role here. Another interpretation found in the *Petavatthu* is based on the assumption that 'it is not the food and clothing offered by the donor that the *peta* enjoys but food and clothing that have been *miraculously transformed* through the template of the merit field so as to be effective in another level of existence' (White 1986: 209; original emphasis). The gifts to the *petas* materialise themselves in a wholly other place than the original place of offering, but in this account they are still linked to the notion of merit. Masefield, however, rejects the idea of a transfer of merit and simply states that 'this practice, wrongly referred to as transfer of merit, involves no transfer of merit whatsoever; rather, the *peta* is simply assigned the divine counterpart of the alms offered to the *saṅgha* on the *peta*'s behalf' (Masefield 2004: 310).

What one finds in the complex development of the idea of the 'transfer of merit' is a multi-vocal discourse about the possibilities of transferring material objects directly, or as the fruits (*phala*) of a meritorious act. In practice, very often all three forms mentioned by Langer are mixed up and complement each other. Although most of the Lao I know pay little attention to these more doctrinally inspired discussions, it might be worth following up on this as the objects or substances that are transferred (and/or transformed) might help us to understand the modes in which people relate

[28] I take this point from Jeff Shirkey's (2008: 216–17) reading of the *Petavatthu*.

to the dead in a more profound way.[29] It might be crucial to look at the materiality of food offerings and their roles in the ritual. Food as an offering might contain more hints to the understanding of the ritual than merit, or rather the combination of merit and food might reveal something about the nature of the relationships cultivated in the ritual.

As was discussed, we have two processes at work in BKPD. In the morning the laypeople directly present food to the *phiphed*, the ancestors, the protective spirit of the temple and later to the spirit of the rice field. At 7am a transfer of merit with the help of monks is addressing the *vinyan* ('soul') of the deceased. In the dedication prayer words such as *uthid* (dedicated to) are used; a vocabulary not employed during the ritual in the early morning.[30] If we see these transactions, as has been done in some of the previous ethnographic literature, only as a transfer of merit to a rather homogenous group of 'the dead', we would miss an essential point: some of the beings that are addressed in the ritual offering at 5am cannot actually receive merit, but have to be 'fed' directly. The Lao spirits deriving from a pre-Buddhist conception (the *phi*) are usually fed (*liang*), and to my knowledge are never receivers of merit. Whereas the *vinyan* of the deceased can receive merit, the *phiphed*, the *phi dta haek* and the *phi cau vat* are fed directly, without the intermediary role of the monks. The feeding of the ancestors taking place at the bone *stūpas* of deceased relatives can also be seen as a feeding of a *phi* residing in the *stūpa*.[31] The Lao term *liang* is used for people, animals and spirits, but it also has clear connotations of 'fostering'.[32] So we actually have only one case in which we can speak of a transfer of merit, whereas the other beings addressed in the ritual are all fed. Although these acts doubtlessly produce merit for the giver, to speak of a transfer of merit here would neglect several important aspects and could lead to an over-generalised view.

One could speculate that the focus on merit of so many previous studies is rooted in the disregard of the significance of materiality in the study of

[29] Most informants just see it as Davis (1984: 193) has described it for the two festivals among Thai-Lao of northern Thailand: 'Although the offerings are given to monks, they are thought to be used by the deceased as well.'

[30] The Lao term *uthid* derives from Pāli *uddisati* and *ādisati*, words often used for merit transfer in the *Petavatthu* and other sources relating to this practice. They can be translated as to make over, to transfer, to ascribe the merit or virtue of a gift to someone (Gehman 1923: 421).

[31] See Keyes and Anusaranasasanakiarti (1980: 17) for the idea that a bone *stūpa* actually is an ancestor shrine. Several Lao informants have also stated that it contains the spirit (*phi*) of the deceased.

[32] This is also obvious in the English etymology: 'The identification of feeding and fostering is buried in our own language: Old English 'foster' means 'food'' (Young 1971: 41). The Lao term *liang* also has strong connotations of 'care' and 'bringing up someone'.

world-renouncing religions. Why, one could ask, have the relationships between the living and the dead so often been exclusively framed in the discourse of the transfer of merit? Studies of the materiality of religion have only recently become popular. In religious studies in general, and even more so in studies on world-renouncing religions, materiality has been quite neglected. There has been a tendency to 'abstract away from the sensuous materiality of objects' (Manning and Menely 2008: 289–90) in studies of religion and the focus has often been too heavily on human agency and intentionality. Gregory Schopen's (1991) analysis of 'protestant presuppositions' in the archaeology of early Buddhism might also apply here: scholars have often looked at sources that confirmed a certain philosophical image of world-renouncing religions, but neglected the polyvocality of the textual and material sources available. Looking at the ritual practice of BKPD, the 'material evidence' is readily available. Indeed, the production and significance of food in the ritual, and the link to the agricultural cycle are, even in the urban environment of Vientiane, still visible. In Lao Buddhism, as in most of the Buddhist traditions of mainland Southeast Asia, food plays a central role in establishing relations between people, between laypeople and the saṅgha.[33] Andaya (2002: 11) points out: 'The remark that contemporary monasteries in northern Thailand seem "preoccupied" with food should equally be considered in light of a cultural heritage where communal feasting was a significant component in village life.' John Strong (1992: 51) has labelled this a 'commensal community' involving a hierarchical chain of beings not only involving humans, but also other entities like *peta*. In my opinion this relatedness constructed via food offerings among the living is therefore also valid for the relationships between the living and the *phiphed*.

It might seem that I am suggesting dividing notions of merit and food, but the interplay of merit and food could, for example, be analysed here through the notion of container or vehicle. Merit needs a container, a vehicle on which it can jump and be expressed in its materiality. O'Flaherty (1980: 10) mentions that already in the Vedas food is a 'vehicle' for merit. Hayashi (2003: 125) interestingly remarks that among the Lao in northeast Thailand merit is understood as a kind of food: 'Merit is like food. Merit nurtures oneself and others.' Food as a material object can shift between different contexts and be used for feeding several entities. Webb Keane (2006: 416) speaks of a form of 'bundling' or 'contingency' in relation to objects, because '[...] part of the power of material objects in society consists of their openness to "external" events and their resulting potential for mediating

[33] See also Wijeyewardene (1986: 36) on the role of food and emotions in Thai Buddhist culture.

the introduction of "contingency"'. They can shift across contexts and circulate in different orders of value and regimes of communication. All recipients addressed in the first ritual get the same object – the *ho khau* – but it circulates in different orders of consumption and is received by entities that, at first sight, seem to belong to the same ontological sphere (the dead), but which is made up of a multitude of beings with different needs. Some of the latter have different ways of consumption and have to be fed in particular ways. In order to make communication function, objects introduce a sort of mediation that is crucial for the upkeep of relationships. A detour in relationship building via the object as a 'floating signifier' with its openness – what Keane calls contingency – is not simply a crystallisation or reflection of relationships, but food has the capacity to 'nurture' relationships in the real sense of the term. Food as an object is needed to reinscribe the relationship into the social – a capacity that the transfer of merit alone would hardly accomplish.[34] A focus on the offerings that are given, their ways of circulation and their directionality, reveals more than the general reference to the transfer of merit.[35] I think that seeing the connection between moral agents and the 'objects' they use for establishing relationships is crucial here. Thevenot (2002: 59) remarks that 'the autonomous intentional individual is usually regarded as a prerequisite for moral agency. But it achieves such moral agency only with the support of other elements: the functional agency of objects.'

Part of this functional agency is also the sensuality of the object. Life histories, memories of people and emotions of care for the dead might be 'materialised' in food as an object. Food can act as a 'carrier object' and 'container', whereas merit on its own is less tangible and not corporeal. Here food allows for expressions of commensality and relates to Lao notions of feeding and fosterage. I believe that the efficacy of rituals such as BKPD is more often achieved through metaphors of the body and nurturing, for example, than through abstract concepts. Sutton (2001: 46–7) skilfully elaborates on the role of food in rituals linked to death, remembrance and

[34] Bruno Latour (1999: 197) therefore asks: 'Why must society work through them [artefacts] to inscribe itself in something else? Why not inscribe itself directly, since the artefacts count for nothing?' He thinks that the function of objects 'is not to mirror, congeal, crystallise, or hide social relations, but to remake these very relations through fresh und unexpected sources of action'; objects are therefore needed to reestablish relationships and regenerate them.

[35] This is also a question of methodology of research, as Appadurai's (1986: 5) idea to focus on the 'biography of things' extrapolates. Instead of looking at actors and intentionality, he proposes another point of view: 'Even though from a theoretical point of view human actors encode things with significance, from a methodological point of view it is the things-in-motion that illuminate their human and social context' (*ibid.*).

care for the dead in an exchange system that spans generations and includes the dead:

> Even the ephemeral and perishable medium of food, then, can be extended into the future through memory of the act of giving. Indeed, food may be a particularly powerful medium exactly because it internalizes the debt to the other [...] Furthermore, in carefully preparing food one is once again projecting the self, in this case the caring, nurturant self, into an external object – the food – which is meant to inscribe a memorable impression on the receiver.

What we end up with is an image of a ritual economy of food and merit that includes various kinds of the dead and aims at caring for them. In return, and following the law of reciprocity, the living receive blessings and well-being from the deceased, as exemplified by the offering prayers mentioned previously. With reference to the spirit of the rice field and the spirit of the first abbot of the monastery, the living understand these as protective spirits of places which have to be cared for as well. Specifically in relation to the *phiphed* and the narratives attached to them, we find even a higher telos of the ritual – the liberation from continuous torture and their reintegration into other realms of the Buddhist cosmos. Jeff Shirkey (2008: 327) has argued that the *Petavatthu* 'implicitly, if not explicitly, demonstrates that reintegration of *peta*-s back into an ideal Buddhist order is the soteriological goal of these ritual exchanges'. Shirkey sees a ritual economy at work here that he rightly understands as a moral economy with distributive principles aiming at the well-being of Buddhist communities. McWilliam, following Steven Gudeman's (2001: 27) analysis of markets and societies, speaks of 'spiritual commons' and defines them as the 'varieties of symbolic and religious behaviour designed to nurture and protect the well-being of a community' (McWilliam 2009: 164). I would like to suggest that the various forms of deceased and spirits addressed in the rituals I have discussed are an active part of this community and that the care for them is also a form of care of the community.

CONCLUSION

Among the ethnic Lao, the relationship with various kinds of deceased is marked by ritual exchanges in which an intensified 'care for the dead' is to be observed. Whereas most accounts frame the (re)construction of these relationships in Buddhist concepts subsumed under the notion of the 'transfer of merit', a close examination has revealed that an analysis based on concepts related to materiality and food might be more appropriate to understand this particular ritual. I have focused in my discussion largely on the *phiphed* addressed in the ritual, but have also shown that a multitude of other beings are integrated through the offering of food, mostly without the mediating role of Buddhist monks. I have argued that merit and food should be understood as a synthesis of container and contained, but I have also shown that a single focus on merit is insufficient as certain beings – all those slotted into the category of *phi* – cannot be receivers of merit, but have to be fed. Feeding (*liang*) was identified among the Lao as being linked to ideas of care and fosterage. In particular, the relationships with ghosts show that the welcome of these refugees from hell, the act of feeding and their socialisation are essential parts of the rite. Avery Gordon (2008: 8) argues that 'the ghost is not simply dead or a missing person, but a social figure'. I have tried to understand the *phiphed* as social figures as part of a larger ontology that extends beyond death. I have described them as invading strangers who are socialised to the world of the living during the rite through feeding and the reactualisation of a kinship bond.

Coming back to the statement in the introduction to this chapter about the boundary between the living and the dead as a locus of transformation and the perpetuation of being, we can now see how the interactions of the living and a heterogeneous category of the deceased are embedded into a larger ritual economy. Local adaptations of well-known Buddhist stories and characters (Bimbisāra, Moggallāna and Phra Malai) in this context remind the living of their duties towards the deceased. When they are aware of these and present offerings, the living receive protection from the deceased. As ancestors and spirits of the place they protect places and families, and as agricultural divinities, they also regenerate fertility. Moreover, a fulfilling of the responsibility towards the *phiphed* – and the investment into the ritual economy – has the soteriological goal of liberating liminal ghosts from their misery in hell. The ritual exchanges of BKPD thereby contribute to the construction of a moral universe, in which protection, fertility and compassion are intimately linked and contribute to the well-being of a community that has been understood as being fundamentally constituted by the living and the dead.

BIBLIOGRAPHY

Abhay, T. N. and Kene, T. (1958), *Buddhism in Laos*, Vientiane: The Literary Committee.

Adorno, T. W. and Horkheimer, M. (1997), 'On the theory of ghosts', in eds. T. W. Adorno and M. Horkheimer, *Dialectic of Enlightenment*, London: Verso Books.

Agasse, J.-M. (1978), 'Le transfert de mérite dans le Bouddhisme Pāli classique', *Journal Asiatique* 3–4, 311–32.

Andaya, B. W. (2002), 'Localising the universal: women, motherhood and the appeal of early Theravāda Buddhism', *Journal of Southeast Asian Studies* 33(1), 1–30.

Appadurai, A. (1986), 'Introduction: commodities and the politics of value', in ed. Arjun Appadurai, *The Social Life of Things. Commodities in Cultural Perspective*, New York: Cambridge University Press.

Archaimbault, C. (1973), *Structures Religieuses Lao (Rites et Mythes)*, Vientiane: Vithagna.

Barraud, C., De Coppet, D., Iteanu, A. and Jamous, R. (1994), *Of Relations and the Dead: Four Societies Viewed from the Angle of Their Exchanges*, Oxford: Berg.

Bechert, H. (1992), 'Buddha-field and transfer of merit in a Theravāda source', *Indo-Iranian Journal* 35, 95–108.

Bloch, M. and Parry, J. (1982), 'Introduction', in eds. M. Bloch and J. Parry, *Death and the Regeneration of Life*, Cambridge University Press.

Brereton, B. P. (1995), *Thai Telling of Phra Malai: Texts and Rituals Concerning a Popular Buddhist Saint*, Tempe: Arizona State University Program for Southeast Asian Studies.

Buakham, S. M. (2001), *Preachings of 108 Anisong*, Vientiane [in Lao].

Choulean, A. (2006), 'Vom Brahmanismus zum Buddhismus: Betrachtungen zum Totenfest in Kambodscha', in ed. Wibke Lobo, *Angkor: Göttliches Erbe Kambodschas*, Berlin: Priestel Verlag.

Collins, S. (1993), 'The story of the Elder Māleyya', *Journal of the Pāli Text Society* 18, 65–96.

Condominas, G. (1975), 'Phiban cults in rural Laos', in eds. W. Skinner and T. Kirsch, *Change and Persistence in Thai Society*, Ithaca, NY: Cornell University Press.

Davis, R. (1984), *Muang Metaphysics: a Study of Northern Thai Myth and Ritual*, Bangkok: Silkworm Press.

Denis, E. (1964), *Brah Maleyyadevatheravatthum: Legende Bouddhiste du Saint Thera Maleyyadeva*, unpublished PhD thesis, Paris: Sorbonne.

Duangmala, C. (2003), *Culture and Lao Traditions*, Vientiane [in Lao].

Finot, L. (1917), 'Recherches sur la litterature laotienne', *Bulletin de l'École Française d'Extrême-Orient* 17 (5), 5–224.

Gehman, H. S. (1923), 'Ādisati, Anvādisati, Anudisati, and Uddisati in the Peta-Vatthu', *Journal of the American Oriental Society* 43, 410–21.

Genau, G. and Thamamone, B. (2000), *Drei Palmblätter aus dem Tempel Sayaphum gestatten Einblicke in den 'Laotischen Volksbuddhismus'*, Düsseldorf: private publisher.

Gifford, J. (2003), 'The insight guide to hell: Mahā Moggallāna and Theravāda Buddhist cosmology', in eds. John Holt, Jacob Kinnard and Jonathan Walters, *Constituting Communities: Theravāda Buddhism and the Religious Cultures of South and Southeast Asia*, Albany, NY: State University of New York Press.

Gombrich, R. (1971), 'Merit transference in Sinhalese Buddhism', *History of Religions* 11, 203–19.

Gordon, A. F. (2008), *Ghostly Matters: Haunting and the Sociological Imagination*, Minneapolis, MN: University of Minnesota Press.

Gudeman, S. (2001), *The Anthropology of Economy: Community, Market and Culture*, Oxford: Blackwell.

Hayashi, T. (1999), 'Preliminary notes on merit transfer in Theravāda Buddhism', *Ronshu: Studies in Religions East and West* **26**, 29–55.

Hayashi, Y. (2003), *Practical Buddhism among the Thai-Lao: Religion in the Making of a Region*, Kyoto University Press.

Hertz, R. (1960), 'A contribution to the study of the collective representation of death', in eds. R. Needham and C. Needham, *Death and the Right Hand*, New York: Free Press.

Holt, J. C. (1981), 'Assisting the dead by venerating the living: merit transfer in the early Buddhist tradition', *Numen* **28** (1), 1–28.

Kapstein, M. T. (2007), 'Mulian in the land of snows and King Gesar in hell: a Chinese tale of parental death in its Tibetan transformations', in eds. B. Cuevas and J. Stone, *The Buddhist Dead: Practices, Discourses, Representations*, Honolulu: University of Hawai'i Press, 345–77.

Keane, W. (2006), 'Subject and object', in eds. C. Tilley, W. Keane S. Kuechler-Fogden, M. Rowlands and P. Spyer, *Handbook of Material Culture*, London: Sage Publications.

Keyes C. and Anusaranasasanakiarti, P. (1980), 'Funerary rites and the Buddhist meaning of death: an interpretative text from northern Thailand', *Journal of the Siam Society* **68** (1), 1–28.

Kourilsky, G. (2008), 'Note sur la piété filiale en Asie du Sud-Est theravādin: la notion de guṇ', *Aséanie: Sciences Humaines en Asie du Sud-Est* **20**, 27–54.

(2012), *Parents et Ancêtres en Milieu Bouddhiste Lao: Étude de Textes Choisis et de Leurs Applications Rituelles*, PhD thesis, École Pratique des Hautes Études, Paris.

Kwon, H. (2008), *Ghosts of War in Vietnam*, Cambridge University Press.

Kyaw, U. and Masefield, P. (1980), *Elucidation of the Intrinsic Meaning so named the Commentary on the Peta-Stories by Dhammapāla*, London: Pāli Text Society.

Ladwig, P. (2002), 'The mimetic "representation" of the dead and social space among the Buddhist Lao', *Tai Culture: International Review on Tai Cultural Studies* 7 (2), 120–34.

(forthcoming), 'Visitors from hell: hospitality to ghosts in a Lao Buddhist festival', *Journal of the Royal Anthropological Institute*.

Lambek, M. (1996), 'Afterword: spirits and their histories', in eds. J. M. Mageo, A. Howard and R. Levy, *Spirits in Culture, History, and Mind*, London: Routledge, 237–50.

Langer, R. (2007), *Buddhist Rituals of Death and Rebirth: Contemporary Sri Lankan Practice and its Origins*, Abingdon and New York: Routledge.

Latour, B. (1999), *Pandora's Hope: Essays on the Reality of Science Studies*, Cambridge, MA: Harvard University Press.

Manning, P. and Meneley, A. (2008), 'Material objects in cosmological worlds: an introduction', *Ethnos* 73 (3), 285–302.

Masefield, P. (2004), 'Ghost festival', in ed. Robert Buswell, *Encyclopaedia of Buddhism*, New York: Macmillan Reference, 307–10.

McDaniel, J. (2008), *Gathering Leaves and Lifting Words: Histories of Buddhist Monastic Education in Laos and Thailand*, Seattle, WA: University of Washington Press.

McWilliam, A. (2009), 'The spiritual commons: some immaterial aspects of community economies in eastern Indonesia', *The Australian Journal of Anthropology* **20** (2), 163–77.

Nginn, P. S. (1961), *Les Fêtes Profanes et Religieuses au Laos*, Vientiane: Literary Committee.

O'Flaherty, W. D. (1980), 'Karma and rebirth in the Vedas and Puranas', *Karma and Rebirth in Classical Indian Traditions*, in ed. W. D. O'Flaherty, Berkeley, CA: University of California Press.

Parry, J. (1994), *Death in Benares*, Cambridge University Press.

Peltier, A. (1982), 'Iconographie de la légende de Brah Malay', *Bulletin de l'École Française d'Extrême-Orient* **71**, 63–76.

Philavong, P. (1967), *Costumes, Rites and Worthy Traditions of the Lao People*, Vientiane [in Lao].

Porée-Maspero, E. (1950), *Cérémonies des Douze Mois: Fêtes Annuelles Cambodgiennes*, Phnom Penh: Institute Bouddhique.

Pottier, R. (2007), *Yû dî mî hèng, Etre Bien, Avoir de la Force: Essai sur les Pratiques Thérapeutiques Lao*, Paris: École Française d'Extrême-Orient.

Premchit, S. and Doré, A. (1992), *The Lanna Twelve Months Traditions*, Chiang Mai.

Rajadhon, A. (1955), 'Me Posop, the Rice Mother', *Journal of the Siam Society* **43** (1), 55–61.

Rozenberg, G. (2005), 'Anthropology and the Buddhological Imagination: Reconstructing the Invisible Life of Texts', *Aséanie: Sciences Humaines en Asie du Sud-Est* **16**, 41–60.

Schmitthausen, L. (1986), 'Critical response', in ed. R. Neufeldt, *Karma and Rebirth*. Albany, NY: State University of New York Press.

Schopen, G. (1991), 'Archaeology and protestant presuppositions in the study of Indian Buddhism', *History of Religions*, **31** (1), 1–23.

Shirkey, J. C. (2008), *The Moral Economy of the Petavatthu: Hungry Ghosts and Theravāda Buddhist Cosmology*, unpublished PhD thesis, University of Chicago.

Simphon, R. (2007), *Handbook for Making Merit according to Lao Culture*, Vientiane [in Lao].

Strong, J. S. (1992), *The Legend and Cult of Upagupta: Sanskrit Buddhism in North India and Southeast Asia*, Princeton, NJ: Princeton University Press.

Sutton, D. (2001), *Remembrance of Repasts: an Anthropology of Food and Memory*, New York: Berg.

Tambiah, S. J. (1970), *Buddhism and the Spirit Cults in North-east Thailand*, Cambridge University Press.

Teiser, S. (1988), *The Ghost Festival in Medieval China*, Princeton, NJ: Princeton University Press.

Thevenot, L. (2002), 'Which road to follow? The moral complexity of an "equipped" humanity', in eds. John Law and Annemarie Mol, *Complexities: Social Studies of Knowledge Practices* Durham and London: Duke University Press.

Viravong, M. (1996), *The Twelve Rituals*. Vientiane: National Library [in Lao].

Walters, J. (2003), 'Communal karma and karmic community in Theravāda Buddhist history', in eds. J. Holt, J. Kinnard and J. Walters, *Constituting Communities: Theravāda Buddhism and the Religious Cultures of South and Southeast Asia*. Albany, NY: State University of New York Press.

White, D. (1986), 'Dakkhina and agnicayana: an extended application of Paul Mus's typology', *History of Religions* **26**, 188–213.

Wijeyewardene, G. (1986), *Place and Emotion in Northern Thai Ritual Behaviour*. Bangkok: Pandora.

Young, M. (1971), *Fighting with Food. Leadership, Values and Social Control in a Massim Society*, Cambridge University Press.

Zago, M. (1972), *Rites et Cérémonies en Milieu Bouddhiste Lao*. Rome: Università Gregoriana.

CHAPTER 7

Funeral rituals, bad death and the protection of social space among the Arakanese (Burma)

Alexandra de Mersan

INTRODUCTION

Data presented in this article is based on fieldwork conducted between 1998 and 2001 at Mrauk U, the ancient capital of the former Buddhist Kingdom of Arakan, now a Burmese state.[1] Thus hypotheses were developed neither in response to pre-existent questions, nor in relation to Buddhist texts or dogma; rather my first aim has been to understand the meaning of mortuary ritual in this Burmese Buddhist society starting with this ethnographic data, describing 'the Buddhism at the village' (Condominas [1968] 1998). Funerals resulting from 'normal' death are detailed and analysed, and are compared with those associated with bad death. Funerals governed by village rules (*gama paññat*) constitute the most prominent manifestation of the village as a social unit, showing the value of good neighbourly relations in this society devoid of ancestor or founder cults. In this aspect, as shown by Hertz, death is eminently a social fact (Hertz 1928). Members of this local society, part of wider Burma, redefine their living space through ritual practices (as seen here in funerary ritual) and this constitutes one of their peculiarities.

Gama paññat

Mrauk U is a small town located in the fertile plains between the Kaladan and Lemro rivers. A river and its different tributaries or arms divides the town into a number of small 'islands' or quarters. Each quarter is like a village (*rva*), and is sometimes called so. Villagers live under a set of customary rules named *gama paññat*, which literally means 'ruling

As a token of my gratitude, this article is dedicated to the memory of Sara Gri U Kyaw Kyaw Hla, thanks to whom everything began. I would also like to express many thanks to U Shwe Maung Tha and gratitude to Natacha Collomb who read this article and provided her useful comments.

[1] See details in my PhD dissertation, de Mersan (2005: 108–53).

the village'.[2] These prescriptive and proscriptive rules, to my knowledge unwritten, are known to everybody and indicate social and moral conduct appropriate to the welfare of the village, and thus define the village as a social unit.[3] They govern participation in many aspects of social life including questions relative to funerals such as delivering the authorisation for a funeral procession to pass through a quarter other than that of the deceased.

It was precisely while studying funerals that I first heard of the expression *gama paññat*, which is due to the importance of the rules pertaining to the treatment of death, a particularly threatening event concerning all the inhabitants. *Gama paññat* are about preventing risk, misfortunes or danger, and repairing damages. Not following or breaking the rules (*khyui: phok*) affects the village causing it to 'suffer' (*rva na*). In May 1999, the death by drowning of a young man quickly caused a surge of anxiety among residents. It was then decided to carry out a ceremony to expel the evil. But the headman of the quarter delayed his decision on fixing the date. Persistent fevers among several children including the headman's own nephews ended his reticence. A ceremony was then performed involving every house in the quarter.[4] In this case, as it appears, the wholeness of the village was at stake.

Many *gama paññat* have been told to me without my being able to say how rigorously these normative rules are observed. A number of them will be provided in the description of funerals.

CORPORAL COMPONENTS

Although there is a 'classical conception' of the human body, inherited from India, made up of five elements, or *dhat* (earth, fire, water, wind and space, this latter keeping all the others in motion), rites observed in the cycle of life deal with other components, which seem to refer to a different conception of the person.[5] They are primarily the body or corporeal part or material envelope (*kon*) and the *lippra* (romanised for English readers as 'leip-bya',

[2] The expression is composed from Pāli-derived terms: *gama* is the 'village' and *paññat* means 'to prohibit, to regulate, to make rules in the name of a civil or religious law' (my translation; D. Bernot 1978–92, f.9: 187). Romanisation of Arakanese and Burmese terms follows the Library of Congress. However, for technical reasons, some diacritics are omitted.

[3] Some written texts describing rites and observances in case of violent death among the Lao are similar to a certain extent to what is said in Arakan (especially rules concerning death by drowning and those indicating the limits of the village). See the translation of *Mula kut* in Archaimbault (1963, vol. II). It raises the hope of finding similar texts in Arakan or elsewhere in Burma in the future, which could constitute a common corpus with Theravāda societies.

[4] 'House' means members of a family living in the same compound.

[5] See Macdonald (1979 [1879]: 21–2). This conception is found mostly in traditional medicine but is also linked to astrological practices.

'leippya'), the 'immaterial component of a person' (Brac de la Perrière (1989), my translation): usually translated as butterfly [*lippra*]-spirit by anglo-saxon writers.[6]

The *lippra* is at the same time an identification and animation principle. Several authors have pointed out this fragile relationship between the body and the *lippra*. This component evolves throughout the life of a person. A newly born baby's *lippra* must be treated by the traditional one-week-long birth-fire, which is said to warm it (L. Bernot 1967: 514). A child's *lippra* is supposed to be more tender, fragile and volatile (*lippra nu/nay*). The *lippra* can temporarily leave its support, the body, specifically when a person is sleeping (Shway Yoe 1963: 391, ch. XL). It can also be captured by malevolent spirits or insects (L. Bernot 1967: 515).

The *lippra*'s prolonged absence from the body can provoke illness and even death. It leaves the possibility of a bad spirit entering the body, taking its place and becoming the spirit, which governs a person's body.[7] The removing of the *lippra* implies a loss of consciousness. *Lippra* as a life-principle is thus also a principle of consciousness and reason (in the sense of the ability to act and evaluate one's own activity). This idea is also illustrated by the fact that the corporal envelope (*kon*) means 'material body whether animate or not', 'a physical person' but also 'an animal', 'a being'. The Arakanese also use the Pāli term *wiññañ* (*viññāṇa*) which means 'consciousness', 'mind', 'soul', 'spirit' and 'life' as a synonym to or associated with *lippra*.[8] In this chapter, I shall show that rites are conducted in order to bring the deceased person – meaning his or her physical remains and life-principle (*lippra*) – out of the domestic and village space so that the 'karmic' progression can be accomplished.

Bernot has shown the link between cotton threads seen as 'clothes of thread' and *lippra* in the life-cycle of the Marma (Arakanese; see L. Bernot 1967: 413–15). As he demonstrated, threads (*krui:*) that will encircle different parts of the body temporarily have a simultaneously protective, economic, religious and aesthetic purpose.[9] They are always 'a protective sign, a

6 See Shway Yoe (1963: 390–5), Temple (1906: 10). It is also translated as 'soul', see Spiro (1967: 33–4, 69–70). For this article, I also used French sources: Brac de la Perrière (1989: 91–4, 2001: 236, n. 4), L. Bernot (1967: 412–15, 514–15) and Robinne (2000: ch. V). See also Chapter 8 by Robinne in the present volume.

7 This is fully described and analysed in Brac de la Perrière's works on possession cults among the Burmese, (1989: 91–2) and (2001).

8 Tambiah has compared the different meanings of these terms among the Burmese and the Thai (1970: 57–9, 191–4). Lack of data for Arakan does not allow this comparison.

9 The word *krui:* is always used in these cases although it can also be a large piece of cotton, as for the mother after giving birth.

socialisation, the recognition of a new state' (L. Bernot 1967: 415, my translation). Thread, depending on interpretations, is the *lippra*'s support, symbolises it or materialises it (Brac de la Perrière 1989: 92, my translation). Depending also on the context, thread can erect a barrier (separate) or conduct.

DEATH IN BUDDHIST SOCIETY

How Buddhist is death? Two aspects stand out: the type of death (ordinary or 'green') and the status of the deceased. Although there is a link between them, I will mostly consider the former after saying a few words on the question of the person's status.

The funerary rites of a Buddhist monk can be distinguished from those of a layman, and, among the latter, differences in rites and sequences indicate the relative social position, prestige (cf. *oja/ana*) and spiritual powers of the deceased.[10] Social position depends on material welfare and on family pedigree (*myui: rui:*, see below), but also on redistributive ability and on the capacity to behave and live with others in accordance with rules and values inherited from Buddhism. Those are based on self-control, gift-making, non-attachment, absence of desire and so on. The social status also depends on *karma*, based on merit accumulated throughout their entire life and on respect for Buddhist precepts (*sīla*). Briefly put, the higher the spiritual accomplishment, the more sumptuous, happier and longer the funeral, as is the case with monks. People insist on the importance of behaving according to the Buddhist moral code and to *gama paññat*, even if it is sometimes difficult to say where one or the other of them originated. Some rules (*gama paññat*) and texts mention differences of treatment during funerals according to the deceased's life-cycle stage and sex.[11] These indicators are linked with karmic progression but my data on the subject are incomplete.

I shall now return to my former question: apart from the fact that only death in the life-cycle requires the participation of Buddhist monks, 'Is death Buddhist?' There is a kind of ideal death or ordinary death, which is

[10] *Oja* as opposed to a kind of coercive power (*ana*) has been developed in the context of Burma in general. Also *oja* ('influence, prestige') has to be linked with spiritual powers *bhun* and *tan khui:*, (see M. Nash 1965: 76–93; Schober 1989: 103–7, 120–36; Houtman 1999: ch. 6). See also Brac de la Perrière (2001). On monks' funerals see among many references, Hla Pe (2004: 153–60).

[11] See the writings of the Arakanese monk Venerable Cakkinda (1969: 34–6). On the question of sex, see also L. Bernot (1967: 571) and Lewin (1869).

illustrated in the very last moments before dying.[12] Discourses oppose a quiet, peaceful death to an agitated one. Indeed a person who is dying without expressing suffering, who can maintain self-control until the very last moment, thinking or meditating about the Buddha and taking refuge in the Three Jewels, is considered to have followed the precepts of Buddhist morality or practised meditation regularly. This person then behaves according to the Buddhist notion of non-attachment. Some say that if someone thinks about an animal, for example, at this moment, he may be reborn as such in his next life.

It is sometimes said that a person is dying because he or she has decided so and has chosen to leave, or has preferred not to be accompanied in death by other members of the family (*khyan tha kha re*).

Here then is the 'ideal Buddhist death' or 'ordinary death' (*rui: rui: se khran:*) as opposed to a sudden, violent or accidental one, known as a *a cim: se:*, a 'green death' or 'unripe death'. The terminology is explicit. Indeed, the word *cim:* means (1) to be green, unripe (for plants); (2) to be raw. Obviously, the term suggests a shortened or not fully accomplished life. Literally, 'to be raw' means 'unprepared', but is also used for a stranger. One can meet someone, see and know him by sight but this person will be considered 'raw', until introduced by a third party who indicates his name, occupation, the reason for his presence and so on. Then, the stranger is 'cooked' or 'known'. In this case, it has a positive connotation. Syntactically *a cim: se:* suggests both precocious death and the notion of a stranger. Indeed the word 'stranger' (*cim: su*) is composed from *cim:*. Someone who died a sudden death or who died away from home, which often comes to the same thing, is then considered a stranger to his village or house.

This is exemplified when women die in childbirth or just before, as well as their baby (Foley 1835: 90–3 and L. Bernot 1967: 511–14). In this case, it is important to separate them physically, the child being inhumed outside the village (on the other side of the river) because he is a stranger and can even be qualified as a monster (*bhilu:*) who devoured the woman from inside. The newborn does not belong to the village until it has been integrated by the proper rites. Funerary rites and ceremonies depend also on where death occurred. Several *gama paññat* indicate how the corpse should be transferred to the cemetery according to the place of death. For example, in Mrauk U, if a person dies at the hospital, the corpse must be carried by boat on the river and not on a 'government road' and should be laid on a mortuary bed in front of its house.

[12] The same preoccupation occurs in Sri Lanka with recitation of some verse (*pirit*, see *parit* in Burmese) at this 'vulnerable moment', see R. Langer (2007: 14–23).

Someone who dies a 'green' death has to be buried as quickly as possible or at least wait unburied at the cemetery. To have the deceased brought back home would endanger the lives of the inhabitants. In this case, the corpse also has to be transferred to the cemetery by water on a pirogue. These rules seem to concern more specifically those who die in the water, a common cause of 'green' death in Arakan.

FUNERALS (*ASUBHA*)[13]

The Arakanese bury or cremate their dead depending on their wealth. Cremation is more valued but more expensive. Nevertheless, in Mrauk U this only provides a partial explanation, as poor people are sometimes cremated with old tyres, which is cheap. Some categories of people are never cremated: victims of 'green' death – of murder, suicide or drowning – and people with goitre or affected by elephantiasis. In these two latter cases the excrescence is supposed to be full of water.

I will base my description here on a ritual observed in May 1998, completed by later observations and explanations given by inhabitants or found mainly in Arakanese texts. Daw Kra Khyac Phru died at home of old age at seventy-five. The woman's funeral was important both in terms of the number of people coming to pay their respects at her home and accompanying her to the cemetery, and of the money spent (for her catafalque, offerings to the monks and so on). Her father had been headman of a village about 10 km from Mrauk U before the second world war. Although the woman had left her former village forty years earlier and settled in Mrauk U, and although the village headman system had been suppressed after Burma gained independence, it was explained to me that people still remembered her father's position. This was why many people attended the funerals. In addition the woman had fourteen grandchildren and as many great-grandchildren. Funerals usually last three days, except when family members live far away, the rule being that the corpse should be conserved for an uneven number of days. As soon as the dying person breathes his last (*a sak*), the eyes and mouth are closed and the body is washed and dressed in fresh or new clothes. The washing of the body initiates a new status for the dead person because from this moment on, things and movements are supposed to be reversed with regards to what is

[13] *Asubha* is made up of *a* privative + *subha*, a Pāli word which means 'impure, unpleasant, bad, ugly … ' (Rhys-Davids and Stede 1997 [1921–5]: 89). Funerals are inauspicious (*amangala)*.

done in daily life.[14] For example, in this case the blouse is worn back to front.

The body is covered with a cotton cloth or shroud, leaving the face free. A coin (or even a betel leaf) is placed in the dead person's mouth. This is required to pay to cross the river in order to leave the human world (*lu praññ*). It is called the 'tax for the ferry' (*ka/ku tui kha*).[15] The two big toes are then tied together with strip of white cotton cloth called 'the thread of toes'. Sometimes the mouth and nose are obstructed with a piece of cotton or something else (i.e. leaves) in order to preserve the body and prevent the spread of unpleasant smells.

The corpse, laid on its back on a cloth on a 'bed' (*khat*) – with a post at each corner – covered by a mosquito net, is thus exposed during several days.[16] The corpse is laid out in the guest or reception room, which is also where the Buddha altar is located, with the head oriented towards it and the feet pointing towards the house's entrance. This is the usual position for people when sleeping.

A silver bowl is set on a small table beside the bed for the visitors to toss bank notes into (e.g. 200 kyats, 10 kyats). This money will be donated to the monastery.

When someone has died, the house doors and windows are opened and friends, neighbours and family are informed. A collection is organised in the quarter by a neighbour who goes from house to house asking for money for the funeral (*asubha ca rit*). Participation in the funeral expenses is a social obligation (*gama paññat*) whatever the sum given. In the street in front of the house a notice details the identity of the deceased, age, date of death and the day and time of the cemetery burial. Throughout this period the deceased stays in the house. A loudspeaker or a band of musicians (neighbours) relays songs day and night interrupted only by inaudible prayers.

Outside in the street, in front of the house, a group of men (neighbours, members of the family) build a temporary bamboo pavilion to shelter guests and visitors on the day of the burial. Another group of men prepare the coffin (*khon:*) and the catafalque. Three words are used for this: first is *ta la:*, defined in Burmese dictionaries as a coffin.[17] Second is *ma sa tham: can*, which is the

[14] This point is common to Burmese and many other groups, (see L. Bernot 1967: 559, 580–1 and F. Robinne 2000: 142).

[15] *Kha* in general, more than a tax, is a payment; a consideration for services rendered.

[16] Except *kon*, already mentioned, another word for the physical part of the body is *alon*, which indicates a transitory state, in progress. The deceased is also called *ma sa*, literally 'the unpleasant'.

[17] Alternatively, 'any receptacle in which a corpse is placed to receive funeral rites' (Judson 1953: 473). Ferrars and Ferrars (1901: 193–6) mention the same name with the same use as in Arakan. In general, description of Burmese funerals at the beginning of the twentieth century is similar in many points to what is described here for an Arakanese one.

palanquin or the 'hand-barrow for the unpleasant' (see Judson 1953: 517). This expression is commonly used when people carry the corpse to the cemetery. Finally the last word is *mran: phon* or *phon* alone, which means 'barge'.[18] This can be a simple bamboo structure decorated with tinsel-paper carried on the shoulders, with one or two stepped tiers. It can also be more elaborate and decorated, higher, with a multi-tiered roof (three, five or seven tiers, or even nine when reserved for monks, and named *prasad*), with a pyramidal form and mounted on a wheeled cart, as in the present case. These are a material indication of the degree of the deceased's spiritual accomplishment, the expression of social recognition. The front of the cart represents the head of a bird, a *karaveik*. The craftsmen who make these are *sangaja*, a term not found in dictionaries. However, this occupation is despised, as is that of the gravedigger and others connected with death.[19]

PLACING THE CORPSE IN THE COFFIN

As soon as the coffin is ready, a short ceremony is organised inside the house to place the body in it (*khon: svan re*). A monk arrives and sits under the Buddha's altar. The coffin is brought inside the house by the same main entrance and put on the floor. It is opened; and charcoal and then lime are put inside. If all the doors to the house are not opened yet, they are opened now, and the women pay homage to the deceased by prostrating themselves (*rhi khui:*). The body with the cloth is lifted up and placed in the coffin. A white strip of cotton is also put inside before the coffin is closed (see below). The face can be seen through a small window. The coffin is put on the bed under the mosquito net decorated with fresh flowers. Then the monk recites some short Pāli verses for less than ten minutes, and leaves. Until the time comes to carry the corpse to the cemetery, friends and neighbours come to exchange condolences. They enter the house, sometimes prostrate themselves in front of the coffin, then look at the face and put money in the bowl. Some crumple a betel leaf, rubbing it lightly on themselves and then throw the leaf on the coffin (*kan: pvan: tuik/kuin*, see below).[20] They sit for a short while and talk with the women of the family in the room (often a daughter, or granddaughter), after which they leave or

[18] Literally 'the horse barge'. Judson (1953: 786) defines it as 'a Burmese bier'.

[19] This is similar to the *sandalas* and the *thubayazas* mentioned by Maung Tha Kin (1922: 142), and by Shway Yoe (1963: 594), who qualifies them as 'outcasts'.

[20] This is done on several occasions during the life-cycle.

lend their help. The days of preparation are spent in this way while relatives arrive from the surrounding villages and from more distant towns.

A monk may be invited every night to recite a Buddhist verse (called *ñña va*).[21] Evenings spent watching the dead are pretty noisy and animated in the compound of the house. They are similar to ones organised in other key moments in life (noviciate, wedding ceremonies), when neighbours and friends watch over the person concerned, in this case the deceased, who is never left alone. Some neighbours and relatives cook while others play cards and gamble the whole night.

THE DAY OF THE CEMETERY

An 'offering of the law' (*tara: pve)* – usual gifts for a ceremony performed by monks – made of a coconut with its stem, bananas, paddy and betel quid, is installed near the coffin.[22] There is also a reel of white cotton. Near this bowl of offerings, there are also some fresh flowers, an apple and a cup of water with instant coffee, the latter representing the deceased's breakfast. These items, nice things that she liked (and which also indicate that she belonged to a wealthy family) are offered to her as a final meal. While waiting for the monks, five or six women prepare hundreds of betel quids, which will be given to participants before and at the cemetery.

FILLING THE ALMS BOWL

Around 10:30, a monk arrives and sits near the coffin under the Buddha's altar for his lunch offering. This is specially made when there is a funeral and called 'filling up the alms bowl of food for monks' (*sa pit phraññ. chvam:*). Those taking part then pay homage to him by prostrating themselves. The deceased woman's brother places food inside the monk's bowl and two apples on its lid. The monk then recites a protective formula, which is also an exorcism (*parit*).[23] It ends with a pouring of water (*re cak khya*), a regular performance at all almsgivings testifying to the performance of a good deed

[21] The monk Siri Okkantha (1990: 157) writes that 'yamaka' and 'pathana' from the Abhidhammapiṭaka are recited. 'The lay-people come to listen to the teaching of the master, take practice of Asubha Kamathâna (contemplation of loathsomeness of the body)'.

[22] There should be two hands of bananas – instead of the usual three – and also an even number of betel leaves.

[23] *Parit*, from the Pāli *paritta*, is a kind of prayer, used to ward off evil, being an extract from 'suttam pitakat', Judson (1953: 624). They are often recited by monks on different occasions and belong to a more powerful set of eleven (*parit kri: chay tac sut*) and four lesser ones *(parit khye*). See de Mersan (2005: 495–6), also Spiro (1970: 264–9) and Tambiah (1970: 199–222).

and the sharing of merit.[24] This offering is thus an occasion to earn merit even though the intention is to obtain it for the deceased.

SEPARATING THE *LIPPRA*

When children and grandchildren arrive inside the house, an elder sister of the deceased (or another elderly member of the family) performs a rite that separates the butterfly-spirit of the living from that of the deceased. She takes the reel that was placed inside the offering, hooks one end around the right big toe, unreeling it until it reaches the top of the head, breaks the thread, winds it up, passes it over the face three times with a circular movement in front of the mosquito net and then throws the thread on the coffin. It is said that 'life is asked to leave and the *lippra* are separated' (*khre krui: nai. asak kui tuin pri: lippra khvai te*). By so doing, it means metaphorically that ties are cut. By doing so, children in particular who are supposed to have a fragile *lippra* should not be bothered by the deceased's *lippra*, which also will leave the house more easily. Outside preparations are nearly complete, and people are slowly arriving and waiting under the temporary pavilion or in the shadow of a tree. While small prayer booklets with Buddhist verses, usually one of the eleven protective verses, are distributed among them, in the house the women finish dressing.[25]

DEPARTURE TO THE CEMETERY

Then, at around 1:00 pm, everything accelerates. A son of the deceased takes the offerings for the monks and the pan with offerings (*tara: pve*) prepared earlier in the mourning house. The posts of the mortuary bed are broken. The mosquito net, flowers and the mat on which the coffin was placed are wrapped up. Everything will be deposited at the monastery. Men (mostly sons) quickly carry the coffin out of the house by the usual stairs. An old woman follows, sprinkling water on the bed, the floor and the stairs. In two or three minutes everything is packed up and cleaned. It is important (although I never saw it) to turn a scale upside down so that the deceased will not find the way back. Emotion at this moment is at its height and several relatives are crying loudly with grief.

[24] The libation refers to a famous episode in the life of the Buddha, just before Illumination when the goddess of the earth, Wasundhare, testifies of his good deeds which then puts Māra's army to flight (See Raymond 1998).

[25] The verses are as *mettā bhāvanā*, or in this case *dharana parit*.

The coffin is placed on the wheeled cart (*phon*), with the feet in front. It is tied down and the catafalque is closed. Whether the *tala:* is brought to the cemetery by cart or on men's shoulders (young men of the village, neighbours, sons or other relatives), there is a rule always strictly observed not to put the coffin on the ground between the house and the cemetery.

THE PROCESSION

A two-hundred-metre long rope has been fixed to both sides of the front of the catafalque. People spread out along it and take it in their hand. The cord delimits thus a long closed space and people stand outside it. Mostly women carry it, the eldest woman in the family being at the head. Sometimes people will only carry it for a short distance. The procession then starts to move. At its head come the offerings intended for the monk, followed by the deceased's eldest son, then the cart pulled by the women and behind them the men and monks. There are no explicit rules concerning the order in the procession (i.e. an order indicating social rank in the society), but the monks always walk behind the cart. Cars are following those on foot.

The procession starts, and the son of the deceased throws puffed rice mixed with small sweets or presents along its path. The children of the quarter throw themselves at the latter. It is said here that the procession sets a 'golden and silver way' (*rvhe lam: nve lam: khan: re*) or that it provides a 'ride on a peaceful road for the dead body'.[26]

THE CEMETERY

The cemetery is in the northwest part of Mrauk U aside from the houses. There is a small roofed area on the top of a hillock where ceremonies take place. It is surrounded by uncleared ground on which are scattered a few small tombstones hidden in the vegetation. Except for these, there is usually nothing to mark a grave's position for future years. The cemetery is reached after about fifteen minutes, the coffin is placed under the roofed area, with the head to the east, facing the monks. The brightly coloured catafalque is thrown on the ground where it is left to decay. Only its decorative bird's head will be recovered by the *sangaja*. While the crowd gradually takes places on mats under the roof, the monks are seated on a bench, and the women of the family distribute prayer booklets, sweets, ice-cream and betel to the mourners, and drinks to the monks. The son of the brother of the deceased opens the

[26] Note *khan:* in this expression, which means 'to set out in order'.

coffin and cuts 'the thread of toes' with a razor blade, which is then deposited in the coffin. This rite is important as it is a preliminary to the summoning of the butterfly-spirit. One end of the cotton cloth from near the head is drawn out of the coffin so that it lies on the ground.

The ceremony will last about half an hour. When everybody is ready, monks and mourners recite the formula for taking refuge in the Three Jewels (Buddha Dhamma, Saṅgha). Formulae are also pronounced to take leave of the deceased; they are blessings. Then the five precepts are pronounced. Monks may give a sermon about the fear of the consequences of sin, in a future state (*samvega*). Offerings (robes, money) are then given to the monks and merit is shared with the deceased (*sarana gun tan re*) and all beings. This concludes with a final libation. In this case, the water is poured directly onto the strip of cotton. This is also the moment to 'call the butterfly-spirit' (*lippra kho re*) for the aim of the rite is to invite it to leave; the poured water indicates the way out. As soon as the last drop has been poured, family, relatives and close friends can (or are then allowed to) cry loudly of grief. These few minutes are highly emotional. Among the mourners some are already leaving, while many come to view the corpse for the last time.[27] The coffin is then nailed closed and the monks leave.

The deceased is then quickly buried with the head pointing towards the north. Some of the relatives throw earth on the coffin. Nobody lingers in a cemetery. It is a frightening place where many invisible creatures and evil spirits prowl. People almost run as they leave it. I once witnessed a cremation. The sons of the deceased kindled the fire together but most of the relatives left after that. Ashes and bones are usually left in place but are sometimes collected and put in an urn. I have not witnessed this.

Relatives may go back to the mourning house where the floor will have been washed and where nothing that had any contact with the deceased will remain. A small fire will be burning at the entrance to the house. Those who wish to purify themselves will step over it.

THE LAST MEAL

One week after the day of death, mourning household members offer a meal to the monks, usually at the monastery. This is called the 'seventh day meal offering' (*7 rak laññ chvam: kyve: pve*) or 'filling the alms bowl with food'. This last meal is another occasion to gain and share merit with the deceased. I have

[27] While approaching the coffin, some people lightly rub a betel leaf on their body before throwing it to the coffin.

never witnessed it. A monk told me that it was not obligatory and that the tradition came from India. However all my interlocutors considered that it was only after this meal that the rules and interdictions linked to the funerals ended and, with them, this transitional period.

ELEMENTS OF ANALYSIS

When studying funerals, one faces an apparent contradiction. A monk told me that as soon as the dying person dies, he/she can be reborn, and he explained that the donation at the cemetery is made to be shared with the deceased. However, why share the merit if the deceased has already departed or is already on its way? The analysis reveals it is the treatment of the *lippra* that determines the progression of the *karma*.[28] It is the main point, a process that usually lasts seven days, which also aims to show the way towards the outside, a progressive exclusion of the deceased – *lippra* and corpse – from house and village.

TREATMENT OF THE *LIPPRA*

During this period, it seems that everything is done to show the butterfly-spirit the path it must take, to control it, so as to break (*kyvat*) the link with the living, despite its attachment for people and the living world. Different steps are taken in this process of guiding the *lippra*: maintaining, separating and making it leave.

As already said, the person's last moments and their control of 'mind' are crucial. We have pointed out that this can be understood in terms of Buddhist notions of the extinction of desire. This is also because at this moment people can be transformed into spirits (*nat*). This attitude allows a gentle transition from life to death, which is also a way for the *lippra* not to be afraid, not to leave and to be controlled. I cannot say if the *lippra* is fixed to the body – as the strip which links the big toes would suggest – throughout the period between the moment of death and the procession, or if it is detached and stays wandering about the house.[29] However, it does not leave the mourning house compound. Besides the continuous presence of people is a way of accompanying the deceased, to watch, and to 'please' it: its corpse is kept at home,

[28] As Brac de la Perrière (2001: 244–8) has demonstrated.

[29] According to Brac de la Perrière (2001: 241–2), rites such as opening of doors allow the circulation of the *lippra* in the house.

dressed and arranged with the bed and mosquito net decorated. All this social activity doubtlessly aims to repulse evil spirits particularly active at night.

Then comes the rite of separating the *lippra* both from members of the household and from the house itself.[30] This is illustrated by the next gesture: physically cutting the links between related people.[31] When the coffin is taken out of the house, all is done as if to clean, erase and purify: destruction and removal of everything that has been in contact with the deceased, immediately followed by the pouring of water. This indicates that there is only one general movement: towards the exit.

ONLY ONE POSSIBLE WAY

Several rules concern the ways to use the space created by the procession as is indicated by the different protective coverings, which conceal the deceased. These are first the clothes and shroud that swathe the corpse, which is inside the closed coffin, which is itself put inside the bier that is also closed. Then men carrying this bier surround it on all sides. When it is a wheeled bier, there is a closed space in front of it created by the rope pulled by the mourning females. On auspicious (*mangala*) occasions (when transporting a Buddha image from a craftsman's workshop to a monastery, for example) two ropes are used to form an open space in front of the vehicle, and this is probably not coincidental. In funerals, the rope delimits a space and this is reminiscent of the fact that an enclosed protective space is created whenever there is a danger.

Afterwards, everything is done to prevent the *lippra* from attaching itself to anything other than the one 'retained'. Rules prohibit the corpse and coffin to touch the ground before reaching the cemetery, and establish the route the procession should follow, taking for example main or government roads (*lam: ma kri:* or *a cui: ra lam:*).[32] The danger arises when the *lippra* takes another path or is possibly captured by malevolent spirits, which haunt the ground.

At the head of the procession, puffed rice is scattered with small presents. As well as being a generous gesture to the children and a kind of respectful

[30] According to Robinne's description among the Intha in Shan State of Burma, this rite allows the *lippra* to leave its house by refastening it to its corporeal component and it is called 'to re-fix *the lippra*', (2000: 191, n. 64).

[31] When a mother dies after or soon after giving birth, a rite is performed to separate the two *lippra* to prevent the one of the mother keeping that of the baby. See Shway Yoe (1963: 393), L. Bernot (1967: 514), M. Nash (1965: 154–5) and Robinne (2000: 191, 232).

[32] During Burmese funerals, too, the procession follows 'conventions', see Hla Pe (2004: 156).

compensation for the inhabitants of the quarter crossed, it is also a way of diverting children away from the coffin (the sweets are thrown to the sides in front of the houses rather than in the middle of the road). These are also implicit precautions taken towards the spirits: feeding them, whatever they are, may induce them to leave the *lippra* alone. What seems important here is that the rice must be dry. This confirms the rule that forbids the use of water during the procession. Thus the whole village, relatives and neighbours conduct the deceased to the cemetery down a marked and protected path. The coffin tied securely to the bier, its processional support, is also a way of controlling and bringing the *lippra* safely to the cemetery.

The 'calling of the *lippra*' is the key moment at the cemetery. Its release is made possible after cutting the toe-string. The end of the final libation corresponds precisely to the moment of the *lippra*'s departure. The mourners can then express their grief, showing their own attachment without fear because the *lippra* has gone. The separation accomplished, the conclusion of the ritual is focused on the coffin that is quickly nailed shut and burned or inhumed. Here again there is no way back. Nothing that has been in contact with the coffin is recuperated.

ACTION ON KARMA

The monks' participation may also be helpful for the progression of the *karma* of the dead. Two aspects emerge in funerals consequently and interdependently: the treatment of the *lippra* and the action on *karma*. In at least three situations – at the house 'filling the alms bowl' before the rite of 'separation of the *lippra*', at the cemetery before the 'calling of the *lippra*' and then offering a meal to the monk one week after the death – donations to monks (*a lhu atan:)* mean to obtain merits and share them with the deceased.[33] On two occasions in Mrauk U, I met men who had been ordained monk or novice for several weeks after the death of one of their parents. This was a way to meditate on suffering in order to overcome the death as well as to increase the deceased person's karmic capital.[34] The last offering to the monks is seen as a last necessary merit for the dead in order for the *lippra* to be completely free (*kyvat*). Among the Burmese, there are examples of donations to gain merit performed when the *lippra* of the

[33] In some places of Arakan, this donation is made after calling the *lippra* to participate. See Cakkinda (1969: 36–8).

[34] Also noted by Foley (1835: 33). Tambiah (1970: 194) points out this fact in Thailand, and Archaimbault for Laos (1963 vol. I: 5).

deceased seemed not to have departed properly (J. Nash 1966: 129–32 and Brac de la Perrière 2001: 246–7).

THE INVISIBLE WORLD: RITES OF PROTECTION AND SOCIAL COHESIVENESS

In facing death, relatives and even villagers themselves feel threatened (see also Siri Okkantha 1990: 158). Rules and gestures indicate the threat to the living, as seen with the need to separate the *lippra.* Nothing from the deceased is left in their house: things are either brought to the monastery or left at the cemetery. It is believed that anybody who is weak, sick or vulnerable (pregnant women, children in particular) or even has a small scratch, is exposed to danger in the presence of death. This is why people rub betel leaves on themselves at the mourning house or at the cemetery. It purifies them and the (dangerous) impurity is removed and thrown onto the coffin.

Finally, the most significant point about danger lies in the role played by the monks. Indeed, they participate at specific moments during the funeral, when their spiritual power (*tan khui:*) seems necessary to prevent evil, and each time as an indispensable preliminary. Furthermore, most of the chants recited on these occasions are *parit,* which are protective formulae. As N. Tannenbaum (2001) convincingly demonstrated about Buddhism among the Shan, but which is relevant to the Arakanese, the spiritual power of monks is primarily a protective power. This is most significant in cases of 'green' death (see below).

TIME AND SPACE

In the description of funerals the mourners participate in what might be called a collective 'circular movement'. This movement results from the union of the forces of the villagers with cosmic and cyclical forces. As astrology decisively matters in daily life, different aspects of the timing of funerary rituals are determined by the position of the planets. There are special days that require the burial of the deceased the same day (day of the week of birth, Wednesday, moonless night). Those constitute 'social units of time'. This is not the place to examine the details of this.

Also, although I was given no specific rule, the moment of the deceased's departure from the mortuary house always takes place at the sun's zenith. The return from the cemetery always occurs around 2:30 pm. This lapse of time (between 1:13 pm and 3:36 pm on one of my calendars), which in astrological calculations is called the 'three moments' (*sum: khyac ti khyin*), corresponds to another social unit of time. There is then a conjunction between the position of the sun and the moment when the body is borne in a collective movement through the village. It is thus delimited and as such protected both in space and time.[35]

As with other steps in the life-cycle, funerals ideally last a week, ending with the offering to the monks. The expression used for this last meal is '*7 rak lañ*'. *Lañ* as a verb means 'to turn, to revolve, turn around' and, in a figurative sense, 'return to one's original state'. It is also 'to go about, to wander' and figuratively 'to work well, to function properly'. The expression *7 rak lañ* indicates thus that there is a necessary seven-day cycle for funerals, and that in relation to this offering the *lippra* has been processed.[36] As the terminology suggests, the living may return to their previous state. The normal course of life can begin anew.

SUDDEN OR 'GREEN' DEATH

The analysis of funerals of an 'ordinary' death shows that the principal characteristic of a green death is its suddenness because proper ritual treatment of the *lippra* becomes impossible, and this loss of control impairs the deceased's karmic progression. Bad death gives rise to an immaterial component of a person, in search of a base, which therefore endangers the living (see Brac de la Perrière 2001: 251). This also explains the absence of a monk for the funeral rites. However, confronted with this kind of death, the village community has no choice other than to perform an expulsion rite.

SPIRITS OF THE DECEASED

People say that spirits (*nat*) never die. This affirmation becomes clear when one considers that *nat* are spirits of people who died sudden deaths. The 'green-dead' will be evergreen. Prisoners of the karmic cycle, they cannot be reborn, condemned to live in an intermediary state. They are in nature close to ghosts, and the expression '*a cim: mya:*' or 'the greens' is sometimes used to describe malevolent spirits who catch people at night. The most powerful spirits, the Lords of Arakan, are those of rivers. Sometimes they are said to be those of people who died violently in the water. However, there is no

[35] Tannenbaum (2001: 159–77) develops a similar conception in a chapter with the significant title 'the bounded nature of space, time and person'.

[36] The verb from which the substantive *a phat* (week) is derived means also 'to go round, encircle, to encompass'.

clear distinction in Arakanese between the theoretical nature of *nat* in general and *lippra*.[37]

FUNERARY RITES IN CASE OF 'GREEN' DEATH

The death by drowning of a teenager in May 1999 and the discovery of the corpse on the bank of the small island where I was living alone with a couple who were caretakers, produced many worries. The wife told me that she could not sleep anymore, she was scared and wanted to go back to her home (as the island was a temporary residence for the duration of my stay). Several friends asked me also whether I was afraid, enquiring about how I slept. One evoked the presence of ghosts. All these questions and discussions stopped after the village performed a rite.

The family of the victim very quickly buried the body and the next day performed a small rite. I did not witness it. It took place where the corpse was found, in the presence of members of the dead boy's family. The main element of this rite was the raising of a green bamboo pole, three or four meters high, on the spot where the water touched the land. A white cloth (mosquito netting) was tied to the top of the pole. Inside it were five circular bamboo ribs that held the cloth in a cylindrical shape. Both ends were closed. This is called *tam khvan*, 'the streamer [for the dead]'. L. Bernot (1967) describes a similar object for the Marma, but used for ordinary deaths. In former times, a new earthenware pot with its bottom pierced was filled with water at the spot where the person had died. Someone then carried the pot as far as possible until the water ran out and this then indicated the place where the corpse should be buried. This practice had ceased in Mrauk U because the increased demographic density in each quarter prevented the mourners crossing from one part of the town to another. We should therefore limit ourselves to the hypothesis that the pole might be a way of offering support to the spirit of the deceased.

In short, the ritual in this case is greatly simplified, in terms of both time, people, publicity and money, which is also suggested in the ethnographic literature.[38] Whatever the explanation, green death releases a dangerous, wandering immaterial component into the environment.

[37] Contrary to typology developed by Formoso (1998).

[38] See M. Nash's description (1965: 151–2) and J. Nash (1966: 129–32).

PURIFICATION RITE

The rite known as *kammavaca ññhap te*, which consists of reciting Pāli verses (*kammavācā*), is performed whenever beings such as ghosts and evil spirits (*bhilu, tacche, pritta*, and so on) need to be driven away.[39] In Mrauk U, the ceremony used to be organised each time a green death occurred (drowning, suicide, a murder) inside the village. Illness or fever striking several inhabitants of the same village simultaneously is a symptom of disorder that is also interpreted as requiring performance of the rite.[40] The inhabitants do not always specify the link with violent death. A similar ceremony celebrated annually on the very last day of the year in each quarter has the same aim of protecting and purifying the site.[41]

Recitation of the *kammavācā* is common in many different situations for lay people when a place or thing needs to be purified, because impurity creates dangers.[42] The term is composed of two Pāli words *kamma*, (act, action, deed) + *vācā*, (word, saying, speech). The meaning indicates that action is made essentially through words, and this significantly illustrates the focal point of the ceremony. The texts come from rituals in the *Vinayapiṭaka* used for the ordination of monks.

THE CEREMONY

The first step is to delimit the space requiring purification by ritual. The gates (*rva van va*) of the village are closed at the time of the ceremony so that entering or leaving is forbidden. Breaking this rule would invalidate the ceremony. In the case observed, there were four gates corresponding to the four cardinal points of the compass and indicated by a rough row of bamboo sticks. In daily life, nothing materialises them.[43]

In the evening when everybody's day is usually finished, nine invited monks arrive and sit at the main crossroads, in this case near the market at the 'centre' of the village. The number of monks represents an auspicious and powerful Buddhist totality. In front of them, in addition to the usual

[39] This is also known as *kammowa ññhap te*, literally 'to introduce the word action'. The word used by Burmese instead of *ññhap* is *rvat* which means 'to recite, read aloud'.

[40] This kind of ceremony is also performed among the Burmese in case of epidemics. See Shway Yoe (1963: 236–7, 396–400) and Spiro (1967: 37).

[41] This 'positive' rite, named 'listen to the verse to ward off evil' (*parit na*) follows other rites done to purify the body of people and the houses.

[42] It is also popular elsewhere in Burma. See Schober (1989: 142, n. 35) who indicates some situations in which these texts are recited.

[43] In Mrauk U when villages are 'islands', their gates are at the bridge.

offering for monks, many receptacles filled with water have been deposited along with a mango or *sapre* (*Eugenia*) branch from each house. There are also some pots of uncooked rice. The inhabitants leave their receptacles and go home. When everything is ready (ideally at 9 pm), the monks ask the headman of the village three times if he likes evil spirits. He says no and consequently the monks start in unison to recite the *kammavācā*, each of them reading his own text. This will last about thirty minutes. The monks then stand up and in pairs walk through the village towards a gate while the ninth, the most venerable, that is to say the most powerful, remains at the recitation place. A bicycle-sidecar goes through the village informing the inhabitants that they can retrieve their receptacles and the rice that are now 'imbued' with the spiritual power necessary to purify and protect their home. A few minutes later, one hears a noise (*cam ko ti sam*) coming from the houses. It is made by the inhabitants striking a tray with a big spoon used for cooking rice. As they do this they also shout 'Leave! Leave!' or 'Out! Out!' so as to frighten and expel all malevolent spirits. For purification, the owner of the house sprinkles the water or rice first on the Buddha's altar, then on the main poles of the houses (starting with the one dedicated to the tutelary spirit of the house) and on each threshold (bottom of the steps, main entrance, windows, etc.). If there is a second house within the compound, it is treated the same way. After that, the village is reopened and tea and biscuits are shared by the villagers where the recitation had taken place.

The afflicted village is identified and enclosed with the aim of restoring order (*rva khan: re*). All houses are concerned. Spatial purification is accomplished by recitation of Pāli verses as well as the ritual circulation of monks, whose moral and spiritual power (*tan khui:*) acts as a protection against spirits while the most powerful of them stays in the centre. This movement is similar to the wheel. Tambiah also tells a story of the Buddha teaching his disciple Ānanda another powerful verse (*ratana sutta*), who after reciting it while walking about and sprinkling water to ward off evil spirits, restored order to a wrecked city.[44]

The joint actions, of the monks for the whole village and of the villagers in their own houses, are accomplished by the efficacy of power transmitted to rice and water. The integrity of the village is then restored through the action on its ritual space. Houses, which also constitute a unit, are interdependent and represent a whole, physically limited in this case by its gates. Here, as shown, power to be efficient must be limited (Lehman 1981: 104).

44 Tambiah (1970: 202). Tambiah (1968) and (1970: 195–227) has described and analysed the efficient and magical power of words in Buddhist rituals.

The entire funeral period constitutes a threat to villagers, which necessitates the erection of protections for both the deceased and the living. These are materialised by envelopes, barriers that are set up both in space and time.

CONCLUSION

Analysis of funerals reveals that death constitutes a progressive separation process that lasts ideally seven days. One of the words used for the corpse indicates that during this period the deceased is no longer alive but neither has he yet attained his definitive status. Indeed '*alon:*', the corpse, is probably the substantive term derived from the verb '*lon:*', which means 'to be in the course of completion'.[45] This is a significant indicator of death as process. The dead belong to an intermediary state during this period, both temporally and 'spiritually'. It is a dangerous time, both for the dead – because the *lippra* might not go where it is meant to go, thus preventing karmic progression – and for the living – who might become the victims of the wandering *lippra*, as it seeks a new host in which to incarnate. The whole village then contributes to the success of the process, accompanying the deceased until the very end, to show the *lippra* that it must go outside its domestic sphere and place of residence, supplied with something to pay for its trip, to cross the river or whatever. This essential guiding of the *lippra* is also achieved by preventing it from attaching itself to other things or to be captured by other spirits. This is the indispensable collective treatment for the *lippra*, so the living are left in peace and so that rebirth may be possible. The participation of both laymen and monks is crucial in this case and, for the monks, is said to be unnecessary in that of a 'green' death, because there is no *lippra* to treat, as it has already 'escaped'. However, data presented show that their spiritual power, which prevents and protects, is nevertheless required in another ritual to restore the social order of the village. The characteristic suddenness of bad death prevents the cutting of ties or bonds with family members in the proper way as materialised by the cotton thread.

The separation of the *lippra* takes place in two stages in two social units of space, house and village. Separation is detachment. Its meaning refers to a concept based in Buddhist morality. The most significant element here is the separation of the *lippra* of the dead from those of the living in the household.

[45] Also 'to bring into an incipient state with a view to finishing', Judson (1953: 927).

BIBLIOGRAPHY

Archaimbault, C. (1963), 'Contribution à l'étude du rituel funéraire lao (I) et (II)', *The Journal of the Siam Society* **51** (1), 1–57.

Bernot, D. (1978–92), *Dictionnaire Birman–Français*, Paris: Editions SELAF (Asie du Sud-Est et Océan Indien), 15 fascicules.

Bernot, L. (1967), *Les Paysans Arakanais du Pakistan Oriental: L'histoire, le Monde Végétal et l'Organisation Sociale des Réfugiés Marma (Mog)*, Paris, La Haye: Editions Mouton and Co., Ecole Pratique des Hautes Etudes, 2 vols.

Brac de la Perrière, B. (1989), *Les Rituels de Possession en Birmanie: Du Culte d'État aux Cérémonies Privées*, Paris: Éditions Recherches sur les Civilisations.

(2001), 'Malemort et "bonne mort" en Birmanie (Myanmar)', in ed. Brigitte Baptandier, *De la Malemort en Quelques Pays d'Asie*, Paris: Karthala, 235–58.

Cakkinda [U:] and Man on pi ya (1969), *Rakhuin Yañ Kye: Mhu Mya:* [Arakanese traditions], Yangon.

Condominas, G. (1998), *Le Bouddhisme au Village: Notes Ethnographiques sur les Pratiques Religieuses dans la Société Rurale Lao (Plaine de Ventiane)*, Vientiane: Editions des Cahiers de France [originally published as (1968), 'Notes sur le bouddhisme populaire en milieu rural lao', *Archives de Sociologie des Religions* **25**, 81–110 and **26**, 111–50].

de Mersan, A. (2005), *Espace Rituel et Construction de la Localité : Contribution à l'Étude Ethnographique d'une Population de la Birmanie Contemporaine: les Arakanais*. Unpublished PhD dissertation in social anthropology and ethnology, Paris: Ecole des Hautes Etudes en Sciences Sociales.

Ferrars, M. and Ferrars, B. (1901), *Burma* (2nd edn.), London: Sampson Low, Marston and Company.

Foley, W. (Lieut.) (1835), 'Journal of a tour through the Island of Rambree, with a geological sketch of the country and brief account of the customs, and of its inhabitants', *Journal of the Asiatic Society of Bengal* **4**, 82–95.

Formoso, B. (1998), 'Bad death and malevolent spirits among the Tai peoples', *Anthropos* 1–3, 3–17.

Hertz, R. [1907] (1928), 'Contribution à une étude sur la représentation collective de la mort', in ed. R. Hertz, *Mélanges de Sociologie Religieuse et de Folklore*, Paris: Felix Alcan, 1–98 (1st edn. *Année Sociologique*, 1st series, vol. 10).

Hla Pe (Dr.) (2004), *The Myanmar Buddhist: His Life from the Cradle to the Grave*, trans. Dr. Tin Hlaing, Yangon: Don: ca pe.

Houtman, G. (1999), *Mental Culture in Burmese Crisis Politics: Aung San Suu Kyi and the National League for Democracy*, Tokyo: Institute for the Study of Languages and Cultures of Asia and Africa.

Judson, A. (1953), *Judson's Burmese–English Dictionary: Unabridged Centenary Edition*, Rangoon: Baptist Board of Publications [1st edn. 1852].

Langer, R. (2007), *Buddhist Rituals of Death and Rebirth: Contemporary Sri Lankan Practice and its Origins*, Abingdon and New York: Routledge.

Lehman, F. K. (Chit Hlaing) (1981), 'On the vocabulary and semantics of "field" in Theravāda Buddhist society', *Contributions to Asian Studies* **16**, 101–11.

Lewin, T. H. (Capt.) (1869), *The Hill Tracts of Chittagong and the Dwellers Therein; with Comparative Vocabularies of the Hill Dialects*, Calcutta: Bengal Printing Co.

Macdonald, K. N. (1979), *The Practice of Medicine among the Burmese. Translated from Original Manuscripts, with an Historical Sketch of the Progress of Medicine*, Edinburgh: Maclachlan and Stewart [1st edn. 1879].

Maung Tha Kin (1922), 'Depressed classes of Burma', *Journal of the Burma Research Society* **12** (3), 140–4.

Nash, J. C. (1966), 'Living with nats: an analysis of animism in Burman village social relations', *Anthropological Studies in Theravāda Buddhism*, Cultural Report, Series no. 13, Southeast Asian Studies, Yale University, 117–36.

Nash, M. (1965), *The Golden Road to Modernity: Village Life in Contemporary Burma*, New York: John Wiley and Sons.

Okkantha (Siri, Ashin) (1990), *History of Buddhism in Arakan*, unpublished PhD thesis, University of Calcutta.

Raymond, C. (1998), 'Wathundayé, divinité de la terre en Birmanie et en Arakan', *Études Birmanes en Hommage à Denise Bernot*, Paris: École Française d'Extrême-Orient, 113–27.

Rhys-Davids T. W. and Stede, W. (1997), *Pāli–English Dictionary,* Delhi: Motilal Banarsidass [1st edn. London, 1921–5].

Robinne, F. (2000), *Fils et Maîtres du Lac: Relations Interethniques dans l'État Shan de Birmanie*, Paris: Centre National de la Recherche Scientifique/Maison des Sciences de l'Homme.

Schober, J. (1989), *Paths to Enlightenment: Theravāda Buddhism in Upper Burma*, unpublished thesis in anthropology, University of Illinois, Urbana.

Shway Yoe [George Scott] (1963), *The Burman, his Life and Notions*, New York: W.W. Norton [1st edn. 1882].

Spiro, M. E. (1967), *Burmese Supernaturalism: a Study in the Explanation and Reduction of Suffering*, Englewood Cliffs, NJ: Prentice-Hall.

(1970), *Buddhism and Society: a Great Tradition and its Burmese Vicissitudes*, London: George Allen and Unwin.

Tambiah, S. J. (1968), 'The magical power of words', *Man* **3**, 175–208.

(1970), *Buddhism and the Spirit Cults in North-east Thailand*, Cambridge University Press.

Tannenbaum, N. (2001), *Who Can Compete Against The World? Power-Protection and Buddhism in Shan Worldview*, Association for Asian Studies, Monograph and Occasional Paper Series, **51**, Ann Arbor [1st edn. 1995].

Temple, R. C. (Sir) (1906), *The Thirty-seven Nats: a Phase of Spirit-worship Prevailing in Burma*, London: W. Griggs, Chromo-Lithographer to the King.

CHAPTER 8

Theatre of death and rebirth: monks' funerals in Burma

François Robinne

RITUAL REWRITING OF THE BUDDHIST CANON

Temporary substitute for death

Among the nine Buddhist congregations officially recognised in Burma, the Tudhamma congregation has the largest number of saṅgha members. It is particularly renowned for the size of its ritual performances which include the funeral ceremonies of a superior monk.[1]

To my knowledge, only two vernacular texts describe these in detail. The one concerns royal funerals – but also those of monks and Shan sawbwa – at the court of Ava from the second half of the seventeenth to the first half of the eighteenth century (Sīri Ujuanā 1962), the other the funeral of a monk who lived in the nineteenth century under the Konbaung dynasty (Anonymous 1 1988).[2] Valuable information is sometimes contained in the eulogies published on the death of a monk: besides the deceased's biography, we also find in these the texts recited on the occasion by the Buddhist community and the groups of women as well as a detailed account of the festivities (Anonymous 2 2003). Though these vernacular documents

[1] Louis Gabaude did a critical reading of a first draft of this chapter, which has been totally rewritten, including the title, which uses one of his suggestions. I take the opportunity of thanking him sincerely for this. My kindest regards go to Guillaume Rozenberg, with whom I conducted two field investigations. The actors U Win Thun and Daw Tebyè, along with their daughter who is a dancer, played a decisive role in my comprehension of the ritual. Maé helped me translate the whole two and a half hour recording of this theatrical genre known as *eyiṅ*. Despite these different contributions, any errors that may be found, like the opinions expressed, are the author's sole responsibility. Unless otherwise specified, Burmese terms are given in a literal transcription and in italics; for technical reasons, the dot that should be over 'n' is written 'ṅ', while the dot that should be over 'm' is missing (as in *cam* for 'model' or *kam* for 'karma'). The vernaculars are in normal characters when romanised; this is the case notably for Buddha, Dhamma, Saṅgha or sawbwa, referring to the 'Shan princes' whose administrations were dissolved after the 1962 Burmese coup.

[2] This text was given to me in August 2004 by Daw San San May, the librarian in charge of the Burmese department at the British Library in London (shelf mark MYAN.A.857). It is also the document on which B. Brac de la Perrière (2006) recently based her 'Analyse des rituels de la royauté birmane'.

are extremely valuable, they are not sufficient to make up for the lack of anthropological analysis.

The shortage of studies on the subject contrasts with the splendour of the ceremonies of a monk's funeral, one of the most impressive ritual performances I have ever seen; during the three days and two nights this ritual lasts, festive and funerary elements combine in the same show staging Buddhist rebirth and the concepts related to it.[3] This funeral performance appears in a way to be a ritual rewriting of the Buddhist canon when the latter proves insufficient or, at the very least, when the texts' ambiguity leaves open this space of liberty Buddhism allows.

The Buddhist concepts of not-self (*anattā*), suffering (*dukkha*) and impermanence (*anicca*) dictate the ritual performances' conceptual framework. Nonetheless, in this domain as in others, the same norms refer to different forms. The two cremations undergone by the abbot's corpse in the village of Tèkè-Khyin were an unexpected example of this. Casts had been made of the deceased's face and feet before the body was cremated two days after death, thus avoiding the trouble entailed in evisceration. The ashes and the uncalcined pieces of bone were retrieved and put in a reliquary. This, in turn, was placed between the two reconstituted parts of the body then covered with a saffron robe, as if the monk were draped in it. In the glass coffin the body thus gave the impression of having been preserved intact as is usually the case. Another cremation took place three months later, at the close of the funeral properly speaking. This is the only attested instance – though certainly not an isolated one – of a double cremation, first of the corpse then of the reconstituted body. And it is likely that many other variants are in use here and there.

But the purpose of the comparative approach is not of an encyclopaedic nature. It is a matter of understanding the process that makes rebirth, which some say takes place simultaneously with the last breath, the subject of a ritual performance which extends the operation both in time and space. Just as the first step of – or preliminaries to – the funeral, a few days after the last breath, makes the decomposition of the body into a kind of temporary substitute for death, so the cremation or burial ceremony organises the

[3] It was possible to observe several ceremonies of a superior monk's funeral (cremation and burial as well) in the villages of central Burma: the first time at Pagan Nyaung-Oo in January 1995; then a few years later, in the village of O-Phaw south-west of the Chindwin river on the third, fourth and fifth day of the waning moon in the lunar month of Tebawdwè (February 2002). In March 2004 I was able to observe two entire funeral rituals which took place one after the other in February 2004 in the village of Ton-Zè-Pé, then in that of Tèkè-Khyin. Three films were made: the nine hours of film are currently being edited; a first film of about forty-five minutes was shown at the Rangoon cultural service in January 2004, and again in March 2010 in Paris at The Musée du Quai Branly.

process of rebirth which we literally see take place before the very eyes of the monk's pupils. Though the endless cycle of rebirths is subjected to social control during the ritual, it also acts locally as the demonstration – 'the proof' – of its reality and the reality of the Buddhist concepts related to impermanence.

As the approach adopted here consists in letting the monks, pilgrims and troupes of actors speak, our analysis is governed by the discourse of the people who participated in the rituals observed; therefore, there will be no analysis of canonic texts or of the comments they can occasion but a study of the texts recited, declaimed or sung. In particular, the recording of the two and a half hours or so the *eyiń* initiatory performance lasts – between the moment the coffin leaves the monastery and the cremation of the deceased – will constitute the main theme of my analysis. It is on the observation of these ritual performances in several central Burmese villages, on the recording and the translation of the plays acted and on inquiries carried out among the participants, whether monks or lay people, that the following analysis of the interpretation of the conditions of existence and the process of rebirth, as they are shown to us, will be based.

LULLABIES FOR THE BABY AND LAMENTATIONS FOR THE DEAD

In accordance with the Buddhist canon, the ritual staging of death and rebirth takes place in a temporary pavilion called *cam kyoń:*, that is to say '[built on the] model (*cam*) of a monastery (*kyoń:*)'. This can be erected in the monastery grounds, as was the case in the villages of O-Phaw and Ton-Ze-Pé, or in the village square as at Pagan Nyaung-Oo and Tèkkè-Khyin. Intended to be taken down and put up again, the framework of the temporary pavilion is made of bamboo and decorated with gilt. On the first day of the ritual a play is acted in it at the beginning of the afternoon. In some cases, a second performance is given the next day, before the cremation. There may also be several pavilions, thus creating a kind of competition between the troupes performing: the audience judges the quality of the show by its presence or lack of interest. Improvisation – and therefore the acting and the richness of the actors' repertoire – is decisive in the show's success. It is not an easy genre for, besides the principal actress's performance, it involves Buddhist concepts and Pāli terms. They would remain incomprehensible for most people if they were not part of the framework of a story which unfolds throughout the show known by the name of *eyiń* and if, within the story itself, famous legends from a Burmanised Buddhist heritage were not enacted.[4]

In its original meaning, now obsolete, the noun *eyiń* and its verbal form *eyiń kyū* designate a lullaby sung for a prince (Myanmar–English Dictionary 1998: 614).[5] Nowadays *eyiń* is the name of a play systematically performed on the death of a monk. The lullaby has been replaced by the lamentations of a woman who sings the virtues of the departed monk while desiring to keep him with her. During the performance, the term *pukhak* (pronounced 'pekhè') is substituted for the term *eyiń*: both mean 'cradle' but whereas the latter refers to the cradle of a member of the royal family, the former is the word commonly used for children's cradles. Here the 'cradle' designates the bamboo structure hanging at the back of the stage on which the monk's coffin is placed and remains throughout the performance.

The cradle will be pulled vigorously back three times during the part of the play in which the main actress confronts Sakra's messengers; afterwards it will be swung three times in the opposite direction when the actress finally resigns herself to the monk's departure: she then gently rocks the cradle while singing a melancholy lullaby. Whereas, in the one case, both sides quarrel over the coffin, in the other, the fight has given way to tender resignation: the actress has come round to the views of Sakra's messengers and pays her last respects to the deceased monk by rocking his corpse as a mother would her baby. Birth and death will thus be recurrently correlated throughout the ritual including during the process of mental and corporeality separation and aggregation.

The *eyiń*'s central theme is the pain of the living mourning the departed. The main actress's long, uncombed hair, her cries, her tears, the blows she inflicts on herself and on others and those she receives, all contribute to the staging of despair. Through her, the villagers express their wish to keep the deceased with them, even to bring him back to life or to find a substitute (*acā: thuī: kyoń:*) for death which would put an end to the process of rebirth. The pointlessness of this attempt is illustrated by the fight – and, as we shall see, it really is a matter of physical confrontations – between an actress symbolising the humans and two male characters representing Sakra's messengers. It is through them that during the two and a half hour long

[4] This is the case, for example, for Maung Seitta the beekeeper, the only man capable of lifting the corpse of the venerable Shintamwara, a theme found in another form in Cambodia (Adhémard Leclère 1906: 5).

[5] *Eyiń* designates a royal cradle while *kyū* means 'to emit a melodious sound'.

show, the Buddhist concepts of not-self (*anattā*), impermanence (*anicca*) and suffering (*dukkha*) – the three conditions of existence – are developed.

The story is taken from a dual Buddhist and Burmese legend heritage whose framework forms the basis around which the Buddhist concepts related to death are developed. Although the story's theme is the death of a monk, this is not strictly speaking the monk in whose honour the funeral is taking place. His presence is nevertheless recurrent throughout the play: physically because his coffin is placed on a 'cradle' and in thought because the villagers constantly recall the dead man's merits, associating them with the details of the monk's life and death: his age, his education, the date of his robing ceremony, the name of the monasteries he had been to, or even the three stomach operations he had undergone before dying and his death throes. But these references to the dead monk's life course are added to legends famous throughout Buddhist Burma which are thus personalised. In other words, the basic story is more or less identical from one funeral ceremony to another, its variants depending on the different theatrical troupes.

SHOWING IMPERMANENCE

The *eyiń* show, which is predominantly religious – with a background of sadness and violence – is presented alternately with scenes of dance and singing and predominantly sexual sketches; these secular interludes come from the theatrical genre known as *ańyen:*. I shall come back to it later.

After a short offstage prelude spoken by Sakra, the *eyiń* itself is composed of four acts.

Act 1: The brother and sister's dreams

On the way to go and give their brother, the monk, a present of a saffron robe, the brother and sister talk. The younger brother interprets the fall he had as a bad omen; in her turn his elder sister then tells him about her dream and the bad omens she saw in it. In fact, this is a long monologue declaimed by the principal actress and addressed to the Sakra's messengers:

[The younger brother]: Lord Bonze, I was saying to myself that as soon as I arrived at your monastery I would go and get something to eat and drink in the stores. Yes, I was saying to myself that I would do that. I was telling myself that I would be happy there and I would have something to drink and to eat. Elder sister, how come, elder sister, how come the easiest roads are always, always paved with obstacles for your young brother? The dirt road was flat, straight and level – you don't see many like that. Big sister, it wasn't like a village road but like one in town. The road was a real pleasure. So why did I trip up on that road then? Oh well, it was like a bad dream, yes like a bad dream. It really was. When I tripped, I broke my big toe. I stayed sitting there, stuck, not able to get up, as if I was dead, beloved elder sister.

[The elder sister]: Listen to the nightmare I had. It was full of signs and I haven't felt calm ever since. Sunday's dream: offerings to the king, Monday's dream: husband, Tuesday's: close relations, Wednesday's dream or Buddha's day: children and family, Thursday's dream: friends, Friday and Saturday's dream: buffaloes, cows, elephants, horses, Sunday's dream: about myself, and the dream I had was in the night between Tuesday and Wednesday, yes, yes, that's it. That dream was to do with bad omens. Yes, bad omens. Everyone will tell you so, it's in the astrological treatises, no possible error, the dream I had on Tuesday night was very frightening. How can I ignore the omen in it, violent death cannot leave me serene. It's an ocean of sadness [which is overwhelming me], your dear older sister is terribly scared of this omen, as if she was going to be brought to court for malpractice.[6]

When they get to the monastery where their brother, the superior monk, lives, they learn he has been dead for three days.

Act 2: The minister's anger

By order of the minister – the story is meant to take place in the days of the monarchy – the common people may pay their last respects to the deceased monk on the first day; the second day being reserved for merchants and the third day for court personalities. As they arrive on the third day, the monk's brother and sister are not allowed to pay their respects to him. Because of their family ties with the monk, the minister's representative does them the favour of letting them spend an hour at the dead man's side. But the brother and sister want to stay longer than the time allotted and anger the minister and his assistant. The verbal exchange is stormy.

[The minister]: The Buddha and Dhamma cannot be unaware of it, nobody, not even the most ignorant or the greediest, not even the Buddha nor the Dhamma nor the saṅgha members can be unaware that you're treating us like louts, like louts, aren't you? Come here, come here. You've been with the monk and you are insulting me, are you? Yes, you are insulting me.

[The monk's sister]: Don't come near, don't come near me!

[The minister]: Come here, come here! Like louts!

[The monk's sister]: Don't come near! Don't come near!

[6] Wednesday is called *bhuddhahū*, or Buddha's day. The usual expression for 'violent death' is *acim: se*, 'green death'. However, it is the Pāli term *upaccetaka* the actress uses.

[The minister]: Hey! What do you think of me to insult me so? For you have insulted me. I'll pull your teeth out, I'll kill you, that I will. Your skin is tender, soon it will bear the very visible marks of my five fingers, I'll hit you, I'll hit you, go away or I'll beat you until your teeth fall out!

[The monk's sister]: Listen, we [she and her brother] will cook big pieces of pork and rice, very big pieces of pork and perfumed rice, for you both [the minister and his subordinate].[7] Is it true? Yes, it's true. It's true. And we'll also make you vermicelli soup with peas and our wonderful savoury *bhalakhyoṅ* with fermented fish paste. And … and … everything you like. Tasty bitter mangoes! Yes yes, alright! All this, with big pieces of pork, it's certain, we'll give you all that! Is it true? Of course it's true! Don't come near me! Don't slap me!

Having finally convinced the minister and his subordinate, the sister turns to the two messengers sent by Sakra. A struggle for power – in the true sense of the term – ensues. As for the brother, he stays in the background contenting himself with coming to his sister's aid, mostly when she is already on the ground.

Act 3: The fight between the dead monk's sister and Sakra's messengers

In order to keep the dead man with her, she first asks for permission to erect a tomb to him:

[Sakra's messengers]: Because of the old monk's praiseworthy deeds we came down to the land of human beings where we do not usually dwell; from there we went to Mandalay division, to Matteya district, to the village of Ton-Zè-Pé, into the grounds of Meizzuma monastery. The donors – all the men and women without exception – from the village of Ton-Zè-Pé want to hold a cremation ceremony [in conformity with the concept] of not-self – this is good, this is good – thus upsetting – this is bad – the relatives from the village of Saung-Kyi.[8] What should we decide? To ascertain this, we must consider everything carefully.

[. . .]

[The monk's sister]: Lords and masters who have Ananda's qualities, I appeal to your great kindness, I will give you the most varied offerings, my hands joined above my head. Let me do this. Oh abbot, your disciples want to accompany you one last time. Oh monk, your older sister wants to take you to the cemetery, this is a good thing isn't it? You lived in Pegu Division, in Pan-Taung district, in the Nay-Ye-Lay group of villages, then you came to Mandalay Division, to the town of Matteya, to the village of Ton-Ze-Pay and your beloved sister's last wish is to lay your coffin

[7] Pork is most appreciated in Burma among Buddhists. The woman just wants to offer to the minister the finest dishes, and, as far as I know, there is in the matter no allusion to the story from the Mahaparinibbāna Sutta where the Buddha died of eating pork.

[8] The expression used is *anattā* (not-self) *ma* (main) *zāpana* (cremation, funeral). The usual expression for 'good' is *sādhu*, generally said three times in succession. Here the actress uses the expression *sādhu kilena*, from the Pāli *sādhu kilana*. The Pāli expression used for 'bad' is *brāpāda*.

where you lived [. . .] Our monk lived for sixty-four years, oh venerable abbot, you were over sixty-four and it is in this monastery that your beloved sister and all your disciples have always seen you and that is why we now want to erect a brick monastery to you, it is the most appropriate place to live and to continue to meet you . . .

Three times the actress tries to approach the hanging coffin and get past Sakra's messengers who bar the way with their bodies. She forces her way past, literally throwing herself onto the cradle, which tilts over under her weight. During one performance, it did not stand up to the violence of the attack and partially collapsed under the impact, almost tipping the coffin off. The *nat* grab hold of the actress and pull her hair. Frenzied, on her knees, lying with head and shoulders on the coffin which she kisses and strokes with her hands, she mourns the deceased monk and begs the Sakra's messengers to let her keep the corpse with her. Twice they push her away, throwing her to the ground, hitting and trampling on her. A third time, the actress is thrown off the stage into the crowd. With difficulty she climbs back onto the podium, in pain and tears. She continues thus to implore the two messengers then, in desperation, she challenges them:

[Sakra's messengers]: Hey all of you, exercising his power, our Lord [Sakra] has ordered the corpse be cremated on earth by the *nat* which heat between the fourth level of the Tawadi region and the summit of mount Wirazein.[9] Hey, if you don't do this, our Lord will use his weapons to smash the brick building containing the corpse.[10] Do as he commands, carry the corpse if you want to avoid punishment.

[The monk's sister]: If that's the way it is, big brother *nat*, to avoid having to fight with you, we shall place the monk's corpse between us, his relatives, and you, the spirits, and a rope will be used to pull it.

[Sakra's messenger]: If that's the way it is, mother Maya, let us place the monk's corpse as you said and pull it with a rope without having to fight each other.[11] It's agreed. You, mother Maya, hey! and you little brother Subhadwaruray, will place the corpse between you, with the divinities on one side and the humans on the other and you will pull it with a rope without having to fight each other. The corpse automatically consumes the fire[12].

9 The Pāli Burmese expresssion used here for 'fire' is *mī: gruiha*, word for word: 'fire (Burmese term) + Pāli term for cremation'. *Nat wiṅ:* 'the spirit penetrates', the equivalent of *nat pū*, that is to say 'the spirit heats'. If the *nat* heat, it means they possess the person they enter or, as here, that they inhabit the region indicated.

10 *Warazin* in its Burmese form, from the Pāli-based *wazira*, a term which also has the second meaning of 'lightning'.

11 The expression used here is *nat rwā cam* 'like the *nat*'s village' *kam tō kun to* 'the consumed karma' *alum:* 'corpse', that is literally: the corpse without karma in the spirits' village.

12 The Pāli-based expression used is *tezō* (fire) *dhāt* (element). At the beginning of her performance the actress enumerates the eleven sorts of fire to which death has put an end: *rāga, bhoga, moha, jāti, jara, maranā, soka, patidewa, dukkha, domanasā, uparāpa*. The same is true for the corpse which, indirectly, itself settles the matter at issue by avoiding any form of quarrel.

[The monk's sister]: It is thus, our monk consumes the fire. It is thus, our very great and venerable monk loves all his relations. And because the monk also loves all his donors [she turns towards the audience], men and women together, they will also pull the corpse with us.

[Sakra's messengers]: Ah well, of course, you humans are very numerous, that's why you provoke the *nat* like this.

[The monk's sister]: The relations [of the monk] are really very numerous. Big brother *nat*, you would do better to give [the corpse] back to us.

[Sakra's messengers]: Give the corpse back to you, you must be joking! All the *nat* together are also very numerous! We'll take you on. Hey, all the *nat*, gather round me! And you human beings, I won't give you two chances, don't forget. We'll go along with the challenge because it will prevent a real battle, come on, let's take up our positions as we said.

[The monk's sister]: Big brother *nat*, you must take up the bet three times, three times, do you hear?

[Sakra's messengers]: We'll take up the bet. And you, the conductor, have the percussion play and don't make any mistakes!

Then we see them go into action: the sister and brother positioned besides the dead man's feet and Sakra's two messengers at his head. Three times in a row they pull the coffin from both sides. The first time the brother and sister win because the spirits' rope breaks and they fall into the orchestra; the second time, it's the turn of the brother and sister's rope to break, making them fall into the crowd and the Sakra's two messengers are victorious; the third time the latter win.

Act 4: The monk's sister's resignation

In tears, the monk's sister is finally convinced by the *nats*' words that it is impossible to keep the dead monk with her, and of the stupidity of trying to escape from the three conditions of existence which are once again enumerated: not-self (*anattā*), suffering (*dukkha*) and impermanence (*anicca*). In the ode she then begins to sing, she tells the story of a woman looking for a substitute for the death of her baby. The didactic purpose of the theme thus chanted uses scenes of everyday life, in the same way that monks illustrate their preaching with concrete examples; here, the reference to Gautami, Gautama Buddha's mother-in-law, gives even more weight to the actress's words:[13]

[13] Thanks to L. Gabaude and F. Lagirarde who indicated some references on Kisa Gotami. One of them, easy to consult via the Internet is: 'Gotami Sutta: Sister Gotami' (SN 5.3), translated from the Pāli by Thanissaro Bhikkhu (www.accesstoinsight.org/tipitaka/sn/sn05/sn05.003.than.html). See also Kloppenborg and Hanegraaf 1995: 163.

[The monk's sister in the role of Gautami]: My son no longer sucks milk from my breast. He no longer yells neither does he cry. So I took him in my arms and I went to find my neighbours. My son no longer breathes, his body is lifeless. Help me. That's when an old man answered me: 'Madam, if you go on tearing yourself apart, you will end up dying. The very venerable Buddha lives over there in the monastery called Zetawun.' So I went there to ask the Buddha if he had a cure, something to bring back life. A remedy for death. I took my child in my arms and I asked the Buddha if there was any medicine for death. 'How can you ask that? Gautami, my beloved daughter, how can you get into such a state of sadness?' But Buddha! Your disciple's son no longer cries and no longer yells. Buddha, he no longer suckles either. Find me a remedy capable of curing my son and bringing him back to life. Treat my child, Buddha. Then the Buddha smiled and said: 'My daughter, go and travel through the Sawadi region, and try just to bring back a handful, or even a mere finger, of mustard seeds corresponding to the number of houses in which there have been no deaths.[14] If you bring back a finger of mustard seeds your son will come back to life.' The beloved daughter then picked up her son in her arms and travelled all through the region as far as the four outer walls. Hey, you mothers, the mothers of all the houses, give me a few mustard seeds if no one has died in your home. Hey, mother! 'But, my good woman, my little boy died in this house a few days ago'. I went to the house next door asking: oh, mother, if no one has died yet, give me a mustard seed. I travelled the whole country again going into seven billion houses, but once more I was told: 'My good woman, my old mother died a month ago.' I couldn't find one. None of the houses I visited had been spared by death. Having been all over the place carrying my son in my arms in search of a remedy for death, I decided to return to Zetawun monastery where the Buddha lives. Very venerable Buddha, I went everywhere but I couldn't find one. So I decided to stay there as a nun to listen to the Buddha's sermons.[15]

The actress goes on to recount the death and the cremation of the monk Shintanwarama Thera, as well as the burial of his bones and ashes under a *zedī*. Although this long passage explains the *eyiń*'s origin, it does not seem useful to reproduce it here. The end of the play marks the coffin's transfer to the tomb or the cremation place and, with this, the crossing of the third and final threshold.

ALTERNATION OF SECULAR AND RELIGIOUS FORMS

As well as the feminine divinities, a man – or a woman dressed as a man – wearing only a loincloth pulled up between his thighs, also boards the *karawik*. While the first are placed at the bows, the second goes to the stern. They remain standing. Seated on either side of the vessel, the women

[14] The Sawadi region is the upper region where Sakra reigns.

[15] The Pāli-derived term for nun used is *bhikkunī ma* and not *sīla rhan*, which is more commonly used.

rowers form the middle part of the tripartite structure, whose recurrence we have noted above. The harmony of this structure restores the contrast between the two opposites. On the one side, the grace and elegance of the dance steps performed by the higher divinities, on the other, the casualness and vulgarity of the human being who gesticulates, jumps, jokes and fools around with his oar; on the one side, a half-naked man, on the other, women dressed in heavy, shimmering clothes. It is the actors themselves who during the *eyiń* justify such a contrast: at the end of the comic show performed intermittently in front of the coffin, they remind the audience that if suffering is part of the order of things, so too is joy. Therefore, this fact is not peculiar to the show performed on Sakra's vehicle. As in initiatory robing ceremonies (Robinne 2000 and 2002), in monks' funerals there is an alternation of religious and secular phases. This is the reason for the presence of the half-naked man and the higher spirits on the *karawik*. The same principle is found in a performance given at night.

Besides the *eyiń*, another theatrical genre, known as *zāt* or *zāt pwè* is performed at funerals. Unlike the *eyiń* show, the *zāt* is not specific to monks' funerals. At pagoda festivals, but also during rituals to spirits of some importance, one or several bamboo marquees are erected for this purpose in the village square. The religious themes developed in the *eyiń* and the *zāt* are respectively the unavoidable nature of the three conditions of existence, with lamentations in the background, and the Buddha's previous lives, which are tending to be eclipsed by the theatrical and musical productions in which the most popular groups perform. Certain scenes of Gautama Buddha's previous lives are, nonetheless, still sometimes acted, hence the name given to the show: for in *zāt* (*jat* in transliteration) we can recognise the Burmese form of the Pāli term *jātaka*. At Ton-Zè-Pé, the scenes danced by the Mandalay National Theatre company gave a folk version of the *jātaka* presented as traditional.

At a monk's funeral, the two shows, *eyiń* and *zāt*, are performed alternately, both in time and in space: the *eyiń* takes place during the day, generally in the monastery grounds, while the *zāt* is performed at night in the village square. The alternation principle is also found within the two predominantly religious theatrical genres themselves in the middle of which is inserted a predominantly secular show known by the name of *ańyen*. The theatre troupe, comprised of both men and women, performs sketches on very different themes during which several prohibitions are transgressed. One of them, for example, makes fun of the monks' litanies by perfectly imitating the characteristic tone used in Sutta recitation. Another theme, and this is part of the trend of current government propaganda, is the caricaturing of Westerners. For example, a woman interrupts the classical dance she is performing to launch into a gestural and musical parody of rock'n'roll: the orchestra contributes to the comic effect of the scene. But criticism can just as easily be aimed at the junta. On one occasion, one of the actors was dressed as a soldier: with a colander for a helmet and a broom for a rifle, unusually audacious in the context of the Burmese dictatorship. Only the show called *añyen* and the puppet shows, which are in the same vein, can break the rules like this. The sketches vary from one troupe to another depending on the actors' improvisation talents.

Sexuality is a dominant theme which continues and exacerbates the conception/death relationship staged in the *eyiń*. During these sketches, a favourite gag is the disproportionately large end – mirroring the actors' exaggerated gestures and words – of the garment the men drape themselves in; they use the protuberance formed by this in a mime to represent an enormous erect phallus with which they run after their female partner. Another sketch consists in a play on the words 'little sister' to designate a 'girlfriend'; using the description one of the actors gives of his younger sister whom he praises, another actor begins to measure the 'smallness' of the sister, who gets smaller and smaller as he lowers the flat of his hand towards the ground until, when he is nearly touching it, he concludes: 'your sister is really very small, no bigger than a clitoris': the audience's laughter accompanies the faces the actress makes.

In some cases, the theme of sexuality is illustrated in a much more spectacular way. This was the case in the village of Tèkkè-Khyin, the only one of the four villages where the second funeral involved a bamboo tiger whose size was as impressive as that of its sex. This tiger, placed at the top of framework also made of bamboo and fixed to a cart, was jointed: attached to a central axis, it could turn in all directions; in addition, the jaws and the erect sex – painted pink – were operated by two men hidden inside the animal. The tiger was big enough for it to be able to pick up in its mouth a woman lying on her back, her legs and head hanging in thin air on either side of the animal's jaw. The tiger had been commissioned to replace another older one during the lifetime of the monk whose funeral was being celebrated that day. Some claimed that this practice was more common in the past than it is today. These informants gave as an example the funeral of the monk of Mingun, famous throughout the country for having recited the whole Tipitaka from memory.[16] When he died, in the

[16] Situated on the river bank opposite Mandalay, a little further upstream, Mingun is a major tourist destination because of a monumental temple built there in the Konbaung era.

early 1990s, the donors wanted to place his coffin in the mouth of a bamboo tiger but the government is said to have forbidden this, on the pretext that tourists would have been shocked.

According to my informants, the origin of the tiger scene at a second funeral ceremony refers to the death of Sariputta, the disciple on the Buddha's right: his corpse is said to have been carried off in the mouth of a tiger built by villagers. In the village of Tèkkè-Khyin, the reason the dead man's coffin was not put in the tiger's mouth would seem there again to rest on the monk's decision; he is said to have expressed the wish while alive that a 'princess' or an 'actress', depending on the translation of *mań: samī:*, be placed in it.[17] The scene of a feline carrying off a young woman between its jaws also goes back to an old legend which is very well known in Burma. It is about the 'two brothers' of Taunbyon, a spot near Mandalay where once a year, in August, a ritual centred on these two spirits, represented iconographically by a tiger, is held (Brac de la Perrière 1992). The story was described briefly by Daw Tebye, the principal actress of the *eyiń* described here:

> A very long time ago, Ko Yin Maung, who worked as a woodcutter in the Taunbyon region had married Ma Shwé U. Two messengers from King Anawratha [the founder of Pagan], Shwé Pyin the elder and Shwé Pyin the younger, went to China to get one of the Buddha's teeth. On their way back, they stopped at Taunbyon. The two brothers fell in love with Ma Shwe U. But she rejected them. So they sent a tiger to kill her. They became *nat* but still remained in love with the young woman. Having taken on the appearance of a tiger, they tried to kidnap her when she was weaving on the verandah of her house.

These two spirits are known as 'outside' spirits (*aprań nat*): outside the Buddhist pantheon and therefore outside the cycle of rebirths because of the bad death which characterises them. They must be distinguished from those called 'inside' spirits (*atwań: nat*). The latter 'inside' spirits are reborn in one of the thirty-one regions which comprise the *samsāra*, while the former 'outside' spirits become wandering spirits (Robinne 2000). Some are identified and iconographically represented: these are the '37 Lords' whose cult Bénédicte Brac de la Perrière studies (1989). The Taunbyon spirits are here the counterpart of the two inside spirits sent by Sakra and presented in the *eyiń*, just as the weaver and her husband are the counterpart of the principal actress and her brother.

[17] It would seem this was a good decision for the scaffolding on which a little house had been built and in front of which the young girl was weaving collapsed during the performance.

Whether it be the meaningfulness of popular beliefs, the challenging of Buddhist concepts or of accepted hierarchies, the fundamentals of society – Burmese, royal and Buddhist society and its contemporary metamorphoses, no sphere escapes caricature. The comic tone makes it possible to point out failings, limitations and excesses, even of the junta represented with a colander on its head or of monks who make everybody laugh when they are imitated. Relations between men and women, an underlying theme throughout this theatrical performance, are a pretext for staging the most serious concepts in a humorous form or using a dramatic approach. At once entertaining and didactic, the exercise lends itself to an interpretation of the process of rebirth which it invites us both to watch and to reflect on. The theme of corporeality and mental separation and aggregation is part of this: linked to the process of the body's decomposition, it is implicit throughout the ritual performance.

SHOWING REBIRTH

Conceptual amalgams

During the initiatory show called an *eyiń*, the troupe of actors stages the fundamental Buddhist concepts related to death. Thus the principal actress begins her lament in front of the 'cradle' holding the coffin:

> Today, the poor and the rich come despite themselves to pay their last respects to your body, oh lord monk. Food (*ahara*), the cycle of the seasons (*udu*), desire (*cit*) and karma (*kam*) are sources of suffering against which one cannot fight and death's generals exercised their art successfully when they caused your death, venerable abbot. Because of the three conditions of existence *rūpa nāma anicca* (impermanence), *rūpa nāma anattā* (not-self) and *rūpa nāma dukkha* (suffering) you have departed, venerable monk.[18]

In this reminder of the three conditions of existence, the latter are associated with the nouns *rūpa* and *nāma*. These two terms are of Pāli origin. They refer respectively to the corporeality and mental components of all living beings.

Rūpa refers to the corporeal order, with the connotation of 'physical form', of 'appearance', of 'matter'.[19] It is from this term, for example, that

[18] The Pāli-Burmese expression used for 'Existence' is *lakhana sum: pā*.

[19] *Rūpa* must be distinguished from the human body itself designated by the term *khandha* and used to form several compounds: *khandhamara* or *khandha upadhi*, 'the five aggregates of existence' (Anonymous 1996: 302); *viññanakkhandha*, 'consciousness aggregate' (*ibid.*: 336).

the Burmese words for 'sculpture', 'puppet' or even the neologism 'cinema' are derived.[20] The four main elements (*dhāt krī:*): water, earth, fire and air – with which even numbers are associated – condition the corporeality element. *Rūpa* is symbolised by a square in esoteric treatises.

As for *nāma* it refers to the mental order: it is on this term that the three words for 'name' in Burmese are based: *nām, amañ, nāmañ* or *nāmañ nāma.*[21] The three constitutive parts of *nāma*: the spirit, acts and seasons – with which uneven numbers are associated – condition the mental element. *Nāma* is symbolised by a triangle in esoteric treatises.

The corporeal and the mental are interactive and a source of harmony. It is on the combination of each constitutive part of the two orders, and on the combination of the two orders in a general sense, that the harmony of everything depends. This is the reason why, in the many astrological representations arising from the concepts of *nāma* and *rūpa*, even and odd numbers are alternated. We can thus understand why, during the *eyiṅ* funeral performance, the actress associates these two elements *rūpa* and *nāma*, symbolising harmony, with the three conditions of existence (*anicca, anattā* and *dukkha*), symbolising suffering. It is for this reason too that the triangular representation of the mental and the quandrangular representation of the corporeality are intertwined and surrounded by a circle, the symbol of entity; this is the model on which the *zedī*, at whose base the relics of the Buddha are said to have been placed and under which, in Burma, monks' ashes and bones are only placed exceptionally, are built.

Let us pause a moment to consider the concept of *nāma*. The translation given by Adoniram Judson ([1852] 1966: 568): 'mind, spirit' is quite close to the 'mental order' chosen here. On the other hand, Melford Spiro (1971: 85) has shown this and investigations carried out recently have confirmed it, the Burmese first make an amalgam between the concepts of *nāma* and *wiññyan* which are indiscriminately translated by 'soul':

> Using the Pāli-Burmese term as *nan-teiya* (Pāli, *nāma*) or the Burmese *wiññyan* (Pāli *viññāna*), to refer to a person's spirit, consciousness, mind or soul – for Buddhism distinguishes between the psychological (*nāma*) and the physical (*rūpa*) dimensions of all organisms – the more sophisticated villagers agree that this entity is impermanent; it comes to an end with a person's death.

[20] The life-size cast of a monk is called *rup tu*, a term built on the root *rūpa;* the definition given of this bisyllabic word in the Myanmar–English Dictionary (1998: 411) is: 'image; idol; statue; sculpture'.

[21] Judson (1966: 568); Robinne (1998: 91–105).

The definition given in the Myanmar–English Dictionary (1998: 475) for *wiññyan* is 'consciousness', 'spirit'[22]. As an identification principle, it is acquired when the name is given: this is not surprising when we remember that 'name' and 'mental' are built on the same root; and, because its medium is the body, it disintegrates at the same time as the corpse decomposes at death. An initial conclusion seems obvious: the *wiññyan* is not – contrary to what is generally thought – at the origin of death.

The notion of 'consciousness' is, theoretically, indissociable from the notion of self, or more correctly of no-self, designated by the Buddhist concept *anattā*. Yet, just as the Burmese generally confuse *nāma* and *wiññyan*, they also tend to reduce the notion of not-self (*anattā*) to that of impermanence (*anicca*) – a second amalgam. According to Spiro (1971: 86), this is partly due to the fact that 'in adopting the Hindu doctrine of reincarnation while rejecting that of a self or an eternal soul (*ātman*), Buddhism created a serious paradox'.

This idea is continued in the assimilation – a third amalgam – of the non-Buddhist concept of butterfly soul (*leippya*) and of the Buddhist one of consciousness (*wiññyan*). In their popular sense, butterfly soul, consciousness and mental order refer to the same notion, often translated – inappropriately – by soul. But if *nāma* and *wiññyan* are two distinct yet Buddhist concepts, this is not the case for the *leippya* which, after a transitionary period after death, becomes a wandering spirit in search of a new corporeality medium. The very concept of butterfly soul, and that of the life principle which is attached to it, is in opposition to the two fundamental concepts of the Buddhist doctrine which are, on the one hand, the impermanence of all things and, on the other, the non-existence of a soul associated with the negation of the egocentric principle, 'this illusion of the self as an entity' (Anonymous 3 1996: 282). Instead of imprisoning them in an impossible antinomy, the Burmese interweave these two notions, that of self-contained in *leippya* and of not-self-contained in *wiññyan*, in their complementarity.

A fourth amalgam is made between consciousness (*wiññyan*) and 'life' in the sense of 'breath' designated by the term *asak*. Yet the distinction between the two is fundamental. Consciousness is an identification principle: a baby, for example, only acquires its own identity several weeks or months after birth when it is given a name: this is the moment when its *wiññyan* is supposed to separate from its mother's. It disintegrates at death

[22] In order to avoid any confusion with *nat* translated by 'spirit' and to be done with the notion of 'soul' with which it is often inappropriately associated, the term of Pāli origin *wiññyan* refers here to the Buddhist concept of 'consciousness'.

at the same time as the body decays. As for the concept of life, it is the fruit of the aggregation of the corporeality component (*rūpa*) and the mental component (*nāma*). In other words, the entity *asak* – the uniting of *rūpa* and *nāma* – is a life principle: it is the separation of the mental and the corporeality which is at the origin of death, while *wiññyan* is an identification principle.

These amalgams or confusions cannot be simply attributed to ignorance. From the point of view considered here they are meaningful. It is particularly in this space of liberty Buddhism contains that the idea of consciousness associated with life (*asak*) is interpreted, at the very point where the notion of self is fundamentally alien to the doctrine, at the very point where the Pāli word acts as a conceptual tool denouncing the very concept it designates.

Explanatory metaphors

What is reborn – or, possibly, reincarnated? The question often sows confusion. Investigations on this subject have not been confined only to people – monks or lay people – present at funerals; they have been undertaken for many years, in urban and rural settings, in central Burma as elsewhere in Shan State. It is generally accepted that it is the dead person's *wiññyan* or *leippya* which follows the cycle of rebirth. In almost all cases, the answer is identical: the *wiññyan* 'clings', the literal translation of the expression *wiññyan tway* that the Myanmar–English Dictionary (1998: 475) gives as 'to come into another existence'.

A case in point is the notion of identified reincarnation according to which a dead relative's *wiññyan* or *leippya* has again taken on a human form in the person of one of their descendants: the physical signs or the resemblances to a dead person are presented as 'the proof' that the person 'eaten' is the reincarnation of someone who has died (Robinne 2000).[23] The people concerned – and the case is very frequent – say they are both themselves and someone else. A well-known Burmanisation process is based on this type of identified reincarnation: the Burmese king Alaungsithu (1112–67) is thus presented both as the grandson of Kyanzittha and as the identified reincarnation of the Indian prince Pedikaya (Pe Maung Tin and Luce 1960: 105–6). Let us briefly recall this episode. While he was travelling through the air, Pedikaya heard from some monks of the marriage of his beloved, the

[23] The Burmese expression associated with this concept is *lū wan cā:*, literally: 'person + to enter + to eat'.

Burmese princess; stupefied, he let fall from his mouth the ball of mercury which gave him supernatural powers: the ejection of the ball not only caused the Indian prince's death but also impregnated the Burmese princess who gave birth to Alaungsithu, the future king. Such a principle of identified reincarnation contains the idea of the *wiññyan*'s perenniality and the continuity of the rebirth process. As such it is in opposition to the two Buddhist notions of impermanence and not-self.

Some, on the other hand, claim that the *leippya/wiññyan* couple disintegrates at death. When someone dies, their consciousness also ceases to exist: it is 'gagged', this being the semantic value of *khyup* in the expression *wiññyan khyup*, that is to say 'to die'. This was, in particular, the opinion of a monk from the village of Tèkkè-Khyin, who strongly and spontaneously opposed the idea that the *wiññyan* is reborn in one of the thirty-one regions. The monks from the Tudhamma congregation of 'Pariyeitta', the Buddhist University in Mandalay and those of the Shwe Kyin congregation from Mahandhayon monastery in Amarapura share this opinion. These monks, without exception, give as a synonym for *wiññyan* the term *asak*, that is to say 'life', with the connotation of 'breath'. According to this meaning, life stops when consciousness disintegrates with death. It is significant that the terms *wiññyan* and *leippya* are not mentioned once during the two and a half hours the *eyiń* performance lasts and this could be analysed as follows: though the *wiññyan* and *leippya* are identification principles, neither of them is at the origin of death.

Opinions are divided on the *wiññyan*'s continuity or discontinuity. Two metaphors are generally used to illustrate the rebirth process: the flame of a candle passed on to another candle or one's own reflection in a mirror. Neither of them, however, explains the modus operandi of rebirth. This vagueness is maintained in the very expression meaning 'to die' when talking of a monk: *Bhawa nat tham* ***pram*** *[pyan] lwan tō mū*, that is to say '**flight** to the land of the spirits'. Written *pram*, according to the most common spelling (Anonymous 1: 89–90), this term means 'to fly' in the cycle of rebirths, just like a bird continues to fly from branch to branch to return to the metaphor generally used; this expression appears to infer a principle of continuity. On the other hand, if this term is spelt *pyan*, as some recommend it to be, it has the meaning of 'to return', thus inferring the idea of discontinuity peculiar to rebirth.

Discontinuity and continuity, both processes have their followers. The ritual shows links to an individual's initiatory path – the family ones for the giving of a baby's name, those concerning the whole community for the robing rituals or the holistically orientated ones of a monk's funeral – seem to have resolved the question.

Analytical reconstruction

Far from explaining a process, the metaphors are part of the continuity of the amalgams made: they illustrate the difficulty of conceptualising the process of rebirth. The ritual stagings of death and rebirth belong to the same empirical process. Therefore, let us now try to go a step further by giving a conceptual dimension to the process.

The *rūpa/nāma* association is not only a source of harmony; it is also a source of life (*asak*). The principal actress of the *eyiń* reminds us of this, death is the result of the separation of the corporeality and the mental, for if they separate permanently, life, in the sense of breath, expressed in the term *asak*, stops: most monks agree on this.[24] Then the body's decomposition commences; having once more sung the pointlessness of trying to struggle against death, the actress of the *eyiń* begins a detailed description of the process:

On the first day after death, the joints can no longer move; and even though the five aromatic substances are applied, one mark, then two gradually appear on the cheekbones; the cheeks and the eyelids cave in.

On the second day, the food rots, the intestines overflow, the stomach loses its shape and swells up out of all proportion.

On the third day, it is impossible to love the deceased any longer, the heart feels only hate; the veins on the corpse swell and liquid seeps out of all the orifices.

On the fourth day, protuberances appear on the body which, through lack of air, looks like a bag of skin on the bones.

On the fifth day, it's really disgusting, the two eyes bulge from their sockets and the tongue hangs out like a monster's.[25]

On the sixth day, pus flows out: it would be a lie to say it smells nice, it stinks, it's disgusting and you want to be sick.

On the seventh day, it is impossible to love the deceased, the kidneys and the liver mix as they decompose, the guts are in shreds, shit flows out constantly.

On the eighth day, a breath of air is enough to detach the skin, the body withers and falls away like rotten fruit before disappearing into the ground, it is written in the Dhamma that all is doomed to disappear and die.[26]

[24] *Khandhā khwè swā: pyi. Rūpa nè. Khwè swā: tè. charatō bhurā*, that is: 'the body has separated. The monk's *rūpa* and *nāma* have separated.'

[25] 'Tebè', *sabhak* in transliteration, a category of *pratta* located in the lower regions of rebirth.

[26] The term used here is *krwe*, which means 'to fall' when talking of fruit and, by extension, 'to die'.

On the ninth day, it's disgusting to see the marrow coming through the bones and these whitening in places like depigmented skin.

On the tenth day, the veins and arteries are in shreds and the body in pieces. There is no hope of escaping the endless cycle of *samsara*, the Buddha himself was not spared it.

The *wiññyan* is meant to roam around the corpse for a time, then around the spot where it lay in the house: several days after the funeral of a layman, the dead person's circle of family and friends put his clothes on the mat where he used to sleep; for a week food is placed there specifically for the *wiññyan*, to prevent it wandering about. The end of this offering marks the definitive disappearance of the body and consciousness which is sanctioned by offerings to the monks and the preaching of the latter at a final ceremony.

The process of the corpse's decomposition is designated by the Pāli-Burmese expression 'the ten meditations on impurity', *asubha chay pā*. The different stages in the body's decomposition are punctuated by the growing physical disgust and the concomitant erasure of feelings. And it is only when the body merges with the earth and when feelings have completely disappeared that the concept of impermanence openly and publicly finds its full expression. Here we find, applied to the Buddhist concept of rebirth, Robert Hertz's analysis (1928: 32) of the transmigration process: 'Death is consummated only when decomposition has ended: only then does the deceased cease to belong to this world so as to enter into another existence.' Decomposition is also a process of separation: when, on the one hand, the corpse decomposes, on the other, rebirth takes place. Just as the giving of a name (*nām* or *nāman*) to a child or the giving of a new name to a novice marks the fact that the mental component (*nāma*) has combined with a new medium, the *nāma* of a dead person undergoes a change of the same order.

The corpse's decomposition is both hastened, because the entrails are scooped out, and partially interrupted because the body is embalmed in order to preserve it temporarily. The artifical preservation of the corporeality component can be explained by the necessity of stopping the concomitant disintegration of the mental component which is alone destined to be reborn. For this, it must go through a preliminary stage which enables it to separate from the corporeality component – of which the body is the human form (*khandha*) – and then to aggregate to a new corporeality component whose form and nature vary according to the region of rebirth. The upper regions inhabited by the Brahma are of two sorts: the first, *rūpa brahma*, possess a corporeality dimension, the others, *arūpa brahma*, have no corporeality dimension; at this level of rebirth, the mental dimension is self-sufficient. Although rebirth in one of the regions inhabited by the Brahma is potentially possible, it is on one of the six levels inhabited by the *nat dewa* that rebirth is generally envisaged. *Rūpa* and *nāma* reunited generate in their entity a 'breath' principle (*asak*), from which a new life course (*bhawa*) can begin. In the absolute, a new consciousness should be added to this entity, just as a baby acquires its own identity when a name is attributed to it.

According to this pattern, the principle of 'consciousness' (*wiññyan*) is no more a source of life than the origin of death: its disappearance or reappearance is merely the result of one or the other, it is not the agent of it. It disintegrates at the same time as the corpse decomposes and this is probably one of the reasons why an earthenware pot at the dead person's feet is broken when the coffin is taken out of the monastery: it is no longer necessary to feed the *wiññyan* of the deceased whose end is physically marked by the fragments of the earthenware pot.[27]

As we have seen, opinions are divided on whether the *wiññyan* is reborn or not. The fact of considering it in the absolute is the only way to see clearly the structure inherent to the rebirth process. This involves, on the one hand, abandoning the idea of the *wiññyan*'s rebirth and, on the other, considering the *rūpa/nāma/asak* trilogy as an entity and in its internal dynamics. If the separation of the mental and corporeality is the explanation of death, this separation is itself at the origin of the stopping of life (breath) just as the aggregation of the mental to a new corporeality medium gives rise in the absolute to life or rebirth[28]. *Rūpa* and *nāma* are connected 'for life and beyond the grave' as it were. But whereas the corporeality element and consciousness are doomed to follow the same course of decomposition, the mental component is destined to undergo a metamorphosis enabling it to aggregate to another corporeality medium in the region where it is meant to be reborn.

To summarise, after death, the process set in motion is the following:

By separating, the corporeality (*rūpa*) and mental components (*nāma*) cause death (*ase*).

The body (*khandha*) decomposes at the same time as consciousness (*wiññyan*), an identification principle, disintegrates.

Embalming temporarily delays the decomposition process.

The mental component must find a new corporeality medium in a rebirth region, if not it too will disintegrate.

[27] Lagirarde (1998: 55), writing about funeral rites in Lanna and Laos, talks of the 'pot of disgust or of separation' and, quoting Terwiel (1994: 155) recalls a similar practice among the Tai of Assam (*ibid.*).

[28] A concept expressed by the Pāli term *paṭisandhi*.

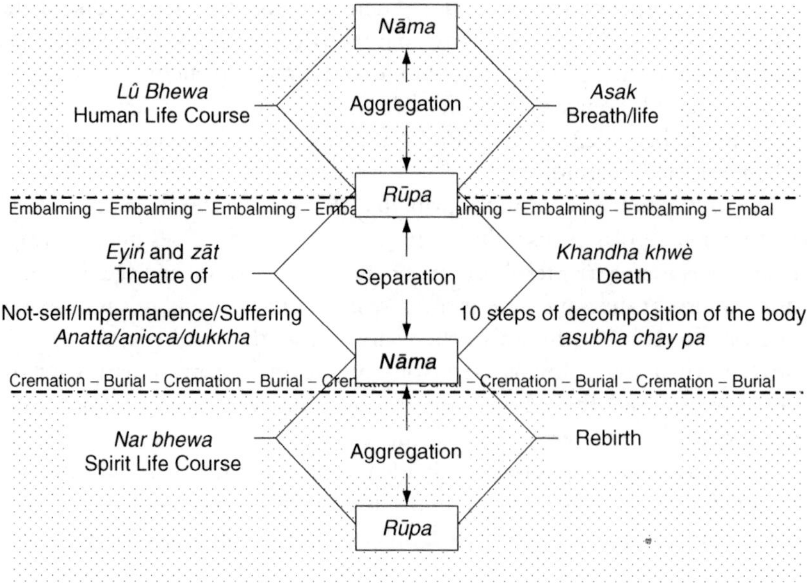

Figure 8.1 Process of separation and aggregation

The initiation's purpose is to enable the mental component to pass from a human corporeality medium to a corporeality medium whose nature depends on the region of rebirth.

The new corporeality and mental entity generates life (*asak*).

In theory, a new identification principle should be given to this entity.

This process is synthetised in Figure 8.1.

We now understand why it is necessary to delay the body's decomposition during the funeral: it is a question of preserving its mental alter ego in order to subject it to the initiation without which the process of separation from the human body and that of aggregation to a new corporeality component would not be possible. If the mental component decomposed like the corporeality component, there would be no rebirth possible.

The intermediate vigil period between the lying in repose of a lay person's body and its cremation – or burial – is, in the case of a monk's second funeral, the corollary of the *eyiń* theatrical performance. The lying in repose, for a few hours in the case of a lay person or for several months in a monastery for a monk, does not only allow anyone who so wishes to come and pay their last respects, but also is the prelude to an initiatory phase during which the separation of the corporeality and the mental component, the metamorphosis of the mental element, followed by the aggregation of the mental to a new corporeality component occur. Even though it is not expressed in these terms, this is essentially the reason why the body's decomposition must be temporarily interrupted. It is also the reason why the funeral takes place in three stages.

The tripartite structure of the *eyiń* initiatory performance is found not only in the form of the second funeral but also in the first and second funeral ritual taken as a whole. In the first stage, during first funerals, the concomitant disintegration of the body (*khandha rūpa*), of consciousness and of the mental component (*nāma*) is controlled. The second stage is the intermediate phase – 'preliminary' in Arnold van Gennep's terminology ([1909] 1981) – between the first and second funeral, during which the corpse is presented in its glass coffin so that the disciples (*tapañ*) and donors (*dakā* and *dakāma*) can pay their last respects to the deceased monk. The third stage is the ritual performance of the rebirth process. The necessity of a transitional initiatory phase, be it in the form of an *eyiń* or simply a vigil of a few hours or several months, is the reason for the existence of a first and second funeral.

REPRESENTATIONS OF SUPERIOR MONKS

Far from challenging the concepts related to rebirth, the variants observed from one village to another highlight, sometimes in an almost caricatural fashion, the fact that they are deeply rooted in social life. Thus the play known as an *eyiń* accentuates the terms of the conception/death relationship by giving them an extension of a sex/violence kind, a tendency which is further accentuated by the scene connected with the bamboo tiger. At the same time, the variants indicate, under a guise of 'tradition', a leitmotiv running all through the ritual wherever it is performed, certain paradoxes or vaguenesses contained or maintained in the Buddhist canon. This is the case, as we have seen, for the confusion generated by the concepts of butterfly soul, consciousness, life in the sense of 'breath', or of the mental element, which are used in place of one another. It is also the case for that between the astrological short term and the long term of the rebirth cycle: if astrological calculations are used, it is doubtless in order to harmonise the social and the cosmic order and to endow the rituals with the best signs but it is also – above all even – in order to organise and purify a life course. During a ritual, the notion of merits shared by all the men and women donors gives the life course its collective dimension. The ritual shows both stages of the canonic texts by visualising the process of rebirth and emphasises the social bonds by transgressing some interdicts such as relationship between genders or between military authorities and civil society.

Alongside these variants, some more radical changes are also emerging. For instance, the proliferation over the last few years of iconographic representations of monks. In agreement with the villagers, during their lifetime the latter sometimes commission a life-size statue of themselves. To celebrate his forty fasts, that is to say the number of years he had been ordained, the monk of Ton-Zè-Pé commissioned a cast of himself, a practice which is becoming more and more common in Burma as in Thailand (Gabaude 2003). Protected by glass walls, the iconographic representation of the monk stood imposingly first beside the mortal remains, then in the teaching hall (*dhamma rum*), before being moved into the monastery where pilgrims will be able to continue to pay him their posthumous respects. In doing this, the villagers are not so much trying to acquire some form of power (*dago*) contained in the hyperrealist representation – the monks all reject this interpretation which the villagers tend to adopt – but paying their respects to the acknowledged qualities (*guṇ*) of the dead monk.[29] The members of the Shwe-Kyin congregation are not exempt from this tendency: two sculptures, representing the two previous superior monks, stand outside Mahagandhayon monastery at Amarapura, on the east side, in vaults built on the actual spot where their cremations took place.[30]

Such hyperrealist representations which endure after the monk's death call into question, to say the least, the contemporary meaning of the Buddhist concepts of not-self and impermanence. These representations should not be put on the same level as the use of medicinal injections instead of evisceration. Embalming the body provisionally stops the decomposition process in order to make possible the ritual passage from life to death and from death to rebirth; because of its perennial – and not temporary for ritual purposes – nature, the presence of statues of dead monks in monasteries seems on the contrary to be a response to the actress in the *eyiń* in search of a substitute for death. In the one case, embalming

[29] *Dago* is *Tankhui:* in Burmese, a term doubtless of Mône origin; the Sanskrit equivalent is *pratihaya* (Myanmar–English Dictionary 1998: 186). *Guṇ* is from the Pāli *guṇa*. The definition given in the Myanmar–English Dictionary (1998: 86) is '(a) qualities; characteristics; attributes; (b) prestige'. The Burmese Pāli expression used for the monk is *ārum pyu*, 'evoke the good characteristics' [of the dead monk].

[30] The Pāli term designating this building is *bhimān*.

provides a short-term transitory solution needed for the ritual process of separating the corporeality from the mental; in the other, the iconographic representation is a choice in the long term.

The paradox created by the dead man's statue with regard to the concept of impermanence is not new in itself. It is found in the practice, which is very rare in Burma, that consists of burying a dead monk's ashes under a *zedī*. The expression designating this funeral practice is 'to gather the bones together', *arui: kok pwè*. It is not attested in the Ava era (Sīri Ujanā: 1962) and the author of the document about the death of a monk who lived in the Konbaung period says it was reserved for the Buddha's disciples and lesser Buddhas (Anonymous 1 1988). I have never to date had the opportunity of observing this final phase. The last ceremony of gathering together the bones was, to my knowledge, that performed at the funeral of Ledi Seyadaw, a spiritual authority whose charisma spread beyond the Tudhamma congregation alone. The *zedī* under which his ashes were buried was built within the actual monastery grounds and the spot was later abandoned. The reason for this was given to me indirectly by the monks of the village of Tèkkè-Khyin. The remains of a superior monk had been placed in a building erected on the other side of the outer walls of a *zedī*. 'How could I bow down before this *zedī* if the ashes of a monk younger than I, with perhaps less fasts than I, [the dead monk had in fact sixty-nine fasts, a kind of record] and whose karma is perhaps inferior to mine, were in it?' Contrary to what seems to be practised in Laos (Ladwig 2003), there is, therefore, in Burma no phase for the reintegration of the deceased into social life. It is the opposite that happens: if a monk's ashes are found to have been buried under a *zedī*, it is social life which moves away from the dead man.

BIBLIOGRAPHY

Anonymous 1 (1988) [2532 of the Buddhist era, 1350 of the Burmese era], [*Mandalay, Mahanindhasenara monastery, gratitude, cremation ceremony of the dead Bhaddanta Mahāthera Abhidazamaharúaguru. Cremation ceremony*], Mandalay: Mahānindhasenārāma monastery (in Burmese).

Anonymous 2 (2003) [2547 of the Buddhist era, 1365 of the Burmese era], 1996 AD, [*Mandalay division, district of Myiò Khyan, village of Takkèkhyiò, Uttarārā monastery, in gratitude, biography of the monk Mahāthera Bhaddanta U Sāsana and programme of the cremation ceremony*], Mandalay: edition published by the author (in Burmese).

Anonymous 3 (1996) *A Dictionary of Buddhist Terms* [*Buddhadesanātō Wohāra Abhidhan*], Rangoon: Ministry of Religious Affairs (in English and Burmese), with an Introduction by Nyunt Maung.

Brac de la Perrière, B. (1989), *Les Rituels de Possession en Birmanie: du Culte d'État aux Cérémonies Privées*, Paris: Éditions Recherches sur les Civilisations.

(1992), 'La fête de Taunbyon: le grand rituel du culte des naq de Birmanie (Myanmar)', *Bulletin de l'École Française d'Extrême-Orient* 79 (2), 201–31.

(2001), 'Malemort et "bonne mort" en Birmanie (Myanmar)', in ed. Brigitte Baptandier, *De la Malemort en Quelques Pays d'Asie*, Paris: Karthala, 235–58.

(2006), 'Le traité des apparences du monde: analyse des rituels de la royauté birmane d'après un traité du dix-huitième siècle', in eds. B. Brac de la Perrière and M.-L. Reiniche, *Les Apparences du Monde: Royautés Hindoues et Bouddhiques de l'Asie du Sud et du Sud-Est*, Paris: École Française d'Extrême-Orient, 265–94.

Gabaude, L. (2003), 'A new phenomenon in Thaï monasteries: the stūpa-museum', in eds. P. Pichard and F. Lagirarde, *The Buddhist Monastery: a Cross-cultural Survey*, Paris: École Française d'Extrême-Orient, 169–86.

Gennep, A. van, [1909] (1981), *Les Rites de Passage: Etudes Systématiques des Rites*, Paris: Editions A. et J. Picard.

Hertz, R. [1907] (1928), 'Contribution à une étude sur la représentation collective de la mort', in *Mélanges de Sociologie Religieuse et de Folklore*, Paris: Félix Alcan, 1–98 (1st edn. *Année Sociologique*, 1st series, vol. 10).

Judson, A. [1852] (1966), *A Burmese–English Dictionary*, Rangoon: Baptist Board of Publications.

Kloppenborg, R. and Hanegraaf, W. J. (1995), *Female Stereotypes in Religious Studies*, Leiden: E. J. Brill.

Ladwig, P. (2003), *Death Rituals among the Lao: an Ethnological Analysis*, Berlin. Seacom Edition, Tai Culture Interdisciplinary, Tai Studies Series 15.

Lagirarde, F. (1998), 'Une interprétation bouddhique des rites funéraires du Lanna et du Laos: le sutta apocryphe de Maha-Kala', *Aséanie* 2, 47–77.

Leclère, A. (1906), *Cambodge: la Crémation et ses Rites Funéraires*, Hanoi: Schneider.

Mya Tin [Daw] (trans.) [1985] (1995), *The Dhammapada: Verses and Stories*, Yangon: Myanmar Pitaka Association.

Myanmar Language Commission (1998), *Myanmar–English Dictionary*, Yangon: Ministry of Education.

Myint Swe [U] (1994), *Jātkrī: Chay Bhwè – The Ten Great Jataka Stories*, Yangon: Mandalay, nawarat cāpe (in Burmese and English).

Obādā Bhi Wam Sa [vénérable] (no date), *Saruppra Abhidhān – Précis de la Nature Humaine*, phyāpum tuik san, saraktō tuik (in Burmese).

Pe Maung Tin [U] and Luce, G. H. (trans.) [1923] (1960), *The Glass Palace Chronicle of the Kings of Burma*, Rangoon: Rangoon University Press.

Robinne, F. (1998), 'La notion de reste dans le choix du nom personnel en Birmanie (Myanmar)', *Aséanie* 1, 91–105.

(2000), *Fils et Maîtres du Lac: Relations Interethniques dans l'Etat Shan de Birmanie*, Paris: Centre National de la Recherche Scientifique/Maison des Sciences de l'Homme.

(2002), 'L'initiation bouddhique au marriage: formes rituelles en Birmanie', *Aséanie* 10, 11–37.

(2003), 'The monastic unity: a contemporary Burmese artefact?', in eds. P. Pichard and F. Lagirarde, *The Buddhist Monastery: a Cross-cultural Survey*, Paris: École Française d'Extrême-Orient, 75–92.

Shway Yoe [George Scott] (1963), *The Burman, his Life and Notions*, New York: W. W. Norton. [1st edn. 1882].

Sīri Ujanā (1962), *Lawka Byuha Kyam – le Traité des Apparences du Monde*, 2nd edn., Rangoon: Govt. Printing Press (in Burmese).

Spiro, M. E. (1971), *Buddhism and Society: a Great Tradition and its Burmese Vicissitudes*, London: George Allen and Unwin.

Terwiel, B. J. (1994), *Monks and Magic: an Analysis of Religious Ceremonies in Central Thaïland*, 3rd edn., Bangkok: White Lotus.

Than Tun, [U] (1978), 'History of Buddhism in Burma, AD 1000–1300', *Journal of the Burma Research Society* **61** (1/2).

CHAPTER 9

From bones to ashes: the Teochiu management of bad death in China and overseas

Bernard Formoso

INTRODUCTION

The idea, widely spread in Asia, that each human being is a microcosmic emanation of the whole universe, reduplicating on a small scale its basic elements and ruling principles, commonly leads to theories of social epidemiology and to related rituals, which closely link treatment of the physical and of the social bodies. For the Chinese case, several studies have richly documented the central function that the proper manipulation and geomantic placing of the dead, conducted during the funeral, assumes for the regeneration of life and the redistribution of status within the line of descent.[1] James L. Watson has also convincingly demonstrated that the standardisation by the state of death rituals was a major political issue in the pursuit of cultural unity and of social cohesiveness in late imperial China (Watson 1993: 80–9). In this cultural context, however, little attention has been paid to the treatment of those who die at the fringe of the social structure, that is, without descendants to take care of them. Because their 'orphaned' remains are believed to pollute the environment and their souls to transform into hungry and wandering ghosts who threaten the living as well as the social order, these dead occupy a core position in the Chinese folk theories of social epidemiology, and therefore constitute a topic of great epistemological relevancy.

The present study intends to fill this gap through examination of a ritual, named *xiu gugu* 修孤骨 (Teochiu: *xiu kouku*, 'refining of the orphaned bones') that the Teochiu, generally considered an ethnic subgroup of the Han people, of Chaozhou (in northeast Guangdong province) perform periodically. In addition to the analysis of the meanings associated with the manipulation of human bones during the ritual, my purpose is to explore the political economy of the event in contemporary China, and in

[1] See notably Ahern (1973); Watson (1982: 155–86); Watson and Rawski (1988).

the countries of Southeast Asia, namely Thailand and Malaysia, where Teochiu immigrants adapted the ritual to local needs. Between 1993 and 2005, I attended several *xiu gugu* in these three areas. Through comparing different versions of this ritual in China and Southeast Asia, I present a threefold argument. First, I assume that the changes imposed by the Thai Buddhist and Malay Muslim environment to the original *xiu gugu* framework shed light on core conceptions underlying the ritual. The second statement is that the contrasting modalities of adaptations of the ritual to Thailand and Malaysia reflect the patterns of interethnic relations that the Chinese minority entertains with the native populations of these two countries. Concerning the Thai situation, my assumption is that Buddhism, whatever the doctrinal differences between Theravāda and Mahāyāna traditions, is a key factor to bridge differences between the groups in contact. Lastly, I suggest that overseas, in cultural and political environments challenging the perpetuation of a Chinese specificity, the management of bones by the means of this ritual brings ethnic issues to the fore. This is particularly true in Thailand where, for various reasons explored in the following pages, most of the 'orphaned bones' that the Teochiu 'adopt' at the occasion of the *xiu gugu* are those of Thai natives.

HISTORICAL BACKGROUND AND PRACTICE OF THE RITUAL IN CHINA

According to oral accounts that I recorded in Chaozhou, the idea of organising *xiu gugu* was devised during the twelfth century, under the Song Dynasty, by a Buddhist monk named Dafeng 大峰 (Teo. Tai Hongkong) who had settled in Chaoyang County (Chaozhou). Legends about this monk, recorded by the modern scholars Lin Wushu and Zhan Tianyan, present him as a miracle-maker who used his magical powers to relieve the local folk from periodical disasters.[2] He is portrayed in Chaozhou as a local bodhisattva who became an object of worship after his death. During the late Ming Dynasty (seventeenth

[2] Lin Wushu (1995, 1996: 1–17); Zhan Tianyan (1997: 150–65). According to Lin Wushu (1995: 25–41), Dafeng was born around 1039. Having passed the civil service examination, he was appointed governor of a district in Zhejiang, but gave up the position because the corruption of the imperial bureaucracy disgusted him. He then chose to become a Buddhist monk in the neighbouring province of Fujian. Afterwards, he settled in the ruins of an old monastery located on a hill, in the present-day Teochiu (Chaozhou) district of Chaoyang. He rebuilt the monastery and became famous by employing compassion to rescue the needy. He offered free medical treatments for the people, donated coffins and sponsored funerals for those who passed away in poverty. He also raised funds to build a stone bridge at the mouth of a local river whose floods were devastating. According to legend, Dafeng wrote to notify the Gods of the Water of the project and to seek their blessing. They then interrupted the

century), devotees made of his hermitage a Buddhist hall for good deeds, or *shantang* 善堂 (Teo. *xiangteng*), which sponsored charitable activities. This charitable body, called Baode Shantang 報德善堂 ('*shantang* for the recompense of virtue', Teo. *Potek Xiangteng*) is the mother temple of about 70 per cent of the 350 halls for good deeds operating today in the Chaozhou area (they numbered more than 500 before 1949).[3]

The manager of Baode Shantang at the time of the study told me that the first *xiu gugu* in history was performed in the 1640s, because of the large number of deaths during the Qing overthrow and a plague epidemic that followed.[4] To face the crisis, the local gentry quickly founded new *shantang*, and put into practice Dafeng's instructions concerning a ritual device – the *xiu gugu* – whose aim was to protect the living from epidemics by burying the corpses, and to offer the orphan dead an adoptive family, through reintegrating them into the cycle of reincarnation by means of the ritual and continuous devotions.

Although in contemporary Chaozhou most *xiu gugu* activities are organised by *shantang*, some of them are performed independently of this institutional framework, either by village communities or lineage associations. More fundamentally, the ritual seems to be rooted in the practice of secondary burial which was traditionally widespread in Guangdong, Fujian and the South of Taiwan.[5] Even though my informants deny the practice of private secondary burials among the Teochiu, the basic goals they pursue by performing the *xiu gugu* are similar to those put forward by Timothy Tsu in discussing the south of Taiwan, namely purification of the remains, revival of the purified bones and definition of the geomantic property of the grave (Tsu 2000: 2). In the specific case of the Buddhist cult communities, the practice also resonates with Buddhist notions of compassion and the

flood tide for seven days, the time needed to complete the work. He passed away when he was 86 years old (1125), but his remains were never discovered. As in the case of Bodhidharma his grave, located in Heping, is said to contain one of his shoes.

3 See Ma Ximin (2002).

4 In actuality, the involvement of lay Buddhist societies in China devoted to burying the unwanted dead goes back at least as far as the sixth century. See Liu Shufen (1995: 19–46). This seems to have been a popular innovation lacking canonical sources to sustain it.

5 See Lin Xunsheng (1955: 25–42); Freedman (1971: 118–23); Ahern (1973: 163–219); Watson (1982); Thompson (1988: 71–108). Watson notes that in China the secondary burial complex is limited to the Southern Han peoples (e.g. Cantonese, Hakka and Hokkien). According to him: 'There can be little doubt that the custom is historically linked to close interactions with the non-Han (or more precisely pre-Han) cultures of the region. The pattern of burial and reburial, which plays on the distinction between flesh and bones, is found throughout the highlands of Southeast Asia and extends down the Peninsula into Borneo and New Guinea. Somehow, during the long history of sinicisation in South China, indigenous burial practices appear to have been transformed and incorporated into the local versions of Han culture' (1993: 90–1).

correlative acquisition of merits. In addition, conditions specific to Chaozhou no doubt also played an important role in the development of the ritual. Surrounded by ranges of mountains, this remote area was, and is still today, one of the poorest and most populated parts of Guangdong province. Consequently, the cyclical epidemics and starvations, which affected the southeast of China for centuries, were locally amplified. Informants also suggest the coastal location of Chaozhou as a factor. According to them, a significant part of the unclaimed bodies processed through the ritual were victims of typhoons and shipwrecks.

The main requirement to organise a *xiu gugu* is, of course, to have gathered an amount of unclaimed remains large enough to justify either the building of a new collective grave or the opening of an old one. In the past, fresh corpses were left to decay from seven to ten years in temporary graves, but over the last decade the share such corpses constitute in the stock of orphaned bones has decreased significantly. Nowadays, local police collect the remains of the unidentified dead for identification and forensic evidence. Moreover, following an official document by the government in 1956, the generalisation of cremation became a national objective. Chinese citizens were prompted and even compelled during the most repressive periods to cremate their dead, though the enforcement of the successive regulations outside of cities was not uniform.[6] As a consequence, the remains collected in present days are mainly old bones and skeletons, which are either discovered accidentally, for example in building sites, or are located in private graves, which must be shifted from the farm land they occupy to other places.[7] Such resettlements, caused by overpopulation,

[6] Fang Ling and Vincent Goossaert (2008: 51–73) have shown that the KMT had already launched in 1934 a policy based on notions of hygienism, frugality and civism that encouraged Chinese citizens to disown the traditional 'costly' and 'superstitious' funeral rites. Later on, the Communist Party followed this policy. It compelled the peasants to incinerate their dead at the occasion of the 'Great leap forward' campaign (1958–61), and destroyed, at large scale, graves and coffins during the Cultural Revolution. Although, after 1978, funeral processions, banquets and burials were again tolerated, the regulation of February 1985 (*Guowuyuan guanyu binzang guanli de zaxing guiding* 國務院關于殯葬管理的暫行規定) planned to progressively extend cremation to densely populated areas and to restrain burial practices to non-arable land. In 1997, this regulation was replaced by the *Bindang guanli tiaoli* 殡葬管理条例, which recommends a strict control of the concessions' size and duration.

[7] The number of bones gathered through this mode is far from insignificant. To take a few examples, Baode Shantang, the oldest Teochiu benevolent hall devoted to Dafeng, collected in the 1990s more than 20,000 bones by prospecting in the construction site of an industrial plant in Heping (Chaoyang), while during the same period it offered temporary graves to 180 fresh corpses (客尸, *ke shi*, 'guest bodies', Teo. *kêhshi*). According to Lin Juncong (1998: 569, 597), the Haimen branch of Baode Shantang buried more than 14,000 bones exhumed from building sites, while Chengde Shanshe 诚德善社 of Shantou, at the request of the authorities, took away and buried, in the early 1990s, more than 1,000 skeletons from the site of what is now the Shantou University.

urbanisation and agricultural intensification, saw a peak during the Maoist period. At that time, local Communist officials proved to be pragmatic by relying mainly on the *xiu gugu* tradition to smoothly manage this sensitive issue: the scattered remains were put into collective graves under the supervision of Dafeng or other deities. This is why, despite the ban on *shantang* activities enforced in the 1950s, the ritual was preserved, even during the Cultural Revolution.

Such a pragmatic attitude was certainly favoured by the practice of collective burial which characterises the *xiu gugu*, and which opportunely met the collectivist objectives then pursued by the Communists. More fundamentally, this pragmatism may be interpreted with reference to the political centrality of funeral practices in pre-modern and contemporary China. The Teochiu materials confirm the statement made by James L. Watson about late imperial China that: 'The exclusion of burial rites from the roster of the prescribed death rituals can thus be seen as an implicit concession to ethnic and regional sensitivities.' He adds that: 'This may well have been the consequence of a conscious policy by imperial officials and educated elites, given that any attempt to control burial practices would have been disastrously expensive, and impossible to enforce' (Watson 1993: 91).

Although Communists of the 1950s and 1960s often proved to be more dogmatic, they rapidly faced a sound resistance in rural areas, prompting them to adopt a policy of flexibility in the application of the Beijing policy. More recently, the regulations of 1985 and 1997 urging families to cremate their dead and restraining the granting of grave concessions gave rise to the same local adjustments.[8] This is notably the case in Chaozhou, where the temporary burying of unclaimed fresh corpses in preparation for eventual *xiu gugu* is widely tolerated, some counties or districts going so far as to supply local *shantang* with unclaimed bodies from other provinces or corpses of individuals sentenced to death.

Finally, owing to the short supply of burial land, Chaozhou has recently seen an increase in the number of 'normal dead' initially buried privately, but who are reprocessed to a collective grave through the festival. In the view of the organisers, these dead enter nevertheless into the category of 'orphaned bones', because their descendants have to abandon the corpse to the *xiu gugu* committee prior to their transfer into the collective grave. A few weeks before the closure of old burial places, signposts are put on the graves stipulating to the owners the deadline for reclaiming the remains and

[8] For details about these regulations see Fang Ling and Vincent Goossaert (2008: 59–60).

suggesting that they 'rely on the benevolence of Dafeng', i.e. let the corpses be reburied at the occasion of a forthcoming *xiu gugu*. This arrangement is attractive because Dafeng is believed to be a paragon of virtue and a powerful protector, and because most families are unable to afford the cost of secondary burials, and prefer inhumation to incineration. Similar arguments and the fact that Dafeng is an emblem of local identity lead some overseas Teochiu, motivated by post-mortem repatriation, to entrust *shantang* specialised in this business with the ritual processing of their corpse during a *xiu gugu*.

If we now turn to the ritual process, its first sequence consists of the participants digging out the corpses from their temporary graves and bringing them to their final burial place by the way of a procession headed by a statue of Dafeng carried on a palanquin. Next, the bones are washed with 'pure' water drawn from a natural place chosen by the gods, and are left to dry in the sun. Afterwards, they are put into jars allegorically called *hua jin* 花金 ('blossoming gold', Teo. *huê kim*), to express an auspicious transfer of the dead to the other world and a desirable prospective rebirth. The skull is placed on the top of the whole set of remains, facing the front of the grave. The corpse is supposed to be placed sitting curled up in the container, thus evoking a foetal position, an analogy that some informants validate by assimilating the 'blossoming gold jar' to the placenta. If we add that scholars usually compare the omega-shaped tumulus typical of Chinese graves to a matrix, we can logically conclude that the dead bones are believed to 'live' in gestation in the vault, a vault that the Teochiu evocatively call 'mother mountain' 母亲山 (Teo. *bhocing sua*), in the specific case of the *xiu gugu*.

Because the jar is supposed to receive the bones of only one person, it assumes, from a symbolic point of view, an important function to preserve the integrity of the dead. This integrity is, however, conceived as spiritual rather than physical. Indeed, in a large number of cases the diggers are unable to exhume the whole set of remains. In their view, though entire skeletons are preferable, the partial reconstruction of the body does not impede the transfer of the dead to the other world and his or her aptitude to rebirth. While the bones are important because they provide a physical focus for purification, the main aim of the festival is nevertheless the salvation of the *linghun* 灵魂 (Teo. *lênghung*), the spiritual component of the person. Thus, in addition to the exhumation, mediums go over the seashore, crossroads and nearby countryside to locate wandering souls without remains, and to attract them to the grave by means of sutra recitations and paper offerings burnt on the spot.

The little emphasis put on the physical integrity of the dead in the case of the *xiu gugu* seems to conflict with other vernacular conceptions which, on the contrary, consider it important for the deceased to go 'intact' into the other world. According to evidence provided by Dan Waters, those ideas have long hindered surgeries and autopsies in China.[9] However, the contradiction loses some of its force if we consider that the preservation of bodily integrity becomes all the more relative for corpses reduced to bones and that, in the case of *xiu gugu*, this issue gives way to other, more compelling goals to cleanse the environment of the uncontrolled forces which pollute it and to subdue their energy by incorporating them into a holistic order. The integrity of the social body then subsumes its components.

The way the jars are arranged into the collective grave perfectly expresses this holism. It also illustrates the universal pattern analysed by Mary Douglas (1966), according to which pollution and disorder are co-extensive ideas. Thus, the purification of the bones through their cleaning combines with a layout of the jars respecting the basic principles of a well-ordered sociocosm. The group grave, which can contain in some cases thousands of dead persons, reproduces the basic divisions of a house, with a central hall called a *hui yiting* 会议厅 ('meeting hall', Teo. *huê ngitian*), two lateral bedrooms (*fang* 房, Teo. *bang*) and two bathrooms, one for each gender. These bathrooms are allegedly used by the dead for periodical repurification of their bones. While the house of the living is believed to be dominated by the *yang* principle and is called accordingly *yang zhaiju* 阳宅局 (Teo. *iang têhgêg*), the house of the dead is called a *yin zhaiju* 阴宅局 (Teo. *im têhgêg*), certainly because its purpose is to serve as symbolic flesh to the bones, thus creating a new balance between life principles needed for an auspicious destiny in the other world, and in prospect of further rebirth. Within this '*yin* house', and according to a symbolism well-studied by Marcel Granet (1973: 43–58), the skeletons identified as male are arranged in rows on the left half, while those seen as female are put on the right side. When the pots are so numerous that they need to be put one above another, in several levels, the grave is called a 'pagoda grave' (*fen tazhong* 坟塔塚, Teo. *pung tahtong*), thus emphasising the Buddhist dimension of the ritual.

[9] Waters (1991: 104–34). The author refers to the Confucian dictum, according to which: 'One should not inflict harm on one's body, not even hair and skin because they were inherited from parents.' As other evidences of the traditional concern for bodily integrity after death, he notes that eunuchs in Imperial China kept their castrated parts in jars to be buried with them on their death, and that not until 1913 did an official edict in China grant permission for autopsies. According to his own observations, in Hong Kong, up to the 1950s and even later, if a patient had an operation and then died, some families would request that any removed organs be buried with the corpse (1991: 106).

Dafeng or other deities who supervise the different steps of the *xiu gugu* through the channel of mediums performing *wuji*, not only define the proper geomantic setting of the grave, its size and the identity and gender of the bones, but they also appoint among them a king, a queen and a court of six ministers whose function is to rule the whole cohort.[10] The jars of these leaders occupy the front row of the grave. The ability of the king to enact decrees and laws is symbolised by an inkpot put into his jar, together with the usual items accompanying the dead, namely gold paper, paper on which there is printed furniture, clothes and valuables, and a Buddhist sutra called *wang shengzhou* 往生咒 ('Rebirth Incantation', Teo. *uang sênziu*). Lastly, before rebuilding the 'roof', i.e. the tumulus, jars containing the bones of dogs are placed at the four corners of the grave. The function of these domestic animals is to act as watchers, thus preventing malevolent forces from threatening the new community that has just been settled by means of the ritual.

To conclude this brief description of the *xiu gugu* as it is performed nowadays in Chaozhou, I want to come back to the contribution of Mary Douglas concerning anomalous categories. The orphaned bones manipulated during the festival are anomalous dead and because of this status, they are perceived as possessing power and danger. In this context, the main aim of the festival is to neutralise the danger they embody by integrating them into a well-governed community. In so doing, their power is domesticated and they become benevolent.

THE ADAPTATION TO THE THAI CONTEXT

Before analysing the adaptation of the ritual to the Thai context and the aggregate of shared meanings which underlies it, there is a need to briefly describe the Chinese community in Thailand. The social integration of this

[10] *Wuji* (武乩 'spirit-writing of the warrior' Teo. *bhuki*) is alongside *wenji* (文乩 'spirit-writing of the scholar', Teo. *bhungki*), one of the two main types of *fuji* 扶乩 (Teo. *huki*). *Fuji* is a technique of spirit-writing where two mediums hold a forked branch to write oracles or charms, to point to a place or to cure a patient through application of the divine stylus on painful parts of his/her body. The forked branch symbolises the *luan*-bird, a mythical bird believed to be the privileged conveyor of heavenly gods. The mediums are a pair because they express the *yin/yang* complementarities as well as the heaven/earth spiritual encounter. The medium who holds one arm of the fork with his right hand, but stands on the left side while facing the altar, is considered the *yang* and 'heaven's hand' 天手 (*tianshou*, Teo. *tiangcu*). His fellow medium, who holds the other arm of the fork with his left hand, and stands on the right side, serves as an assistant and embodies the *yin* aspect. For its part, the warrior/scholar opposition represents two basic and complementary attributes of imperial power. Whereas *wenji* consists mainly in the gentle writing of moral poetry, *wuji* is usually rugged, since the mediums fight against malevolent spirits they try to subdue. For a good ethnography of this technique see Jordan and Overmyer (1986). See also more recently Lin Fushi (1995: 159–64).

'middleman minority' in Thailand was made easier than in most other Southeast Asian countries.[11] Thai and Chinese elites have merged their interests for centuries to the point of forming nowadays a common upper stratum, more and more dominated by businessmen and politicians of Chinese ancestry (Ockey 2004). Intermarriages with Thai women among the first generations of immigrants and the policy of the ultra-nationalist governments (1932–1960s) prompted the Chinese to display overt signs of Thaisation, and to restrict the activities of their own institutions (Landon 1973 [1941]). The economic dynamism of the Chinese, mostly Teochiu, does not seem to create the interethnic tensions and resentment observed in other countries of Southeast Asia (Malaysia, Indonesia and the Philippines). Some have argued that the relatively peaceful assimilation of Chinese entrepreneurs into Thai society is rooted in religious beliefs.[12]

Economic factors may also explain the symbiotic relations that Chinese migrants and Thai natives maintain. I refer here to the long-lasting prosperity the Thai peasantry benefited from up to recent times and which sharply contrasts with the demographic pressure and harsh poverty that several generations of Chinese from Guangdong experienced; hence the massive emigration of Teochiu males to the southern seas during the late nineteenth and early twentieth centuries. Through their willingness to work hard for low profit and their ethnic solidarity, they filled unexploited niches of the economy and progressively became the capitalist elite of the host country. From a sociological point of view, high rates of intermarriage, the fact that generations of Chinese have been educated in Thai as a result of the policy of assimilation, and that they employ a large part of the native manpower, lead most Teochiu to be quite familiar with Thai culture, habits and relational norms. In the religious sphere, such intimacy is enhanced by the fact that the two populations share a basic set of Buddhist ideas and values. Chinese and Thai-Chinese are active supporters of the local Buddhist institutions. Although few Chinese are ordained as monks, they do, however, make important donations to monasteries in return for lucky charms, amulets and other protective or divinatory devices. To the same

[11] See Mackie (1988: 217–60); Cushman (1991); Winichakul (1994); Suryadinata (2007).

[12] William Skinner and Richard Coughlin stress the influence of Theravāda Buddhism, which emphasises the accumulation of merits and the spiritual development of the individual, rather than the acquisition of wealth. See Skinner (1954: 113); Coughlin (1960: 197). Karma and transmigration are also significant issues for Mahayana Buddhism. Should we believe the doubtful statement of Max Weber, who asserts that the motivations these issues raise among Chinese are lessened and blurred by the worldly achievements that the Daoist magical goals and the Confucian familism emphasise (Daoism and Confucianism rationalising man-in-nature and man-in-society respectively)? See Weber (1951).

ends, they involve themselves significantly in the cult of *phi*, the Thai spirits which control the invisible dimension of the world.

The institution of *xiu gugu* was introduced into Thailand at the beginning of the twentieth century by the local branch of Baode Shantang, the first Buddhist hall for good deeds to have been created in Chaozhou. The association had informally started its charitable activities as early as 1897, but the top leaders of the local Chinese community who managed it were looking for royal patronage before opening it officially. King Chulalongkorn agreed to give his patronage, but under two conditions: that the charitable activities of the association benefit the whole population of the kingdom without ethnic distinction, and that the *ngan kep sop rayat* that Baode Shantang intended to organise respects the Thai customs concerning the unfortunate dead.[13] The custom that the king was referring to is linked to the Thai belief that unfortunate dead are those whose destiny on earth is shortened by a bad karma. Before being properly processed through cremation these dead must make repentance on earth during at least three years, which correspond to the Buddhist Triple Gem, namely Buddha, Dharma (the teaching of Buddha) and Saṅgha (the monastic community in charge of propagating the truth). Accordingly, they are buried, preferably in the vicinity of Thai monasteries which serve as protective umbrellas against their malevolent power. In actuality, the feeling of fear that these bad dead arouse among the Thai, especially among the poor and less educated, entails in most cases their desertion. They remain buried forever, their souls being consequently condemned to haunt endlessly some carefully avoided places of the human world.

Following the royal requirements, Baode Shantang quickly modified the *xiu gugu* and performed its first ritual in 1910, as part of the ceremonies marking its official opening. If most of the 100 bodies ritually processed for the occasion were those of Chinese coolies, on the following occasions the share of Chinese bodies decreased progressively to the point that from the end of the second world war onwards most of the orphaned bones processed were Thai. The statement applies both to Baode Shantang, which cremated between 1910 and 1999 more than 153,000 bodies, and to the other *shantang* operating in Thailand. In a national context where the people originating from Chaozhou constitute about 70 per cent of the Chinese community, the *shantang* and *shantang*-like organisations have spread widely in Thai territory, especially from the 1960s onwards, thanks to the spectacular

[13] The Thai compound created by the king to name this new and alien custom is close in meaning to the Chinese expression, since it can be translated by: 'ritual to collect the corpses without parents'.

economic growth of the country. Nowadays more than 150 Teochiu *shantang* or affiliated associations perform their own *xiu gugu* in Thailand, once every seven to ten years.

Several reasons explain why most orphaned bones taken into charge are Thai. The weakening of the patrilineal ideology among overseas Chinese is one of them, especially in Thailand, where most lineage associations have either disappeared or have lost a large part of their influence. In this context, it is admitted that a daughter or other parent may worship the ancestor instead of a failing son. Orphaned dead have therefore almost totally disappeared among these overseas Chinese. The second reason lies in close conceptions between Chinese and Thai concerning bad death and its management, as well as in the Teochiu efforts to adapt the festival to the Thai requirements. The third and last reason is the usual combination of *xiu gugu* with other charitable activities, which give the *shantang* the opportunity to collect corpses.

In practice, most of the dead bodies these associations gather are not brought to their premises, but come from direct or indirect prospecting by their teams of volunteers. Thus, a majority of the halls for good deeds operating in Thailand have rescuers who assist police and fire-fighters in case of disasters such as floods, fires, landslides, plane crashes, or train derailments. For example, these rescuers intervened massively in Phuket Island after the tsunami of December 2004. The most dynamic of them also manage twenty-four hour emergency squads whose ambulances rescue victims of traffic accidents in close connection with police and hospitals. In addition, it is admitted that they also appropriate the unclaimed bodies and those abandoned by their families. Following the Thai legislation, this appropriation is validated after a period of three years, during which the corpses, duly identified, are kept in temporary vaults of the Chinese cemeteries, but can be reclaimed by their family. Afterwards, they lose their personal identity and are placed in group vaults. Another good way to collect skeletons on a large scale is to prospect the places near Buddhist monasteries where Tai untimely dead are buried. In return for permission to take away the remains, the *shantang* usually make generous donations to the monasteries.

If we now turn to the *xiu gugu* as it is performed in Thailand, the first sequences of the ritual are similar to what can be observed in Chaozhou. Under the supervision of Dafeng or other gods communicating through the channel of mediums, the remains are exhumed and washed with pure water. It must be said that to purify efficiently the dead bones from the pollution attached to them, the participants to the ritual must be pure themselves.

Accordingly, and it is also true in China, they eat vegetarian food, drink water purified by gods, refrain from sexual intercourse and should theoretically dress in white clothes. Menstruating women are prohibited from attending the festival. The bone gatherers also wear charms to protect themselves against the danger of handling this category of dead. After their cleaning, the bones are arranged in rows to be dried by the sun.

Most symbolical aspects related to the hierarchical and gender arranging of the refined bones have been maintained in Thailand. During the whole ritual process, the skeletons identified as male and female are clearly separated. A king and a queen are also appointed by gods. Certainly under the influence of the Thai, the skull is covered with golden sheets of paper. Another adaptation to the Thai context is the fact that the dead identified as monks are draped with a monastic saffron gown and put aside. For their part, the mummified bodies have a special status, especially when they are embryos or bodies of young children. In the latter case, the mummies are called *jintong* 金童 ('gold boys', Teo. *kimtong*) or *yunü* 玉女 ('jade girls', Teo. *yêknung*) according to their gender. The epithets 'gold' and 'jade' are usually applied in China to young associates of deities. In the present case, they express both the decay-resistance of these dead and the high value conferred on them. One of my informants explained that these dead have resisted the process of decay because of an exceptional imbalance in favour of their *yang* aspect. Consequently the mummies are believed to have turned into very powerful spirits.[14] It needs to be stressed that these mummies draw their power from a natural process of mummification and not as the result of thanatology. For this reason, they do not enter into the typology of Justin Ritzinger and Marcus Bingenheimer, who make a distinction between mummification as a form of burial and mummification as a mode of the relic cult (2006: 37–94, 38). In Chaozhou, their jars are set at the back of that of the king, whereas in the Thai context they are put on the top of the stacks, just behind the skulls of the rulers. Although

[14] The unusual power radiating from mummified corpses is a significant theme developed in China by both Buddhist historical texts and popular beliefs. Recent case studies, in Taiwan, show that enshrined and worshipped mummies of Buddhist monks are alternatively called 'bodhisattvas' (*roushen pusa* 肉身菩薩), 'dharmic bodies' (*fati* 法體) or 'golden bodies' (*jinshen* 金身). See for instance Lin Fushi (1995: 104–5), or Gildow (2005: 3–4). According to Gildow, the historical origins of mummification in China are opaque. Evidence suggests, however, that this practice by Buddhist circles preceded efforts at doctrinal explanation, according to which mummies were produced through the virtue of the deceased. This author adds that 'unlike the relatively impersonal bone relics [. . .] the souls of these flesh bodhisattvas persist inside the mummy, and they are worshipped as fully conscious agents capable of communication and interaction as they bestow favors and provide guidance to devotees' (2005: 4).

acknowledged for their exceptional spiritual power, they do not become objects of specific relic cults.

The main change introduced in Thailand is that the skeletons are not set into jars, but are piled up according to their gender into two large chimney pyres called, by means of Buddhist metaphors, *baota* 宝塔 ('treasure pagoda', Teo. *botah*) for males, and *lianhua chi* 蓮花池 ('lotus lake', Teo. *loihua ti*) for females. These chimneys may be seen as big collective jars because the bones are laid inside so that they form a single mega-corpse, with the bones of the feet and legs at the bottom, those of the trunk and arms occupying the intermediate position and the skulls arranged to form a pyramid at the top. Such a device confirms the observation made about China that the ritual subsumes individual integrity to holistic aims. The symbolism of a well-ordered social body is thus preserved, though in a vertical rather than a horizontal way. Two local adjustments, however, characterise the device. An umbrella, which is the symbol of the king in Thailand, overhangs the skulls of the rulers, and if the remains of a Buddhist monk have been identified, they are set at the apex, in order to represent the overwhelming spiritual power of the Buddha. Lastly, on the night preceding the cremation, mediums go to places of allegedly frequent violent death – such as crossroads, jails or military fields – and determine the number of wandering souls haunting them. The same number of paper offerings is burnt on these spots to make the spirits rally the cohort of dead to be sent to the other world.

Indicative of the organisers' desire to give evidence of acculturation, local representatives of the state and of the Thai Buddhist clergy, together with daily newspaper and TV reporters, are invited to attend the cremation. Afterwards, the ashes are left to cool for three days, following the Thai custom. Finally, devotees put the ashes into white bags whose name, *baona* 宝拿 ('to hold treasure', Teo. *bona*) perfectly expresses the prospect for wealth related to the manipulation of the bones of the dead. A procession headed by a statue of Dafeng carries these bags to the *shantang* graveyard. There, they are stored in the collective grave that the association maintains for the remains from successive *xiu gugu*. Following the symbolism in use in Chaozhou, the grave is identified with a *yin* house and comprises a vault for each gender, but without lateral bathrooms, because the transformation of bones into ashes has made the bathrooms useless and even dangerous. Although the ashes still retain the *yang* aspect that bones embody, they are the result of a final process of purification through fire which impedes further contact with the antithetic water element. According to informants, such contact would dissolve the dead matter and identity, hence compromising his chances of rebirth. This interpretation discloses a belief in a strong interactive relationship between the earthly remains and the souls transferred to heaven. In other words, the welfare and destiny of the dead *spiritus* is closely related to the way his bones/ashes are managed on earth. Such a belief explains why the arrangement of the jars/bags into the grave follows the pattern of an ideal house and society. This pattern is supposed to accompany the cohort of souls to the other world, thus offering them both the domestic and political frame for a prosperous and harmonious life in the new environment. The fact that in Confucian philosophy the household epitomises the core relational values of the society may explain why the grave is conceived as a house.

The adaptation to the Thai context inspired a significant change in attitudes towards the physical integrity of the dead. Whereas in China each jar is associated to a corpse in gestation, symbolising the placenta, in Thailand the bags contain a mix of ashes which admittedly belongs to several persons of the same gender. The only exceptions concern the king, the queen, the monks and the mummies whose ashes are isolated through the channel of mediums, and put into specific bags which occupy, as in China, the front stage in the grave. The holistic conceptions underlying the ritual device appear more clearly through this change. The basic requirement to preserve the *xiu gugu* efficacy lies in the clear distinction of status and gender roles which feature the social body to which the refined cohort of dead is identified. Apart from leaders, whose symbolic embodiment is functional, the identification of 'commoners' does not need to be elaborated out of the gender roles they assume collectively, as groups of males and females whose intercourse is crucial for the society's reproduction. Consistently, in Chaozhou the bones kept in jars were only defined according to their gender. Contrary to normal dead, subject to funerals and whose personal identity is written on the front tablet of the grave, the corpses managed during the *xiu gugu* remain unnamed throughout the ritual process. Commonly referred to on the tombstone as 'revered parents from all generations and origins', they are reduced to a group identity, hence the emphasis put on their treatment as a whole. In this case, the lack of parts to the individual body and even its merging with others of the same kind is of secondary importance. What is conversely of great concern is the integrity of the entire 'social body' which encompasses it, an integrity that a clear arrangement and geomantic setting of the grave is supposed to ensure. Finally, the ultimate storage of the remains in the grave respects the Chinese tradition without infringing radically on the local requirements, since the Thai bury part of the ashes and put the rest into an urn stored within the Buddhist temple's compound.

THE AMBIGUITIES OF INTERETHNIC COOPERATION

Interethnic cooperation underlies the ritual in its Thai context. First, for both the Thai and the Chinese, bad death is of special concern as a major source of disorder and danger.[15] The mythology of both folk traditions emphasises these malevolent ghosts of human origin who haunt the world and threaten the whole society. Against this threat the strategy that the Teochiu and the Thai develop is also quite similar. The process corresponds neatly to the traditional tripartite pattern of the rites of passage that Arnold van Gennep identified (van Gennep 1960). They confine these dead during a liminal period into specific places which radiate the protective power of Buddhist institutions, namely the Thai monasteries or the *shantang*, before sending them ritually to the other world. In contemporary Thailand, however, because of the reluctance of most Thai to achieve the last step of the process, and because of the acculturation of the *xiu gugu* imposed by Rama V, the Teochiu became progressively the main performers of an acculturated version of the Thai ritual. Interestingly, they often refer to the terms of this idiom of shared ideas and practices when they ask the Thai monasteries for permission to gather bones. Expressed roughly, the argument is then: 'We are both Buddhist, we both share the same concern for these fearsome ghosts, we can reintegrate them into the cycle of reincarnation according to Thai custom, so let us do the job for you!'

This set of common ideas combines in turn with complementary conceptions which enhance rather than weaken interethnic cooperation. Among them, the most significant are those concerning the essence of bad death. For the Thai and the Chinese, bad dead are persons whose destiny on earth was shortened by untimely death, violent or otherwise. For the Chinese, however, lack of male progeny is prior in the chain of causations: the unfortunate dead are those who failed to have sons to worship them. In other words, while the Thai think in terms of individual fate by reference to the doctrine of *karma*, the Chinese favour position in the social structure and put forward the Confucian values of filial piety. Furthermore, the feelings that the unfortunate dead arouse among the Chinese and the Thai are not the same. For the Chinese, these feelings are ambivalent. The orphaned bones generate both fear and compassion. Although they are factors of virulent pollution and social disorder, their prevailing image is, nevertheless, that of pitiful beggars (see Wolf 1974: 148–55; Weller 1987: 61–7). Hence the Buddhist concern

[15] On Thai attitudes toward 'bad death' see Tambiah (1970). Concerning the Chinese, see Jordan (1972); Katz (1987: 197–215); Lin Fushih (1994: 117–44, or 1988: 56–7).

for their salvation conflates in the case of *Xiu gugu* with the aim of absorbing the *yang* property of the bones. For the Thai, on the contrary, the untimely dead arouse an unambiguous feeling of fear and also a sentiment of shame because his bad karma sullies the honour of his parents, suspected to be bad Buddhists. It is certainly why the Thai are so prompt to dissociate themselves from such dead and to abandon their remains to outsiders. Another difference between the two groups lies in the handling of bones. If the Thai believe that such handling may result in protective power, the belief only applies to the remains of forest Buddhist *arahants* whose ashes and bone splinters are mixed with clay to produce very efficient amulets (Tambiah 1984). For their part, the Chinese are less restrictive. If they are along the same lines as the Thai by conferring great magical power to mummies and bones of Buddhist saints, they also believe that whatever the status and origin of the dead, the proper ritual manipulation of their bones allows those who do it to take on the *yang* property that these bones embody (Watson 1982: 179). In this respect, and to borrow a formula of Kenneth Dean (1993: 14), the *xiu gugu* implements a 'Daoist alchemy of the society', since part of its *raison d'être* is to convert into positive energy (happiness, wealth, longevity) a negative one (emanating from the restless ghosts), through the manipulation and transformation of dead bones.

The set of different or common ideas which underlies this interethnic cooperation gives rise to ambiguous images from both sides. On the one hand, because of their apparent concern for the salvation of Thai dead, the Teochiu give evidence of their identification with the national community, of their Buddhist compassion and of their desire to rid the country of the malevolent spirits who haunt it. But on the other hand, by displaying sympathy towards fearsome ghosts, they arouse suspicion and lead some Thai to question their status as 'civilised people'. In return, the Teochiu feel contempt for the natives who abandon their bad dead and saturate the landscape with malevolent ghosts. Whereas the Thai believe they are taking advantage of the interaction by disposing of their bad dead at the lowest cost and by letting the Chinese carry out this dirty work, the Chinese are in return convinced of their own superiority. This feeling is based on the idea that their community plays a key role in the regeneration and control of sociocosmic forces, and that they are taking advantage of local resources. Thus, while the economic hegemony of the Chinese gives them patronage over a large part of the local population, they seem to extend this relationship to the religious sphere by patronising part of the Thai dead. Just as their prosperity depends on Thai manpower, so they try ritually to augment their prosperity by taking over, manipulating and geomantically settling the ashes of the Thai unfortunate dead. As we can see, rather than bringing together the Thai and the Chinese, this interethnic cooperation enhances the prejudices they apply to each other and strengthens their social and cultural boundaries.

Finally, despite the acculturative pressure exerted by the Thai host society, the semiotic structure and goals of the festival remain unchanged. Although the dead are now cremated, this step does not prevent the devotees from absorbing beforehand the bones' properties through their manipulation, nor is it an impediment to the storage of the remains (in this case the ashes) in collective graves whose layout respects the Chinese categories of a well-ordered sociocosm. Even if the idea of an individual matrix for the bones, symbolised by the jar, has not been transposed to Thailand, the *yin/yang* balance necessary to the regeneration of life is still conveyed by the *yin* house enclosing the *yang* ashes. Another slight difference is that prior to their incineration the bones are cleaned for the one and only time, whereas in Chaozhou periodical reopenings of graves may lead to successive manipulations and cleanings of the same remains. This change and, more generally, the symbolical consequences of the transformation of bones into ashes should not be overemphasised, however, particularly given the contemporary funeral practices of the Chinese. In several countries of Asia, including the People's Republic of China, Singapore and Malaysia, laws and fines against burial compel them to cremate their dead. Such a change does not seem to affect ancestor worship as long as the descendants may keep the box or the urn containing the dead remains in a shrine.

THE MALAY HINDRANCE

The fact that in Thailand the acculturation of the *xiu gugu* has only entailed minor changes to the Chaozhou ritual should not lead us to underestimate the impact of external factors in more agonistic contexts of interaction. The marginal and minimalist adaptation of the *xiu gugu* to the Muslim environment of Malaysia is all the more enlightening in this respect. The Malaysian Teochiu, a small minority of whom live in the fishing towns of Kuala Kurau and Tanjung Piandang (North of Perak State), gave up performing a version of the ritual locally. The stubbornness of the Perak fishermen in performing the ritual whatever the local conditions may be explained by the fact that Kuala Kurau is one of those few towns of Malaysia where the Chinese immigrants, mostly Teochiu in this case, form a majority of the population. Moreover, among them the people originating from Huilai County dominate, this rural and coastal area being the main place of Chaozhou where *xiu gugu* are performed nowadays. In this town of about 65,000 inhabitants, seven Teochiu *shantang* and affiliated organisations were providing charity in 2003. Despite these very specific and favourable conditions, the devotees perform a minimal and spiritual version of the festival, consisting of catching the souls of wandering ghosts through mediums' prospecting in the town and nearby natural places. These orphaned souls are then identified by the mediums as male or female, king, queen or commoners and are confined, accordingly, to small jars hermetically closed by means of lids and charms. These jars are temporarily stored in a specific room of the *shantang*. Their transfer to the other world occurs during the seventh lunar month, as part of the *pudu* 普度 (universal salvation festival), a Buddhist calendar event, the general purpose of which is to display compassion towards poor people and hungry ghosts. *Pudu* is devoted to the feeding of normal dead, orphaned souls and beggars. The latter scramble for the coins, sweets and cakes that the priests throw out (Feuchtwang 1992). *Pudu* is also a liturgical framework for the transferral of merits to both normal dead and hungry ghosts (Teiser 1988). The president of Zhen An Ge, an association of Tanjung Piandang which performed a *xiu gugu* in 2003, put forward congruent goals and features to justify the local merging of the two rituals. He argued that their liturgies bring together living and orphaned dead with the intention of securing the prosperity of the former through displays of compassion towards the latter.

In the days preceding that ritual, volunteers set up, in the temple courtyard, altars devoted to Dafeng and to prominent gods of heaven, earth and hells. The liturgical framework of the event was basically similar to what I observed in other *pudu* performances in Thailand and Malaysia. The only difference concerned the search for wandering souls, a *xiu gugu* sequence which was reproduced in Tanjung Piandang. At nightfall, mediums acting under Dafeng's guidance prospected in the town and natural areas. Local spirits named *badi* were among the ghosts to be captured. For Malay people, *badi* are parts of human or animal souls which remain by bones in case of violent death (see Skeat 1900: 427; Endicott 1991: 66). Like the Thai, the Malay regards victims of violent or otherwise unusual death with a great deal of fear. According to Kirk Endicott, *badi* is an independent entity which does not prevent the murdered Muslim to whom it is attached from enjoying the delights of Paradise (Endicott 1991: 71, 86). The usual Malay strategy to neutralise the power of this entity consists in isolating the corpse in a deserted place, and occasionally in separating the *badi* from the skeleton through magic. This is precisely the kind of separation that the Chinese mediums of Tanjung Piandang intended to carry out during their prospecting – without, however, digging out the bones. When I asked them how the power of Chinese gods could apply to Muslim souls, they answered that, unlike *nyawa* (the breath of life that goes to heaven), *badi* has nothing to do with Islam. This view, which echoes Malay beliefs, proves an intimate knowledge of the religious context. It is related to the frequent association in business of the local Malay and Chinese fishermen. In Malaysia, such intercultural intimacy varies significantly from place to place (Carstens 2005). It seems to be more accentuated in rural areas (Winzeler 1986) and in cosmopolitan cities like Penang than in other places (DeBernardi 2006).

In Tanjung Piandang, the orphaned souls that the mediums captured were confined to small jars hermetically closed by means of lids and charms. Back to the temple, the participants distributed the jars into male and female groups, and arranged them in front of the altar to Dafeng. The saint chose amid the jars a king and a queen to rule the cohort. As in Chaozhou and Thailand, during the whole ritual process the participants dressed in white and ate vegetarian food. On the *Pudu* day, Buddhist monks performed a service for the transferral of merits to the dead, and the participants offered food to their dead and to the hungry ghosts, according to the *Pudu* liturgy. They also gave rice, dried fish and cakes to the local Chinese and Indian needy. The president of the association justified the absence of Malay in this distribution by the fact that Muslims had their own charities. Lastly, the mediums pierced the jars' lids, and the recitation of Buddhist sûtras by priests guided the orphaned souls to the otherworld. Although Malay do not believe that hell or heaven are possible destinations for the *badi*, the mediums of the Chinese association claimed that, upon arrival at the otherworld, the *badi* would be secluded into a specific place by Lenyo Wang, the Chinese ruler of the hell. This view does not disturb Malays since none of them attend the ritual. Compared to their fellows of Thailand, the Chaozhou of Tanjung Piandang share some general goals in performing the *xiu gugu*, that is, to rid the local area from the ghosts who haunt it and to transfer them to the otherworld. They also intend to take control of the Malay bad spirits, though secretly and without benefiting from the bones' *yang* properties. As a consequence, they cannot use this ritual as an overt sign of social integration.

Several reasons may be put forward to explain the inability of the Malaysian Teochiu to celebrate the *xiu gugu* on a larger scale and in a fuller form. The fact that they count for only 12 per cent of the Chinese living in the country is one of them (Purcell 1965: 224). In the present case, however, internal demography is of secondary importance when compared to interethnic issues. A long and harsh competition for the control of the national economy between Chinese immigrants and Malay 'sons of the soil' (*Bumiputra*), and the native fear of being outnumbered by aliens, led to decades of interethnic tensions, punctuated by overt conflict, during and after British colonial rule. In 1971, the Malaysian government, through its New Economic Policy (NEP) tried to shift the balance of power in favour of the *Bumiputra* by implementing a policy of positive discrimination.[16] In return, it tolerated the creation of schools, clinics and other welfare services managed by 'Chinese for Chinese'. This policy pursued in another way the special provisions for ethnic customs that the British colonial power had instituted during the nineteenth century (Hall 1986: 546, 549). One of its effects was to reinforce the trend to mutual segregation ensuing from interethnic tensions; hence a low rate of intermarriages, a turning inward by both communities and, more generally, the reduction of interactions to a minimum.

In this context, an interethnic cooperation in hosting the *xiu gugu* was unlikely to happen. Another impediment, closely related to the NEP, was a regulation severely restricting the foundation of non-Muslim temples and shrines. The local *shantang* had therefore no option but to register as welfare associations; as a result it was impossible for them to display too overtly signs of religious activity outside their own premises. Last but not least, the reluctance of the Malay Muslims to let their bodies, either living or dead, be manipulated by non-Muslims was another hindrance to the extensive search for skeletons and bones characterising the festival.

BUDDHISM AS A CROSS-CULTURAL BRIDGE

The 'matter' that the *xiu gugu* processes has evolved from Chaozhou to Southeast Asia. In Thailand, bones are transformed into ashes while the Malaysian version is limited to the search for immaterial souls. However, from one site to another the basic goals that the ritual pursues are the same. Their aim is: (1) to put away the remains and the fearsome influences they materialise from the human environment they pollute and threaten; (2) to incorporate, as a means of control, these scattered 'free electrons' into a burial frame, which reproduces on a micro-scale a well-governed society, properly located according to geomantic rules; and (3) to transfer to the otherworld, at the same time and as a whole, the spiritual aspect of the

[16] For instance, 80 per cent of the positions in the police, army and civil administration would henceforth be reserved to *Bumiputra*, and these latter would have privileged access to public health and welfare services.

social body thus created. In so doing, the 'orphaned' souls are reintegrated into a *socius*, and cannot anymore be considered as anomalous. However, they do not enter the category of normal dead for all of that. They remain specific in the sense that they are not persons to be worshipped as ancestors, but anonymous and communal deceased, whose implicit function is to transcend the kinship structure and ethnic boundaries and to become the collective emblem of the corporate solidarity and good deeds achieved by a Buddhist cult community. In other words, and in some analogy with the British 'Unknown Warrior' devised by King George V in 1920, their depersonalisation makes of them an ideal subject to impersonate encompassing identities. Overseas, this function took logically a new dimension. The *xiu gugu* then became a symbol of the Teochiu religious identity, but also, in the specific case of Thailand, a metaphorical means to express the Chinese claim to take over the control of local resources. Conversely, in Malaysia, its marginal and minimalist performance reflects the political and cultural hindrances opposed to such a claim. In both contexts, however, the adaptation of this ritual provides a good indicator of the way the Chinese minority interacts with the host society.

The *xiu gugu* ritual not only reflects the attitude of different Southeast Asian polities towards Chinese migrants, but also highlights the role that religious ideologies may play to pattern interethnic relationships. Thus, by emulsifying a nexus of symbols and values shared by both Theravāda and Mahāyāna traditions, this Teochiu ritual has built in the Thai context a bridge of cross-cultural communication and co-operation concerning crucial issues such as bad death pollution and danger, socio-cosmic regulation, individual salvation and social integration.

It is noteworthy that this cross-cultural communication flourished outside of the monastic institution. Although Thai Buddhist monasteries provide bones and Chinese monks are sometimes invited to chant sutras, the devotional impetus for organising *xiu gugu* comes from businessmen and other grass-roots worshippers, independently of any clerical hierarchy. Most officiants (either 'priests' or mediums) are self-taught and well-read laymen, whose activity is firmly rooted in the Chinese popular religion, as it involves openness to fonts of the three doctrines (Buddhism, Daoism, Confucianism), and is 'the true product of a "ritualistic culture" where the proper performance of rites is of paramount importance' (Watson and Rawski 1988: 4). Syncretism is also traditionally the rule in the *shantang* where they officiate.

These 'halls for good deeds' emerged and expanded during the late Qing dynasty as an attempt by the gentry and the merchant elites to combine local cults with welfare and rescue services that public institutions had deserted. According to several sources, they emulated features of guilds, of Buddhist and Confucian private associations (*shanhui*) and of government-funded welfare bodies (*tang*).[17] However, as noted by William Rowe, their emergence represented a major change in attitudes about responsibility for community well-being, which was the sign of a new kind of urban society in the making (Rowe 1989: 92). I have suggested elsewhere that the poverty and the harsh experience of uprooting that faced the first generations of migrants encouraged the spread of 'halls for good deeds' throughout Southeast Asia (Formoso 2003: 833–56). In Malaya, for example, a group of ten *shantang*, called the Blue Cross Charitable Society, formed in 1942 to rescue the victims of the Japanese occupation. In Thailand, their cults, centred around Dafeng, served to gain both the Teochiu elite's support and legitimacy from the authorities. They thus contributed to the continuity abroad of typical aspects of Chinese religious thought and of an ethno-linguistic identity under the opportunist flagship of Buddhism.

Finally, the present analysis of a specific institution – the Teochiu halls for good deeds – and of a ritual – the *xiu gugu* – reveals the crucial role that folk organisations and syncretised cults might play for the preservation and adaptation of Buddhism to fluctuating circumstances. Often dismissed by native elites and Western orientalists, who both consider their achievements as impoverished and heterodox versions of an alleged 'great tradition', these local organisations and cults are, on the contrary, the main fabric of the constantly renewed Chinese culture. Their mushrooming in prior and post-Maoist China, outside of state control and doctrinal orthodoxy is, in my view, the main tool of the outstanding Chinese religious revival observed today in the People's Republic of China and overseas. They assumed this function, which is not differentiated from the other forms of social activity, because they operate without dogmatism, profession of faith or doctrinal allegiance (Granet 1988: 586; Schipper 1982: 15). As Maurice Freedman pointed out, they embody 'a civil religion – not austere and cunningly calculated to serve political interests, but based upon a view of the inter-penetration of the society and the universe, and upon a conception of authority that in the last analysis would not allow the religious to separate off from the secular' (Freedman 1974: 19–42, 40). In those conditions they offer a digest of the basic ideas, values and ritual procedures to be performed and memorised by most grass-roots worshippers.

[17] See Yang (1961: 335–6); Smith (1987: 309–37); Naquin (2000: 652).

BIBLIOGRAPHY

Ahern, E. (1973), *The Cult of the Dead in a Chinese Village*, Stanford, CA: Stanford University Press.

Carstens, S. (2005), *Histories, Cultures, Identities: Studies in Malaysian Chinese Worlds*, Singapore: National University of Singapore (NUS) Press.

Coughlin, R. (1960), *Double Identity in Modern Thailand*, Hong Kong University Press.

Cushman, J. (1991), *Family and State: the Formation of a Sino-Thai Tin-Mining Dynasty (1797–1932)*, Singapore: Oxford University Press.

Dean, K. (1993), *Taoist Ritual and Popular Cults of Southeast China*, Princeton, NJ: Princeton University Press.

DeBernardi, J. (2006), *The Ways That Lives in the Hearth: Chinese Popular Religion and Spirit Mediums in Penang, Malaysia*, Stanford, CA: Stanford University Press.

Douglas, M. (1966), *Purity and Danger*, London: Penguin Books.

Endicott, K. (1991), *An Analysis of Malay Magic*, Singapore: Oxford University Press.

Fang Ling and Goossaert, V. (2008), 'Les réformes funéraires et la politique religieuse de l'état chinois, 1900–2008', *Archives de Sciences Sociales des Religions* **144**, 51–73.

Feuchtwang, S. (1992), *The Imperial Metaphor: Popular Religion in China*, New York: Routledge.

Formoso, B. (2003), 'Marchands et philanthropes: les associations de bienfaisance chinoises en Thaïlande', *Annales Histoire, Sciences Sociales (HSS)* **58** (4), 833–56.

Freedman, M. (1971), *Chinese Lineage and Society: Fukien and Kwangtung*, New York: The Athlone Press.

(1974), 'On the sociological study of Chinese religion', in ed. A. P. Wolf, *Religion and Ritual in Chinese Society*, Stanford, CA: Stanford University Press, 19–42.

Gennep, A. van (1960), *The Rites of Passage*, Chicago, IL: University of Chicago Press [1st edn. 1909 in French].

Gildow, D. M. (2005), 'Flesh bodies, stiff corpses, and gathered gold: mummy worship, corpse processing, and mortuary ritual in contemporary Taiwan', *Journal of Chinese Religion* **33**, 3–4.

Granet, M. (1973), 'Right and left in China', in ed. Rodney Needham, *Right and Left: Essays on Dual Symbolic Classification*, Chicago, London: University of Chicago Press, 43–58, [1st edn. 1953 in French].

(1988), *La Pensée Chinoise*. Paris: Albin Michel [1st edn. 1934].

Hall, D. G. (1986), *A History of Southeast Asia*, London: Macmillan [1st edn. 1955].

Jordan, D. K. (1972), *Gods, Ghosts, and Ancestors: Folk Religion in a Taiwanese Village*, Berkeley, CA: University of California Press.

Jordan, D. K. and Overmyer, D. L. (1986), *The Flying Phoenix. Aspects of Chinese Sectarianism in Taiwan*, Princeton, NJ: Princeton University Press.

Katz, P. (1987), 'Demons or deities – The *Wangye* of Taiwan', *Asian Folklore Studies* **46**, 197–215.

Landon, K. (1973), *The Chinese in Thailand*, New York: Russell and Russell [1st edn. 1941].

Lin Fushih (1988), *Handai de wuzhe* [漢代的巫者, '*The Shamans of the Han Period*'], Taibei: Daoxiang Chubanshe.

(1994), *Chinese Shamans and Shamanism in the Chiang-nan Area during the Six Dynasties Period (3rd–6th Century AD)*, unpublished PhD dissertation, Princeton, NJ: Princeton University.

(1995), *Guhun yu Guixiong de Shijie* [孤魂與鬼雄的世界, '*The World of Lonely Souls and Heroic Ghosts*'], Taibei: Beixian Wenhua Chubanshe, 159–64.

Lin Juncong (1998), *Chaoshan Miaotang* 潮汕庙堂, Guangzhou: Guangdong Gaodeng Jiaoyu Chubanshe.

Lin Wushu 林悟殊 (1995), *Taiguo Dafeng Zushi Chongbai yu Huaqiao Baode Shantang Yanjiu* [泰國大峰祖師崇拜與華僑报德善堂研究, '*Studies in Chinese Worship of the Founder Dafeng and Poh Teck Tung Charity in Thailand*'], Taibei: Shuxin Press.

(1996), *Taiguo Dafeng Zushi Chongbai Shulüe*, [泰國大峰祖師崇拜述略, '*A Narrative Sketch of the Cult of Dafeng in Thailand*'], *Minjian Zongjiao* [*Popular Religion*] 2, 1–17.

Lin Xunsheng (1955), 'Dongnan yade xiguzang qi qihuan taiping yangde fenbu' [东南亚的洗骨葬其迄环太平洋的分布, 'The bone-washing burial custom of Southeast Asia and its circum-Pacific distribution'], *Zhongguo Minzu Xuebao*, 25–42.

Liu Shufen (1995), 'Art ritual and society: Buddhist practice in rural China during the Northern Dynasties', *Asia Major*, new series 8 (1), 19–46.

Ma Ximin 马豨民 (2002), *Chaoshan shantang daguan* [潮汕善堂大观, '*The Magnificent Spectacle of the Benevolent Halls of Chao-Shan*'], Shantou: Shantou Daxue Chubanshe.

Mackie, J. A. C. (1988), 'The changing economic roles and ethnic identities of the Southeast Asian Chinese: a comparison of Indonesia and Thailand', in eds. Jennifer Cushman and Wang Gungwu, *Changing Identities of the Southeast Asian Chinese since World War II*, Hong Kong: Hong Kong University Press, 217–60.

Naquin, S. (2000), *Peking, Temples and City Life, 1400–1900*, Berkeley, CA: University of California Press.

Ockey, J. (2004), *Making Democracy: Leadership, Class, Gender, and Political Participation in Thailand*, Honolulu: University of Hawai'i Press.

Purcell, V. (1965), *The Chinese in Southeast Asia*, London: Oxford University Press.

Ritzinger, J. and Bingenheimer, M. (2006), 'Whole-body relics in Chinese Buddhism – previous research and historical overview', *The Indian International Journal of Buddhist Studies* 7, 37–94.

Rowe, W. T. (1989), *Hankow: Conflict and Community in a Chinese City (1796–1895)*, Stanford, CA: Stanford University Press.

Schipper, K. (1982), *Le Corps Taoïste*, Paris: Fayard.

Skeat, W. (1900), *Malay Magic: an Introduction to the Folklore and Popular Religion of the Malay Peninsular*, London: Franck Kass.

Skinner, W. G. (1954), *A Study of Chinese Community Leadership in Bangkok, together with an Historical Survey of Chinese Society in Thailand*, unpublished PhD dissertation, Ithaca, NY: Cornell University.

Smith, J. F. Handlin (1987), 'Benevolent societies: the reshaping of charity during the late Ming and early Ch'ing', *Journal of Asian Studies* **46**, 309–37.

Suryadinata, L. (2007), *Understanding the Ethnic Chinese in Southeast Asia*, Singapore: Institute of Southeast Asian Studies (ISEAS).

Tambiah, S. J. (1970), *Buddhism and the Spirit Cults in North-east Thailand*, Cambridge University Press.

(1984), *The Buddhist Saints of the Forest and the Cult of Amulets*, Cambridge University Press.

Teiser, S. (1988), *The Ghost Festival in Medieval China*, Princeton, NJ: Princeton University Press.

Thompson, S. J. (1988), 'Death, food and fertility', in eds. James L. Watson and Evelyn Rawski, *Death and Ritual in Late Imperial and Modern China*, Berkeley, CA: University of California Press, 71–108.

Tsu, T. (2000), 'Toothless ancestors, felicitous descendants: the rite of secondary burial in south Taiwan', *Asian Folklore Studies* **59**, 1–22.

Waters, D. (1991), 'Chinese funerals: a case study', *Journal of the Royal Asiatic Society Hong Kong Branch* **31**, 104–34.

Watson, J. L. (1982), 'Of flesh and bones: the management of death pollution in Cantonese society', in eds. Maurice Bloch and Jonathan Parry, *Death and the Regeneration of Life*, Cambridge University Press.

(1993), 'Rites or beliefs? The construction of a unified culture in late Imperial China', in eds. Samuel S. Kim and Lowell Dittner, *China's Quest for National Identity*, Ithaca, NY: Cornell University Press.

Watson, J. and Rawski, E. (eds.) (1988), *Death Ritual in Late Imperial and Modern China*, Berkeley, CA, London: University of California Press.

Weber, M. (1951), *The Religion of China: Confucianism and Taoism*, Toronto: The Free Press.

Weller, R. (1987), *Unities and Diversities in Chinese Religion*, London: Macmillan.

Winichakul, Thongchai (1994), *Siam Mapped: a History of the Geo-body of a Nation*, Honolulu: University of Hawai'i Press.

Winzeler, R. (1986), *Ethnic Relations in Kelantan*. Singapore: Oxford University Press.

Wolf, A. (1974), 'Gods, ghosts and ancestors', in ed. A. P. Wolf, *Religion and Ritual in Chinese Society*, Stanford, CA: Stanford University Press, 148–55.

Yang, C. K. (1961), *Religion in Chinese Society*, Berkeley, CA: University of California Press.

Zhan Tianyan 展天眼 (1997), 'Song dafeng pusa xingjiao ji' ['宋大峰菩萨行教记, 'Record on the teachings and behaviour of the bodhisattva song dafeng'], in *Dejiao Qiyuan* 德教起源, Bangkok: Zi Zhenge.

CHAPTER 10

For Buddhas, families and ghosts: the transformation of the Ghost Festival into a Dharma Assembly in southeast China

Ingmar Heise

INTRODUCTION

In this chapter I discuss the transformation of one of the major religious festivals in the Chinese coastal province of Fujian 福建, which is traditionally known as the 'Yulanpen Assembly' (*yulanpen hui* 盂蘭盆會) or 'Ghost Festival' (*guijie* 鬼節). The festival is celebrated during the seventh lunar month, usually around the 15th – in traditional Chinese calendrical terms, the 'Middle Primordial' (*zhongyuan* 中元). It is said that on the 29th of the sixth lunar month King Yama, Lord of the Underworld, opens the gates of his realm and allows the spirits of the dead to visit the world of the living. During this time they receive food offered by the living.

This research is based on fieldwork I undertook in 2008 in the context of my research project on Buddhist death rituals in three cities of Fujian, namely Xiamen 厦门, Quanzhou 泉州 and Fuzhou 福州. Together with my camera assistant, Zhang Han, I observed and filmed the various rituals held in the monasteries of Quanzhou in August 2008, the so-called 'Ghost Month' (*guiyue* 鬼月).

This research is part of the Bristol project on Buddhist Death Rituals in Southeast Asia and China sponsored by the Arts and Humanities Research Council (AHRC). In addition to the financial support from the AHRC, I also received several Read-Tuckwell Bursaries and a Sheng-yen Education Foundation Grant. I would like to thank in particular my camera assistant, Zhang Han, who filmed the Buddhist rituals in August 2008 and with whom I edited a short documentary on these rituals entitled *The Spirits' Happy Days*. Furthermore, I would like to thank my PhD supervisor, John Kieschnick, for the constant patient support during my research and corrections of this chapter. My thanks also goes to the editors of this book, Patrice Ladwig and Paul Williams, for their assistance, and to Els van Dongen for her help during the final efforts to complete this chapter. I would also like to extend my thanks to Professor Xu Jinding of Quanzhou's Huaqiao University and to Mao Wei and his friends for their help during my research in Quanzhou.

In order to better clarify the transformation this major festival has undergone during the last hundred years, I first provide a short historical background of the festival, including a summary of the first detailed ethnographic description given by the Dutch Sinologist de Groot in the late nineteenth century. This I will contrast with the modern situation, of which one of the main characteristics is the separation of practices related to food offering outside of the monastery on the one hand, and the religious practices related to recitation of Buddhist scriptures inside the monastery on the other hand.

I hope to demonstrate that, despite the religious revival since the initiating of the reform policy of the late 1970s, in the cities religious, communal or public rituals have undergone a significant transformation. This transformation is due, so I believe, not only to the strict control of public religious activities in the cities still maintained by the Chinese state, but also by the rapid development of urban modernity and idealised notions of Buddhism mainly serving the living instead of performing rituals for the dead.

HISTORICAL BACKGROUND OF THE GHOST FESTIVAL IN CHINA

The origin of the Ghost Festival is traditionally attributed to the first version of the story of the monk Mulian saving his mother, which is found in the *Yulanpen Sūtra* and the *Sūtra on Offering Bowls to Repay Kindness* (Teiser 1988: 48–9). The story goes like this:

The Buddha's disciple Mulian (Sanskrit: Maudgalyāyana; Pali: Moggallāna; Chinese: 目蓮) sees with his divine eye his deceased mother in the realm of hungry ghosts.[1] He sends her a bowl of rice, but when the food reaches her mouth it turns into flaming coals. Mulian is overcome by grief and asks the Buddha for advice. The Buddha instructs Mulian to offer food, candles, oil lamps, mattresses and the 'sweetest thing' in a bowl to the assembly of monks on the 15th of the seventh lunar month in order to help her. On that day the bodhisattvas, saints and virtuous monks emerge from the three-month summer retreat. This is the day the buddhas rejoice, witnessing the spiritual progress the members of the assembly have achieved. By making offerings to the monks on that day for the sake of

[1] See Patrice Ladwig's Chapter 6 in this volume for a discussion of contemporary Laotian rituals of the Ghost Festival. For the Tibetan transformation of the 'Mulian saves his mother' story, see Kapstein (2007).

seven generations of ancestors, one's parents and six kinds of family relatives will be released 'from suffering in the three evil paths of rebirth'. After Mulian presents the offerings to the saṅgha on the 15th day, his mother is released.[2]

The Yulanpen Festival has been celebrated since at least the second half of the sixth century in South China. Over the centuries its popularity increased as it spread out from the monasteries and was transformed into the 'Ghost Festival', one of the most popular and important public or communal religious festivals in China. Our evidence for the origins and development of the festival comes from a wide range of documents scattered in a variety of genres until the first detailed ethnographic descriptions of the festival's celebrations appear in the nineteenth century.[3]

The ethnographer and Sinologist Jan Jacob M. de Groot (1854–1921), who first arrived in Amoy (as Xiamen was then called) in 1877, gives a detailed account of the celebrations of the Ghost Festival (1977: 403–35). According to him the main activities of the Ghost Month consisted of the holding of a *pudu* 普度, 'a rite of universal salvation'. As described by de Groot, every neighbourhood would hold a *pudu* at a certain day during the seventh month. During a *pudu*, food was offered on tables, together with incense and flowers outside the house. A procession of temple chiefs, monks and musicians accompanied by lanterns and banner holders, proceeded through the streets. At each table the officiant would stop and put incense sticks on the table from his incense holder. The monks recited mantras to transform and multiply the food for the wandering spirits. After the procession had left, paper money for the spirits was burned and the food was moved inside the house. In the evening the family feasted together with invited relatives and friends. Additionally theatrical performances were held, often including the 'Mulian saves his mother' play. According to de Groot, the Ghost Month can therefore also be called a month of banqueting.

In addition to the offering of food in front of the individual houses, a large or communal *pudu* was held in the local temple of the district. Before the start of the Ghost Month a 'Yulanpen Assembly' would be formed by local

[2] See Teiser (1988: 49–54) for a translation of these two sūtras (T. no 685 and T. no 686); and also Stevenson's translation of the *Yulanpen Sūtra* (2004: 329–34).

[3] See Teiser (1988: 48 and 56–8) for the first clear mention and description of the Yulanpen celebration in South China in a secular source. See also Teiser (1988: 107–12 and 1989: 191–223) for a short discussion of the Ghost Festival after the end of the Tang dynasty and until 1900. For the appearance of the 'Mulian saves his mother' story in a wide range of literary genres, from sūtras to opera plays, see Mao Gengru 茆耕茹 (1993).

residents and temple administrators charged with collecting funds to sponsor the *pudu*. Inside the temple a huge scaffold or gigantic table several floors high was erected, filled with 'pyramids' of food, mostly sacks of rice, and adorned with all kinds of ornaments, incense and flowers. On the scaffold or nearby an equally impressive large paper figure of *Pudugong* 普度公, the 'Lord of the Pudu', also known as King of Ghosts, (*gui wang* 鬼王), was placed. This lord was seen by some to be a transformation body of the bodhisattva Avalokiteśvara (Guanyin), whose statue was placed on top of his head. His responsibility is to take care that every ghost receives his fair share of the food and that the *pudu* proceeds in an orderly manner. Additionally paper figures of King Yama and his scribes were placed in the temple, sometimes together with scrolls depicting the various hells.

After the monks returned from their procession through the nearby streets they were seated at a table and started a longer ritual of food-bestowal, during which musicians performed. People streamed into the monastery and offered incense to the temple's god and the two kings (the King of Ghosts and King Yama) and placed food offerings on the scaffold. The officiants sprinkled water with a long green branch and threw coins to the spirits, which were then gathered by the people who scrambled for the coins. As soon as the gong was hit to announce the end of the ritual, what is called 'pillaging the abandoned [ghosts'] scaffold' (*qiang gupeng* 搶孤棚) began. While the crowds of the living fought over the food offerings, the red memorial with the name of the sponsors of this *pudu*, which had been read aloud previously, were burned for the dead, together with the paper effigies of *Pudugong* and King Yama, huge amounts of paper money, paper houses, gardens and even horses, sedan chairs and a boat.

De Groot paints a portrait at the end of the nineteenth century of the Ghost Festival of Fujian as a flourishing communal rite, marking one of the most important periods in the ritual calendar. In the twentieth century, however, the traditions de Groot described came under attack from various sides, culminating in the disappearance of the public celebrations of the festival during the turbulent years of the Cultural Revolution (1966–76).[4] It is only since the end of the twentieth century that the festival has begun to recover some of its former importance.

[4] See Welch (1972) for the suppression of Buddhism under Mao. Wang Mingming (1993: 107) recalls from childhood memory that during the 1960s and 1970s public or communal rituals in Quanzhou were 'domesticated', i.e. performed clandestinely *within* the household.

THE FESTIVAL TODAY

Since the opening and reform policy of the late 1970s, Buddhism has flourished in Southeast China. Monasteries and temples have been reconstructed, a new generation of monks and nuns ordained and since the 1990s the ritual tradition has been reestablished.[5] One of the most visible immaterial signs of the resurgence of Buddhism is the holding of large-scale recitation rituals lasting several days, the so-called dharma assemblies (*fahui* 法會). In Quanzhou, one of the old cultural and religious centres of Fujian province, and ancestral home to many inhabitants of Taiwan and overseas Chinese, some of the most popular rituals held in this city are those related to the Ghost Festival.

Yet one of the legacies of the last century is that during the course of the twentieth century the Ghost Festival was increasingly seen as a relic of the 'feudal' past by successive Republican and Communist governments. This hostility to the festival was not, in other words, new with the Communist government. For instance, the violent 'plundering of the abandoned' part of the Ghost festival was already banned by the imperial government.[6] Under the People's Republic of China (PRC), the Ghost Festival, like all religious activities, especially the public ones, was severely suppressed.

With the reform policy of the late 1970s, when the state moved from suppression of religion to control of religious activities (Potter 2003: 11–31), the practice of offering food, incense and paper money to ancestors and ghosts during the Ghost Month has been revived. In contemporary times, however, it seems that the authorities in the PRC have been even more successful than their imperial predecessors in constraining public religious activities, at least within larger cities. Tan Hwee-San (2003: 8–9) reports that, owing to governmental clamp-down on any large-scale event possibly linked to the Ghost Festival, almost no sign of any activities related to the festival could be detected in Xiamen (an international trade hub) in

[5] For a survey of contemporary Chinese Buddhism, see Birnbaum (2003: 122–44); and for the popularity of Buddhist rituals for the dead in Southeast China, see *ibid.*: (136–7). For the resurgence of the major Buddhist monastery in Xiamen, Nanputuo 南普陀寺, with its famous Minnan Buddhist College 閩南佛學院, see Ashiwa and Wank (2006: 337–59); for the reintroduction of large-scale rituals for the dead since the 1980s, with the help of training ritual masters in Hong Kong and Singapore, see *ibid.* (352).

[6] See Weller's study (1987) of the Ghost Festival in northern Taiwan in the 1970s for a discussion of the (largely futile) attempts of the various imperial, Japanese and Republican governments to control and suppress the Ghost Festival and especially its most chaotic and violent aspect of the 'plundering of the scaffold of offerings for the abandoned souls'.

1997. In nearby Quanzhou she witnessed only low-key activities such as three-day *sūtra*-recitations in monasteries and the performance of a street-opera.

Lagerwey (2005: 225–6) states that in various parts of western Fujian, the festivities during the Ghost Festival seem to be more subdued activities conducted separately by each family or by individual lineages who invite Buddhist monks to perform offerings for the unhappy dead in their ancestral halls. In the Putian coastal plain north of the Minnan region, mid-size Buddhist monasteries offer troupes of monks performing rituals during the Ghost Month (Dean and Zheng Zhenman 2010: 166). In a village in Yongchun county, Tan Chee-Beng (2006: 105–6) reports that each lineage sections offers food for the ghosts and *Pudugong* in the afternoon on a different day of the Ghost Month in front of their ancestral house. In the evening each family takes its food back home.

In short, despite the opening and reform policy of the central government, local city governments tightly control and occasionally crack down on any public religious activities connected with the Ghost Festival and occurring outside the walls of orthodox monasteries.[7] To appreciate the significance of the festival today, and to evaluate how it has changed, it is useful to examine the festival in two distinct spheres: outside the Buddhist monastery, and within the monastery.

Outside the monasteries

The most common practices related to the dead observable in urban Quanzhou during the seventh lunar month are the neighbourhood offering of food for the wandering spirits (i.e. spirits of the dead who for various reasons have failed to become settled 'ancestors') and the public recitation rituals in the monasteries.[8] From the 29th of the sixth lunar month until the last day of the seventh lunar month residents conduct the 'rite of universal salvation' in the streets and neighbourhoods of Quanzhou. In the *pudu* I observed in the beginning of the seventh lunar month of 2008 on

[7] According to Wang Mingming (1993: 139), in 1990, governmental anti-superstitious inspection teams were roaming the neighbourhoods during the Ghost Month trying to hunt down the *pudu*, and even sometimes clashing violently with locals, but more often the warned residents simply evaded them.

[8] Persons who have failed to die a 'good death', that is at old age, peacefully with (plenty) of descendants at their own homes, with the proper funeral and burial rites performed, are prone to become one of the *guhun yegui* ('abandoned souls and wild ghosts' 孤魂野鬼, commonly abbreviated as *guhun*), wandering homeless spirits (i.e. without ancestor tablet at which sacrifices are held). Children who have died a sudden and violent death are particularly at risk of becoming unfortunate wandering spirits after death. See Feuchtwang (2010: 135–9) on 'good death' and 'bad death'.

Houcheng 后城 street, a small street parallel to Quanzhou's Xumen 涂门 main street, along which Quanzhou's famous Qingjing 清净寺 mosque and the important Guangyu 关于庙 temple are situated, a few residents placed tables at the entrance to their residence loaded with cooked food, including fish and crabs still alive. On the doorframes they inserted incense sticks and flowers. Sometimes a little paper money was burned in old woks on the street. In a nearby side-alley surrounded by apartment blocks and thereby shielded from public view, fireworks and large amounts of high-grade, large red-and-golden paper money (usually burned for gods like Tudigong 土地公, the local 'Earth God') and low-grade 'silver money' for the spirits were burned.

These offerings are supposed to be for the unfortunate anonymous dead or, as one middle-aged female resident said, 'the ones who died outside, the ones who were killed outside'. Another middle-aged male resident specifically mentioned that the *pudu* is for dead soldiers, and not for ancestors. This answer points to the main focus of the *pudu* and its ambiguity: although the *pudu* includes like all major Chinese religious rituals and festivities offerings to the ancestors conducted *inside* the house in front of the family altar (and/or in the temples and lineage halls), its main focus is the delivery of offerings to the unknown and unnamed wandering spirits *outside* the family home (at the entrance of the house, on the street or in the monasteries).[9] However, this group of wandering spirits or 'abandoned souls' (*guhun* 孤魂) of, for example, deceased soldiers, are at the same time inevitably *some* family's ancestors or family relatives. Similarly, seen from a Buddhist angle as the Buddha pointed out, referred to in the sixth-century commentary to the *Petavatthu* ('Stories of the Departed'), there exists no family which has no family members reborn as hungry ghosts (P. *peta*, Skt. *preta*, *egui* 餓鬼; Dhammapāla 2007: 30). One could say that offerings to ancestors inside the home in front of the family altar (or at the ancestor tablets in monasteries and clan halls) focus on the 'family' aspect of the known and cherished deceased person, whereas offerings outside the apartment focus on the strange, unfamiliar, pitied and perhaps also feared wandering ghosts.

Generally speaking the rite is now held by middle-aged to elderly women. When I inquired with a group of old men enjoying themselves in the park

[9] Neither I nor de Groot witnessed offerings to the ancestors inside family homes during the Ghost Month. I however assume that food is also offered at the ancestral shrine inside the home. See for example Lombard-Salmon's article (1975: 457–86), which describes offerings and libations conducted in the home of Chinese immigrants for the ancestors during the Ghost Month in nineteenth-century Java.

where the *pudu* would be found, I harvested only dismissive comments about the *pudu*: 'What do you want to see? There is nothing to see.' They further lamented that, unlike today, once the *pudu* was a splendid (*fengfu* 豐富) festival. For many younger people it seems the *pudu*'s main meaning is that of a feast one is invited to by friends. On the streets, the religious connotation and Buddhist roots of the Yulanpen Festival are, to many, completely unknown. Even the local puppet troupe, which normally performs the 'Mulian saves his mother' (*Mulian jiu mu xi* 目蓮救母戲) or another piece during funerals and religious festivals was out of town touring the nation.[10] It is the Buddhist monasteries one has to turn to if one wants to see something which at least resembles a communal or public religious festival.

Inside the monasteries

In the monasteries, the rituals associated with the Ghost Festival are called 'Buddhas' happy days' (*fo huanxi ri* 佛歡喜日, e.g. in Kaiyuan 開元寺 and Nanshaolin Monastery 南少林寺) or dharma assemblies (e.g. in Chengtian 承天寺and Chongfu Monastery 崇福寺). Only a small monastery such as Shijia Monastery 釋迦寺 would call its three-day ritual a *pudu*. The association of the term *pudu* with a backward folkloristic and superstitious degeneration from the noble-spirited religious and culturally splendid Buddhist Yulanpen Festival as it is seen by the (local) state agencies and some Chinese researchers, and modern Buddhists, leads monasteries to avoid the term and instead use the word dharma assembly or *chaodu* 超度 'rite of release and crossing over [the spirits of the dead]'.[11] However, if seen technically as a 'rite of universal salvation', the monasteries' dharma assemblies of the Ghost Month can be regarded according to Chongfu Monastery's abbot as a kind of *pudu*.

The public is informed weeks in advance with a red poster hung outside the monasteries' gates or at the entrance of their main Buddha hall of the date and main content of the ritual, with the contact details of the responsible monks or lay-people in charge of registering the names of the dead for whom the laity wants to sponsor a so-called 'Lotus-seat' (*lianwei* 蓮位).

[10] On the state's agencies', like the Cultural Affairs Bureau 文化局, futile attempts to purify and upgrade local 'backward' and 'superstitious' practices into glorious embodiments of five-thousand-year-old Chinese national culture in Quanzhou, see Wang Mingming's essay (2006: 1–34) on the '"Great Tradition" and its enemy' and his study of yearly rites of Quanzhou (1993).

[11] See, for example, Wu Youxiong 吳幼雄 (1994: 60–7), where the contemporary *pudu* is characterised as an 'undesirable custom' *lousu* 陋俗, which has to be transformed and changed.

These lotus-seats are small yellow strips of paper, on which in the middle the name of the dead family member is written and on the lower left the name of the living sponsor. Thousands of these paper slips are pasted on large boards or panels and installed in one of the halls of the monasteries around an altar.

In these halls, which are temporarily transformed into what is formally called 'Halls of Rebirth' (*wangsheng tang* 往生堂, in Chongfu's official programme) or rather informally 'the place where the release of the dead occurs' (*chaodu difang* 超度地方, as a participating monk called it), the accumulated merit resulting from the recitation of sacred sūtras, penance-texts or the names of buddhas is transferred to the dead.[12] Sometimes the price is also mentioned (Kaiyuan), which is usually fifty Yuan (around five Euros in 2008) for a single slip and five hundred Yuan (about fifty Euros) for one of the large paper steles, on which one is allowed to place several names of dead family members and which are usually installed in the centre of the hall on the altar. The ritual efficacy is the same for both, paper-slip or paper tablet, according to an abbot's attendant, 'but people like to see [and display] their name written large'. Below I translate one of these 'dharma announcements' (for the Chongfu Monastery):

This is held in order to carry out the Tathāgatha's method of filial piety and to carry forward bodhisattva's Kṣitigarbha's magnificent vow, 'As long as hell is not empty, I vow not to realise Buddhahood.' The seventh month is the month all buddhas are fond of. The Yulanpen Festival on the 15th and bodhisattva Kṣitigarbha's holy day on the 30th offer the best opportunity to release the souls of the deceased: the parents and teachers of previous generations, the ancestors of nine successive generations, the family members of the six relations, the creditors to whom one has caused misfortune and injury, and the creditors whose lives one has taken.[13] It is also a satisfactory realisation of the Buddhadharma's enlightening of the people through the method of filial piety.

For this reason this monastery will compassionately initiate procedures to save all living creatures from misery by holding a dharma assembly from the 1st to the 30th of August 2008 (1st to the 30th of the seventh lunar month), in which the 'Scripture of the Merit of the Past Vows of Bodhisattva Kṣitigarbha' – which is an outstanding guide to lead the suffering beings away from misery towards happiness – will be recited, for the benefit of beings in this world and of the world beyond, universally causing beings to be happy in this life, to fulfil all good wishes, allow all who have

[12] These halls could also be called Pure Land Altars (*jingtu tan* 淨土壇), as they are in other public Buddhist rituals.

[13] The 30th day of the seventh lunar month is the day when the transformation and response body of the bodhisattva Dizang, the Korean prince-turned-monk 'died' (or entered nirvāṇa) during the Tang dynasty.

died to be liberated from suffering and give them the opportunity to hear the Dharma and hence practise Buddhism, and satisfy the Path of the Buddha.

All believers of the ten directions are welcome to participate. Participants please go to the Guest Office (*ketang* 客堂) to register.[14]

In my discussion of these dharma assemblies below, I focus on the rituals of two of the largest monasteries of Quanzhou, namely Chengtian Monastery and Chongfu Monastery. These two monasteries form, together with the largest and most famous Kaiyuan Monastery, with its iconic twin-pagodas, a major religious centre not only for the Buddhist community, but also for the general populace in Quanzhou city and beyond.

These dharma assemblies share the tripartite structure of Chinese religious festivals of, first, inviting the buddhas and gods (and summoning the souls, *qingfo zhaohun* 請佛招魂) on the day before the official start of the ritual; second, hosting or welcoming the invited guests by making daily offerings to them of incense, food, sacred recitations and the resulting merit, and huge quantities of paper money, whose climax is the *shanggong* 上供 noon-offering, during a ritual lasting several days and culminating in the Yulanpen Festival on the 15th; and finally, sending off the transcendental, celestial and netherworldly guests (*songsheng* 送聖) on the last day, which formally concludes the ritual.[15]

They at the same time share the essentially dual structure with both private (generally one-day long) Buddhist *chaodu* rituals for deceased family members and the largest Buddhist 'Death Ritual' of all, the famous seven-day long *shuilu fahui* 水陸法會 or 'Dharma Assembly for the Universal Release of All Water, Land [and Air] Beings'. They basically consist in the daily recitation of a text, like the *Sūtra of the Past Vows of Bodhisattva Kṣitigarbha* (*Dizang pusa benyuan jing* 地藏菩薩本願經, T. no. 412) or the *Precious Penance of the Liang Emperor* (*Lianghuang baochan* 梁皇寶懺, T. no. 1909) or the name of Amitābha Buddha, Lord of the Western Paradise, in one of the major halls in front of the Buddha Altar (*fotan* 佛壇).[16] The resulting merit is then transferred to the dead at least twice daily (at the end of both the morning and afternoon sessions) in a separate

[14] Chongfu Monastery 'Dharma News' posted at the monastery's entrance, 2008.

[15] Next to motivations such as 'filial piety', commemoration, Buddhist compassion for the unfortunate dead and devotion to the Buddhas, one may also add the general idea of hospitality as a motivation for these offerings and rituals. See for example Feuchtwang (2010: 175). On the tripartite structure of inviting, welcoming and sending off divinities in northern Chinese rituals, see Overmeyer (2009: 5–6; 56–7; 93–4).

[16] The recitation of a Buddha's name (*nianfo* 念佛) is usually done walking in the monastery's courtyard. But each recitation session begins and ends at the Buddha Altar.

hall, where the Spirit Altar (*lingtan* 靈壇) surrounded by the thousands of 'Lotus-seats' has been established.[17]

Essential for these dharma assemblies as for all Buddhist rituals, not only the ones for the dead, is the holding of a rite for feeding and releasing the ghosts in the evening. The accumulated merit is again transferred at the Spirit Altar.[18] Equally essential for all dharma assemblies is the release of animals rite (*fangsheng* 放生) held in the morning. The resulting merit is received by the living donors.

With the exception of the *Yulanpen Sūtra*, which to my knowledge is only recited once a year, namely on the 15th of the seventh lunar month, none of the hymns, chants, gāthās, mantras and main texts or Buddha names recited and rites held are specific to these dharma assemblies of the Ghost Month. What makes them distinctive is the fact that all monasteries hold them in the same month, the Ghost Month, and that they are second in importance only to the dharma assemblies of the New Year, which are mainly dedicated to the welfare of the living members of the family. The rituals held during the Ghost Month are for the welfare of the deceased part of the family, but also for deceased persons and beings thought to be capable of influencing and possibly threatening the fortune and well-being of the living family, as well as for deceased persons unrelated to the family but for whom one feels compassion, like the victims of the Sichuan earthquake of May 2008.

These dharma assemblies of the Ghost Month are not only major events for the Buddhist communities themselves, but are in my observation the only activities of the Ghost Month that, at least to a certain extent, deserve the name of public (or if one prefers, communal) religious festival. I intend to provide a more detailed description of these rites in my PhD thesis.[19] Here I want to focus instead on several aspects of the rites that highlight changes the festival has undergone in its most recent manifestation.

[17] The use of the terms Buddha Altar (*fotan*) and Spirit Altar (*lingtan*) is taken and follows from Tan Hwee-San (2003: 104).

[18] For a classical anthropological treatment of food offerings in Chinese religion, see Ahern (1973: 166–74), quoted in Chang (1977: 17–19). Basically, it correlates the state of the food, namely raw, half-cooked, dried or cooked, to the relationship and the distance between the offerer to the beings who receive the offering. For example, recently deceased persons receive cooked food from the descendants, whereas Tiangong 天宫, the supreme god of the Chinese popular pantheon, receives raw food. In the contemporary Buddhist rituals, this notion is still visible, but there are considerable differences. First of all, only vegetarian food is offered and the monasteries seem to follow the principle of economic frugality. Generally, cooked food is particularly visible in the offerings to the dead of the family in the Rebirth or Merit Hall, but all offerings seem to consist of a mixture of cooked, dried and uncooked food. On the rise of Buddhist vegetarianism, see Kieschnick (2005).

[19] Ingmar Heise, *Buddhist Death Rituals in Fujian* (forthcoming).

TRANSFORMATION OF THE GHOST FESTIVAL: MODERN MONASTIC CRITICISM AND STATE CONTROL

One of the most influential monks of twentieth-century Chinese Buddhism, Taixu 太虛 (1889–1947), is generally considered to be one of the major critics of Buddhist services for the dead within the Buddhist community.[20] According to Pittman (2001: 101), one of Taixu's main concepts of modern Buddhism is the use of Buddhism and the saṅgha to help and improve the society of the living, rather than making money out of the dead.[21] Nevertheless it is important to note that even Taixu did not question the rituals and their efficacy itself. He once even participated, when asked to replace another monk, as an assistant cantonist (*zhu biao* 助表) at the Inner Altar (*neitan* 內壇) of a *shuilu* dharma assembly.[22] His main critique focused not on the efficacy or utility of the rituals, but on the commercialisation of Buddhist rituals for the dead and its 'corrupting' influence on the saṅgha. For Taixu, who attempted, according to Bingenheimer (2004: 78), to 'de-ghostify' ['*ent-geistern*'] Buddhism, nevertheless 'the divine beings, heavens and hells, and all devotional practices are [. . .] a legitimate part of Buddhism' (*ibid.*: 103).

Almost as influential in the movement to challenge Buddhist death rituals was Yinshun 印順 (1906–2006), a disciple of Taixu's ideas, who also spent time at Nanputuo's Minnan Buddhist College, where Taixu was director.[23] Unlike Taixu, however, he seems personally to have distanced himself from all things ritual. After receiving ordination he was asked to help out reciting the *Precious Penance of the Liang Emperor*, at a monastery in Hangzhou where he stayed during his travels but, uncomfortable with the ritual, he quit the monastery (and reciting) on the second day and stayed instead at an inn.[24] Nevertheless even Yinshun who went, according to Bingenheimer, one step further than Taixu, by attempting to remove the 'deification' of buddhas and bodhisattvas and denied that 'heaven and divine beings ('*Göttergestalten*') should be a substantial part of Buddhist

[20] On the various secular critics and government attempts at reforming Chinese funeral traditions, of which the Buddhist *chaodu* rites form an important but autonomous part, see Fang Ling and Goossaert (2008: 51–73).

[21] See also Welch's classic chapter (1968) on Taixu's life and work, whose assessment differs from Pittman's rather positive one.

[22] See Taixu's autobiography *Zizhuan* 自傳 (n.d.: ch. 9, 28) in his collected works *Taixu Dashi Quanshu* 太虛大師全書.

[23] On the life and work of this eminent scholar-monk, see Bingenheimer (2004).

[24] See Yinshun's autobiography *Pingfan de yi sheng* 平凡的一生 (n.d.: ch. 4, 19) in his collected works *Miao yunji* 妙雲集 .

practice', did not question the ritual efficacy itself.[25] Rather, Yinshun attempted to reinterpret the meaning of the Ghost Festival, shifting the focus from the dead to the living.

In a lecture on the Bodhisattva Dizang, for instance, Yinshun devotes much of his discussion to how one avoids falling into hell, listing the various crimes (most of which are directed against the Three Jewels) which will lead to downfall. Its last part deals with the conduct and rites one should undertake when relatives are approaching death, or after their deaths. Yinshun emphasises again and again the importance of proper behaviour before death, and repeats that the most important 'salvation' is the undertaking of good deeds during one's lifetime. Then the next crucial point is to hold the rites for the deceased as soon as possible during the forty-nine day period of the intermediate state, between two rebirths. Rites conducted later would be too late to help the dead, though he concedes that in special cases deliverance from hell even after forty-nine days is possible by filial sons and daughters (ibid.: 111–13).

In sum, modern reformers like Taixu and Yinshun began to call into question the propriety of monastic dependence on death rituals, including the Ghost Festival rituals, as a major source of income and a focus of monastic energy. Their influence continues to today when Buddhist reformers consistently express discomfort with the centrality of the death ritual in the monastic calendar. Nonetheless, the views of reformer monks like Taixu and Yinshun seem not to have decreased their popularity. Take, for example, a short passage from the monk Zhenhua's biography, a very important source on the life and practice of the majority of China's 'rank-and-file' monks during the first half of the century. Zhenhua, during his wandering in search of the Dharma, was forced by the monasteries where he lived to participate in rites for the dead. He started to 'work funerals' on the 15th of the seventh lunar month 1946, the month when, as he says, the monks of Taiwan (and South China) are most busy. Zhenhua writes:

> Originally, sūtras were the recorded words of the Buddha, and requiems were devised in accordance with the teachings of virtuous men of long ago. For a monk to chant sūtras, conduct requiems or 'release the ravenous ghosts' after a person's

[25] Bingenheimer (2004: 78). See also p. 103 for Taixu's critique of Yinshun's 'reduction of Buddhism to the human realm, which unduly limits Buddhist thought'. As long as Buddhist rituals are held within 49 days after death, with sincere heart and correctly by both monks and lay-people, they may help prevent the deceased from downfall into hell or other unfavourable destinations. See his published Yulanpen Festival lecture titled '*Dizang pusa zhi shengde ji qi famen* 地藏菩薩之聖德及其法門' in *Fofa shi jiushi zhi guang* 佛法是救世之光, vol. 25 of his collected works *Miao yunji* 妙雲集 and especially part six '*Lin duo yi duo zhe baji* 臨墮已墮者之拔濟': 98–114.

death, if done properly and honestly, is a 'door of expediency' [. . .] which benefits himself and others: there is nothing to be said against it. The sad thing is that some people view this beneficial door of expediency as a business deal. Because of this, the result of performing funeral services is that others are not benefited and harm is done to oneself and the Buddhist religion. In the half-year that I worked funerals in Nanking, I saw gifted, talented young monks spit blood and die because of bad habits they had acquired while working funerals. I also saw large, respected monasteries which, because they were doing funeral business, fostered a number of degenerate sons and thus brought shame upon their good names. Did these young monks not harm themselves by working funerals? Did the monasteries not harm the Buddhist religion by making a business of funerals? I make bold to say one thing: the demoralization of today's monastic order and the decline of Buddhism are influenced largely by the flourishing of funeral services – conducted for money. In hopes of persuading young monks to resolve [that it is] 'better to freeze and starve to death sitting on a bask prayer mat, than to be a funerary monk in this world of men', I do not shrink from 'coming forth in person to preach the law' and exposing my own faults, to show the disparity between working funerals as I knew them and the ideal of the saṅgha.[26]

The above examples outline the main arguments of the monastic critique of these rituals, with some of the concerns dating back several centuries. One of the young monks who did recite the *Dizang Sūtra* at Chongfu Monastery, and former attendee of the Minnan Buddhist College, for example, told me he preferred to meditate and read Buddhist texts rather than to recite with a dry throat for hours and days. He mentioned among his various critiques the fact that he and his young co-reciters were not spiritually accomplished enough to hold these rites for the dead, and would rush through the recitation. In the golden age of the Liang Emperor Wudi (sixth century), he continued, old spiritually well-accomplished monks, who could actually see the ghosts, would hold these rites in a slow, dignified manner.[27]

The most radical critique of these rites I have heard came from a north-eastern monk, engaged in Kaiyuan Monastery's charity work, who described

[26] Quote from Zhenhua (1992: 80). On Buddhist funeral services and commercialism see chapters III and IV and especially pp. 80–8, and also Yü Chun-fang's introduction in Zhenhua (1992). See also Günzel's introduction to the German translation of the first part of Zhenhua's biography (Zhenhua 2000).

[27] This criticism is not new. The sixth-century monk, Huijiao 慧皎, in a section of his *Biographies of Eminent Monks* (*Gaoseng zhuan* 高僧傳) devoted to professional composers and chanters of Buddhist hymns, complained about the lack of spiritual and technical accomplishment in chants of his own day. As he comments at the end of the chapter on the *Sūtra Master* (*jing shi* 經師): 'All these numerous songs were made by famous masters. The compositions made by later generations continuing [the work of the famous masters] had many mistakes and omissions. Perhaps this is because *śrāmaṇeras* (novices) and little boys would transmit and receive them to and from each other [in absence of skilled teachers of Buddhist psalmody], and so not even one of the formerly established perfect rules has been passed on. Isn't it a pity!' See Huijiao (497–554, T. 50, no. 2059, p. 415c).

himself as a monk serving the living and not knowing about rites for the dead. He advocated Theravādin *vipassanā* meditation as the ideal occupation for monks, and said he believed not only that the Buddha was a human (as opposed to a 'god'), but also that the southern tradition's doctrine of instant rebirth after death was, in fact, accurate. Taking the critique of the 'wrong time' when rites for the dead are usually held for the lay people to its most extreme, he exclaimed: 'Do these rites have any use at all?!'

One of the ways that leading monks today temper the criticism that they are performing old-fashioned, empty rites is by combining the Ghost Festival rituals with Dharma talks, thus balancing recitation and ritual with teachings and doctrine. At Chongfu Monastery the senior monk would occasionally hold a talk on the *Dizang [Kṣitigarbha] Sūtra* right after the *shanggong* offering for the laity. The other monks would already have proceeded to the refectory for lunch. Some Buddhist devotees, however, usually stayed with the senior monk to listen to his exposition, moving afterwards to the refectory.

The talks were given on the monk's own initiative and are not a regular part of dharma assemblies in Minnan. Indeed one acquaintance, a young college-educated woman from Quanzhou who accompanied us once at the end of the Ghost Month to Chongfu Monastery's ritual, was quite surprised to see a monk 'preaching like a Christian priest'. The senior monk (who did not attend a Buddhist college, but was nonetheless very learned), used Venerable Yinshun's sūtra-exposition on the 'Holy Virtue of Bodhisattva Dizang and his Dharma-Gate' held in 1963 in Taiwan on the 15th of the seventh lunar month as a base for his own lecture.[28] He held these lectures feeling that it is the duty of monks to spread the Dharma (*hongfa* 弘法) and so that the devotees can actually 'understand what they are reciting' (i.e. the *Dizang Sūtra*).

During the last days of the ritual, the senior monk was (according to our acquaintance) discussing the sins, like killing an arhat ('Buddhist saint', *luohan* 羅漢) which lead to downfall into Avīci, the deepest hell. He seemed, according to her, at pains to explain to the middle-aged and elderly women the concept of an arhat. She doubted that the women's education would be high enough to understand his exposition. The lecture was held in the local dialect (Minnan), as 'otherwise they [the lay-people] would not understand [my lecture]'. The incorporation into the Ghost Festival rituals of Dharma talks that attempt to explain the ritual and to educate devotees in Buddhist teachings seems to be a modern innovation.

[28] Yinshun, 'Dizang pusa' in *Foguang* vol. 25 of his collected works *Miao yunji*.

If the primary concern of reformist monks has been what they deemed to be excessive monastic involvement in the Ghost Festival rituals at the expense of self-cultivation and teaching, the primary concern of the state has been large, uncontrollable masses, which could quickly lead to outbursts of social unrest.[29]

Public religious activities in the cities are strictly confined to the monastery and at most to the nearby streets. Large monasteries have their own uniformed and plain-clothed security guards who are present during the rituals, especially during the popular *xuntan* 薰壇 opening, *shanggong* offering and *songsheng* closing ceremonies, when many believers and visitors are expected. They try to help maintain some orderly conduct during processions and rituals. Sometimes during important rites police officers would also appear, who, in contrast to the security guards, would not actively engage in crowd control but behave more like curious onlookers.

These rituals also have to be permitted by the local Religious Affairs Bureau, but this is not a big obstacle for orthodox religious sites, especially Buddhist ones.[30] Despite the proscription against direct participation of state officials and organisations in religious activities, in southern Fujian members of (local) state organisations nevertheless participate either on their own or as representatives of local state bureaus in Buddhist rituals for the dead. On the conclusion of Chongfu Monastery's thirty-day dharma assembly, for example, a pickup van of a local department of the city government unloaded sackloads of rice as a donation for the monks.

CONCLUSION

The small-scale *pudu*, that is the simple offering of food and incense either by individual families or by a whole village for ancestors, and most importantly for wandering ghosts, is still (or again) practised in Fujian but also in other parts of mainland China. The Ghost Festival, a large-scale *pudu*, a spectacular communal event, involving various specialists, monks, priests, musicians and artists, organised by the laity and for the whole community,

[29] One of Welch's informants (1972: 34), a former religious affairs official of Canton in the 1950s, observes relating to crowds attracted to funerals, which were held with the approval of the Religious Affairs Bureau (*zongjiao ju* 宗教局) until the late 1950s in Canton, that 'crowds were what the Party feared most'.

[30] In fact state agencies involved with the monasteries, of which there are quite a few, like the Religious Affairs Bureau, receive a share of the revenues generated by these public rituals (and private ones). For the new monastic economy based on lay donations and income generated from rituals since the 1990s, see Ji Zhe (2004: 2–10) and also Ashiwa and Wank (2006). It is not hard to imagine that these governmental stakeholders are less than hesitant in passing their seal of approval to these rituals.

has been transformed into, on the one hand, a series of *pudu* restricted to a few households of the various neighbourhoods of Quanzhou city and, on the other hand, the large-scale Buddhist dharma assemblies that take place inside of monastic compounds, at least in southeast China. The most direct reason for this shift from large-scale communal festivals to smaller-scale rites in Buddhist temples in mainland China is the government suppression of public religious activities outside monasteries, coupled with official condemnation of such rites as feudal superstition.

In Taiwan and among Chinese communities in Indonesia, despite restrictive government policies, the Ghost Festival, including the aggressive plundering of the ghosts' offering, still continued into the 1930s. But then, owing to increased political and socio-economic safety (modernisation and urbanisation), the nature of the ghosts changed from beings to be fed by the whole community in order to avoid disaster (like socially marginal bandits, corrupt police officers and aggressive beggars) to beings more to be pitied by elderly women, sympathising with the lonely aspect of the ghosts, maybe fearing themselves to be abandoned by their children.[31] In the *pudu* observed by Lombard-Salmon in the early 1970s in Java, after the ghosts have been fed, the fight among the poor for the food is cut short by the orderly distribution of the food to the needy in exchange for tickets distributed to them in advance.[32] What a contrast to the 'plundering of the ghosts' in the late nineteenth century!

In Taiwan, Buddhist modernism is largely responsible for the disentanglement of Buddhist monks from what is now considered a Daoist or folk religion. The large *pudu* witnessed by Weller (1987: 18) in the 1970s in northern Taiwan was held by 'black-capped' lay ritualists using Buddhist texts (probably similar to the incense and flower monks described by Yik Fai Tam in Chapter 11 of this volume), not Buddhist institutional personnel, who seem to be rather withdrawn from local society in the region Weller studied.

In mainland China, ironically, the government-enforced distinction between religion and superstition and control of public religious activities

[31] See Weller (1987: 74–85) for his theory on the change of the ghosts' nature from 'bandit to beggar'.

[32] See Lombard-Salmon (1975: 483). Although Lombard-Salmon mentions the presence of Indonesian militia at the *pudu*, who also receive sackloads of rice as a compensation for their help, and the government prescription against the offering of food to the ghosts in the streets, restricting the *pudu* celebrations to the temple, it seems that she attributes the changes the *pudu* celebration has undergone solely to reform efforts *within* the Chinese-Indonesian community. For an early attempt in 1900 to 'reform' the *pudu*, see *ibid*.: 471–8. For an example of a debate between 'Confucian' opponents of the Ghost Festival, criticising among other things the 'waste' of food, and the 'traditionalists' who defend the *pudu* as a Buddhist method of filial piety, admitting however that the way food is offered (and plundered) has to be reformed, see *ibid*.: 474–8.

has led to the situation that the Buddhist monastery seems to have a monopoly of large-scale rituals for the dead, like the Ghost Month recitation rituals. These dharma assemblies and the monasteries where they are held therefore contain remnants of the beliefs and practices the state has long derided, although on a much reduced scale. The fact that the Ghost Festival comes back to the Buddhist monastery even in a protestantised form of preaching and recitation rituals, however, leads to considerable tension between monks influenced by Buddhist modernism and their actual practise of these rituals for the dead. A tension between, on the one hand, lay demands to perform death rituals coupled with the economic benefits to monasteries of performing them and, on the other, monastic reservations about their dependence on the routine performance of these rituals, may have existed for quite some time before the advent of modernity, and will continue to remain, as long as the demand for these rituals – which is increasing, partly due to growing economic prosperity and the necessity for financial and religious reasons – continues.

The change from *pudu* to dharma assembly has had a considerable impact on how the festival is perceived. Communal religious festivals, as they once existed in the cities and as they seem to exist in some parts of rural China, are organised by the (mostly male) laity, temple chiefs and local leaders. They are a source of social prestige, power, influence and even money. As the public rituals in the cities are in monastic hands, local leaders and men in general lose interest. Furthermore, taking care of the family (including its dead) members seems to be considered the responsibility of women.[33] Work and leisure in the cities pulls the young away from the monasteries and the old men prefer to spend their time in the park (which often is in the very same monastery where the ritual is held).[34] Additionally, rural religious festivals offer a lot to see, *renao* 热闹, 'hot-and-noisy' sociality and a lot to do, in contrast to Buddhist recitation rituals, which may be seen by some as quite boring.[35] Nevertheless, it is astonishing that these dharma rituals are, according to monks and devotees, growing in popularity from

[33] In Vietnam there also seems to be a difference between the genders in their practice of Buddhism: whereas the elder educated men would *read* and discuss sūtras and be seen and see themselves as knowledgeable about Buddhism, and even instruct nuns in the correct holding of rituals, it is the women who regularly participate in the religious services and rituals *chanting* the scriptures. The women are, nevertheless, seen as not knowledgeable about Buddhism. See Soucy (2009: 348–71). See also Tambiah (1970: 143–4) for a similar picture in northeast Thailand.

[34] Welch (1968: 86) states that already during the Republican Era the young were quite disinterested in Buddhism.

[35] For examples of this *renao* sociality of rural religious festivals in north-central China and Fujian, see Yuet Chau (2006) and Dean (1993).

year to year. This suggests that they can offer something that no other secular or religious event can offer, from free meals, to a kind of group activity in a public space not dominated by commerce, to the offering of a prestigious and solemn place (*longzhong* 隆重), to remember and communicate with the dead family members, to the care for the unfortunate dead children who died during pregnancy or during earthquakes. Hence, while the boisterous large-scale communal rituals that could dominate an entire city during the Ghost Festival are gone from contemporary China, formal rituals in the monasteries continue to play an important therapeutic role, mediating between the dead and those members of the living who choose to participate.

BIBLIOGRAPHY

Ahern, E. (1973), *The Cult of the Dead in a Chinese Village*, Stanford, CA: Stanford University Press.

Ashiwa, Y. and Wank, D. L. (2006), 'The politics of a reviving Buddhist temple: state, association, and religion in southeast China', *The Journal of Asian Studies* **65** (2), 337–59.

Bingenheimer, M. (2004), *Der Mönchsgelehrte Yinshun (*1906) und seine Bedeutung für den Chinesisch-Taiwanesischen Buddhismus im 20. Jahrhundert*, Heidelberg: Edition Forum.

Birnbaum, R. (2003), 'Buddhist China at the century's turn', *Religion in China Today (The China Quarterly Special Issue)*, ed. D. L. Overmyer, Cambridge University Press, 122–44.

Chang, K. C. (ed.) (1977), *Food in Chinese Culture – Anthropological and Historical Perspectives*, New Haven and London: Yale University Press.

Chau, A. Y. (2006), *Miraculous Response: Doing Popular Religion in Contemporary China*, Stanford, CA: Stanford University Press.

Dean, K. (1993), *Taoist Ritual and Popular Cults of Southeast China*, Princeton, NJ: Princeton University Press.

Dean, K. and Zhenman Zheng (2010), *Ritual Alliances of the Putian Plain, Vol. 1: Historical Introduction to the Return of the Gods*, Leiden: Brill.

de Groot, J. M. M. (1977), *Les Fêtes Annuellement Célébrées à Émoui (Amoy): Étude Concernant la Religion Populaire des Chinois*, trans. É. Chavannes, Paris: Annales du Musée Guimet, [1st edn. 1886, vol. 2: 403–35. Reprint San Francisco: Chinese Materials Centre, Inc].

Dhammapāla (2007), *Elucidation of the Intrinsic Meaning: So Named the Commentary on the Peta-Stories*, trans. U Ba Kyaw and edited and annotated by Peter Masefield, Lancaster: Pali Text Society.

Fang Ling and Goossaert, V. (2008), 'Les réformes funéraires et la politique religieuse de l'état chinois, 1900–2008', *Archives de Sciences Sociales des Religions* **144**, 51–73.

Feuchtwang, S. (2010), *The Anthropology of Religion, Charisma and Ghosts – Chinese Lessons for Adequate Theory*, Berlin and New York: Walter de Gruyter.

Huijiao 慧皎 (497–554), *Gaoseng zhuan* 高僧傳, Taishō Shinshū Daizōkyō no. 2059.

Ji Zhe (2004), 'La nouvelle relation état-bouddhisme: un nombre gradissant de croyants entraîne une mutation de l'économie monastique en Chine', *Perspectives Chinoises* **84**, http://perspectiveschinoises.revues.org/665?&id+665 (accessed 4 April 2011).

Kapstein, M. T. (2007), 'Mulian in the Land of Snows and King Gesar in Hell – a Chinese tale of parental death in its Tibetan transformation', *The Buddhist Dead: Practices, Discourses, Representations*, eds. B. J. Cuevas and J. I. Stone, Honolulu: University of Hawai'i Press.

Kieschnick, J. (2005), 'Buddhist vegetarianism in China', *Of Tripod and Palate – Food, Politics, and Religion in Traditional China*, ed. R. Sterckx, New York: Palgrave Macmillan, 186–212.

Lagerwey, J. (2005), 'Ghost Festival', *Encyclopedia of Contemporary Culture*, ed. E. L. Davis, London and New York: Routledge, 225–6.

Lombard-Salmon, C. (1975), 'Survivance d'un rite bouddhique à Java: la cérémonie du pu-du', *Bulletin de l'Ecole Française d'Extrême-Orient* **62**, 457–86.

Mao, Gengru 茆耕茹 (1993), *Mulian Ziliao Bianmu Gailüe* 目連資料編目概略 in the *Minsu Quyi Congshu* 民俗曲藝叢書, ed. Wang Qiugui 王秋桂, Taibei: Shih Hocheng Foundation.

Overmeyer, D. L. (2009), *Local Religion in North China in the Twentieth Century: the Structure and Organization of Community Rituals and Beliefs*, Leiden: Brill.

Pittman, D. (2001), *Toward a Modern Chinese Buddhism: Taixu's Reform*, Honolulu: University of Hawai'i Press.

Potter, P. B. (2003), 'Belief in control: regulation of religion in China', *Religion in China Today* (*The China Quarterly Special Issue*), ed. D. L. Overmyer, Cambridge University Press, 11–31.

Soucy, A. (2009), 'Language, orthodoxy, and performances of authority in Vietnamese Buddhism', *Journal of the American Academy of Religion* 77 (2), 348–71.

Stevenson, D. (2004), 'How a monk freed his mother from hell', *Buddhist Scriptures*, ed. D. S. Lopez, Jr., London: Penguin Books, 329–34.

Taixu 太虛, *Taixu Dashi Quanshu* 太虛大師全書, www.yinshun.org.tw (accessed 4 April 2011).

Tambiah, S. (1970), *Buddhism and the Spirit Cults in North-east Thailand*, Cambridge University Press.

Tan Chee-Beng (2006), 'Chinese religious expressions in post-Mao Yongchun, Fujian', *Southern Fujian: Reproduction of Traditions in Post-Mao China*, ed. Tan Chee-Beng, Hong Kong: The Chinese University Press, 97–120.

Tan Hwee-San (2003), *Songs for the Dead*, unpublished PhD thesis, University of London: School of Oriental and African Studies.

Teiser, S. F. (1988), *The Ghost Festival in Medieval China*, Princeton, NJ: Princeton University Press.

(1989), 'The ritual behind the opera: a fragmentary ethnography of the Ghost Festival, AD 400–1900', *Ritual Opera Operatic Ritual: 'Mu-Lien Rescues His Mother'*, ed. David Johnson, Berkeley: Institute of East Asian Studies, 191–223.

Wang Mingming (1993), 'Flower of the state, grasses of the people – yearly rites and the aesthetics of power in Quanzhou Southeast China', unpublished PhD thesis, University of London: School of Oriental and African Studies.

(2006), '"Great Tradition" and its enemy: the issue of "Chinese Culture" on the southeastern coast', *Southern Fujian: Reproduction of Traditions in Post-Mao China*, ed. Tan Chee-Beng, Hong Kong: The Chinese University Press, 1–34.

Welch, H. (1968), *The Buddhist Revival of China*, Cambridge, MA: Harvard University Press.

(1972), *Buddhism under Mao*, Cambridge, MA: Harvard University Press.

Weller, R. (1987), *Unities and Diversities in Chinese Religion*. Houndmills and London: Macmillan.

Wu Youxiong 吴幼雄 (1994), 'Quanzhou Pudu Minsu Kaotan 泉州普度民俗考谈', *Fujian Qiaoxiang Minsu* 福建僑鄉民俗, ed. Chen Guoqiang 陈国强, Xiamen: Xiamen University Press, 60–7.

Yinshun 印順, *Miao Yunji* 妙雲集, www.yinshun.org.tw (accessed 4 April 2011).

Zhenhua [Chen-hua] (1992), *In Search of the Dharma: Memoirs of a Modern Chinese Buddhist Pilgrim*, ed. with an introduction by Chun-fang Yü, trans. D. C. Mair. Albany, NY: State University of New York Press.

(2000), *Lehr- und Wanderjahre eines Chinesischen Mönches (Canxue Suotan)*, trans. Marcus Günzel: Books on Demand.

CHAPTER 11

Xianghua foshi 香花佛事 *(incense and flower Buddhist rites): a local Buddhist funeral ritual tradition in southeastern China*

Yik Fai Tam

> There has yet to be a detailed study of death-related discourse and practices across Buddhist cultures. Such a project would shed light, for example, on the transformations of Buddhism in different Asian settings and on patterns in its interactions with local religion. It could also be expected to reveal just how integral death-related matters have been – doctrinally, ritually, institutionally and socially – to Buddhist traditions.
>
> Jacqueline L. Stone (2005: 56)

INTRODUCTION

Xianghua foshi is the kind of death-related Buddhist rite to which Jacqueline Stone refers in the quotation above, involving the adaptation of Buddhist ideas and practices to a particular Asian setting (southeast China) through interaction with local religion. This local Buddhist funeral ritual tradition is popular in the vicinity of Meizhou City 梅州 located in the northeastern part of Guangdong province in the People's Republic of China (PRC). The region lies at the intersection of Guangdong, Fujian and Jiangxi provinces, and is commonly known as the motherland of the Hakka people, with Meizhou City commonly referred to as the Hakka Capital.[1] *Xianghua foshi* is solely a Hakka rite and is performed in the Hakka dialect. But not all Hakka depend on this funeral rite to allay their anxieties about death. For those who live in areas where the *Xianghua foshi* prevails, however, the rite is believed to generate vast amounts of religious merit, benefiting not only the deceased, but also the living members of the host family, as well as

[1] Hakka is commonly used to refer to a specific group of Chinese people who claim themselves to be part of the dominant Han ethnic group, though their historical and cultural origins remain obscure and controversial.

wandering souls in the neighbourhood, who can all share in the merits of performing these rites. It is believed that this meritorious rite has three main functions: first, it can expedite the deceased soul's passage through the inevitable legal procedures in the Ten Halls in hell; second, the deceased can achieve a higher level of reincarnation in the next life in *Samsara*; and third, if the merit is sufficient, the deceased may even be able to transcend this world and reach the Pure Land of the Buddha.

The rite has a history of approximately 400 years. Nowadays, three versions of this rite are common, varying in length. The most common version is known as *Quanzhai* 全齋 (Complete Set of Vegetarian Version, hereafter referred to as the Complete Set).[2] The other two versions are known as *Banyeguang* 半夜光 (Light at Midnight) and *Banzhai* 半齋 (Half Set of Vegetarian Version). The performers of this rite are *xianghua heshang* 香花和尚 (incense and flower monks, hereafter referred to as clerics) and *zhaigu* 齋姑 (vegetarian women).[3] Both groups identify themselves as Buddhist religious personnel, but their religious identities are unconventional and subject to disputes. However, among the common people of the region, both the rite of *Xianghua foshi* and the status of the clerics who administer it are accepted as authentically Buddhist.

I shall discuss the rite's religious identity in the conclusion. But first, I provide a detailed description of the most common version of the ritual, the Complete Set, preceded by a brief discussion of the clerics who officiate it. I leave the identity of the vegetarian women and related issues for another occasion.

HISTORICAL AND CULTURAL CONTEXTS

Local oral accounts and documentary evidence agree that the *Xianghua foshi* and the peculiar tradition of local clerics originated with an influential local Chan monk named Muyuan Heshang 牧原和尚.[4] I have argued elsewhere

[2] *Zhai* literally means 'vegetarian meals' in Chinese Buddhist terminology. It derives from the Chinese Buddhist tradition that hosts and sponsors of Buddhist meritorious rituals would provide participating saṅgha members with vegetarian meals. Consequently, *zhai* has become a substitute name for Buddhist meritorious rituals among the common people.

[3] *Xianghua heshang* is a term now commonly used by scholars of folk Chinese Buddhist and ritual studies. The clerics do not call themselves *Xianghua heshang*. For the local people, they merely address them as *heshang* (monks).

[4] All the clerics I interviewed hold that Muyuan was the inventor of the *Xianghua foshi*. A type of modern local history known as Wenshi 文史 (literature and history) has been published quarterly every year by the official government at the county level since the 1980s. The Wenshi of Meixian, Xingning and other neighbouring counties affirm the account given by the clerics. The clerics also trace their unconventional lifestyle back to Muyuan. The Wenshi is silent on this issue.

that it is probable that Muyuan was a major editor of an existing funeral ritual tradition in the early and mid-seventeenth century (see Yik Fai Tam 2007: 122–6). Local clerics insist on the ancestral status of Muyuan when responding to challenges against what some consider to be scepticism of their unorthodox practices which primarily consist of the funeral ritual services they perform for the local people.

A HISTORICAL SKETCH OF *XIANGHUA FOSHI*

By the early seventeenth century, a folk Buddhist funeral rite existed in the Meixian 梅縣 region and was documented in *Chongzhen xingning xianzhi* 崇禎興寧縣志 (1637).[5] This folk Buddhist ritual was performed by a group of unordained clerics referred to by the compiler and editors of the local history as *Xianghua seng* 鄉花僧 (village and flower monks). The compiler and editors, on the one hand, provided a detailed yet disparaging description of the ritual performed by these *xianghua seng*; on the other hand, they neutrally mention the existence of another group of Buddhist monks and their funeral ritual. They called this other group of monks *su seng* 素僧 (vegetarian/plain monks). More importantly, the pronunciations of the words 'village' and 'incense' in both Mandarin (the official and national language) and the local Hakka dialect are the same. The 'village and flower monks' were hence very likely the direct ancestors of what are now referred to as 'incense and flower monks'. Judging from this historical account, it is safe to assume that in the early decades of the seventeenth century a popular folk Buddhist funeral rite, unaccepted by the Confucian elite, co-existed with a more conventional Buddhist funeral rite in the northeast part of Guangdong province. Given the fact that the funeral is the most important rite of passage for the Chinese, and that ritual traditions normally take a long time to become commonly accepted as the norm in a given locality, it is also safe to assume that the *Xianghua foshi* was already a well-established rite in the Meixian region by that time. Although later local gazetteers from the neighbouring areas did not specifically mention this rite, indirect and scattered information from those documents and the current prevalence of the *Xianghua foshi* and the clerics who perform it in the region, suggest

[5] See *Chongzhen Xingning Xianzhi*, Book 1 'Dizhi 地誌 (geography), Section of 'Fengsu' 風俗 (customs) (1973: 314–15).

the continuous dominance of this funeral rite among the local population dates from the first half of the seventeenth century.[6]

XIANGHUA FOSHI AND *XIANGHUA HESHANG* (THE CLERICS)

To understand the *Xianghua foshi*, a closer examination of the phenomenon of the 'incense and flower clerics' is key. Most of the clerics who are active in the Meizhou region have little formation in Buddhist philosophy and doctrines. They seldom follow the monastic discipline that is normal for the Chinese saṅgha. Many of them are married and have families who live in nearby areas. While many of these clerics are affiliated with temples, not all of them actually live there. Their appearance does not differ significantly from that of other conventional Buddhist monks. The most distinctive external difference between these clerics and regular monks is that the *xianghua heshang* do not have disciplinary marks on their foreheads from the burning of *moxa* at ordination. This distinctive difference signifies that they do not observe the traditional Buddhist precepts and disciplinary codes. The *xianghua heshang* do, however, wear Buddhist robes and shave their heads. Another distinctive aspect of these unordained clerics is that they eat meat. They justify this act by two reasons: first, eating meat is said to have been allowed by Muyuan Heshang who insisted on non-attachment to Buddhist precepts. Second, they hold that the performance of *Xianghua foshi* requires a large amount of physical strength which, they say, makes a strict vegetarian diet impracticable.

The primary religious function of these clerics is to perform the rite of *Xianghua foshi* for the local communities and the participation and performance of this rite is the main source of their income. Most of the temples in the region are small, and have a small number of resident clerics. Many, if not all, of the clerics are actively involved in other kinds of secular activities, such as investments and speculations in the stock market or other financial endeavours.

While the current clerics may be thought of as secularised Buddhist monks to a certain extent, their primary religious function of providing meritorious funeral rites to the community has always been an important role for the ordained Buddhist monk. In China, this kind of ritual specialisation was affirmed and enhanced through governmental reform during the

[6] For other historical accounts about *Xianghua foshi*, see *Chengxiang Xianzhi* 程鄉縣誌, volume 1 (1993: 17); and *Qianlong Jianyin Zhouzhi* 乾隆嘉應州誌, volume 1 (1991: 46). Another detailed account of local funeral rites can be found in *Guangxu Jiayinzhou Zhi* 光緒嘉應州誌, volume 8 (2003, 34–5).

Ming dynasty (1368–1644). The founder of the Ming dynasty, Emperor Taizu 太祖, was himself once a monk before he joined a rebel army driven in part by strong folk Buddhist beliefs. Taizu initiated a series of administrative and policy changes in order to achieve the purposes of exalting, rectifying and controlling the Buddhist saṅgha. One change that proved to have long-reaching effects was the administrative classification of the Buddhist saṅgha communities into three categories, namely Chan 禪 (meditation), Jiang 講 (lecturing) and Jiao 教 (literally 'teaching' but here meaning ritual) with the Jiao sector including the majority of the monks and nuns.[7] The classification signified a division of labour, designated by the imperial government, within the saṅgha community. Chan monks and nuns were required to reside in Chan monasteries. According to this system, their primary religious function was to practise Chan meditation and other forms of cultivation and to seek personal enlightenment. Monks and nuns of the Jiang category were those who belonged to Buddhist schools, such as Tian-tai 天臺 and Jingtu 淨土 (pure land). They were to focus on studying and lecturing on the doctrines of their respective schools. The majority of monks and nuns were relegated to the Jiao category. The Jiao used in the Ming Buddhist classification system did not refer to doctrines or sects generally, but specifically referred to liturgical teachings (*yujia jiao* 瑜伽教).[8] Monks and nuns in this category were to dedicate themselves to providing ritual services for the people. They were the Buddhist ritual experts in Ming society, and this gradually became a part of their self-identity and how others perceived them.[9] The classification was to be a strict one. Monks and nuns of the three types were, in theory, not allowed to intermingle and were forbidden from interacting with the rest of the society without official permission. Although the effectiveness of this administrative classification is doubtful, and may not have exerted much long-term impact on the saṅgha community, it showed, at least, the importance of esoteric tradition and ritual

[7] Ren Yimin (2009: 6). See also Chun-fang Yu (1998: 893–952).

[8] In Chinese Buddhism, *Yujia jiao* was the name given to the esoteric tradition that emphasised the transformative and thaumaturgical functions of Buddhist rites and *mantras*. Although esoteric Buddhism did not exist as a separate school in China after the beginning of the ninth century, its beliefs and practices continued to exist in Chinese Buddhism. The widespread influences of esoteric Buddhist tradition in Chinese Buddhism is especially evident in Buddhist rites. For more details about the *Yujia jiao* and the other two types of classification, see Chun-fang Yu (1998: 906–11).

[9] An insulting term, *yingfu seng* (monks who respond to call) has become popular in Chinese Buddhist circles. It is used mainly by those who practise conventional forms of Buddhist religious cultivation to describe monks and clerics whose primary religious function is performing ritual services for the common people in exchange for material and monetary rewards.

service in Chinese Buddhism. It further shaped how the people's religious needs were met and how they understood ritual Buddhism.

Given this background, it is safe to assume that the predominance of the ritual role of the monk in China today is owed in part to the Ming classification of the saṅgha. Historically, then, the local funeral rite of *Xianghua foshi* probably developed gradually by the monks and nuns charged with liturgical duties during the Ming period, and might have been significantly revised by the monk Muyuan at the end of the Ming dynasty.

The active role of clerics (as well as of the *zhaigus*) in revising the rite can still be witnessed today. Comparison of different copies of the ritual manuscripts used for the *Xianghua foshi* reveals that monks and clerics continuously made adjustments to the structure and contents of the rite. It is actually in this sense that the *Xianghua foshi* rite and the clerics who perform them are two sides of the same coin: the power of folk and local Buddhism in China. Indeed, neither of these phenomena can be fully explored and understood without a parallel probe of the other.

XIANGHUA FOSHI TODAY

Xianghua foshi is the only Buddhist death rite for the Hakka people in Meizhou and its vicinity. This does not suggest that it is popular in all counties and districts in the region. Meizhou is a prefecture-level city and administers one urban district (Meijiang 梅江 district Meizhou city proper), one county-level city (Xingning 興寧) and six counties (Meixian 梅縣, Dabu 大埔, Jiaoling 蕉嶺, Pingyuan 平遠, Wuhua 五華 and Fengshun 豐順). But the rite is the standard death rite mainly in Meizhou City, Meixian, Dabu, Pingyuan and Jiaoling counties. The death rite at Xingning City, Wuhua and Fengshun is predominantly Daoist and civic.

Under the umbrella of the three most common versions of the *Xianghua foshi*, there are several variations. First, it is not uncommon for individual clerics to make minor improvisations according to their own understanding of the ritual, and then to pass on these improvised performance details to their own disciples. Second, many young clerics acquired their ritual knowledge and skills from different masters. Third, there are geographical differences among various localities in the region. The most obvious variation is what has been documented by the scholar of folk ritual musicology and drama Wang Kui 王馗. According to Wang, Bingcun 丙村 – an important town located 25 km from Meizhou City – is the geographical dividing point for the practice of the ritual (Wang Kui 2001: 141). The *Xianghua foshi* conducted in Meizhou

City, and in towns and villages along the upper streams of the Mei River above Bingcun, is different from that conducted in towns and villages along the river below the town. Though Wang does not mention any designation for the different formats, it is clear that he is referring to two different formats for the ritual: the *shangshui pai* 上水派 (the upper-stream branch) and *xiashui pai* 下水派 (the lower-stream branch).

The same version of the *Xianghua foshi* rite, such as the Complete Set, is performed in different vocal and musical tones in these two branches. There are some minor differences in the flow of the rite as well. Finally, the structure of the rite itself is flexible and allows the clerics and the host family to add additional ritual sections in order to satisfy their unique needs. The flexibility of the rite is described well by a slang expression that the cleric informants use repeatedly. They describe the bewildering phenomenon of the rite as '*xianghua, xianghua, feili fala* 香花香花 啡哩啡啦', a Hakka dialectic expression with no equivalent in Chinese written characters, meaning 'bewilderingly chaotic'.

According to my informants, there are 200–300 ritual specialists who can perform the *Xianghua foshi* in Meizhou City and its vicinity. Among them, there are slightly more vegetarian women than clerics, so the number of clerics is around 100 to 130. The number of clerics needed for a given rite depends on the version of the rite required by the host family. Generally speaking, the 'Light at Midnight' and the 'Half-set Vegetarian Version' need five performing members in the troupe. For the 'Complete Set' at least seven are required. The troupe is not necessarily all male or female; it is quite common to have a rite performed by a troupe comprised of both male clerics and vegetarian women. It is normal for them to develop a kind of network or informal team to enhance their communication within and without the rite.

Informants reported that most clerics perform the *Xianghua foshi* service ten to twelve times every month. They also mentioned that there are two peak seasons for the funeral rites: the fifth and twelfth months of the lunar calendar. The demand for *Xianghua foshi* ritual specialists (male clerics and the vegetarian women) can be acute. The usual amount of money needed to hold a 'Complete Set' is around 6,000 *renminbi* 人民幣 (about US$800).

THE RITE OF *XIANGHUA FOSHI*

I shall focus the following description of the *Xianghua foshi* rite on the 'Complete Set' version, since it is the most common and can also provide an overview of the rite as a whole, as indicated by its title. The 'Complete Set' is also known among the clerics by the title 'One Day and Two Nights'. In fact, it actually covers three calendar days.

It is technically challenging in a short essay to present and discuss a rite which lasts for one day and two evenings. It is also a daunting challenge to encompass the basic structure of this complex rite without becoming lost in details. In general, the various parts of the ritual can be classified into three main categories: structural sections, sections for the deceased and sections for the living. For a more complete overview of the rite, I provide a table of the ritual processes (Table 11.1.) Finally, I present and discuss the nature of individual ritual sections in order to illustrate the function of the ritual as a whole.

The classification of ritual sections

The first category of ritual segments I term the *Structural Sections*. These segments constitute the basic format of the rite, marking it as a Buddhist ritual and, most significantly, making the event meaningful for the local participants. These ritual segments establish the sacred site for the rite, welcome and greet the presiding deities and send them off after the rite is complete. Details of these sections reflect the basic understanding of the participants of how a proper rite should be conducted.

The second type of ritual segment is the *sections for the deceased*. The primary object of the *Xianghua foshi* is to generate religious merit for the dead. The underlying foundation of the rite is the belief that, as Stone suggests, death can be controlled through Buddhist beliefs and corresponding practices (Stone 2005: 57, 60–3). It is believed that, through a proper Buddhist funeral rite, the deceased will benefit either by attending the Longhua hui 龍華會 (dragon-flower assembly), or by achieving a swift and better rebirth.[10] The ritual sections that belong to this type focus on the expression of the belief in merit and the actual procedure of generating it and transferring it to the deceased.

The last type of ritual segment I term *sections for the living*. As many anthropological studies have demonstrated, funeral rites serve the needs of both the dead and the living. *Xianghua foshi* also shows the dual functions of

[10] The belief concerning the dragon-flower assembly is closely related to the Buddhist belief of the future Buddha, Maitreya. It is believed that Maitreya will descend, after the Dharma of Sakyamuni Buddha ends, and teach a pure form of Buddhist teaching, of three assemblies of beings under a dragon flower tree. It is believed that all beings can attain perfect enlightenment in these assemblies.

Table 11.1 *Ritual processes of the* Quanzhai

Day	Time	Section sequence	Structural sections	Sections for the deceased	Sections for the living
1	2:30 pm	1	*Zhaohun* (summoning the soul)		
		2	*Qitan* (setting up the altars)		
		3	*Faguan* (issuing the official document)		
		4		*Muyu* (bathing the soul)	
		5	*Da naobo hua* (striking the cymbals)		
	Dinner				
		6		*Chushen jiuku* (first appeal for relief from suffering)	
		7		*Ershen jiuku* (second appeal for relief from suffering)	
		8		*Sanshen jiuku* (third appeal for relief from suffering)	
	10:00 pm	9	*Angeng* (settling down for the night)		
2	6:00 am	10	*Kaiqi* (starting the rite)		
		11		*Anfan* (positioning the spirit streamer)	
		12	*Jiefo* (welcoming the Buddha)		
		13	*Shanggong* (respectful offerings)		
		14	*Chaocan* (morning greeting)		
		15			*Bai qixing chan* (seven stars rite of repentance
		16		*Shiwang guokan* (inspection by the Ten Enlightened Kings)	
	Lunch				
		17		*Wanchan* (completion of repentance)	

Table 11.1 (*cont.*)

Day	Time	Section sequence	Structural sections	Sections for the deceased	Sections for the living
		18		*Bai Yaoshi* (paying respects to the Medicine Buddha)	
		19			*Zou Yaoshi* (sending off the Medicine Buddha)
	Dinner				
	8:00 pm	20			*Kaiguang* (opening the vision)
		21			*Xingxiang* (walking with incense sticks)
	10:30 pm	22		*Dugu* (rescuing lonely souls)	
		23			*Jiyu chuanhua* (carp crossing with patterns)
		24		*Lienchi* (lotus pond)	
3		25			*Xuepen* (blood basin)
		26			*Mai xuejiu* (selling bloody wine)
		27	*Jiaoqian* (paying money)		
		28	*Shaoqian* (burning money)		
		29		*Guandeng* (extinguishing the lamp)	
		30			*Bai hongfu* (seeking great blessings)
		31	*Songsheng* (sending off the deities)		
		32	*Dunbing* (settling the divine soldiers)		
		33	*Jizi* (Buddhist hymns)		
	4:00 am			End of rite	

serving both target groups. Death, as an existential crisis, does not merely signify the loss of loved ones; it further poses an ultimate challenge to the meaning of human existence, and the meanings derived from its existence. These sections for the living, on the one hand, provide religious and social comfort to the family members of the deceased and, on the other, take advantage of the ritual occasion to lecture about the basic teachings of Buddhism.

It is important to point out that this tri-part classification does not necessarily reflect the understanding of the ritual performers, i.e. the clerics and the vegetarian women. The function and meaning of some sections of the ritual are meaningful for all parties (including deities) involved in the rite. For example, instruction in Buddhist teachings, usually in the form of lyrics and folk songs, in both the sections for the deceased and sections for the living, serve the function of educating all participants of the event, including, but not limited to, both the deceased and the living. Another example is the 'striking cymbals' section. It is designed as a treat and entertainment for the invited deities; however, the entertaining effect is also shared by the living members of the family. In fact, many bystanders from the neighbourhood come to watch and enjoy this section.

Ritual sections (1): structural sections

The *structural sections* are crucial in defining the rite as Buddhist, as a death ritual and as a source of merit. They include the sections 'summoning the soul' 招魂, 'setting up the altars' 起壇, 'issuing the official document' 發關, 'striking the cymbals' 打鐃鈸花, 'settling down for the night' 安更, 'starting the rite' 開啟, 'positioning the spirit streamer' 安幡, 'welcoming the Buddha' 接佛, 'respectful offerings' 上供, 'morning greeting' 朝參, 'sending off the deities' 送神, 'settling the divine soldiers' 頓兵 and 'Buddhist hymns' 偈子.

The backbone of the whole rite, these sections are essential for virtually any Chinese Buddhist funeral rite, with the exception of the section 'summoning the soul'. This section is normally optional, but is crucial when the deceased did not die at home. In such cases, it is necessary for the clerics to call the soul back home where the rite is usually performed. It is believed that the soul can only benefit from the rite when it is present. After the ritual process of summoning, whether the soul has returned or not is determined by divination in a later section termed 'bathing' 沐浴. This section is usually performed at a fork in the road in front of the house.

'Setting up the altars' signifies the beginning of the rite. The religious functions of this section are not confined to the physical establishment of altars, though setting up altars is the most conspicuous activity in this part of the rite. There are three levels of meaning in this section. First, it establishes the main altars for the rite. Officially, there should be seven altars inside and outside of the house; three of these are essential. The most important altar is for the Three Jewels of Buddhism, and figurative representations of the Three Jewels are set up on this altar. The second altar is for the deceased, where paper houses and other offerings are presented. The third is the *guhun tan* 孤魂壇 (Altar of Wandering Souls) outside the house.[11] Offerings are made to satisfy the needs of these spirits. The second level of meaning for this rite is to establish the ritual site 道場 (*daochang*) as a sacred space in which the rite will be performed. Deities, such as the Buddha and Avalokitesvara, are there to oversee the rite, while wandering malevolent spirits are, through this procedure, excluded from the ritual site. The third level of meaning is to officially welcome the Buddha upon his arrival and to invite him to oversee the rite.[12] Once the Buddha is present, the *Xianghua foshi* becomes a legitimate Buddhist rite, and therefore guarantees the generation of religious merit. It is believed that the presence of the Buddha also signifies the arrival of other major and secondary deities. Divine soldiers are deployed to protect the territory so that no trespassing is possible.

'Issuing the official document' is to issue and deliver an official document ordering the deceased's soul to return from the underworld back to his or her home in order to receive the benefits of the ritual. It is commonly believed that part of the soul is taken away by the divine messengers from hell at the moment of death. Moreover, the way between hell and home is guarded by different territorial deities. It is, therefore, crucial for the returning soul to have an official document issued by a legitimate ritual master to pass through the blockades.

The section of 'striking the cymbals' is usually performed after the section of 'bathing', or in the intervals among the three sections of 'appealing for relief from sufferings'. It does not carry an explicit religious meaning if we

[11] The spiritual beings are classified into different types. Gods and ancestors are benevolent, but wandering souls and ghosts are dangerous and vengeful. Therefore, ways and attitudes of providing offerings to different types of spirits should be conducted accordingly. See Wolf (1974).

[12] Although the Buddha statue used in this section is a Sakyamuni Buddha, it actually represents all kinds of buddhas and bodhisattvas in the Mahāyāna tradition. Details of other ritual sections show that many other buddhas are assumed to be present. So, the term Buddha in the *Xianghua foshi* ritual sections should not be taken narrowly as only referring to the historical Buddha.

approach it literally. However, given that in Chinese religious culture one is normally expected to present deities with tea, incense, other offerings and dramatic entertainment performances during ritual events, it is reasonable to assume that this section of 'striking the cymbals' serves the ritual purpose of entertaining the buddhas, bodhisattvas and other deities. This section is so spectacular and attractive that 'striking the cymbals' is a popular alternative name for the *Xianghua foshi*. Indeed, many local people do not realise what *Xianghua foshi* is, but are able to identify the popular Buddhist funeral rite by the name '*da naobo hua*' 打鐃鈸花 (the striking of the cymbals). This is also the best-attended section in the whole ritual process of *Xianghua foshi*. It is a thrilling display of skills in which the clerics must deftly manipulate a pair of large cymbals.

Other than merely providing entertainment to the divine and mundane guests of the rite, this performance relieves to some extent the grief of the living. The section is performed in an open courtyard where the host family, relatives and neighbours gather. While the neighbours express their admiration by applause and vocal praise, the family members express their satisfaction by tossing money to the performing cleric. In whichever way, the satisfaction and relief of the neighbours and the family members can be witnessed on their smiling faces. In this regard, this section can also be classified as a section for the living.

After the 'striking the cymbals' section, the structural framework of the rite is basically established and the focus switches to the soul of the deceased and those ritual sections designated for it. The last structural section of day 1 is 'settling down for the night'. When the ritual sections for the deceased end after the 'third inquiry to save [the deceased's soul] from suffering', the process of *Xianghua foshi* comes to a tentative end. The 'settling down for the night' section serves as a ceremonial way to ask all the buddhas, bodhisattvas and deities to stay for the night and be ready for the rite the next day.

The rite continues in the morning of day 2 at around six o'clock with a series of structural sections. Similar to the 'setting up of the altars' on day 1, 'starting the rite' signifies the beginning of the second day of the ritual process. It starts with another invitation to the Buddha, bodhisattvas and other deities to return to the site.

After all the deities have been invited once again, a section for the deceased commences. However, the deceased is not the primary beneficiary of the rite. Rather, in this section, 'positioning the spirit streamer', the prime targets and beneficiaries are the nearby wandering souls. Three clerics invite those souls to come and share in the merit of the rite, but they are confined to the Altar of Wandering Souls, and are not invited (or allowed) to enter the house. The whole section is marked by placing a spirit streamer at the Altar of Wandering Souls.

The sections of 'welcoming the Buddha', 'respectful offerings' and 'morning greeting', convey a sense of respect and decorum. The first section, as the title suggests, is to welcome and give thanks to all the buddhas and other deities for their presence in the rite again after the night. The second section is to make offerings to the deities to express gratitude. The third section is for leading the soul of the deceased to greet all the buddhas and other deities in the early morning, and also signifies the readiness of the soul to receive the benefits of the rite.

The sections for the deceased and sections for the living follow, and become the dominant part of the ritual process on day 2. The structural sections reenter the ritual process at the end of the whole rite. There are two sections of 'paying money' and 'burning money' for the deceased. Textual sources from the thirteenth century show that the belief in the Ten Kings was associated with a belief in an individual monetary account in hell. According to this notion, each person has a monetary account in hell from which he or she withdraws funds before birth and during his or her lifetime. But the amount used is merely credit which the individual is required to repay after death (for details, see Teiser 1993: 128). The section 'paying money' is the formal process of repayment; and the section of 'burning money' is the symbolic action of repayment.

Early in the morning of day 3 (approximately 4 o'clock), clerics will accompany the departure of all deities to a fork in the road in front of the house by chanting mantras in the section of 'sending off the deities'. There are different accounts of what kinds of deities are sent off. Some informants report that the clerics send off all the buddhas, bodhisattvas and other deities who attended the rite. Other sources mention that they are sending off all the wandering souls. Participation in this section is restricted. None other than the clerics are allowed to proceed to the fork in the road and observe the rite. Judging from this restricted nature, it is safe to assume that this section is designed to lead away all those wandering souls who gather around the ritual site for benefits, and who may have developed an attachment to the site and the people around. Therefore, the section of 'sending off the deities' serves the purpose of sending off these souls in a polite but determined manner.

The section of 'settling the divine soldiers' cannot be understood literally. It gives thanks to local deities for putting up with the disturbances caused by the rite. When deities who are guests and who have come from other realms have left, it is time to thank and pay respect to the Longshen 龍神 (dragon spirits), who are the local deities. The Meixian Hakka believe that the most important dragon spirits are the Wufang Longshen 五方龍神 (the Dragon Spirits of Five Directions), stationed at a special place in traditional Hakka buildings. The host family is required to offer rice, chicken, pork, coins and paper-made items to inform these Longshen of the completion of the rite. The entire rite usually ends before 5 o'clock in the morning of day 3.

Ritual sections (2): sections for the deceased

The sections for the deceased are formally started with the section of 'bathing the soul'. However, the section of 'summoning the soul' which is performed (if needed) before the structural sections also belongs to this category. Among the sections for the deceased, the first three sections – 'summoning the soul', 'bathing the soul' and 'offering wine' 把酒 – can be understood as part of the structural sections. While the structural sections are about setting up the macro-environment for the rite (e.g. setting up the ritual site and inviting as well as sending off the divine guests), the first three sections of the sections for the deceased are micro and personal, focusing on preparing the soul to receive the religious merit and the consequent rescue from hell.

In the section of 'bathing the soul', the clerics use divination to determine if the soul has returned. The process of divination will continue until it demonstrates that the soul has returned. Once the soul returns, the clerics chant several verses about the Buddhist views on death and emptiness. It aims to convince the soul of the fact of death, and prepares to receive the divine rescue generated from the following rite. In the section of 'offering wine', the clerics treat the soul with wine and tea for its return. At the same time, the living members of the family will mourn the death of the deceased in its presence.

This is followed by three sections of 'first appeal for relief from suffering' 初伸救苦, 'second appeal for relief from suffering' 二伸救苦 and 'third appeal for relief from suffering' 三伸救苦, and these form part of the major ritual sections in the rite. The structure of these sections is roughly the same, the only difference lies in the major Buddhist deities that the cleric will address to witness the merits of the rite. These three Buddhist deities are Sakyamuni Buddha (in the 'first appeal'), Avalokitesvara (in the 'second appeal') and Ksitigarbha (in the 'third appeal'). The clerics send out an invitation to invite the Kings to descend. Once the Kings are presumed to have arrived, the clerics offer them three rounds of wine and burn paper

Table 11.2 *Titles of Ten Enlightened Kings*

Hall	Title of Enlightened King
1st Hall	King of Qinguang 秦廣王
2nd Hall	King of Chujiang (River Chu) 楚江王
3rd Hall	King of Song 宋帝王
4th Hall	King of Five Officials 五官王
5th Hall	King Yama 閻羅王
6th Hall	King of Bian City 卞城王
7th Hall	King of Mount Tai 泰山王
8th Hall	King of Urban Areas 都市王
9th Hall	King of Equality 平等王
10th Hall	King of Wheel Turning 轉輪王

money to express gratitude for their co-operation.[13] Then, the soul is introduced to the Enlightened Kings of the Ten Halls as the main beneficiary of the rite.[14] After the recitation of a series of polite expressions, the main cleric chants three slightly different prose passages entitled 'Lament for the soul of the deceased' 嘆亡魂 in each section. The didactic theme of the prose is the same, that is to exhort the soul that life is impermanent, and that the soul should therefore relinquish any attachments in this world so that it can subsequently 'rise up to Heaven from death after this evening, and become a permanent participant of the Plenary Assembly of All Buddhas, Bodhisattvas and Saints'.[15]

At the end of each of these sections, the main cleric asks the respective presiding buddha/bodhisattva to witness that an official dispatch has been issued so that the soul can travel freely to, and in, the Buddha's paradise.[16]

Depending on external factors, such as weather, time constraints, and the preparation of food, a segment from the structural sections will usually be performed either after the 'offering wine' section or during the interval periods of the sections of 'appeal'. This is the section of 'striking the cymbals' discussed under the structural sections.

[13] It is a disciplinary restriction in Buddhist rites to use wine as part of the offerings to the Buddhist deities. The rite of *Xianghua foshi*, in contrast to this widely accepted disciplinary restriction, does use wine to treat the Ten Kings upon their arrival in the ritual sections of 'appealing for relief from suffering'. Given this, wine is used only for two well-defined targets, the soul of the deceased and the Ten Kings in specific ritual sections. It is not used in those sections, such as 'welcoming the Buddha', when the major Buddhist deities are the main target of offerings.

[14] For more information on the name of the title of the Ten Enlightened Kings, please see Table 11.2.

[15] *Chushen jiuku*, Xianghua Quantao 香花全套, Qixing Si manuscript, p. 17.

[16] *Chushen jiuku*, Xianghua Quantao 香花全套, Qixing Si manuscript, pp. 17, 19, 20–2.

With the completion of the 'third appeal', the ritual process reaches its final stage for day 1. It is followed by the structural section of 'settling down for the night' described above.

In day 2, after the structural sections of 'starting the rite', 'welcoming the Buddha', 'respectful offerings' and 'morning greeting', the ritual process continues with the section of 'performing the seven stars rite of repentance' 拜七星懺 – a section for the living. The subjects of the section are the children of the deceased, discussed in more detail below.

By this stage of the rite, the soul has been ritually purified by the rite of 'bathing' and the clerics have, in day 1, made necessary appeals to relieve the soul from suffering. The soul, with the assistance of the family members, is ready to repay the debt the deceased withdrew from his or her account before birth.[17] The section of 'inspection by the Ten Enlightened Kings' 十王過勘 is the formal ritual process that effects the repayment of the soul's debt. The process is solemn and bureaucratic, centring on a legal document with two identical copies on which the sacrificial items used are listed. Each king is said to approve the content of the document, with the presiding cleric stamping the document with an official seal every time that the names of the Ten Kings are announced.

In the afternoon of day 2, the rite starts with the section of 'completion of repentance' 完懺. It is also classified as a section for the living, and will be discussed later. Unlike the structural sections, which are essential for any performance of the *Xianghua foshi*, many segments of the sections for the deceased are optional, depending on specific circumstances. These include 'paying respect to the Medicine Buddha' 拜藥師, 'lotus pond' 蓮池, 'blood basin' 血盆, 'selling blood wine' 賣血酒 and 'extinguishing the lamp' 關燈. There are two basic criteria employed to determine if these sections should be performed. The first is whether the deceased died of a long-term illness, in which case it is essential to perform the section of 'paying respect to the Medicine Buddha'. If this is not the case, the section can be skipped. The second criterion is the gender of the deceased. 'Extinguishing the lamp' is for men. If the deceased is a woman, the sections of 'lotus pond', 'blood basin' and 'selling bloody wine' are expected.

[17] By the thirteenth century, Chinese people commonly accepted the idea of a purgatory which was divided into ten halls, presided over by ten Enlightened Kings respectively. Stephen Teiser has forcefully demonstrated that the belief of the Ten Kings was the result of successful assimilation of Indian Buddhist beliefs with Chinese ideas. According to Teiser, a tenth-century scriptural source proves that the belief reached a mature form and was probably quite widespread. And, according to sources from the thirteenth century, the belief in the Ten Kings was by that time associated with the belief in individual monetary accounts in hell, from which individuals could withdraw funds during their lifetime, to be repaid after death. See Teiser (1993).

'Paying respects to the Medicine Buddha' is a section to express thanks to the Medicine Buddha. It is believed that long-term treatment of sickness, and the consequential prolonging of the life of the deceased, were owing to the compassion and the blessings of the Medicine Buddha.[18] It is appropriate to express gratitude for the intervention of this buddha. After this, another section follows, 'sending off the Medicine Buddha' 走藥師; this is for the benefit of the living and will be discussed later.

The section of 'rescuing lonely souls' 渡孤 is a dangerous one. Wandering souls are traditionally believed to be malevolent and harmful because they are deprived of proper sacrifices from their families. This is the reason that although these souls can partake of the abundant religious merit derived from the *Xianghua foshi*, they have to be kept out of the house at the Altar of Wandering Souls. These wandering souls, having previously gathered outside of the ritual site, are now allowed to receive religious merit, which will assist them in the journey of rebirth.

'Lotus pond' is a significant section in *Xianghua foshi*. As mentioned earlier, it is an indispensable section for the female deceased. The Buddhist saga of Maudgalyayana rescuing his mother is enacted in the form of ritual dancing. I was told that through the reenactment of the Maudgalyayana story, the soul can be released from the sufferings of hells. However, the logic of the rite suggests that the soul should have been guaranteed salvation in the previous sections. Therefore, it is my suspicion that the emphasis on the story of Maudgalyayana serves the didactic purpose of reinforcing the traditional Confucian virtue of filial piety.[19]

In the case of a male deceased, the section of 'extinguishing the lamp' is essential.[20] However, this section is much less elaborate than the section of the 'lotus pond'. While the 'lotus pond' section is dramatic and full of action, the section of 'extinguishing the lamp' is less energetic and basically consists of the chanting of verses.

[18] Healing has been a central theme in Buddhism since its early stage. There are many scriptural sources of medical healing and spiritual healings in early Buddhist texts. The motif is further elaborated and developed in the Mahāyāna tradition in which the bodhisattvas of healing become a significant part of Buddhist faith and skilful means for the spread of the Dharma. See Birnbaum (1989) for the scriptural foundations of this belief.

[19] The incorporation of Confucian cardinal virtues, such as filial piety, into a Buddhist rite reveals the way Buddhism, as a foreign religion, assimilated into Chinese culture and successfully became an important religious source for Chinese culture.

[20] It is a cultural custom in the lineages of southern China that when a male descendant is born, the family head will light a lamp in their ancestral halls. Although the flame of the lamp will not be kept for the whole life-span of the man, it is a corresponding ceremonial action to extinguish the lamp in his funeral to signify his death.

Ritual sections (3): sections for the living

Although *Xianghua foshi* is a death ritual, and its prime objective is to generate religious merit for the deceased, it also serves the needs of the living members of the deceased's family. These needs are basically two, namely, religious and emotional. The underlying message of these rites is that through the ritual the Buddhist clerics can wield the religious resources and strategies to manage the event of death and guarantee a better rebirth or potentially even ultimate liberation from *samsara*. While the *Xianghua foshi* and other Buddhist funeral ritual traditions form part of those resources and strategies for the deceased, those rites can generate religious merit for the living as well. The ways of generating religious merit for the living in funeral rites include, first, encouraging the living to live a moral life which in karmic terms can guarantee them worldly rewards and Buddhist assistance in all forms; and second, individual participants of the rite can share the religious merit generated by the rite, and will benefit at their death. However, Buddhist funeral rites also provide emotional comfort to the living at a time in which they are experiencing the loss of a loved one. The sections for the living in the *Xianghua foshi* provide the services and functions to meet these needs of the surviving members of the family. They persuade the living to cultivate virtue and morality, promise them various types of Buddhist rewards and salvation, help them to overcome the emotional crises of the death of a loved one and alter their fortunes from the bad luck and pollution associated with death to an auspicious event. These sections, like those for the deceased, provide opportunities for the clerics to promote the worldview and beliefs of Buddhism in the community.

After the section of 'paying respect to the Medicine Buddha' in the afternoon of day 2, it is important to perform the section of 'sending off the Medicine Buddha'. The people believe that, although the Medicine Buddha is gracious and has provided tremendous assistance to the deceased, it is inauspicious for the Medicine Buddha to remain in the household. A prolonged stay of the Medicine Buddha may bring sicknesses to the living. This section is optional if the death is not caused by long-term disease and sickness, however, if that was the cause, then this section is essential. The main purpose of sending off the Medicine Buddha is for the benefit of the living family members.

In the evening of day 2, the section of 'opening the vision 開光 begins after dinner. The purpose of this section is to change the fortunes of the host family: to end the bad luck accompanying the death of a family member, and to bring auspicious energy and good fortune to them. More importantly, this section marks the beginning of the auspicious part of the *Xianghua foshi*. The clerics ignite two pairs of rolled coarse paper (soaked with bean oil) and juggle them in various patterns. They then take the rolled paper to every corner of the house to symbolise the auspicious energy that fills the entire house. An assistant then tears down all paper couplets on the pillars, and cleans up any vestiges of the funeral rite. The atmosphere of the rite turns from mourning and sadness to joy and relief.

Sections of 'walking with incense sticks' 行香 and 'carp crossing with patterns' 鯽魚穿花 are similar in nature, but significantly different in the way they are performed. A section for the deceased, 'rescuing lonely souls' is situated between these sections. The section of 'walking with incense sticks' actually is not related to incense and walking. It is a small-scale version of the 'striking the cymbals' section but the performance is shorter and less exciting. The section of 'carp crossing with patterns' is aimed at creating joyful feelings and a relaxed atmosphere. The family members, by forming a line behind the clerics, need to follow the pace and pattern of their walking (and at times even running). The clerics assume various paces in their performance and intentionally bump into the family members. It is all great fun and usually generates a general good feeling among the living.

The sections of 'blood basin' and 'selling bloody wine' are conditional and optional. Like the section of 'lotus pond', these two sections are performed if the deceased is female. Among the two sections, the 'blood basin' can be repeated in different parts of the ritual process. As a normal practice, the clerics perform the section of 'blood basin' by reciting the *Blood Basin Scripture* twice within the section of 'seven stars rite of repentance', and an additional section of 'blood basin' after the section of 'lotus pond'. In all these occasions, the living, mainly the children, their spouses and their children, lament the sufferings of the deceased as a mother, and express regrets for not being able to repay the gracious sacrifices made by their mother. The section of 'selling bloody wine' is an optional extension of the section of the 'blood basin'. Both sections are a ritual, but concrete, expression of their filial virtues and mourning.

The last section for the living is 'seeking great blessings' 拜鴻福. This section did not originally belong to the funeral rite, but it is still a separate rite for seeking blessings in the Meizhou region. It is now incorporated into the *Xianghua foshi* as a concluding section for the benefit of the living. It enhances the function of the rite in generating religious merit.

After the section of 'seeking great blessings', the structural sections of 'sending off the deities' and 'settling the divine soldiers' follow and conclude the entire ritual. With a short chanting of 'Buddhist hymns' 偈子, the

Complete Set of Vegetarian Version of the *Xianghua foshi* comes to a conclusion at approximately 4 o'clock in the early morning of day 3.

CONCLUSION

Owing to its inextricable relationship with the clerics who do not follow the monastic precepts, its syncretic features (i.e. inviting low-ranking Daoist deities and local deities), and accommodation of local customs and beliefs (i.e. accepting the *fengshui* god – the Dragon Gods), critics hold that *Xianghua foshi* is not an orthodox Buddhist funeral rite. Indeed, the question of how to access normative Buddhist funeral rites remains unanswered in the study of Chinese Buddhism up to the present. Even though a more widespread form of the Chinese Buddhist funeral rite does exist, the issue of what is normative and conventional still needs to be closely examined within local contexts. Scholars of Chinese culture and religions do not fail to realise that local customs vary widely even among neighbouring villages and towns. In this case, *Xianghua foshi* can not be called *the* Hakka funeral rite. It prevails only in certain areas of the Meizhou City vicinity and not for the whole Hakka region. Indeed, Hakka in Xingning City generally do not practise Buddhist funeral rites, and Hakka in the neighbouring Jiangxi and Fujian provinces have local forms of Buddhist funeral rites. A full assessment of the question of normative Chinese Buddhist funeral rites may only be possible after detailed studies of local ritual traditions like *Xianghua foshi* have been carried out. Yet even if such studies are done, I doubt any definitive answer on what constitutes a normative Buddhist death ritual can be given with any precision. In the end, defining a 'standard' Chinese Buddhist ritual is not a particularly useful project. It is much more interesting and revealing to examine how Buddhist elements are employed in death rituals for a particular community.

On a more local level, we may ask the question of whether or not the *Xianghua foshi* is a Buddhist rite at all. Given the material presented here, I think we can safely say that it is. All major presiding deities of the rite are Buddhist. The rite employs the recitation of significant Buddhist scriptures and mantras and, more importantly, repeatedly proclaims basic Buddhist ideas such as emptiness and impermanence. From my perspective, the accommodation of non-Buddhist deities and local customs in the *Xianghua foshi* does not change the basic religious identity of the rite. Yet, the incorporation of non-Buddhist elements and non-conventional traditional Chinese funeral practices (i.e. ritual dancing and singing) reveal the flexibility and skilfulness of Buddhism in its interactions with local cultures.

BIBLIOGRAPHY

Birnbaum, R. (1989), *The Healing Buddha* (revised edn.), Boston, MA: Shambhala.

Ren Yimin 任宜敏 (2009), *Zhongguo Fojiao Shi – Mingdai* 中國佛教史 – 明代 [Chinese Buddhist History – Ming Dynasty], Beijing: Renmin chubanshe (see details in records of *Ming shi lu – Taizu*, Hongwu 15th year).

Stone, J. L. (2005), 'Death', in ed. Donald S. Lopez, Jr., *Critical Terms for the Study of Buddhism*, Chicago, IL: University of Chicago Press, 56–76.

Tam Yik Fai 譚翼輝 (2007), 'The Xianghua heshang and Xianghua foshi ritual tradition in the Eastern Guangdong Province' 粵東的香花和尚與香花佛事科儀傳統, in ed. Tam Wai Lun, *Minjian fojiao yanjiu* 民間佛教研究, Beijing: Zhonghua shuju, 115–28.

Teiser, S. (1993), 'The growth of purgatory', in eds. Patricia Buckley Ebrey and Peter N. Gregory, *Religion and Society in T'ang and Sung China*, Honolulu: University of Hawaii Press, 115–45.

Wang Kui 王馗 (2001), '*Xianghua foshi* – Guangdongsheng Meizhoushi de minjian chaodao yishi 香花佛事 – 廣東省梅州市的民間超度儀式', *Journal of Chinese Ritual, Theatre and Folklore* 民俗曲藝, 134, 139 Ritu.

Wolf, A. P. (1974), 'Gods, ghosts and ancestors', in ed. Arthur Wolf, *Religion and Ritual in Chinese Society*, Stanford, CA: Stanford University Press, 131–82.

Yu Chun-fang (1998), 'Ming Buddhism', in eds. Denis Twitchett and Frederick W. Mote, *The Cambridge History of China*, vol. 8: the Ming dynasty, 1368–1644, Part 2, Cambridge University Press, 893–952.

LOCAL HISTORIES AND RESOURCES

Guangdongsheng Difangshizhi Bianzuanweiyuanhui 廣東省地方史志編纂委員會 (2002), ed. *Guangdongshengzhi–Zongjiao Zhi* 廣東省志一宗教志, Guangzhou: Guangdong Remin Chubanshe, 廣東人民出版社.

Li, Guotai 李國泰 (2002), *Yuanshen Juejue: Shi Ruiji Fashi Zhuan* 緣深覺覺–釋瑞基法師傳, Hong Kong: Hong Kong Tianma Tushu Yuxian Gongsi 香港天馬圖書有限公司.

Li, Shichun 李士淳 (1959), *Muyuan Heshang Tazhiming* 牧原和尚塔志銘 (Epitaph of Muyuan Heshang), in *Rentang Yugao* 訒堂餘稿, collected in *Xingning Xianxian Congshu* 興寧先賢叢書 (A Collection of Sages from Xingning), eds. Yuan Wusong 袁五松, Wang Yinping 王蔭平 and Luo Xianglin 羅香林, 1–7, Hong Kong: Xingning Xianxian Congshu Jiaoyinchu 興寧先賢叢書校印處.

(1994), *Yinna Shanzhi* 陰那山志, compiled in 1622, Guangzhou: Guangdong luyou chubanshe 廣東旅遊出版社.

Liang, Lun 梁倫 (ed.) (1996), *Zhongguo Minsu Minjian Wudao Jicheng (Guangdong Juan)*, 中國民族民間舞蹈集成: 廣東卷, ed. Wu Xiaobang 吳曉邦, *Zhongguo Minzu Minjian Wudao Jicheng*, Beijing: Zhongguo Minsu Minjian Wudao Jicheng Bianjibu 中國民族民間舞蹈集成編輯部.

Liu, Bian 劉抃 (ed.) (1686), *Raoping Xianzhi* 鐃平縣志, Chaozhou: Chaozhoushi difangzhi bangongshi 潮州市地方志辦公室.

Liu, Guangcong 劉廣聰 (ed.) (1781), *Chengxiang Xianzhi* 程鄉縣志, ed. Cheng Zhiyuan 程志遠 等 *et al.*, Guangzhou: Guangdongsheng Zhongshan tushuguan 廣東省中山圖書館. Reprint 1993.

Liu, Xizu 劉熙祚 (ed.) (1973), *Chongzhen Xingning Xianzhi* 崇禎興寧縣志, originally printed in 1637, reprint Taiwan Xuesheng Shuju 台灣學生書局.

Meixian Difangzhi Bianzuan Weiyuanhui 梅縣地方志編纂委員會 (ed.) (1994), *Meixianzhi* 梅縣志, Guangzhou: Guangdong Remin Chubanshe 廣東人民出版社.

Meixian Lingguangsi Bianzuanlingdaoxiaozu 梅縣靈光寺編纂領導小組 (ed.) (1996), *Meixian Lingguangsi Zhi* 梅縣靈光寺志, Meizhou: Guangdongsheng Meixian Lingguangsi.

Meizhoushi Difangzhi Bianzuan Weiyuanhui 梅州市地方志編纂委員會 (ed.) (1999), *Meizhou Shizhi* 梅州市志, 2 vols, Guangzhou: Guangdong Remin Chubanshe 廣東人民出版社.

Xianghua Quantao 香花全套, Panglong Gong 盤龍宮manuscript.

Qixingxing Si 七星寺 manuscript.

Wang Zhizheng 王之正 (1750), *Qianlong Jiayin Zhouzhi* 乾隆嘉應州誌, ed. Cheng Zhiyuan *et al.*, Meizhou: Guangdongsheng Zhongshan Tushuguan Gujibu 廣東省中山圖書館古籍部. Reprint 1991.

Wen Zhonghe 溫仲和 compiled, Wu Zongzhuo 吳宗焯 and Li Qingrong 李慶榮 (eds.) (2003), *Guangxu Jiayinzhou Zhi* 光緒嘉應州志, Zhongguo di fang zhi ji cheng, Guangdong zhou fu xian zhi ji 中國地方志集成. 廣東州府縣志輯 20. Shanghai: Shanghai Shudian 上海書店.

CHAPTER 12

Buddhist passports to the other world: a study of modern and early medieval Chinese Buddhist mortuary documents

Frederick Shih-Chung Chen

INTRODUCTION

In modern-day Taiwan, the official document of the Bureau of Three Treasures (*Sanbaosi dieben* 三寶司牒本) to the Underworld Bureau endorsed by the Amitābha Buddha is a model text for a commonly used Buddhist funeral. The document is similar in form to an imperial Chinese travel document and, in Buddhist funerals, is addressed by a Buddhist priest to the otherworld bureau for the arrival of the deceased. Along with other Buddhist and Daoist ceremonial model texts, the official document of the Bureau of Three Treasures is sold in ritual shops or religious bookstores like the Ruicheng Bookstore 瑞成書局 in my home town, Taichung. Buddhist and Daoist priests use these model texts for the religious ceremony.

The main function of the official document of the Bureau of Three Treasures is to ensure the smooth processing of the soul of the deceased through the netherworld. It is filled in with the personal data of the deceased, including the address of the deceased's family and the time and date of birth and death of the deceased. The completed petition is chanted by the Buddhist priests at the beginning of the funeral ceremony

This research project has been made possible as a result of generous sponsorship from Bukkyō Dendō Kyōkai, which enabled me to undertake research for one year (2004–5) at the Institute of Oriental Studies, University of Tokyo, and also on the basis of a Dissertation Fellowship granted by the Chiang Ching-kuo Foundation (2005–6) and a Post-Doctoral Research Fellowship awarded by the National Science Council of Taiwan Government. I am also deeply indebted to Professor Dame Jessica Rawson, Professor Lance Cousins, Professor T. H. Barrett and my supervisor, Dr. Robert Chard, for giving their invaluable guidance and advice with regard to my research, and would wish to acknowledge their munificent assistance.

and then burned.[1] In the petition, the role of the Buddhist priest is twofold. First, the priest conducts the purgatory rite for the deceased. Assisted by the efficacy of the sacred Buddhist scriptures, the priest performs the funeral ceremony on behalf of the deceased with the aim of making him or her repent of any wrongdoings committed during his or her lifetime. Second, he represents the deceased and related family members in mediation with the Underworld Bureau. The process of mediation is spelt out in the same way as in the secular bureaucracy, with the priest acting as an advocate or lawyer. The Lord of Western Paradise, Amitābha Buddha, is the authority of the other world and the efficacy of the document is endorsed by his authority.

The Bureau of Three Treasures document seems to be a Buddhist adoption of the Daoist funeral petition *die wen* 牒文. The adoption of the metaphor of the rituals of the imperial court and of its bureaucracy in the imagery of deities and structure of the pantheon is a common characteristic of Chinese religion. The strong analogy between the image of the other world authority and that of the secular imperial authority seems to suggest that the replication of that 'imperial metaphor' is crucial for the other world pantheon to gain legitimacy and authority (Feuchtwang 1992). Within this metaphor, writing is one of the pivotal aspects, in particular in religious documents that act as communication between the secular world and the other world. The style and transmission of religious documents bear close resemblance to imperial official documents and the paper-pushing culture of the imperial bureaucracy. Although sources predating the Han dynasty had implied a religious belief in an underworld in a bureaucratic form, it was not until the second century BC of the Former Han that there was unequivocal evidence of mortuary texts in the form of secular official documents.[2] This bureaucratic format of mortuary writing was later absorbed by Daoism.[3]

The earliest adoption of imperial Chinese passport documents in Buddhist mortuary practice can be traced back to as early as the sixth century. From the mid-sixth to the mid-seventh centuries, a type of Buddhist tomb inventory that included a mortuary petition emerged in Turfan and became very popular (hereafter '2a type inventory'). The petition was usually made by a Buddhist monk and was addressed to the

[1] See other samples of model texts in Chen Ruilong and Wei Yingman (2005: 95–9). See also, in relation to the fieldwork research on the practice of the Buddhist mortuary petitional texts in Taiwan, Yang Shixian (2008: 71–2).

[2] Lai Guolong (2005: 5–6); Hubei Sheng Wenwu Kaogu Yanjiusuo (1995).

[3] Seidel (1987: 21–57); Wu Rongzeng (1981: 56–63); Nickerson (1996).

Great God of the Five Paths (*wudao dashen* 五道大神 hereafter 'wudao') in an official bureaucratic format, similar to that of later Han funeral texts and modern Buddhist *die wen* used in the funeral. In these imperial passport-like mortuary texts, the Buddhist monk contacted Wudao about the arrival of the deceased. Why and how did Chinese Buddhism start to appropriate this bureaucratic form of document in its mortuary practice? In this chapter, I use tomb inventories excavated in the Turfan region and dating from the end of the fourth century to the middle of the seventh century (before its conquest by the Tang), as an example to demonstrate how Buddhists adopted the Chinese bureaucratic form of communication with the other world in mortuary practice in early medieval China.

Hundreds of cemeteries dating from the fourth to the eighth centuries have been excavated in the areas of Astana and Qarakhodja, 40 km east of Turfan (Dien 2002: 23; Von Le Coq 1985). A number of manuscripts of various sources including sixty-one tomb inventories have been unearthed from these tombs (Hansen 1998a: 2; Dien 2002: 23). These tomb inventories usually comprise a list of the grave goods in the tomb and a statement, in a similar form to secular contracts or official passports, to contact the otherworld authority for protection of the deceased on their journey to the unseen world and for proof of their ownership of the grave goods in the inventory. Dating from the end of the fourth century to the middle of the seventh century, Turfan tomb inventories can, in general, be subsumed within two categories, each related to two periods, the dividing line between them being the middle of the sixth century. According to historical accounts and written sources, Buddhism had been very popular in Turfan since long before the mid-sixth century. Nonetheless, no clearly Buddhist elements have been uncovered in Turfan tombs dating before then (Dien 2002: 24–30). This confusing cleavage between the historical accounts of Buddhism in Turfan and the paucity of Buddhist elements in the Turfan tombs before the mid-sixth century has baffled scholars for many years. Turfan specialist Ma Yong 馬雍 holds that it is probably because Buddhism only circulated among the highest aristocrats and did not spread among the populace (Ma Yong 1990: 120). Ma Yong's inference rested on the premise that there should be coherence between the religious beliefs of the tomb occupant and his related family and the religious beliefs demonstrated in the tomb. Valerie Hansen interprets the adoption of the Chinese bureaucratised form of mortuary document in the 2a type inventory as a suggestion that Buddhism came to Turfan from the east and not the west. She, however, questions the applicability of this premise of correlation in the case of Buddhism (Hansen 1998a: 6; 1998b: 41–2). In this paper, I shall further examine this premise in the first place.

To clarify why and how the Buddhists in Turfan appropriated the use of Chinese mortuary bureaucratic documents for the funeral rite, it is essential to inspect this change in the Turfan mortuary documents before and after the mid-sixth century. In this study, I wish to demonstrate how this transformation suggests a Buddhist attitude towards indigenous local funeral practice during its expansion and the role of Buddhist monks in the funeral rites.

WHY ARE THERE FEW BUDDHIST ELEMENTS IN EARLY TURFAN TOMBS?

The format of the first-period Turfan inventory is similar either to the official certificate or the imperial passport. For example, after a list of inventory goods, the funerary statement in one of the earliest extant first-period inventories, the inventory of Liu Hongfei 劉弘妃, reads as follows (Ogasawara 1960: 255–6):

> On the twenty-second day, *jiazi*, of the first month which starts with the day *kuimao* of the twenty-second year of *Jianyuan* (386 AD), the personal clothes and miscellaneous objects of the adult woman, Liu Hongfei, cannot be claimed by other people under her name. The witnesses: the blue dragon on the left and the white tiger on the right wrote the contract and illustrated the record of what they knew at the time.

The statement resembles an official certificate for individual property rights. It comprises three parts: first, the date of the statement and the identity of the tomb occupant; second, the claim of the tomb occupant's ownership of the property in the tomb and the guarantee of her ownership right against identity theft; and third, the celestial endorsers of this document. In many first-period inventories, the statement ends with the formulaic official ending, 'promptly, promptly, in accordance with the statutes and ordinances'.

The sentence which protects the tomb occupant's ownership of the objects in the graves from identity theft is an innovation of the early medieval period. Ursula-Angelika Cedzich has revealed that, during the early medieval era, there were religious beliefs and related practices aimed at achieving personal immortality by impersonating other people's identities to mislead the otherworld bureaucrats as to the registered lifespan of such an individual (Cedzich 2001: 1–68). The claim against the infringement by identity thieves here seems relevant to this religious belief.

PASSPORTS TO THE OTHER WORLD

In several first-period inventories, the claim of ownership of the tomb occupant over the objects in the grave is accompanied by a formulaic sentence for the freedom of the deceased in his or her journey to the other world. For example, the inventory of Wei Yirong 隗儀容 of tomb no. 96 in Qarakhodja reads as follows (*Turfan manuscripts I*, p. 28):

> I sincerely list the number of personal clothes and objects of the deceased. Other people cannot falsely claim them under her [the tomb occupant's] name. I wish that at the check-points for ferry crossing and river bridges, she should not be detained or troubled. In accordance with the statutes and ordinances.

Arakawa Masaharu 荒川正晴 has pointed out that this formulaic sentence runs parallel to a formulaic sentence in the Han dynasty passport.[4] At the end of a damaged first-period inventory found at tomb no. 91 in Qarakhodja, it was written 過所 *guosuo*, which means passport (*Turfan manuscripts I*, p. 55). This seems to suggest that first-period inventories at Turfan functioned like passports for the tomb occupant for their journey to and in the other world.

Buddhist elements in the first-period Turfan tombs

There are very few Buddhist items unearthed in the first-period Turfan tombs. One of the few Buddhist remains are fragmentary manuscripts of a Buddhist sūtra, the *Foshuo qi nü jing* 佛說七女經 (the *Sūtra of Seven Daughters*), discovered in tomb no. 13 in Astana.[5] Another, in tomb inventory S. no. 6251 dated to 420 AD, was supposed to have been excavated in one tomb in Astana, and yet mistakenly included in the Dunhuang collection as S. no. 6251.[6] The text ends with the following sentences:

> The contemporary witnesses are the blue dragon on the left and the white tiger on the right . . .
>
> to write the numbers of the items, the barbarian monk (received?) to . . .

[4] Arakawa Masaharu (2004: 113–14); Zhongguo kexueyuan kaogu yanjiusuo (1957: 77).

[5] *Turfan manuscripts I*, pp. 113–14; *Foshuo qinü jing*. T. 14, no. 556, pp. 907c –909b. This text claims to be a translation from an Indian original, but no attempt has been made to reconstruct a Sanskrit title.

[6] Chen Guocan (2004: 95–6); Hou Can and Wu Meilin (2003: 698–9).

It seems that a non-Chinese monk was involved here in this first-period inventory. Unfortunately, because of damage to the manuscript, we are not certain as to what he actually did. He might have been a kind of endorser or scribe. This case implies that Buddhist monks of the first period might have been involved in burial practice in certain cases.

Lady Peng's tomb

Among the tomb inventories of the first Turfan period, the inventory of Lady Peng, the only silk manuscript of the first Turfan period found so far (tomb no. 383 in Astana, dated to 458 AD), is deserving of our attention.[7] According to the content of the inventory, we know that Lady Peng was one of the wives of Juqu Mengxun 沮渠蒙遜, the founder of the non-Chinese regime, Northern Liang (401–39 AD), based in Liangzhou 涼州, mainly Gansu 甘肅. Mengxun was noted for his patronage of Buddhism. One of his well-known feats is the construction of the Buddhist stone caves in Liangzhou.[8]

According to an inscription recording the establishment of a temple dedicated to Maitreya and the excavated manuscripts of Buddhist sūtras that all attribute their sponsorship to the later ruler Juqu Anzhou 沮渠安周 (r. 444–60 AD), we know that the ruling Juqu family continued to patronise Buddhism after they moved to Turfan.[9] As the wife of the deceased ruler Mengxun, Lady Peng was therefore very likely also a devout Buddhist. However, no item relevant to Buddhism has been excavated from her tomb, and neither was any listed in the inventory.

In response to Ma Yong's question, Lady Peng's tomb shows that Buddhist elements were also absent even in the tomb of the member of the ruling Buddhist family in Turfan. In my opinion, this also raises the question as to whether we could detect a conversion to Buddhism merely through the grave goods in the tombs. Does the absence of Buddhist elements in the first-period tomb suggest that Buddhist monks in Turfan did not take part in their follower's funeral ceremony or that they just did not get involved in the presentation of the tomb? To unravel this puzzle, two issues are essential: Buddhist burial culture, and the attitude of Buddhism towards indigenous local religious beliefs and mortuary practices when it was introduced to local areas.

[7] Tulufan diqu wenwu baoguansuo (1994: 75–80); Liu Hongliang (1997: 146–57).

[8] *Ibid.*; Fang Xuanling, (1974: 129, 3197).

[9] Rong Xinjiang (1998: 65–92); Ikeda on (1985: 102–20).

Buddhist burial culture

The Buddhist adoption of the idea of communication with the otherworld bureaucrats over the coming of the deceased in second-period Turfan tomb inventories is considered by scholars as evidence of Buddhist involvement in the funeral. This presumption usually implies that it was not until Buddhist monks were able to syncretise their ideas with local Chinese burial culture that they managed to step into funeral practice. Ancient Chinese burial culture was conspicuously different from the treatment of the dead in India. One of the differences was that, in China, cremation was scarcely practised. However, there is no canonical Buddhist source instructing whether cremation or interment leads to a better rebirth (Ebrey 2003: 152). Theoretically speaking, this does not necessarily mean therefore that the Chinese way of interment was seen as being in conflict with Buddhist doctrine. The question would be rather whether it is possible that the Chinese burial culture and Buddhism might have been able to co-exist, and how.

In practice, there was a preference for cremation in India. In the Vinaya of Mūlasarvāstivāda, which according to Gregory Schopen (2004: 96) was probably compiled during the period between the beginning of the Common Era and 500 AD, there is an account on the proper ways of dealing with the corpse of a monk. According to the passage in question, cremation was the first preference. Only when cremation was impossible were disposal in the river or burial considered acceptable alternative options (*ibid.*: 108; also Schopen 1997: 215–18). Burial here is depicted as an easy economic alternative option, not like the Chinese luxurious underground chamber style. This account reminds us that cremation was the top preference for disposing of the dead, along with other methods practised in ancient India and Sri Lanka which varied according to social class and economic considerations (Basham 1954: 176–7; Langer 2007: 70–3). In the *Mahāparinibbāna Suttanta*, the Buddha instructed Ānanda to cremate his remains like that of a King of Kings (Rhys Davids 1910: 155–6, 182–91). The cremation of the Buddha's body just followed that established custom.

The attitude of Buddhism towards indigenous local religious beliefs and mortuary practices

Cremation was not only alien to the ancient Chinese but also inimical to Confucian values of not harming the personal body. According to work by current scholars, cremation was scarcely practised among Chinese Buddhist followers, and the Buddhist clergy was not known for its participation in funerals in early medieval China.[10] Since the Chinese style of burial was not in the Indian Buddhist funeral tradition, when Buddhism was introduced to China, would it have been a dilemma for the Buddhist missionaries from India to face the options of either persuading their Chinese followers to observe what they did in India and Central Asia, or just following or adapting the indigenous tradition as early Buddhists did in India? Current available sources seem to suggest the latter. Why?

Schopen, drawing on accounts of the funerals of monks in the *Mūlasarvāstivāda-vinaya*, has argued that, in order to avoid social censure of improper mortuary practice by indigenous local communities, which would not only jeopardise the image of the Buddhist saṅgha, but also annoy their lay followers, the Buddhist saṅgha had a tendency to adjust their practice to local values (Schopen 1997: 204–37). This tendency is also expressed in certain early medieval Chinese Buddhist scriptures. In the *Foshuo Guanding Jing* 佛說灌頂經 (*Sūtra of Consecration*), an apocryphal sūtra allegedly translated from an Indian original by Śrīmitra 帛尸梨蜜多羅 (? –343 AD?), but in fact composed in China, we see a similar, accommodating attitude to mortuary matters. In the chapter on graves and tombs, the Buddha tells Ānanda that there are numerous types of mortuary rites, and that in India these included cremation and disposal in water. Then, the Buddha explicates three aspects of burial in graves and stūpas. He firstly praises the conventional mortuary practice in China, where Buddhism, he says, is also practised. Then, he condemned the conventional mortuary practices in two minor states, where Buddhism was, in one case, not respected, and in the other, unknown. The Buddha praises the burial practice in China as follows:

> There are three matters on burial in stūpas and graves. In the world of *Jambu*, there is the Cīna state [China]. I have dispatched three sages there to transform and guide, and people are kind and sympathetic and are endowed with propriety and justice. There are no disobedient people among both upper and lower classes of people. In the China state, the way of burial is endowed with dignity. There are gold, silver, precious treasures, and carved and engraved vehicles. The flying celestial beings consider it dignified. Musicians perform with drums and bells, and songs of eulogy are used as funeral music. The corpse of the deceased is fully provided with clothes. The inner and outer coffins are delicately scented with fragrances. Hundreds and thousands of people see the deceased off in the rural countryside. The ritual is held solemnly in the mountain forest. The wood is flourishing. Each line is of the same value without anyone being too extravagant or

[10] Seidel (1983: 573–85); Ebrey (2003: 152); Liu Shufen (2000: 7–8, 11).

too poor. The cypress tree in the cemetery appears flourishing, and the stele monumental archway is dignified. No one who sees this does not rejoice.[11]

This apocryphal account seems to attempt to justify Chinese indigenous interment culture as a good burial model as long as it is under Buddhist authority. It demonstrates a similar mechanism of flexibility in Chinese Buddhism to avoid social conflict by adopting local customs. This flexibility also shows that compatibility with other religious beliefs was not necessarily in contradiction with Buddhist doctrine (Gombrich 1995: 58–9).

The monk's role in mortuary culture

However, the fact that monks were willing to accept local burial customs does not necessarily mean that Buddhist monks did not take part in mortuary practice. There is at least a basic role for monks found in various sources. In Xuan Zang's 玄奘 (602–64 AD) account of Buddhist funeral practice in India, he states 878a):

For the Buddhist Saṅgha, the funeral custom does not include wailing. When their parents die, Buddhist monks chant (sūtras) to pay their debt of gratitude towards their parents. By doing this, they carefully perform the funeral rites for their parents and follow them when gone with due sacrifices. It will therefore increase the merit (to their parents) in the other world.

Schopen's research on the monks' funerals in the *Mūlasarvāstivāda-vinaya* also shows that, in addition to disposing of the body, fellow monks carried out a Buddhist recitation (in certain accounts, it was referred to as teachings on impermanence, the Dharma of the Three Sections [*tridaṇḍaka*]) in the name of the deceased monk, through which they would direct merit to the deceased (Schopen 2004: 97, 106–7). Nowadays, reciting the Buddha Dharma (in the form of sūtras or verses) is still the major essential role for Buddhist monks in both Theravāda and Mahāyāna traditions.[12] In this regard, is it possible that in the case of Lady Peng, who was very likely a Buddhist follower, there may have been a compatible division of work between the Buddhist monk and local ritual specialists in her mortuary service. The Buddhist monk would have recited the Buddhist Dharma for prospective merit to be gained by the deceased in the funeral, while the ritual specialist would have taken charge of burial matters.

In modern-day Chinese society, the role of Buddhist monks in funerals is generally only that of chanting Buddhist sūtras and verses, while the

[11] *Foshuo guanding jing*. T. 21, no. 1331, p. 512b; Strickmann (1990: 75–118).
[12] Gombrich (1995: 255–6, 282–4, 320–1); Langer (2007); Shi Shengyan (1999: 53–5).

arrangement of the funeral ritual is mainly directed by ritual specialists from funeral service companies (Shi Shengyan 1999: 53–5). In Taiwan, cremation and burial are two major options for Buddhists in dealing with the body of the deceased. When a person dies, his family generally first contacts the funeral specialist, who will instruct the family about funeral matters. According to the family's religious preference, either Buddhist or Daoist priests will be called to hold a service for the deceased. If the family prefers to bury the deceased, the burial is normally overseen by ritual specialists and geomancers, not by monks. Therefore, the arrangement and content of the tombs of the Buddhist followers is usually not determined by Buddhist monks, but by ritual specialists. Occasionally, certain individual Buddhist priests who possess the knowledge of burial rites may extend their role to burial. But in general, the arrangement of tomb and burial is mainly based on the interpretation of the ritual specialist on what the proper religious presentation for the welfare of the deceased in the other world would be, usually according to the budget of the family of the deceased. As no orthodox Buddhist sources give instructions on standard burial rites, the burial rites for Buddhists generally follow traditional Chinese burial customs, sometimes with a Buddhist flavour, for example, by the application of Buddhist images or texts on paper money or on the coffin, which is also normally overseen by ritual specialists, not Buddhist monks.[13] This compatible division of work between the Buddhist priest and local ritual specialists in mortuary services in Taiwan shows that the role of the Buddhist monk is not necessarily demonstrated in Buddhist tombs and brings into question the approach of previous scholars which attempts to judge whether there was an involvement of a Buddhist monk in the funeral or a conversion to Buddhism of the deceased by merely examining the grave goods in the tomb; and it suggests the very likely possibility that, during the first period of Turfan, Buddhist monks may have played a role in funerals for their followers by reciting the Buddha Dharma or sūtras as Buddhist monks otherwise do, even though this role does not emerge in tomb evidence.

THE SECOND-PERIOD TURFAN TOMB INVENTORY

From the middle of the sixth century, a type of tomb inventory which was petitioned by Buddhist monks to Wudao became a dominant type of tomb inventory in Turfan (2a type inventory). Besides the essential information

[13] Chen Ruilong and Wei Yingman (2005: 31–8, 62–3); Walshe (1908: 450–4); Shi Jinglin (2008); Welch (1967: 191–7).

we have seen in the first-period inventory and Chinese popular mortuary religious ideas, the 2a type Turfan tomb inventory also comprises Buddhist ideas about the other world. The appearance of Buddhist monks as petitioners in the 2a type inventory has been considered evidence of not only the involvement of Buddhist monks in funeral practice, but also of their adoption of the imperial bureaucratic metaphor in religious communication.

The 2a type inventory generally consists of two parts: a list of grave goods and a petition in a form similar to that found in official documents from a Buddhist priest to Wudao. The sequence of these two parts can be reversed and in certain cases these parts are mingled. While the petitionary part explicitly describes Buddhist involvement, no unequivocal Buddhist character emerges in grave goods of the 2a type inventory. Apart from clothing, bolts of silk, jewellery and other personal commodities, certain tomb inventories also include the *Xiao Jing* 孝經 (the Classic of Filial Piety) and tin figures 錫人: burial items whose origin can be traced back to Confucian tradition and to late Han burial practice respectively.

The structure of the petitionary part of the 2a type inventory is generally based on the format of a Chinese imperial travel document, which typically starts with the date of the petition, then makes contact with the divine counterpart of the priest in the other world and ends with the official closing phrase 'Promptly! Promptly! In accordance with the statutes and ordinances'. It usually includes a formative sentence: 'Regardless of whether [the deceased] wants to seek the east end of the sea, or find the east wall of the sea, [the deceased] should not be detained or hindered for even a brief moment 若欲求海東頭, 若欲覓海東壁, 不得奄遏停留'. (In many cases, the east wall of the sea was referred to as the west wall of the sea.) The clause, '[the deceased] should not be detained or hindered for even a brief moment' is a common term used in Chinese official travel documents.

The content of the petitionary part of the 2a type inventory is a hybrid reservoir that comprises both Buddhist concepts as well as concepts from Chinese popular religion. The Buddhist concepts include Wudao and its related concepts: the Five Paths, the Five Precepts and the Ten Merits, and the Buddhist monk as a this-world petitioner. The ideologies of popular religions include the Daoist concept of longevity: the deceased ought to live to an advanced age, and always maintain himself and not age 宜向(享)遐齡, 永保難老; the idea of the two celestial witnesses or endorsers of the petition: Zhang Jiangu and Li Dingdu 張堅固, 李定度 (there are some minor variations of the characters of the names in certain cases).

THE PROBLEMS OF THE IDENTITIES OF THE BUDDHIST MONKS IN THE 2A TYPE INVENTORIES

The salient feature of the 2a type tomb inventory is the intervention of Buddhist monks in the process of the transition of the deceased to their next destination. Representing the secular world, the Buddhist monk in the 2a type tomb inventory makes a petition to his counterpart, Wudao, in the unseen world. This role runs parallel to that of the local bureaucrat in the former Han funeral texts and that of the Celestial Emperor's Envoy in the later Han tomb-quelling texts.[14]

Among the Buddhist monks mentioned in the 2a type tomb inventories in Turfan, Guoyuan 果願 is the most prominent name. The identity of Guoyuan has perplexed scholars for many years. The difficulty in determining his identity is due to the fact that the time gap between the extant earliest and last inventories mentioning Guoyuan extends from 543 AD to 637 AD – almost a century. If the 2a type tomb inventory of Turfan had been read during the funeral ceremony and then placed in the tomb (Oda Yoshihisa 1988: 51), then this monk would have had to have lived an exceptionally long life. This prompts one to ask whether *Guoyuan* in these tomb inventories in fact denotes the same man.

Another problem of the 2a type inventory is the frequent and seemingly inconsistent absences of either the name of the tomb occupant or of the identity of the Buddhist monk, or in some cases, of both of them. The omission of the name of the tomb occupant and of the Buddhist monk was carried out simply by not mentioning their names, by leaving a blank space or by including the term 'so and so', *mojia* 某甲. Simple omissions appear to have been the result of a direct replication of these texts from a model petitionary text without any modification. Omissions left with a blank space or with the term 'so and so' were usually displayed in the female inventories and it has been suspected by scholars that this might have been owing to certain religious taboos on deceased females (*ibid.*: 51–2; Hansen 1998b: 56). Apart from this, linguistic errors such as typos

[14] Celestial ordinances for the dead are documents written on pottery jars to ward off evil from the tomb and the deceased. They are also called tomb-quelling texts, *zhenmu wen* 鎮墓文. Seidel described them as a passport endorsed by the Supreme Celestial Deity (or the Yellow God) and his envoy to introduce the dead to the subterranean administration. Apart from the third to fifth century AD tombs in Dunhuang, celestial ordinances on jars have been found only in the tombs of later Han (Seidel 1987: 25, 48).

and fragmentary sentences are also frequently found in the petitionary part of the 2a type Turfan inventory. Both the omissions and linguistic errors were often considered to be the result of the scribe's inefficiency in classical Chinese and insufficient understanding of the content of the texts (Hansen 1998b: 56–7).

To unravel how 2a type inventories were actually practised in Turfan during the second period, it is crucial to unravel these two puzzles. First of all, it is essential to clarify the definition of the terms 'inconsistencies' and 'omissions'. Inconsistencies and omissions usually imply that procedures were not done properly in accordance with a standard model. In the case of the 2a type inventories, the concept of a correct observance of the 2a type inventory usually rests on two assumptions believed by many scholars: first, that the 2a type inventory was undertaken by the Buddhist monks in Turfan as a part of funeral practices, and second, that there was a standard way of doing this.

However, the frequent inconsistencies and these seemingly linguistic errors suggest that many 2a type inventories were not done properly. Rather than merely attributing them to the scribe's incompetence, we may need to consider the possibility that the 2a type inventory could have been practised with more than one standard interpretation in the second period of Turfan. Specifically, the 2a type inventory could have been a format observed by different groups of people with different interpretations.

In this regard, instead of the conventional approach by previous scholarship, which often only selects more completed individual texts from different tombs to re-establish a standard model form of the 2a type inventory, it is necessary to include those seemingly exceptional cases into account. Accordingly, besides inspecting certain essential individual inventories from individual tombs, my research approach will be based here on an examination and comparison of the 2a type inventories from family tombs, which means that I will examine and compare the 2a type inventories from the same family tomb first, and then examine and compare groups of inventories from different family tombs. Through this twofold analysis, I wish to demonstrate that, although the practice of 2a type inventories was at the beginning very likely a collaborative product of Buddhist religious ideas and local ritual tradition, the 2a type inventory was not necessarily practised exclusively by Buddhists. Further, the 2a type inventory was not the exclusive type of tomb inventory adopted by Buddhists.

Buddhist intervention in the Turfan tomb inventory: participation under a triangular structure of mortuary management

The extant earliest 2a type inventory, the inventory of Xiaozi 孝姿, was excavated in the tomb of Zhang Hong 張洪 and his two wives Xiaozi and Guangfei 光妃 (Astana tomb no. 170). All three tomb occupants had tomb inventories. The petition part of the inventory of Xiaozi reads as follows (Tang Changru, *Tulufan Chutu Wenshu* vol. 1, 143):

On the thirteenth day *jiaxu* of the first month, which starts with the day *renxu*, of the thirteenth year, *shuihai*, of Zhanghe, *bhikṣu* Guoyuan sincerely transmits (this document) to the Great God of the Five Paths. The Buddhist disciple Xiaozi who observed the Five Buddhist Precepts and devoted herself to the practice of the Ten Merits passed away on the sixth day of this month. She is wading through the Five Paths. May she be allowed to go wherever she wants to go. The items listed to the right are all of the objects that she used in her life. The contemporary men are Zhang Jiangu and Ji (Li) Dingdu. Regardless of whether the deceased would like to seek the east end of the sea, and look for the east wall of the sea, she should not be scolded or detained even for a brief moment. Promptly! Promptly! In accordance with the statutes and ordinances.

This text literally depicts how a Buddhist monk filed a petition to hand over the dead to the authority of the other world. His counterpart in the bureaucracy of the unseen world is Wudao, the deity in charge of the destinations of the deceased. In the 2a type inventory, the fulfilment of the Five Precepts and of the Ten Merits in life by the deceased is always addressed in the beginning of the petition as a condition to request guarantees from Wudao to secure their liberty and rights in the unseen world. The report of the fulfilment by the deceased of the Buddhist moral deeds to Wudao in the 2a type inventory seems to embody the instruction from the Buddha to Wudao that a good destination for the deceased is determined by their fulfilment of the Buddhist Five Precepts and the Ten Merits during their lifetimes as stated in the *Puyao jing* 普曜經 (one Chinese version of the life of the Buddha), alleged to have been translated by Dharmārakaṣa 竺法護 in 308 AD.[15]

[15] *Puyao jing*. T. 3, no. 186, pp. 507c–508a. The God of the Five Paths was from an obscure origin in the Chinese Buddhist scriptures and became one of the most important Buddhist bureaucratic deities associated with human rebirth in the light of the person's life deeds during the early medieval and medieval period. Oda Yoshihisa (1976: 14–29); Dudbridge (1996–7: 65–98). I have presented a new study on the origin and the transformation of the deity in the UK Association for Buddhist Studies conference 2010.

Although in content the 2a type text is a funeral petition which includes a Buddhist intervention, the text itself is still a tomb inventory in nature, and no grave goods with an unequivocal Buddhist feature are listed in the 2a type text. While it is possible that in the very beginning the 2a type inventory was undertaken by a Buddhist monk who also possessed the knowledge of burial tradition, still, in terms of practice, the implementation of the 2a type text may have necessarily required the participation of a ritual specialist. That is to say, the real picture of funeral practice beneath the 2a type inventory should include a triangular participation, including the ritual specialist, the Buddhist monk and the family of the deceased. In practice, the role of the ritual specialist in the previous first period context would hardly have been completely replaced by the Buddhist monk.

Diversity of mortuary management of the Turfan inventory during the second period

This triangular relation in practice was probably more complicated than that of a standardised model. First, the 2a type inventory was not the only type of inventory practised in Turfan during the second period and was not the only standardised inventory for the Buddhists. There were other options like the inventories of Astana tombs no. 313 (07/1 and 07/2), 303 and 335 (hereafter the 2b type inventory) during the second period. The 2b type inventory seems to have been thought to be compatible with either Daoist or Buddhist elements. There is a Daoist talisman found in tomb no. 303, and the inventories of no. 313 (07/2) and no. 335 both mention Buddhist monks as endorsers of the inventories (Huang Lie 1981: 51–5).

For example, after an inventory list, a Buddhist monk's name is mentioned in the endorsement of tomb no. 313 (07/2) as follows:

On the eighteenth day . . . of the eleventh month of the eighteenth year, *wuchen*, of Zhanghe. The Most Virtuous master Huiyan endorses for this. [. . .] witnesses: Zhang Dingtu and Li Jiangu [. . .] settles in water.[16]

[16] Tang Changru (1992–6, *Tulufan Chutu Wenshu* vol. 1, 288). The meaning of '*shui zhong ding* 水中定' is not clear. It might be associated with the water concentration *shui ding* 水定, also called *shui guan* 水觀, which means visualising the West Paradise as water; or *bagongde shuixiang* 八功德水想, which means visualising the West Paradise as eight precious lotus ponds. They are both of the sixteen visualisations of the Amitābha paradise described in the *Foshuo guan wuliangshuofo jing* 佛說觀無量壽佛經 (Sūtra on visualisation of the Amitābha Buddha) translated by fifth-century Jiangliang yeshe 畺良耶舍 (T. 12, no. 365, p. 342). Karetzky (1997: 33–56); Soper (1959: 144); Silk (1997: 181–256).

The appearance of Buddhist priests as the endorsers in the 2b type Turfan text in Astana tombs no. 313 (07/2) and no. 335 shows that, apart from the 2a type inventory, some Buddhist monks participated in another type of tomb inventorial practice which was not exclusive to the Buddhists.

Also, even in the same family tomb, not every family member's inventory was of the same style. In Astana tomb no. 48, we see that, in contrast to the 2a type inventories of the male and female occupants dated 604 AD and 596 AD respectively, the female inventory dated 617 AD is not of the 2a type. The inventory ends with a statement which reads like an ordinary contract (Tang Changru 1992–6, *Tulufan Chutu Wenshu*, vol. 1, 336):

> On the right is the list of goods that grow or that are used every year. It is recorded on the second day of the sixth month of the fourth year, *Dingchou*, of *Yihe*.

The inventory does not express any specific religious preference. This suggests that, even in the same tomb, the inventory of each tomb occupant was not necessarily undertaken with the same religious interpretation over the inventory, and not necessarily by the same group of people.

The examination of the name of the tomb occupant and the identity of the Buddhist monk in the inventories from the four family tombs

Among the 2a type inventories, the observation of these inventories could vary according to each individual case. Here I investigate the 2a type inventory by analysing and comparing the inventories in the four family tombs of the second period: which are tombs no. 170, 169, 386 and 48 of Astana.

Tomb no. 170 is an example of a family tomb in which all three inventories of a husband and his two wives seem to have derived from a standardised model text. Except for the personal information, the petitionary part of the inventories of Zhang Hong and his two wives is almost identical and the Buddhist monk in all three inventories was Guoyuan. The great similarity displayed in the petitionary part of these three inventories seems to assert that the funeral service of the three was presided over by Guoyuan. Yet, it is also noteworthy that the scribes were different (given the different handwriting in each text).

Tombs no. 169 and 386 represent two cases where information about the deceased and the Buddhist monk in the inventory is handled differently according to gender. While the names of Zhang Xiaozhang 張孝章 and of Buddhist master Falin 法林 were well documented in Zhang's inventory of tomb no. 169, their counterparts were left blank with the term 'so and so' in his wife's inventory. In tomb no. 386, the names of the male tomb occupant, Zhang Shi'er 張師兒, and that of the Buddhist monk, Yiyuan 義[亻+荊] were both well recorded in Zhang's inventory, while in the female occupant's inventory, although the name of the Buddhist monk was given as Guoyuan, the name of the female deceased was left blank with the term 'so and so'.

Tomb no. 48 is probably another example showing this gender difference. We have seen that the female inventory of 617 AD is not of the 2a type. The other female inventory dated 596 AD is of the 2a type and the names of the Buddhist monk and of the deceased were both left blank with the term 'so and so'. Although the male tomb inventory did name Guoyuan as the monk, unfortunately, owing to manuscript damage, we cannot determine if the name of the male tomb occupant was included in the inventory.

What do these inconsistencies and absences of essential information about the deceased and the Buddhist monk among the 2a type tomb inventories suggest?

Through my examination of the inventories in these four tombs, three questions arise which are essential to the issue of Guoyuan in the 2a type inventories. To begin with, as in the male inventory of tombs no. 169 and 386, the monks' names referred to other monks and not Guoyuan. It seems reasonable to assume that Guoyuan was as much a real figure as these Buddhist monks. However, unlike the case of other monks who had a first character in their names which appears also in Turfan manuscripts in relation to other monks, and whose names in some cases even appeared in other Turfan documents, no monk's name started with the first character *guo*, as that in *Guoyuan* found in the Turfan manuscripts. In the later Han tomb-quelling texts and later early medieval Daoist mortuary texts, the priest is only referred to as the Messenger of the Celestial Emperor, the first person or the speaker of an edict from a Daoist authoritative god without mentioning their names. Is it possible that Guoyuan could also have been a celestial title, as other scholars have suggested?[17]

[17] Oda Yoshihisa has suggested a link between the two characters on a Northern Liang votive stūpa and those of the 2a type inventory that Guo Yuan could literally embed a meaning of 'to accomplish the wish' (1988: 49, 81); Shi Yan (1956: 56).

Secondly, if Guoyuan was a real figure, then the almost one-century gap between the extant earliest and last inventories mentioning Guoyuan would be extraordinary. Some other Buddhist monks were also referred to in the 2a type Turfan inventories as petitioners for the deceased, for example, the monk Yiyuan in the inventory of the prominent General Zhang Shi'er of tomb no. 386. Even if we presume that Guoyuan was a very popular priest in the funeral service, why could not the presence of the centenarian priest in the petition have been taken over by another younger monk like Yiyuan who also would have been capable of presiding over services for high-profile figures? In particular, when Zhang Shi'er's wife, Lady Wang, died, eighteen years after his death, why would her inventory not have been petitioned by a younger capable monk like Yiyuan, but rather by the centenarian Guoyuan?

In addition, according to available specimens of the 2a type inventory, the names deliberately left blank with a space or with the term 'so and so' are all of deceased women. As the dates of death and the petition were both well documented in these female inventories, it seems that these omissions might have been owing not to simple typos, but to certain religious taboos on women. According to our available sources, the limited numbers of inventories, such as the inventories of Xiaozi, Guangfei of Astana tomb no. 170 and Niu Chenying 牛辰英 of Astana tomb no. 88 (Tang Changru 1992–6, *Tulufan Chutu Wenshu* vol. 1, 198), where the names of the deceased females were well documented, are all of the early second period. None is later than 567 AD. There seems to have been an increasingly popular religious penchant in Turfan which led to the omission of the names of deceased females in the inventory. In my opinion, the diverse interpretations on this matter could have derived from the fact that there were probably different religious interpretations or beliefs among Buddhist monks or ritual specialists.

Among these available female inventories without names, the names of Buddhist monks were left blank, substituted with the term 'so and so' – as was the case in the female inventories of tomb no. 169 and of 596 AD of tomb no. 48 – or were referred to as Guoyuan, as happened in the female inventories of no. 386 and of 601 AD of the Otani collection (Ogasawara Senshu 1960: 254, fig. 31). There seem to have been different interpretations among the scribes as to the name of the Buddhist monk, one upholding that it was to be indicated as Guoyuan, and the other that it was to be left blank like a direct copy from a model text. The exceptional case is that of the female inventory of tomb no. 23. In this manuscript, it reads: 'the most virtuous *bhikṣu* "so and so", Nanguang 南光', with two dots next to the characters of 'so and so' signifying deletion (Tang Changru 1992–6, *Tulufan*

Chutu Wenshu vol. 1, 306). In contrast to this correction on the name of the Buddhist monk, the name of the deceased in this inventory was still left blank with the term 'so and so'. It seems to me that it was left blank deliberately as in the other female inventories. Like the scribes of those female inventories which referred to Guoyuan as the Buddhist priest, yet did not mention the name of the deceased, the scribe of the inventory no. 23 seems to have shared a similar idea, namely, while the name of the female deceased was to be omitted, it was essential to indicate the identity of the Buddhist monk in the inventory.

Nonetheless, before we jump to this assumption, one should consider that there were two types of interpretation with regard to the name of the deceased in the female inventories which made reference to Guoyuan: it was thought either that it was to be mentioned or that it was to be left blank. In the two female inventories of tomb no. 170, the names of deceased Xiaozi and Guangfei were both well documented, while in the female inventories of Lady Wang of tomb no. 386, and of 601 AD of the Otani collection, the name of the deceased was left blank with the term 'so and so', or a spare space respectively. If Guoyuan was the monk taking charge of the petitions, my third question is on why he adopted different attitudes towards declaring the name of the female deceased in the inventories of Xiaozi and Guangfei, and the female inventories of tomb no. 386, and of 601 AD of the Otani collection. Could it have been that there was a certain religious taboo for the deceased in the later two inventories?

The threefold questions prompt my suspicion that in many second-period inventories, 'the most virtuous *bhikṣu* Guoyuan' in the 2a type, like 'the most virtuous *bhikṣu* so and so' was also a part of the format of a model text, not really indicating an identical Buddhist monk in the service, if there was one in every case. Although we cannot exclude the possibility that Guoyuan was once a real eminent figure participating in certain 2a type inventories, these three questions, in my opinion, seem to point to a possibility that in particular during the late second period, in the 2a type inventory, Guoyuan was a formative title for the this-world Buddhist petitioner, much like the Messenger of the Celestial Emperor in the later Han tomb-quelling and the speaker of the celestial edict in the early medieval Daoist mortuary text, and not a real indication of a Buddhist monk called Guoyuan in the real funeral services corresponding to this text. I think that this is a better possible explanation of these inconsistent confusions among the 2a type inventories found so far.

Thus we see that Guoyuan could have been a part of the format of a model text in some tomb inventory, like the term 'so and so' of the monk's name in those inventories which did not mention the identity of the monk. Including the inventories that refer to the names of other monks, and not Guoyuan, there seem to be at least three different interpretations among the scribes on whether the monk's name in the inventory should actually correspond to the real figure in the ceremony. Besides these formats, there is also an abbreviated version of a 2a type inventory, for instance, the inventory of Niu Chenying, which does not even mention the Buddhist monk, nor Wudao.

In my opinion, these seemingly trivial inconsistencies and variations among these texts suggest that an overall consensus among the scribes may have existed about the content of the model text of the 2a type inventory, even while there were also different interpretations on the input of the information about the Buddhist monk and the deceased among them. The dissimilar understandings on these issues could have resulted from different religious ideas on these issues or even possibly from a misunderstanding of the initial practice by the scribe.

Furthermore, not all 2a type inventories necessarily suggest Buddhist intervention on the funeral ceremony. In the unnamed inventory found in the tomb of Fan Faji 氾法濟 (Astana tomb no. 151) the petition part of the inventory states awkwardly that the deceased Buddhist disciple 'so and so' is to contact Wudao, not a Buddhist monk as in other 2a type inventories. It is unusual that the deceased should be making a petition for himself, as is the case here, which makes the whole sentence sound irrational. In addition, the text comprises several fragmentary sentences which make the meaning of the text also fragmentary. It seems that the scribe was not well aware of the content he was writing from a model text that he memorised.

Chinese archaeologists have also pointed out that, because the handwriting and the colour of ink are different from the rest of the text, the grave goods object, called the five grains in full 五穀具, which were considered to be paid as tax in the underworld, were probably added in the inventory later. This suggests that the list of grave goods was checked before the text was placed in the tomb.[18] While the grave goods in the inventory had been proof-checked, the linguistic mistakes in the petitionary part were disregarded.[19] It seems to me that, for the scribe or the ritual specialist, the correctness of the petitionary part is not the issue that they were really concerned about, but that of the grave goods. This might imply that, for

[18] Tang Changru (1992–6, vol. 2, 85); Zhang Xunliao and Bai Bin (2006: 567).
[19] Hou Can and Wu Meilin (2003: 318–19); Tang Changru (1992–6, vol. 2, 85–6).

some scribes and ritual specialists, it was fashionable to have the 2a type petitionary part in the inventory or that it might merely symbolise an apotropaic function. Yet, whether the content of the text or the information of the deceased in that inventory are correct or not is not important. Another inventory of an unknown female in Astana tomb no. 31, whose petitionary part is also devoid of any personal information of the deceased and is incomplete in content, is probably another example of this kind (Tang Changru 1992–6, *Tulufan chutu wenshu* vol. 1, 358).

Consequently, in certain cases, the 2a type inventory could be just a fashionable and popular apotropaic format applied by the ritual specialist in the burial ritual, and not necessarily a definite indication of Buddhist participation in practice. Even for some of those 2a type inventories which include complete information of the deceased and mention Guoyuan as the Buddhist monk, the name of Guoyuan could have been just a part of the format of a model text, and was not necessarily an indication of Buddhist intervention in practice.

Thus we see a more complicated picture of how Buddhist monks and ritual specialists were possibly involved in the mortuary business in the second period of Turfan. The mechanism in that triangular relation between the Buddhist monk, local ritual specialists and the family of the deceased presented in the 2a type inventory seems versatile rather than standardised.

CONCLUSION

In order to unravel the process of Buddhist adoption of the Chinese mortuary passport, I argue in this research that it is essential to inspect the role of the Buddhist monk in the funeral and to look at Buddhist general attitudes towards local funeral cultures when Buddhism was transmitted to foreign lands in the first place. My investigation shows that universal sources from different Buddhist traditions all testify that chanting the Buddha Dharma to generate merit for the deceased is the major duty of the Buddhist monk in the funeral. In dealing with the corpse of the deceased, rather than creating their own method outside of the established tradition, from the very beginning, Buddhism followed pre-established Indian custom. Moreover, in order to avoid social censure on improper mortuary practice, the Buddhist saṅgha developed a tendency to adjust their mortuary practice to local customs in foreign environments. In this sense, I argue in this context that the premise of a correlation between the religious beliefs manifested in the tomb and the religious beliefs of the tomb occupant and the related family in life by previous scholarship, is not entirely applicable to Buddhism. The 2a type inventory, as an inventory, necessarily requires the participation of the funeral specialists. As a result, the presentation of mortuary beliefs in the tomb is not based merely on the binary relation between Buddhist saṅgha and the related family, but on the triangular relation that also includes the funeral specialists. Like the management of funerals in modern-day Taiwan, the arrangement of tomb and burial in the second period of Turfan was probably also mainly determined by the ritual specialist according to the budget of the family of the deceased, not by the monks.

In respect of the two major problems with the 2a type inventory: the identity of Master Guoyuan and the frequent inconsistent absence of either the identity of the deceased or that of the Buddhist monk, my examination shows that the 2a type Turfan Buddhist inventory could have been a format observed by different groups of people (particularly the funeral specialists) with different interpretations. This means that the mechanism in this triangular relation may have been versatile rather than standardised. In certain cases, the 2a type inventory could just have been fashionable and a popular apotropaic format applied by the ritual specialist in the burial ritual, and not necessarily an indication of the involvement of Buddhist monks.

My analysis of the early medieval Turfan inventories shows that to understand how Buddhism appropriated Chinese mortuary culture into its practice, it is essential to take into account the role of the ritual specialist in the structure of mortuary management. The intervention of Buddhist monks in local mortuary practice generally requires co-operation and compatible division of work with a local ritual specialist. Under the triangular structure, in many respects, the presentation of the burial is usually determined by ritual specialists.

BIBLIOGRAPHY

PRIMARY SOURCES

Daoxuan 道宣, *Xiu Gaoseng Zhuan* 續高僧傳, T. 50, no. 2060.
Dharmarkṣa 竺法護, *Puyao Jing* 普曜經, T. 3, no. 186.
Fang Xuanling 房玄齡 (ed.) (1974), *Jinshu* 晉書, Beijing: Zhonghua Shuju.
Jiangliang Yeshe 畺良耶舍, *Foshuo Guan Wuliangshuofo Jing* 佛說觀無量壽佛經, T. 12, no. 365.
Li Yanshou 李延壽 (1974), *Beishi* 北史, Beijing: Zhonghua Shuju.
Linghu Defen令狐德棻 (ed.) (1971), *Zhoushu* 周書, Beijing: Zhonghua Shuju.
Shi Huijiao 釋慧皎, *Gaosengzhuan* 高僧傳, T. 50, no. 2059.

Shih Daoxuan 釋道宣, *Jishenzhou Sanbao Gantonglu* 集神州三寶感通錄, T. 52, no. 2106.
Śrīmitra 帛尸梨蜜多羅, *Foshuo Guanding Jing* 佛說灌頂經, T. 21, no. 1331.
Wei Shou 魏收 (1974), *Weishu* 魏書, Beijing: Zhonghua Shuju.
Wei Zheng 魏徵 (ed.) (1973), *Sui Shu* 隋書, Beijing: Zhonghua Shuju.
Xuan Zang 玄奘, *Datang Xiyuji* 大唐西域記, T. 51, no. 2087.
Zhi Qian 支謙, *Foshuo Qinü Jing* 佛說七女經, T. 14, no. 556.

SECONDARY SOURCES

Arakawa Masaharu 荒川正晴 (2004), 'Tōrufan kanjin no meikaikan to bukkyōshikō トゥルファン漢人の冥界観と仏教信仰' [Passports to the other world: transformations of Buddhist beliefs among the Chinese people resident in Turfan during the fourth to eighth centuries] in ed. Moriyasu Takao 森安孝夫, *Chūō Ajia Shutsudo Bunbutsu Ronsō* 中央アジア出土文物論叢 *[Papers on the Pre-Islamic Documents and Other Materials Unearthed from Central Asia]*, Kyoto: Hōyū shoten, 111–26.
Asami Naoichirō 浅見直一郎 (1990), 'Chūgoku Nambokuchō jidai no sōsō bunshu – Hokusei Muhei yonnen "O Kō hi zuisō ibutsuso" o chūshin ni 中国南北朝時代の葬送文書-北斉武平四年『王江妃随葬衣物疏』を中心に', *Kodai Bunka* 古代文化 **42** (4), 1–19.
Basham, A. L. (1954), *The Wonder that was India*, London: Sidgwick and Jackson.
Cedzich, U.-A. (2001), 'Corpse deliverance, substitute bodies, name change, and feigned death: aspects of metamorphosis and immortality in early medieval China', *Journal of Chinese Religions* **29**, 1–68.
Chen Guocan 陳國燦 (1999), 'The worship of Daoist celestial deities in the kingdom of Gaochang: a study in burial customs', *Early Medieval China* **5**, 36–54.
(2004), *Sitanyin Suohuo Tulufan Wenshu Yanjiu* 斯坦因所獲吐魯番文書研究, Taipei: Taiwan guji chubanshe.
Chen Ruilong 陳瑞隆 and Wei Yingman 魏英滿 (eds.) (2005), *Taiwan Sangzang Lisu Yuanyou* 台灣喪葬禮俗源由, Tainan: Yuwentang.
Dien, A. E. (2002), 'Turfan funereal documents', *Journal of Chinese Religions* **30**, 23–48.
Du Doucheng 杜斗城 (1998), *Beiliang Fojiao Yanjiu* 北涼佛教研究, Taipei: Xinwenfeng.
Dudbridge, G. (1996–7), 'The General of the Five Paths in Tang and pre-Tang China', *Cahiers d'Extrême-Asie* **9**, 65–98.
Ebrey, P. B. (2003), *Women and the Family in Chinese History*, London and New York: Routledge.
Evison, G. (1989), *Indian Death Rituals: the Enactment of Ambivalence*, unpublished PhD thesis, University of Oxford.
Feuchtwang, S. (1992), *The Imperial Metaphor: Popular Religion in China*, New York: Routledge.

Gombrich, R. F. (1995), *Precept and Practice: Traditional Buddhism in the Rural Highlands of Ceylon*, London and New York: Kegan Paul International.

Hansen, V. (1998a), 'Introduction: Turfan as a silk road community', *Asia Major* 11 (2), 1–11.

(1998b) 'The path of Buddhism into China: the view from Turfan', *Asia Major* 11 (2), 37–66.

Hillebrandt, A. (1908), 'Death and disposal of the dead – Hindu', in ed. James Hastings, *Encyclopaedia of Religion and Ethics, vol. 4*, Edinburgh: T and T Clark, 475–9.

Holt, J. C. (1981), 'Assisting the dead by venerating the living: merit transfer in the early Buddhist tradition', *Numen* **28** (1), 1–28.

Hou Can 侯燦 and Wu Meilin 吳美琳 (2003), *Tulufan Chutu Zhuanzhi Jizhu* 吐魯番出土磚誌集注, Chengdu: Bashu Shushe.

Hu Ji 胡戟, Li Xiaocong 李孝聰 and Rong Xinjiang 榮新江 (1987), *Tulufan* 吐魯番, Xian: Sanqin Chubanshe.

Huang Lie 黃烈 (1981), 'Luelun tulufan chutu de "daojiao fulu" 略論吐魯番出土的 "道教符籙"', *Wenwu* 1, 51–5.

Huang Wenbi 黃文弼 (1954), *Tulufan Kaoguji* 吐魯番考古記, Beijing: Kexue Chubanshe.

Hubei Sheng Wenwu Kaogu Yanjiusuo 湖北省文物考古研究所 (1995), *Jiangling Jiudian Dongzhou Mu* 江陵九店東周墓, Beijing: Kexue.

Ikeda On 池田溫 (1985), 'Kōshō sanhi ryaku kō 高昌三碑略考' [A brief study on the Gaochang 3 stone inscriptions], in *Mikami Tsugio Hakushi Kiju Kinen Ronbunshū* 三上次男博士喜寿記念論文集 *[Essays in Honour of Prof. Dr. Tsugio Mikami on His 77th Birthday*], Tokyo: Heibonsha: 102–20.

Karetzky, P. E. (1997), 'Water, the divine element of creation and early images of the Buddha of the West in early China', *Journal of Chinese Religions* **25**, 33–56.

Kleeman, T. (1984), 'Land contracts and related documents', in *Chūgoku Noshukyō Shisō to Kagaku: Makio Ryōkai Kakiuh Shōju Kinen Ronshū* 中国の宗教思想と科学：牧尾良海博士頌寿記念論集, Tokyo: Kokusho Kankōkai, 1–34.

Lai Guolong (2005), 'Death and the otherworldly journey in early China as seen through tomb texts, travel paraphernalia, and road ritual', *Asia Major* **18** (1), 1–44.

Langer, R. (2007), *Buddhist Rituals of Death and Rebirth: Contemporary Sri Lankan Practice and its Origins*, Abingdon and New York: Routledge.

Lin Wushu 林悟殊 (1987), 'Lungaochang "sushitianshen" 論高昌 "俗事天神"', *Lishi Yanjiu* 歷史研究 4, 89–97.

Liu Hongliang 柳洪亮 (1997), *Xinchu Tulufan Wenshu ji qi Yanjiu* 新出吐魯番文書及其研究, Urumqi: Xinjiang Renmin Chubanshe.

Liu Shufen (2000), 'Death and the degeneration of life: exposure of the corpse in medieval Chinese Buddhism', *Journal of Chinese Religions* **28**, 1–30.

Ma Yong 馬雍 (1990), *Xiyu Shidi Wenwu Congkao* 西域史地文物叢考, Beijing: Wenwu Chubanshe.

Meng Xianshi 孟憲實 (2004), *Hantang Wenhua yu Gaochang Lishi* 漢唐文化與高昌歷史, Jinan: Qilu.

Nickerson, P. S. (1996), *Taoism, Death, and Bureaucracy in Early Medieval China*, PhD thesis, University of California, Berkeley, publication forthcoming.

Oda Yoshihisa 小田義久 (1961), 'Toroban shutsudo sōsōyō bunsho no ikkōsatsu – toku ni "godō taishin" ni tsuite 吐魯番出土葬送用文書の一考察 – 特に "五道大神" について –', *Ryūkoku Shidan* 龍谷史壇 **47**, 39–56.

(1976), 'Godō daijin kō 五道大神攷', *Tōhō Shūkyō* 東方宗教 **48**, 14–29.

(1988), 'Torohan shutsudo sōsō girei kankei monjo no ichi kōsatsu – zuisōibutsuso kara kudokuso e 吐魯番出土葬送儀礼関係文書の一考察——隨葬衣物疏から功德疏へ', *Tōyō Shien* 東洋史苑, 41–82.

Ogasawara Senshū 小笠原宣秀 (1957), 'Kōshō bukkyō no kenkyū 高昌佛教の研究', *Ryūkoku Shidan* 龍谷史壇 **42**, 1–13.

(1960), 'Toroban shutsudo no shūkyō seikatsu monjo 吐魯番出土の宗教生活文書', *Seiiki Bunka Kenkyū* 西域文化研究 3, Kyoto: Hozokan, 251–62.

Rhys Davids, T. W. and C. A. F. (1910), *Dialogues of the Buddha – translated from the Pali of the Dīgha Nikāya*, London: H. Frowde, Oxford University Press.

Rong Xinjiang 榮新江 (1998), '"Juqu anzhou bei" yu gaochang daliang zhengquan《且渠安周碑》與高昌大涼政權', *Yanjing Xuebao* 燕京學報 new series 5, 65–92.

Schopen, G. (1997), *Bones, Stones, and Buddhist Monks – Collected Papers on the Archaeology, Epigraphy, and Texts of Monastic Buddhism in India*, Honolulu: University of Hawai'i Press.

(2004), *Buddhist Monks and Business Matters – Still More Papers on Monastic Buddhism in India*, Honolulu: University of Hawai'i Press.

Seidel, A. (1983), 'Dabi', in eds. Paul Demieville *et al.*, *Hōbōgirin: Dictionnaire Encyclopédique du Bouddhisme d'après les Sources Chinoises et Japonaises* vol. 6, Paris: Institut de France, 573–85.

(1987), 'Traces of Han religion in funeral texts found in tombs', in ed. Akizuki Kan'ei 秋月觀暎, *Dōkyō to Shūkyō Bunka* 道教と宗教文化, Tokyo: Hirakawa Shuppansha, 21–57.

Sha Zhi 沙知 and Kong Xiangxing 孔祥星 (eds.) (1983), *Dunhuang Tulufan Wenshu Yanjiu* 敦煌吐魯番文書研究, Lanzhou: Ganshu Renmin Chubanshe.

Shi Jinglin 施晶琳 (2008), *Taiwan de Jinyin Zhiqian – yi Tainan shi wei Kaocha Zhongxin* 臺灣的金銀紙錢 – 以臺南市為考察中心, Taipei: Lantai.

Shi Shengyan 釋聖嚴 (1999), *Xuefo Qunyi* 學佛群疑, Taipei: Dharma Drum.

Shi Yan 史岩 (1956), 'Jiuquan wenshushan de shiku siyuan yiji 酒泉文殊山的石窟寺院遺跡', *Wenwu Cankao Ziliao* 文物參考資料 7, 53–9.

Silk, J. A. (1997), 'The composition of the Guan Wuliangshoufo-Jing: some Buddhist and Jaina parallels to the narrative frame', *Journal of Indian Philosophy* **25**, 181–256.

Soper, A. (1959), *Literary Evidence for Early Buddhist Art in China*, Ascona: Artibus Asiae.

Strickmann, M. (1990), 'The Consecration Sutra: a Buddhist book of spells', in ed. Robert E. Buswell Jr., *Chinese Buddhist Apocrypha*, Honolulu: University of Hawai'i Press, 75–118.

Tang Changru 唐長孺 (ed.) (1992–6), *Tulufan Chutu Wenshu* 吐魯番出土文書, Beijing: Wenwu Chubanshe 4 vols.

Tiwari, J. N. (1979), *Disposal of the Dead in the Mahābhārata – A Study in the Funeral Customs in Ancient India*, Varanasi: Kishor Vidya Niketan.

Tulufan diqu wenwu baoguansuo 吐魯番地區文物保管所 (1994), 'Tulufan beiliang wuxuanwang Juqu mengxun furen pengshi mu 吐魯番北涼武宣王沮渠蒙遜夫人彭氏墓', *Wenwu* **9**, 75–80.

Von Le Coq, A. (1985), *Buried Treasures of Chinese Turkestan*, Hong Kong: Oxford University Press.

Walshe, W. G. (1908) 'Death and disposal of the dead – Chinese', in ed. James Hastings, *Encyclopaedia of Religion and Ethics, vol. 4*, Edinburgh: T and T Clark, 450–4.

Welch, H. (1967), *The Practice of Chinese Buddhism 1900–1950*, Cambridge. MA: Harvard University Press.

Wu Rongzeng 吴荣曾 (1981), 'Zhenmuwen zhong suo jiandao de dong Han daowu guanxi 镇墓文中所见到的东汉道巫关系', *Wenwu* **3**, 56–63.

Xinjian Weiwuer Zizhiqu Bowuguan 新疆維吾爾自治區博物館 (1960), 'Xinjian Tulufan asitana beiqu fajue jianbao 新疆吐魯番阿斯塔那北區發掘簡報', *Wenwu* **6**, 13–21.

Yang Shixian 楊士賢 (2008), *Shenzhong Zhuiyuan – Tushuo Taiwan Sangli* 慎終追遠 – 圖說台灣喪禮, Taipei: Boyyoung.

Zhang Guangda and Rong Xinjiang (1998), 'A concise history of the Turfan oasis and its exploration', *Asia Major* **11** (2), 13–36.

Zhang Xunliao 張勛燎 and Bai Bin 白彬 (2006), *Zhongguo Daojiao Kaogu* 中國道教考古, Beijing: Xianzhuang Shuju.

Zhongguo Kexueyuan Kaogu Yanjiusuo 中國科學院考古研究所 (ed.) (1957), *Juyan Hanjian Jiabian* 居延漢簡甲編, Beijing: Kexue Chubanshe.

Index

Abhidhamma
  as charm 33, 64
  chanting at funerals 31–33, 59, 64–65, 87
    when incorporated into funerals 41
    why chanted at funerals 32, 64
  illustrated manuscripts of 83
  on transfer of merit 29
accidental death 103, 116
  See also bad death
aggregates 4, 65
agriculture
  relation to death rites 76, 119
  rituals for 60, 70–75, 99, 105
altars 249
Amitābha 226, 261, 262
amulets. *See* charms
anattā. *See* self and non-self
ancestors
  absence of cult to 111
  altars for 101
  in new year ceremony 117
  local cults for 10, 208
  offerings to 124, 219
  Phunoy cult compared to Chinese 8
  pole 102
  reciprocal relations with 3, 5, 130, 137
  source of fertility 113
  tablets 223
animals
  as offerings 252
  release of 227
  sacrifice of 102, 115
animism 11, 67
arahants 207
Arakan 142
ashes
  burial of 189
  charms made from 207
  orphaned bones made into 204
  storage of in temple 205
Astana 275, 278, 281
asubha-kammaṭṭhāna: 83, 87–88
autopsy 198
Avalokiteśvara 220, 249

bad deaths 12–14
  accidental 103
  and lack of male progeny 206
  and non-Buddhist spirits 158, 177
  as strangers 146–147
  burial 103
  drowning 103, 143, 158, 159
  during childbirth 68, 103, 146
  earthquakes 227
  in Buddhist ritual 115–117
  in Laos 99–100
  in Malaysia 209
  murder 209
  private ceremonies for 222
  shipwrecks 195
  similarities between Thai and Chinese 202, 206
  suicide 99, 103, 116
  Thailand 201
Bangkok 81, 89, 91
bells 123
belongings of deceased 103
betal 150
bier 156
Bimbisāra 125, 129–131
BKPD *boun khau padab din*. *See* Ghost Festival
blood basin 254, 257
bodies 143–145
  See also bones; corpses; ashes
bones
  arrangement of 197
  collection of 202
  dried in sun 203
  exhumation of 197, 202
  figurines made of 25, 37
  male and female 198, 203
  of dogs 199
  of saints 207

bones (cont.)
  orphaned 192–213
  placed in jars 197
  protective power of 207
  purification of 198
  washing of 197, 202
  yang property of 207
Boun Khau Salak. *See* Ghost Festival
Brahmā 33
bricolage 23
Buddha
  cremation of 79, 267
  death and funeral of 1–2, 10
  relics of 177
  scenes from life performed at funeral 175
  statues of 106, 107, 108–109, 112
Buddhas 105–107
Bun Pimay. *See* New Year festival
burial
  compared to cremation 197
  differences between Indian and Chinese 267
  of coffin 151–152, 153, 168
  secondary 194, 197
  See also burial urns
burial urns (a.k.a. jars)
  for cleaned bones 197
  for corpse 86
  for unclaimed bones 209, 210
butterfly soul (*leippya*) 143, 180
  See also spirit

candles
  as offering 107, 111, 123
  in hands of corpse 85
cemeteries
  Burmese 152
  for bad dead 103
  for good dead 103
  movement of corpse to 146
  reading of text in 102
  temporary vaults in 202
  See also graves
Chan Buddhism 7
chanting
  and pollution 12, 160
  at Ghost Festival 227
  Dhammacakkappavattana Sutta 33
  Dhammapada 35
  Dhammasaṅgaṇṇī 32
  in Burmese funeral 149
  in Laos 107
  Khuddakapāṭha 24, 28
  Mahāparinibbāna Sutta 80, 86
  of petition 261
  of precepts 153
  on the radio 34
  Pali 22–46
  Paritta 34–35
  Paṭṭhāna 32
  purpose of 34
  reasons for composition of 36
  ridicule of 175
  Tirokuḍḍapetavatthu 29
  Vinaya 160
  See also Abhidhamma
chaodu 224, 225–226
  See also Ghost Festival
Chaozhou 194, 195, 196, 201, 203
  See also Guangdong
charitable organisations for the dead
  Chinese 194, 209
  Thai 202
charms
  as protection against dead 203–204
  closing of bone jars with 209, 210
  made from ashes 213
childbirth 68, 103, 146
children
  corpses of 203
  of the deceased 254
  tombs of 103
Chulalongkorn 201
Classic of Filial Piety 271
cloth
  consecration of 70
  offering of at funeral 37
  under corpse 153
clothing worn at funerals 210
coffins
  before cremation 91, 166
  depiction of 83
  in Burma 148
  in China 268
  in theatrical performance 172
  makers of 149
  removal to cemetery 151
comedy at funeral 175, 178
Communism and death ritual 195
  See also state policy
confession 29–30, 201
consciousness
  and rebirth 185
  Buddhist doctrine of 12
  loss of 144
Consecration sūtra 268
corpses
  binding of 65, 67–68, 85–86
  decomposition of 183–184, 185–186
  depiction of 81
  disposal in river 267, 268

exposure of face 91
flower placed in hand of 85, 86
food placed with 102
isolation of 209
meditation on 80, 83, 87–88
movement of 65
mummification of 203
of children 203
of those sentenced to death 196
orientation of 148, 153
paper in mouth of 32
placement in coffin 149–150
placement in urn 197
preparation of 7, 85, 102, 147–148
preservation of 89, 185, 198
relation to destiny of spirit 205
shrouds taken from 82
transformation of 7
treatment of in *Mūlasarvāstivāda* 267
viewing of 153
See also bones *see also under* body
cotton threads
burning of 107
linking dead to temples 108
used in rituals 112–113, 144, 153
cremation
and not-self 171
as state policy 195, 196, 208
Buddha 79
Burmese 147, 153
casts made previous to 166
compared to burial 197, 267
crematorium 91
depiction of 83
double 166
in India 21, 268
of poor 147
orphaned bones 201, 204
Thai 88
crying. *See* weeping
Cultural Revolution 196
cymbals 108, 111

Dafeng
altars devoted to 209
and reclamation of corpses 197, 202
biography of 193
communication through mediums 199
in Thailand 213
statue of 204
dance 175, 255
Daoism
association with folk religion 233
conversion of negative energy 207
funerals 270
gods of 277
mortuary texts 262, 279
talismans 275
dead
as members of community 3
care for 7
possessions of 157
registering of names for ghost festival 224
socialisation of 137, 194
death
acceptance of 2
as central to Buddhism 1–3, 12, 174
fear of 60, 63, 65, 96
last moments before 146, 154
mask 166
ordinary 146
process of transformation 3, 6, 91
See also good deaths, bad deaths, pollution
death ritual
after long-term illness 254
and gender 254–255, 257, 276, 278–279
and identity 197
as business 230, 241
as renewal 112
criticism of 228–231
flexibility of 244, 269, 281
for women 254–255, 257
function of 6, 13
innovations in 243
place of 167
resilience to change 6, 39–40
See also funerals, festivals for the dead, *Xianghua foshi*, Ghost Festival
separation of dead from living 15, 162
structure of 245–258
timing of 157–158, 244
deathscapes 5, 6
deities 251
deva *See* gods
Dhammacakkappavattana Sutta 33
Dhammapada 35
Dhammasaṅgaṇī 32
Dharma assemblies 221, 224, 225–226
See also pudu
Dharmarakṣa 274
divination 103, 252
double cremation 166
Douglas, Mary 13, 60, 198, 199–201
drowning 103, 143, 159
drums 106, 108

earthquakes 227
entertainment 84, 249, 250
See also theatre

ethnicity
  and Buddhism 200
  and death ritual 196, 201
  and social cooperation 206–208
exorcism 150
eyiń 167

Fahui (Dharma Assemblies) 221
families of deceased
  depiction of 85
  duties in relation to doctrine of non-self 4
  needs of 256
  role in funeral 37, 275
  taking temporary ordination 156
  viewing of open coffin 85, 91
  weeping 88, 151, 153
fangsheng 227
fans (*talaphat*) 85
fertility
  agricultural 73, 99
  and death 15–16, 75
  and death ritual 111, 113, 119
  and liṅga 66
  from spirits 115, 137
  human 117
festivals for the dead
  as second funeral 104
  Cambodia 122
  Laos 99–117, 120
  popularity of 233
  shuilu fahui 226
  structure of 226
  See also Ghost Festival, New Year Festival
filial duty 29
fireworks 109–110, 113, 223
flowers
  as offering 91, 107, 111, 223
  as symbol of cremation 87
  in hand of corpse 85, 86
food
  and merit 131–136
  as offerings to dead 108, 120, 121, 123–137, 227
  at death festival 107
  offered to monks 153
  offerings to spirits 109
  placed with corpse 102
Foshuo guanding jing 268
Fujian 194, 217–235
funerals
  Buddhist hegemony of 12
  business of 17
  Chinese compared to Theravāda 7–8, 9, 16
  comedy at 175, 178
  comparison of Burmese, Thai, Lao and Sri Lankan 38
  cost of 104, 148
  emotional comfort provided at 256
  for monks 7, 14, 145, 165–189
  function of 5
  gifts to monks in 25
  in early Buddhism 10
  in ritual cycle 120, 217
  in Taiwan 233
  inauspicious nature of 256
  lack of prescriptive literature on 22
  length of 38, 145, 147, 158
  location of 10
  main characteristics 8–9
  objects used in 14–15, 27–29
  preaching at 6, 25, 27, 31, 153
  prescriptive literature 21–22
  royal 165
  second 104, 187
  standard Buddhist 7, 10, 258
  theatre at 6
  Theravāda 22–53
  Theravāda compared to Chinese 7–8, 9, 16
  timing of 104
  See also death ritual, offerings, processions, lay ritual specialists

Gautama. *See* Buddha
Gellner, David 11
gender. *see also under* death ritual
geomancy 199, 207
ghost festival
  and Bimbisāra 129–131
  and local authorities 232
  and Yama 219, 220
  announcement of 225–226
  attacked as superstition 125, 220, 221, 230
  beings addressed during 124
  Cambodian 122
  chanting during 227
  Chinese 217–235
  Chinese and Vietnamese versions compared to Laos 4
  commercialism of criticised 228, 230
  conversations with ancestors during 123
  description of 122–124, 219–220, 222–227
  food offerings during 123, 131–136, 222
  goal of 125, 223
  handbooks for 124
  historical background of 218–220
  in Indonesia 233
  in Malaysia 209–210
  Lao 119
  Moggallāna in 127–129
  names of deceased listed during 225
  offerings to monks during 123

opening of doors of hell during 123
Pudugong 220, 222
rationalized explanation for 125
scaffold of offerings during 220
sermons during 231
spirit money offered during 128, 223, 226
ghost money. *See* spirit paper
ghosts
and bad death 12–14, 159
as malevolent spirits 158
feeding of 209
from hell 124
hungry 29, 123, 209, 223
in Laos 125–129
in Sri Lanka 34
king of 220
scaffold for 220
sighting of 230
sympathy towards 207
See also spirits
God of the Five Paths
charged with destinations of the deceased 271, 274
petition addressed to 262, 271, 272, 274
gods
as possible rebirth 3
dislike of human smell 27
invitation to funeral 26, 38
good deaths 8, 146–147, 157, 158
government regulation of death ritual. *See* state policy
graves
apotropaic elements in 281
as homes 38, 198, 205
bathroom in 198
collective 195, 196, 198, 204
compared to womb 197
contents of 264–265, 270, 271, 280
diggers of 149
in China 268
inventories of 263, 270–281
location of 103
not determined by monks 270
of women 272, 277, 278
private 195
reasons for absence of Buddhist elements in 263
reopening of 208
siting of 199
sūtra in 265
symbolism of 198, 204, 205
tablets of 205
temporary 197
tin figures in 271 *see also under* cemetery
green death 8, 146–147, 157, 158
Guangdong 194, 200, 240
See also Chaozhou
Guanyin 220
Guoyuan 272, 276–281

Hakka 238, 252
halls of rebirth 225
handbooks 23–25, 39, 124, 243
See also model texts
hells
Avīci 231
avoidance of 229
depiction of 220
monetary account in 251
path to 102
stories of 84
travel from 249
travel to 80, 83, 124, 125, 127–129
Hertz, Robert
on collective representations of death 6, 15
on death as social fact 142
on death contagion 60
on death ritual as integration and separation 119
on decomposition of corpse 184
Hinduism 12–13, 63
holy days 114

impermanence
and meditation on the corpse 87
of self 4–5
relation to death 2–3, 180
representation in ritual 166, 169
incense
as offering 223
in hands of corpse 85
Indonesia 233
interment. *See* burial
Islam 208, 209, 210, 211

Japan 17
Jar. *See* burial.
Java 233

karma 4, 30, 130
Khandha 4, 65
Khuddakapāṭha 24, 28
Kṣitigarbha 225, 252

Lady Peng 266
laity
chanting at funeral 27
exclamations during funeral 37
importance of for funeral 162
See also families, lay ritual specialists

Lalitavistara 274
lay ritual specialists
  and Chinese popular religion 212
  and division of labour with monks 269–270
  chanting 37
  Chinese compared to Theravāda 9
  cremations performed by 90
  differences from monks 241–243
  in Phunoy funerary ritual 100–101, 102
  in triangular structure of mortuary rites 274–275
  vegetarian women (*zhaigu*) 244
leippya 143, 180
  See also spirit
Lenyo Wang 210
  See also Yama
Lévy-Strauss, Claude 36
liṅga 66
linghun 197
  See also spirit
lippra 143, 180
  See also spirit
lotus seat 224

Mahāparinibbāna Sutta
  as source of death rites 10, 27, 79
  chanting of 80, 86
Maitreya 30, 91, 266
Malaysia 208–213
malevolent spirits
  danger of 65, 155
  exclusion from rites 249, 250
  insulted by offences against nature 60–61
  malevolent female 68
  propitiation of 109, 114, 155, 156
  protection against 65, 108, 201
  See also ghosts, spirits, wandering spirits, bad death
mantra 219
manuscripts 80
Māra 2
Matakavastra. *See* Paṃsukūla.
Maudgalyāyana 8, 127–129, 218, 255
meat 114
media 204
Medicine Buddha 254–255, 256
mediums. *See* spirit mediums
Meizhou 238, 243
menstruation 203
merit
  as food 134
  generation of 255
  sharing of 151, 153
merit transfer
  and social order 16
  common explanation for death ritual 120
  from alms 25, 124
  from chanting 28–29
  in *Xianghua foshi* 245
  limitations as interpretative framework 133
  liturgy for 209
  monks' participation in 131–136
  not spoken of 111
  problems with 29, 120, 154
  to all present at funeral 30, 31, 239
  to ghosts 15, 225, 226
Ming Taizu 242
model text for funeral 261
modernisation 16
Moggallāna 8, 127–129, 218, 255
monasteries. 201 *See* temples
money
  as gift 107, 111
  division of 109
  offered to ghosts 128
  offered to monks 148
  placed in statues 108
Mongkut, Prince 24, 40, 81, 87–88
Mongolia 17
monks
  acceptance of local burial customs 269–270
  and progression of karma 156–157
  as intermediaries in death ritual 90–91, 120, 131
  as recipients of gifts 14
  as representative of the deceased 262
  as socially dead 76
  binding of corpse by 65
  duties in funerals 25, 281
  engaged in activities others avoid 60
  funerals of 7
  limited role in funerals 212
  not involved in cremation 90
  not involved in death ritual in medieval China 267
  power of 63, 157, 162
  role in funeral affirmed by state 241
  role in funeral in contrast to spirit priests 99, 102
  statues of 188–189
  washing of feet 111
mortuary bed 151
mourning 85
Mulian 8, 127–129, 218, 255
mummies 197, 203, 207
music
  cymbals 108, 111
  drums 106, 108
  in funeral 84, 148, 244, 268
musicians 220
mustard seeds 174

murder 209
Muyuan 239, 243

Nāga 106
nāma 179, 183
See also spirit
nat 173
Nepal 85
New Year festival (Bun Pimay)
absence of doctrine of merit from 111
and government purges 101
description of 104–111
main beneficiaries of 111
place in ritual calendar 100
purpose of 101, 111
nibbāna 30, 31, 32, 84
non-self. *See* self and non-self
novels 81

offerings
betal 150
by monks 150
candles 107, 111, 123
coffee 150
fireworks 109–110, 113, 223
importance of monks for 131
manuscripts 80
meat 114
money 109, 128, 148
paṃsukūla robe 62
paper 197, 204, 220
placed with corpse 102
tea 252
to Buddhas 105–106
to dead 104
to monks 105–106, 123, 150, 153, 218
to wandering spirits 222
See also food, flowers, merit
omens of death 169–170

pagoda
ceremonies conducted in 100–101, 106, 107, 115
definition of 105
symbolism of 112
See also stūpas
Pali Canon 24
paṃsukūla
as offering 62
as ritual 63–65
definition of 27, 59–76
in funerary culture 14
origins 61–62, 90
symbolism of 62, 63
white cloth replaced by robe 88–90
paper
covering for corpse 203
offerings 197, 204, 220
slips for the dead 225
Paritta 34–35
passports 265, 271
Paṭṭhāna 32
peta. See ghosts
Petavatthu 28
phed 124, 126
See also wandering spirits
phi 201
See also wandering spirits
phiphed 124, 125
See also wandering spirits
Phra Malai
and meditations on corpse 87
and Moggallāna 128
illustrations of 80, 83, 84–85
local adaptation of 127
symbolism of 91
plague 194
pollution
and bad death 12–14
expiation of 256
fear of 62
monks' ability to resist 60–61
of corpse 90, 198
of menstruation 203
vulnerability to 157
praliṅ 66–68, 73–74
prayer booklets 152
prayer ribbon 86
preaching
Burmese funerals 153
Chinese funerals 231
formal request for 27
Sri Lankan funerals 6, 25, 31
precepts 153
processions
at funerals 79, 143, 152
at Ghost Festival 219
from temporary grave 197
in New Year festival 106, 111, 114
pudu 219, 220, 224
See also Ghost Festival
Pudugong 220, 222
puppets 176, 224
Pure Land 239
purification
by fire 204
ceremonies of 107, 160–162
of remains 194
Puyao jing 274
pyres 204

Quanzhou 221, 222

rag robe. *See paṃsukūla*
rebirth
among men 31
among Phunoy 116
as deity 128
as source of confusion 181–183
forty-nine days after death 3, 5, 228–231
identification of 181
immediately following death 3, 154, 166, 231
in Brahma realm 185
in Buddhist doctrine 3–5
in Laos 123
in upper regions 184
metaphors for 182–183, 197
seven days after death 27, 34, 65, 154, 162
reincarnation. *See* rebirth
relics 177
reliquary 166
repentance 254
rites of passage 1
ritual performance 37–38
ritual specialists. *See* lay specialists
robes
in funeral procession 152, 155
monastic 72, 84, 166
rags from cremation ground 88
See also paṃsukūla

sacrifice 102, 115
Śākyamuni. *See* Buddha
secondary burial 194, 197
self and non-self
and cremation 171
and death ritual 166, 169
and images of the deceased 188
and impermanence 178–181
and rebirth 4–5
sermons. *See* preaching
sex
in funeral plays 176–177
refraining from 203
symbolism of 16
shantang 201
shipwrecks 195
shroud 148, 155
shuilu fahui 226
shuilu festival 226
Siddhārtha. *See* Buddha
sīmā 69–70
Singapore 208
singing 168
skandha 4, 65
socialism 6, 125
See also state policy
soldiers
divine 249
ghosts of 14, 223
soul 12
inadequacy of term 179, 180
of Phunoy 104
summoning of 248
See also spirit, *nāma*
spirit
Buddhist concept of 179–181
leippya 180
linghun 197
nāma 179, 183
release from body 151, 154
wiññyan 179–184, 185
See also phi
spirit mediums
identifying ashes 205
in Malaysia 209
locating wandering spirits 197
possessed by Dafeng 202
supervising ritual 199
techniques of 199
spirit money. *See* spirit paper
spirit paper
for orphaned bones 199
for wandering spirits 219
function of 251
types of 223
See also offerings
spirits
and local cults 10, 100–101, 113
guardian 114, 124
non-Buddhist 60, 69, 106, 114–115
of one who died away from home 248
See also ghosts, malevolent spirits, wandering spirits
Sri Lanka
civil war 6
death rituals of 6
funerals compared with other areas of Southeast Asia 38–39
starvation 195
state policy
and death ritual 195, 241–243
on cremation 195–196, 208
on Ghost Festival 221, 232
on unclaimed bodies 202
regulating temples 211
religious purges by 101–102
standardising death ritual 192
Stone, Jacqueline 238

stūpas
burial in 268
of deceased relatives 123
See also pagodas
suicide 99, 103, 116
syncretism 10–12, 212

Taiwan
cremation and burial in 270
funerals in 282
funerary texts in 261
Ghost Festival in 233
secondary burial in 194
Taixu 228
talaphat (monastic fan) 85
tea 252
temples
and monarch 71
consecration of 69, 74
site of offering to dead 105, 107
spirits inhabiting 70
ten kings of hell 251, 252, 253, 254
Thailand
death ritual in 130
funeral compared with Sri Lanka and other areas of Southeast Asia 38–39
funerary art 79–96
hospices in 17
introduction of Pali liturgy 24–25
theatre
at funerals 6, 167–189
at Ghost Festival 219, 222
eyiń 167
zāt 175
Tirokuḍḍapetavatthu 29
tomb quelling texts 272
tombs. *See* graves.
tributes 110
tsunami 202
Turfan 263
typhoons 195

umbrella 204
underworld
bureaucracy of 239, 249, 261, 262
Chinese compared to Theravāda 9
imperial metaphor applied to 9
tax of 280
See also hell *see also under* heaven
urbanisation 195
urn. *See* burial
van Gennep, Arnold 206

Vedic sūtras 21
vegetarianism
during mourning 210
rejection of 241
Vessantara jātaka 94
Vientiane 122, 134
Vietnam 75, 129, 234
vinaya 76, 160
Viññāṇa 65
violent death. 103 *See* bad death.
Visuddhimagga 28

wandering spirits
altars for 249, 251
and bad death 159
as hell beings 126
between death and funeral 154
catching 209
contrasted with 'inside' spirits 177
dangers of 162, 192, 254–255
determining number of 204
families of 110, 116
feeding of 219
hunger of 128
leading away of 251
offerings 222, 223
search for 197, 209
searching for new body 180
See also ghosts, bad death, spirits
water
forbidden 156
inviting spirit to leave body 153
on offering 114
perfumed 109
pouring of while chanting 29
symbol of merit 37, 150
weeping
actress 168
during funeral 269
relatives 88, 151, 153
wine
offered to deceased 252
offered to deities 253
wiññyan 179–184, 185
women
as ritual specialists 244
death rites for 254–255, 257
responsible for care of dead 233
tombs of 272, 277, 278
writings for dead 108
Wudao. *See* God of the Five Paths
Xiamen 221

Xianghua foshi
cleric of 241–243
description of 245–258
frequency of 244

Xianghua foshi (cont.)
function of 239
history of 240–241
origins of 239–241
Xiaojing 271
Xuanzang 269

Yama
effigy of 220
entry into realm of 62
granting permission to leave hell 129, 217
in Ghost Festival 220
in Moggallāna story 127
seclusion of spirit by 210
Yinshun 228
Yulanpen. *See* Ghost Festival
zât 175

Zhenhua 229

Lightning Source UK Ltd.
Milton Keynes UK
UKOW04f2000190914

238895UK00004B/285/P

9 781107 667877